TRANSNATIONAL ORGANIZED CRIME

TRANSNATIONAL ORGANIZED CRIME

YESTERDAY AND TODAY

Kimberly A. McCabe
University of Lynchburg

cognella
SAN DIEGO

Bassim Hamadeh, CEO and Publisher
Carolyn Meier, Publisher
Danielle Gradisher, Project Editor
Rachel Kahn, Production Editor
Emely Villavicencio, Senior Graphic Designer
Natalie Piccotti, Director of Marketing
Kassie Graves, Senior Vice President, Editorial
Jamie Giganti, Director of Academic Publishing

cognella® ACADEMIC PUBLISHING
3970 Sorrento Valley Blvd., Ste. 500, San Diego, CA 92121

Brief Contents

Detailed Contents

Preface

Transnational crime is a topic often studied within the discipline of criminal justice. When the element of organized crime is added to the criminal action, the topic becomes more significant in its impact on global societies. Specifically, the value of transnational organized crime (hereafter TOC) is estimated at approximately $5 trillion, or over 7% of global GDP annually. The broader impact of organized crime is difficult to assess as it is multidimensional and is shared across the private sector, the public sector, and society itself. The United Nations Convention against Transnational Organized Crime defines *organized crime* broadly as encompassing most forms of profit-motivated crime. Aside from its illicit work with specific markets, TOC affects the social, economic, and political development of countries through its facilitation of corruption, loss of democratic participation, victimization, and efforts to destabilize economies and political systems.

TOC poses a significant and growing threat to national and international security, with dire implications for public safety, public health, and democratic institutions. Criminal networks are not just expanding; they are also diversifying their criminal activities, resulting in the convergence of threats that were once distinct and today have even more explosive and destabilizing effects. As TOC networks expand, they undermine free markets through the operations of black markets as they build alliances with political leaders, financial institutions, law enforcement, foreign intelligence, and security agencies. TOC penetration of governments exacerbates corruption and undermines governance, rule of law, judicial systems, free press, democratic institution-building, and transparency of operations.

For students who are interested in crime and criminal justice, this book, *Transnational Organized Crime: Yesterday and Today*, provides both broad and in-depth information on TOC as well as on the similarities and differences in structure and goals of TOC, and on punishment for these crimes with an emphasis on victims and victims' rights as related to TOC. Within the area of criminal justice, it is common to categorize the functions of the criminal justice systems into policing, courts, and corrections; however, those who study comparative criminal justice study different types of societies, their methods of enforcement, and their different types of punishment. Unfortunately, textbooks that focus TOC are rare, and those that do exist are often focused on organized crime within regions or are limited on their coverage of legal reactions and the global scope of the problem. This textbook helps to address those limitations by discussing the theoretical and practical aspects of TOC.

TOC groups are self-perpetuating associations of individuals that operate, wholly or in part, by illegal means and irrespective of geography. These groups consistently seek power, influence, and monetary gains, with globalization or hyperglobalization fueling the problem. There is no single structure under which TOC groups function—they vary from hierarchies to clans, networks, and cells, and they may evolve into other structures in reaction to criminal justice enforcement efforts and products. TOC groups are typically insular and protect their activities through corruption, violence, international commerce, complex communication mechanisms, and an organizational structure that exploits national boundaries.

With few exceptions, TOC groups' primary goal is economic gain, and they will employ an array of lawful and illicit schemes to generate profit. Crimes such as drug trafficking, migrant smuggling, human trafficking, money laundering, firearms trafficking, illegal gambling, extortion, counterfeit goods, wildlife and cultural property smuggling, and cybercrime are keystones within TOC enterprises. However, as addressed in this book, TOC efforts may also be utilized to facilitate the actions of violent extremists and terrorists.

Features of This Book

TOC groups may encompass both the Eastern and Western Hemispheres and include persons with ethnic or cultural ties to Europe, Africa, Asia, the Middle East, Australia, and the Russian Federation. These groups, however, are able to target victims and execute their schemes from anywhere in the world; thus, the extent of their operations within a particular area does not necessarily reflect the degree of the threat they pose to that rea.

The actions of TOC organizations may be grouped into three broad categories: the provision of illicit goods (e.g., drug trafficking, trafficking in stolen property, weapons trafficking, and counterfeiting), the operation of illicit services (e.g., commercial sexual exploitation and human trafficking), and the infiltration of businesses and government (e.g., fraud and racketeering). This textbook addresses all three broad categories.

This book, although acknowledging its core foundation in the actions of organized crime, attempts to discuss criminal behaviors within the global arena, as it focuses on TOC as well as on national and international efforts to identify and address these criminal activities. This book is organized in three parts for a total of 12 chapters to provide students with information on TOC. In addition, end-of-chapter questions for discussion provide the foundation for further discussions on the chapter's topic. The purpose of this book is to provide students in criminal justice courses with information on TOC within the world. The content includes reactions from police, the courts, and corrections. Information on TOC groups and their actions are provided, as well as case examples of TOC activities, to help students make their own transnational assessments.

Organization of This Text

This text is divided into three parts:

1. Foundations of TOC—Chapters 1-3
2. Issues and Consequences of TOC—Chapters 4–10
3. Global Responses to TOC—Chapters 11–12

In Part I, Chapter 1 introduces readers to TOC and the many crimes associated with TOC. It discusses sources of data on TOC, and offers general discussions on the concept of corruption and globalization and hyperglobalization as related to TOC. Chapter 2 provides theoretical and practical explanations of TOC, beginning with explanations for organized crime from classical and contemporary theories and then discussing the interconnectivity of countries and their cooperative efforts, which facilitate TOC. Chapter 2 also discusses common systems of law, and also the use of technology in expanding the criminal activities of TOC. Chapter 3 serves as an introduction to the structure of organized crime networks as applied to TOC. This chapter includes discussions on leadership and leadership positions within TOC organizations, as well as information on membership in TOC groups and the roles of structure as related to the operations of the TOC group.

In Part II, Chapter 4 introduces demographic country-level variables that are often at risk for victimization by TOC, as well as the concept of corruption as applied to criminal justice systems and those systems' reactions to TOC. The chapter discusses the risk factors for TOC, including community-level and individual-level variables. Hence, Chapter 4 provides an overview of TOC's role in crimes against humanity, crimes against vulnerable groups such as women and children, crimes against internally displaced and/or stateless persons, crimes against LGBTQ individuals, and crimes against the environment. It discusses vulnerabilities in terms of structural risk, potential harm to individuals, and risk to environments and societies as a whole. Chapters 5 through 10 focus on the specific products targeted by TOC.

Chapter 5 discusses TOC's relation to drug trafficking; it includes a brief history, a discussion on the business and profit margins, an identification of specific kinds of drugs by country of origin, and the actions of TOC as related to the manufacture and distribution of illegal drugs; it also covers global reactions to the drug trade and factors that facilitate TOC groups' part in the drug trade. Chapter 6 discusses TOC as related to weapons trafficking, including a brief history, a discussion of the business and profit margins, an identification of specific weapons and arms currently trafficked through TOC and weapons of mass destruction, including nuclear, chemical, and biological; it also covers global reactions to weapons trafficking. Chapter 7 discusses TOC as related to human trafficking. This chapter provides a brief history of human trafficking and a brief discussion of the structure of TOC as it relates to human trafficking. Further, it defines the differences between human trafficking and people smuggling, discusses the business and profit margins of TOC, identifies victim profiles and modes of victim recruitment, and covers countries identified as source, transit, and/or destination countries for human trafficking. In addition, Chapter 7 provides a discussion of legislative efforts to address human trafficking. Chapter 8 discusses TOC as it relates to wildlife trafficking. This chapter discusses environmental crimes and the roles of TOC in facilitating these crimes. This chapter, although dedicated to discussions on all five of the areas of international environmental crime, focuses on TOC and wildlife trafficking to include consequences of wildlife trafficking and the factors that facilitate wildlife trafficking as well as the asserted relationship between COVID-19 and wildlife trafficking. Chapter 9 discusses TOC as it relates to the trafficking of art, antiquities, and other products (e.g., cigarettes and alcohol) in demand on the black market. This chapter includes a brief history, a discussion of the business and profit margins for other trafficked products, a discussion on the demands for products as related to incentives for TOC groups, and coverage of international efforts to address these aspects of TOC activities. Chapter 10 provides an overview of extremist activities perpetrated against a government or its citizens, as well as terrorism. The chapter includes a historical examination of terrorist acts; discussion on the theoretical links between violent extremisms, terrorism, and TOC; and discussion of current demonstrations of violent extremism and terrorism and the facilitating relationship between terrorist organizations and TOC. Chapter 10 continues the discussion of cyberterrorism (begun in Chapter 3) and vulnerable populations (Chapter 4) with discussions on the recruitment or coercion of followers and participants in extremist acts of violence. Lastly, this part provides a brief discussion on the asserted effect of COVID-19 pandemic on violent extremism and terrorism.

In Part III, Chapter 11 introduces the roles of law enforcement in attempting to address the criminal behavior of TOC. This chapter focuses on policing around the world as related to the reality of TOC, including a discussion on concerns about aspects of TOC for law enforcement today and a history of policing efforts in various countries. Also in this chapter is a brief discussion of the three structural models of policing (centralized, decentralized, and integrated); the concept of democratic policing; the vulnerabilities to police that are created by underground economies, diversity, and corruption; and the effects of hyperglobalization and the digital age as police attempt to control the criminal actions of TOC. The final chapter of this book, Chapter 12, focuses on the International Court of Justice (also known as the World Court) by explaining the basis for international courts and the concept of international crime, and by providing examples of such courts around the globe. Chapter 12 also examines the various legal jurisdictions of these courts, and it reviews specific case files. The chapter focuses primarily on the International Court of Justice and the International Criminal Court. In addition, this chapter discusses the concept of TOC as it relates to prosecution, accountability, and potential expansion of prosecution within the international courts and the limitations of those efforts.

Acknowledgments

Many years ago, my research focused exclusively on child abuse and police efforts to protect children. However, a trip to Scotland and a discussion on the 2001 case of a young West African boy whose severed torso was discovered in London's River Thames, although never confirmed as a case of human trafficking, introduced me to the subject of human trafficking. Years later, an observation of members of an organized crime group meeting within a cafe in Serbia further piqued my curiosity on the criminal activities of these crime groups—and specifically the role of TOC in the exploitation of persons.

Over the last decade, my research interests about the scope of TOC have led me throughout Europe for the collection and analysis of data related to TOC. I am grateful to my friends and family members, including my now adult children (Jesse and Mac), who for years have allowed me my soliloquies on factors facilitating TOC as well as my monologues on the consequences of ignoring the criminal actions of TOC. I am especially grateful to Carolyn Henderson Meier and Cognella for supporting the publication of this book. It is my sincere desire that this book will not only be of interest to its readers but will also inspire the newest criminologists to continue to focus on TOC and efforts to reduce the crimes committed by these groups of criminals.

PART I

Foundations

Introduction to Transnational Organized Crime

Key Terms

Black market
Corruption Perceptions Index
Counterfeiting
Cybercrime
Drug trafficking
Firearms trafficking
Fraudulent medicines
Gang
Globalization
Human trafficking
Hyperglobalization
International Organized Crime Intelligence and Operations Center (IOC-2)
Interpol
Irish Mob
Italian Mafia
Money laundering
Organized crime
People smuggling
Pirates
Rational choice theory
Rule of law
Smuggling of goods
Taliban
Terrorism
Trafficking of art and antiquities
Trafficking of natural resources
Transnational organized crime (TOC)
United Nations Convention Against Transnational Organized Crime (UNTOC)
United Nations Office on Drugs and Crime (UNODC)
Violent extremism
Wildlife trafficking
World Factbook

CHAPTER OBJECTIVES

Chapter 1 will enable readers to understand the following:

- the problem of defining *organized crime*
- the history of transnational organized crime (TOC)

(*continued*)

- the common crimes for TOC
- the profits of TOC
- the interconnectivity among products and TOC
- the connection between TOC and acts of terrorism
- the influence of hyperglobalization of TOC

TRANSNATIONAL ORGANIZED CRIME (TOC) is a criminal activity that has gained much attention within the global arena not only for its perceived criminal actions and human rights violations, but also as one of the most profitable aspects of criminal organizations—with annual profits ranging from $1.6 trillion to $2.2 trillion (Clough, 2017). As demonstrated in the July 2021 report above, groups involved in TOC often are made up of many members with a variety or responsibilities and many victims. TOC, as its name infers, involves the criminal actions of groups of individuals that occur not only within national boundaries, but also across international borders and, in many cases, within the virtual jurisdiction-free settings of cyber-communities. The motive for TOC, similar to the motive for most premeditated crimes, is profit (McCabe, 2017). Unfortunately, today's TOC groups are no longer simply specialized criminal organizations; rather, they are often the essential elements for armed groups around the world and a source of funding for terrorists, corrupt politicians, warlords, and rouge governments (International Peace Institute, 2009).

In July of 2021, 286 members of a TOC network were arrested on charges of human trafficking and migrant smuggling across Europe (Interpol, 2021b). This effort resulted in the rescue of over 400 human-trafficking victims and the identification of 4,000 irregular migrants from 74 different countries. These victims, requiring medical, psychological, and housing assistance, were taken into the care of protective services.

Transnational organized crime (TOC)—The criminal actions of groups of individuals within national boundaries, across international borders, and within virtual jurisdiction-free settings.

TOC encompasses many activities, including drug trafficking; the smuggling of migrants; human trafficking; money laundering; and trafficking in firearms, counterfeit goods, wildlife, and cultural property—as well as some aspects of cybercrime, including **black market** exchanges and membership recruitments into violent extremist and terrorist organizations. Even in 2021, as **Taliban** forces infiltrated and seized control of Afghanistan, the majority of the general population failed to recognize the place of the Taliban in

TOC through what is referred to as the *Quetta Shura Taliban* (Peters, 2011). What most citizens do not realize is that the QST engages in smuggling, the drug trade, extortion, and kidnapping for profit and recognition while at the same time destabilizing governments, intensifying conflicts, and fueling corruption. Hence, outcomes of TOC include the victimizations of persons (as illustrated by the July 2021 death discussed below), the victimization of animals, threats to the rule of law, threats to security, and corruption of societies. In other words, TOC encompasses more than simply the perceived **Italian Mafia**, and to date countries and international organizations have largely failed to anticipate the evolution of TOC groups as critical components of strategic threats to governments, societies, and economies (International Peace Institute, 2009).

In July of 2021, Dutch crime reporter Peter R. de Vries was shot and seriously wounded, and died of his injuries just a few days later. Mr. de Vries was well known for his investigations of mobsters and drug lords and had won critical acclaim for his reporting on the Dutch underworld—including the 1983 kidnapping of the beer millionaire, Freddy Heineken (BBC News, 2021b).

Organized Crime, TOC, and History

The history of **organized crime** is the history of TOC. While TOC has existed for centuries (with the history of its involvement in illicit trades discussed throughout this chapter), the last four decades have provided expanded avenues for profit through hyperglobalization and developments in international transactions. When individuals consider the organizations of criminal networks (or organized crime), most Americans reflect upon the American Mafia (commonly referred to in North America as the Italian-American Mafia, the Mafia, or the Mob) and Prohibition in the 1920s and 1930s. However, scholars have supported the identification of criminal groups such as the Sea People, a group of ocean raiders who attacked and robbed ships of the Aegean and Mediterranean civilizations in the 14th century BCE (Pennell, 2001), the biblical accounts of Joseph in Genesis 37:26–28 as a victim of human trafficking, as well as the criminal street groups in London during the 16th and 17th centuries (McMullan, 1982) as depicted in Charles Dickens's 1838 novel *Oliver Twist*.

Research suggests that the history of organized crime accompanies the history of civilizations and the movement of these societies.

In the Hebrew Bible, Joseph was traded into slavery by his brothers and then trafficked into Egypt. During the third century, individuals such as Bulla Felix—later referred to as ancient Rome's Robin Hood as he led and organized over 600 members of his criminal group—pillaged the goods of the wealthy and redistributed such goods to the less fortunate (Valjak, 2017).

In the 13th and 14th centuries, as goods began being massively and regularly transported from one location to another by sea routes, **pirates** or sea people were documented as operating as organized criminal groups by stealing products from one ship, moving the products to another ship for transportation, and reselling to consumers within various destinations (Müller, 1888). During the same period, land-based criminal organizations (i.e., bandits) used violence and coercion to profit within Europe (Hobsbawn, 1985). Barbarians led by individuals such as Genghis Khan operated in the regions between modern-day Mongolia and Siberia (Borst, 1992), and the Turks operated in Asia and Europe (Lunde, 2004).

In the 19th-century Victorian era, as the smaller criminal groups evolved into larger, more organized criminal groups, prostitution, robbery, forgery, and **counterfeiting** became more common criminal actions in Europe. In the United States, groups such as the Cochise County Cowboys, based in the Arizona Territory, focused on the smuggling and illicit trading of contraband between the United States and Mexico (Alexander, 2014). Later, in the United States, groups such as the **Irish Mob**, with enforcers such as Whitey Bulger (as reported here), operated for decades in Boston.

In October 2018, Boston crime boss Whitey Bulger was killed in his prison cell (Schapiro, 2021). Bulger, a leader within Boston's Irish Mob, was thought to be responsible for some of the most brutal murders committed in Boston's history. He was convicted in 2013 of over 30 federal charges and sentenced to life in prison.

Today's criminal groups are referred to as gangs, organized criminals, and TOC groups. While all three of these groups imply a level of business sophistication, the term **gang** generally refers to juvenile delinquents committing more spontaneous criminal actions. Organized criminals or TOC groups are seen to have criminal planning abilities, an established structure, and a degree of organization beyond the juvenile street gang (Klein, 1995).

There is no clear definition of *organized crime*, as it is often difficult to distinguish what constitutes organized crime from what constitutes

Organized crime— Identified by the National Criminal Intelligence Service as crime being perpetrated by a group (1) of three or more people, (2) engaging in prolonged or indefinite criminal activity, (3) motivated by profit or power, and (4) guilty of committing serious criminal offenses (Free Dictionary, 2006).

disorganized crime. However, the National Criminal Intelligence Service (NCIS) identifies organized crime through the following four characteristics: (1) consisting of three or more people; (2) engaging in prolonged or indefinite criminal activity; (3) motivated by profit or power; and (4) guilty of committing serious criminal offenses (Free Dictionary, 2006). Essentially, in the definition of *organized crime*, it is understood that these groups are intentionally organized to achieve their goal (Sondhi, 2015). Historically, most actions of organized crime groups referred to criminal behaviors within a state's or a country's borders; today, however, this is not always the case.

Transnational organized crime, or TOC, refers to criminal actions that involve more than one country. With the use of technology and virtual communities, and without physical land boundaries for police jurisdiction, the reach of TOC has broadened. Given the globalization and interconnectivity of current societies, much of organized crime is actually TOC and therefore must be approached from a global perspective, with cooperation among justice systems within countries. In the simplest of explanations, organized crime is associated with the control of a territory and the demand, supply, and execution of trade, while TOC is associated with demand, supply, and execution of trade without the jurisdictional restrictions for control and profit (Brzenchek, 2020).

Although organized crime may exist in prosperous countries and is not a direct result of the instability of countries, there are those who suggest that organized crime often emerges when economic and political systems are fractured (Godson & Olson, 1995). With the fall of the Soviet Union and the expansion of global markets, the scope of actions and capabilities for TOC increased (Abadinsky, 2017).

Rule of law—The process, institution, practice, agreement, or norm that supports the equality of all citizens.

In addition, with the deterioration of economic conditions, the decline of political control, and the absence of the **rule of law**, individuals who were once under the umbrella of communist control began daily operations outside of the legal framework (Godson & Olson, 1995). These groups, operating outside of this framework, often have the advantages of the availability of weapons, a large resource of immigrants and refugees, and free access to other countries—in other words, a strong foundation to support criminal activities within a larger area. Specifically, in the United States, during the time of

Prohibition and the later embargoes against countries such as Cuba, the mobilization of criminal organizations, and the cooperative partnerships with crime syndicates expanded the criminal organizations' reach to a global scale. Today, TOC groups from Italy, Russia, China, and Mexico are all active in the United States.

To fully explore TOC, one must consider the breadth of the organizations. In fact, research suggests that one of the greatest problems that criminal justice leaders face today involves the difficulties in effectively combating these criminal groups (Brzenchek, 2020). TOC refers to criminal organizations acting across national borders (Abadinsky, 2017), which means the traditional structure of hierarchy and clear lines of power, control, and responsibility that exist with organized crime groups are minimized; structures of loosely connected networks emerge in response to the distribution of products from source countries, through transit countries, and into destination (or consumer) countries. As technology has changed from global to hyperglobal, TOC organizations are able to increase the reach of their criminal activities through apps, through disposable devices, and through the "deep web" and/or "dark web," which conceal criminal transactions and facilitate the networking of those perpetrators of illicit and illegal behaviors. Hence, along with economic failures, underground markets, global communities, and consistent supplies of demand goods, TOC has the capability to become one of the most problematic areas for society today.

Defining TOC

Historically, *organized crime* has been defined as a nonideological enterprise involving a number of persons in close social interaction, organized on a hierarchical basis, with at least three levels or ranks, for the purpose of securing profit and power by engaging in illegal and semilegal activities (Abadinsky, 2017).

In discussing the structure of traditional organized crime networks, research suggests that positions in the hierarchy and positions involving functional specialization may be assigned on the basis of kinship or friendship, or they may be rationally assigned according to skill (such as a documents forger) with a permanency of members assumed to exist within the organized crime group (Abadinsky, 2017). This may not be the case for TOC, however, as the structure of the organization is dependent upon the product(s) of interest, the use of technology for supply and demand, and the product's mode of transport (McCabe, 2017).

To further complicate the clarity in the term *transnational organized crime*, for many individuals the lines of distinction between organized crime and white-collar crime are nonexistent. For clarity in this chapter, white-collar crime is essentially a result of fraud and the criminal action that exists to profit primarily from that specific crime, such as the medical doctor who sells a prescription for narcotics not because the patient needs but because it means an immediate profit for the physician. In organized crime, the actions are a result of continued criminal enterprise with at least two actors involved in the activity (Albanese, 2015). For example, organized crime may be involved in the sale and distribution of narcotics within a specific geographic area; thus, organized crime is not simply a means for profit by one physician. To expand this further, TOC may be involved in the sale or distribution of narcotics within a region, across national and international borders, or through an online black market drug provider. Therefore, in defining *transnational organized crime*, the complexities of numerous countries, the continuation of criminal activities, and the effects on human rights and the rule of law are all aspects of the organized criminal activity. TOC is an ever-changing industry, market-driven and borderless, without consistent definitions of crimes or jurisdictional enforcement.

Controlling TOC is not only difficult for regional authorities but also difficult for most governments, as historically they have focused on specific crimes and the regulatory agency charters that target specific criminal activities such as human trafficking or the drug trade. For example, in the United States, the agency of Immigration and Customs Enforcement (ICE) focuses on people smuggling, the U.S. Drug Enforcement Agency (DEA) focuses on the drug trade, and the Bureau of Alcohol, Tobacco, Firearms and Explosives (ATF) focuses on the trafficking of weapons; however, each of the products (people, drugs, and guns) may be provided to clients or customers through the same criminal organization, yet when the regulatory agencies focus on only the product they fail to see the commonalities within the process. ATF may be investigating gun trafficking and ICE may be investigating people smuggling without acknowledging the commonalities among engaged actors or the elements of TOC. This lack of focus on the criminal action facilitates TOC's ability to adjust products as the market demands.

Definitions of *TOC* vary based upon the perspectives of those defining it. Specifically, the **United Nations Convention against Transnational Organized Crime (UNTOC)** does not provide a precise definition of *transnational organized crime*, nor does it identify the multitude of crimes that may occur through TOC. Instead, the UNTOC provides the general overall definition of *TOC* as an organized criminal group of three or more persons that was not randomly formed, that has existed for a period of time, that acts with the aim of committing at least one criminal offense punishable by at least four years of incarceration, and that acts in order to obtain, either directly or indirectly, some financial or material benefit. This lack of definition was intended to allow for a broader applicability of the UNTOC to new types of crime that emerge constantly as global, regional, and local conditions change over time (United Nations Office on Drugs and Crime, 2020d); for many countries, however, its lack of a specific definition has made the problem worse and has made TOC profits greater.

United Nations Convention against Transnational Organized Crime— Starting in 2000, a United Nations–sponsored multilateral treaty of approximately 150 countries to support efforts against TOC.

The UNTOC definition of *TOC* is specific to those crimes that are "transnational," which includes not only offenses committed in more than one country or state, but also offenses that take place in one country but are planned, controlled, and/or operated in another country or multiple countries. The UNTOC's broad definition is an attempt to account for the complexity of global communities and virtual communities as well as the ever-expanding focus of crimes through TOC. This book acknowledges the generality of the definition and is intended to provide readers an overview of TOC, discussions on its effects throughout the world, and information on enforcement efforts as they currently exist for TOC. This book also acknowledges the cumulative effect of TOC in corroding the capacities of countries, their economic stability, and their public health (International Peace Institute, 2009).

The Business of TOC

TOC is dependent upon market demands and product availability. As suggested by the **United Nations Office on Drugs and Crime,** or UNODC (2017, 2018, 2019, 2020d, 2021b), TOCs include drug trafficking, human trafficking, people smuggling, the firearms trade, trafficking in natural resources, the illegal wildlife trade, the sale of fraudulent medicines and medical information, and cybercrime. TOCs have also been identified as a significant aspect of the smuggling of goods, the trafficking of art and antiquities, counterfeiting, money laundering, and terrorism. The information below provides a general introduction to the business or activities of TOC; common criminal actions will be identified with specific detailed accounts in later chapters.

Drug Trafficking

When individuals think about the illegal activities of organized crime or transnational organized crime, most focus exclusively on the drug trade—and for good reason. **Drug trafficking** has been a major focus of the U.S. government since before the War on Drugs in the 1980s, and it continues today as demonstrated by the July 2021 case shown here. The drug trade has been blamed for the high prevalence of drug-related deaths, for drug violence, and for the many substance abuse addictions experienced around the world. Historically, drug traffickers were perceived as individuals from large urban areas, living in neighborhoods of poverty and oppression, with propensities toward intimidation and violence as a means to an end (Broadhurst et al., 2005). Consistent with this stereotype, those involved in the drug trade were seen to generate respect and the "masculine" persona through toughness, a deference from peers, and stints in prison (Anderson, 1999). However, today's drug traffickers vary in demographics (sex, race, and ethnicity) as well as location and roles of involvement, with many of these variations an indirect consequence of the specific business of TOC (Stryker, 2019). Specifically, the UN's Office on Drugs and Crime (2018) suggests that approximately 10% of those currently arrested as key players in the drug trade are women.

In July 2021, a Mexican national was sentenced in the U.S. District Court for the District of Columbia to 22 years in prison for her role in an international drug-trafficking conspiracy. This TOC, with ties to Mexico, Colombia, Honduras, and others, had the goal of transporting thousands of grams of cocaine and methamphetamine with the intent to distribute within the United States (U.S. Department of Justice, 2021).

Estimates suggest that drug trafficking generates between $426 billion and $652 billion annually (Clough, 2017). Markets for drugs are expanded beyond the historically identified regions and online transactions and are increasing the profits for TOC through diversified products and routes of product delivery. For example, estimates for the global production and distribution of opium increased a suggested 65% from 2016 to 2017, cocaine manufactures are reaching their highest levels ever, countries within Asia and Africa have emerged as trafficking drug hubs, and North America is embracing a leadership role in the trafficking of methamphetamines (United Nations Office on Drugs and Crime, 2018).

The role of TOC in drug trafficking is limited only by the efforts of those involved in the criminal actions. As suggested by **rational choice theory** (Amadae, 2021), as individuals weigh the cost and benefits of participation in the drug trade, they must consider the enormous potential for profit along with the perceived limited risk of detection, conviction, and incarceration to choose "rationally" to participate in the criminal action. Hence, for many people TOC is a rational, thought-based decision.

Human Trafficking

Human trafficking is defined as the use of force, fraud, or coercion from one person to another to obtain some type of labor, some form of commercial sex act, or a human organ (McCabe & Murphy, 2016). The global profits from human trafficking are estimated to be over $150 billion annually, with most research suggesting that this is a conservative approximation (Mavrellis, 2017). Every year, millions of men, women, and children are trafficked from source countries, through transit countries, and into destination countries (McCabe, 2008). For many of those cases of human trafficking, the involvement of TOC goes unnoticed as historically efforts to reduce human trafficking have focused on either prevention through awareness campaigns or on victims' services (McCabe, 2017).

Estimates suggest that the majority of the victims of human trafficking are women and that approximately one half of the victims are under the age of 18 (in other words, children) (McCabe & Murphy, 2016). Human trafficking, although often viewed as a developing-country problem with specific cases in large urban areas, may occur in any community and victims may vary by age, race, gender, or nationality. Traffickers, through TOC, utilize a variety of techniques to deliver their products (i.e., persons) to consumers. Common travel routes from multiple countries into Europe and then into the United States by way of Canada are known to exist (McCabe, 2008). However, once routes are identified by law enforcement authorities, TOC members simply adjust lines of travel and venues across borders in order to continue their enterprises. Techniques that recruiters apply to victims include violence, manipulation, or false promises of well-paying jobs or romantic relationships. Human trafficking not only produces millions of victims but also facilitates the degradation of human rights laws, gender inequality, corruption, and problems in public health. Although human trafficking was once viewed as a "less significant" component of profit for TOC, human trafficking now follows only drug trafficking in terms of public attention, TOC involvement, and TOC profits (McCabe, 2017). Therefore, with the risk to TOC for involvement in human trafficking at a minimum, an endless supply of potential victims for human trafficking, and individuals continuing to be in the market for humans to exploit, human trafficking has become one of the most profitable enterprises for TOC.

People Smuggling

People smuggling, or migrant smuggling, is yet another highly profitable business in which smugglers are rarely detected and/or punished (United Nations Office on Drugs and Crime, 2018). As demonstrated in the January 2021 case, smuggling can result in deadly consequences. In contrast to victims of human trafficking, however, individuals smuggled across a border are often directly involved (i.e., through consent and payment), as they have the desire to enter another country and are willing to do so without proper travel documentation (McCabe, 2008). Those involved in people smuggling are keenly aware of those desires.

> In January of 2021, four men were convicted of the manslaughter of 30 Vietnamese migrants when a TOC people-smuggling effort failed. These victims, smuggled within a container on a ship, were towed to Belgium and then the United Kingdom before their bodies were discovered. Postmortem examinations revealed that within the container the victims had suffered deadly levels of carbon dioxide and temperatures of over 100 degrees (BBC News, 2021a).

Smuggling operations have moved from small one-smuggler operations, with ethnic and geographic connections to the migrant, to operations of a larger scale, organized with professional networks that transcend border operations. TOC has expanded its reach to either a loose "network" without strict lines of command to facilitate border crossing (McCabe, 2008) or a large, well-organized, hierarchical criminal organization with transnational links (United Nations Office on Drugs and Crime, 2018).

In contrast to victims of human trafficking, individuals involved in human smuggling are often directly involved (i.e., consent and payment), as they have the desire to enter another country.

Unique to people smuggling is the fact that in many cases the individuals most connected to the migrants are not involved in major aspects of TOC; in some cases, however, the smugglers do have contacts with violent criminal organizations. People-smuggling networks linked to TOC often engage in systematic corruption at most levels, including grand corruption of the highest level of government authorities (United Nations Office on Drugs and Crime, 2018). Therefore, people smuggling—a well-organized business of moving people around the globe through criminal networks, groups, and routes—is yet another aspect of TOC.

Firearms Trade

The firearms trade is probably one of the aspects of TOC portrayed most often in action movies and on television. Estimates suggest that global profits to TOC from **firearms trafficking** range from $1.7 billion to $3.5 billion annually (Clough, 2017). Unique to firearms trafficking is that the criminal activity, although extremely lucrative on its own, often accompanies other illicit trafficking products such as drugs and people. In many cases, the seizure of firearms is the first indication of other aspects of TOC.

In the firearms trade, seized weapons are overwhelmingly identified as being manufactured outside of the country of seizure. It is only by crossing borders or by TOC that these weapons are delivered to their destination countries (United Nations Office on Drugs and Crime, 2020a). Aside from the United States, which manufactures and seizes the largest proportion of handguns, Caribbean countries report high proportions of imported pistols, Latin American countries report imported revolvers, and Croatia reports a high proportion of machine guns or submachine guns. With firearms coveted in many countries but not available for purchase or with strict limitation on the purchasing, the demands for the product support the activities of TOC most profitably. In some cases, not only firearms but also firearms accessories, such as bipod shooting sticks, rifle scopes, and gun slings, are sought—and all are available through TOC (United Nations Office on Drugs and Crime, 2020a).

Two other aspects of firearms trafficking, often overlooked by law enforcement and researchers, is the trafficking of parts and components of firearms as well as ammunition. In particular, countries in Europe, Africa, and Asia create a market for the parts and components of all firearms, which are not only used for repairs but also used in the modification of weapons for criminals to gain access to small or more powerful weapons (United Nations Office on Drugs and Crime, 2020a). For countries in the United Kingdom, where the purchase of handguns except for antique war-era pistols is prohibited, the desire for antique-weapon ammunition has provided yet another market for profit by TOC. Thus the firearms trade, which often accompanies the trafficking of other products associated with TOC, is not only a criminal enterprise of profit, but also an enterprise that facilitates other aspects of TOC.

Trafficking of Natural Resources

Natural resources, as the name implies, exist globally without the actions of humans. Given that humans neither produce natural resources nor control the quantity of their production, those products in demand within its limited market are often quite expensive to obtain. Hence, when demand exceeds legal availability, TOC plays a role in delivering these resources to the ever-desiring consumer. The **trafficking of natural resources** is another area for involvement by TOC. Specifically, from illegal mining and smuggling of raw materials such as diamonds and rare metals such as gold, estimates of profits to TOC range from $12 billion to $48 billion annually (Clough, 2017), with regions in Africa and South America most often identified as source countries. The trafficking of natural resources depletes the earth, with impacts that are often devastating to the ecosystem and to nonrenewables such as fuel, miners, and logging. Specifically, the trafficking of timber by TOC from areas such as Southeast Asia is estimated to generate annual revenues of over $30 billion (Hunter, 2018).

Recent reports suggest that during the COVID-19 pandemic the trafficking of natural resources has increased significantly, with countries such as Indonesia reporting an increase in illegal logging of over 60% (Chandra, 2021). From a practical perspective, in addition to depleting the environment of natural resources, this activity of TOC reduces tax revenues to source countries, which are already limited in their funding for education, social services, etc.

During the COVID-19 pandemic, the trafficking of natural resources has increased significantly (Chandra, 2021).

The trafficking of natural resources by TOC not only affects a country's tax revenue but also is directly related to child trafficking (McCabe & Murphy, 2016) and to the funding of armed groups in conflict areas (Duarte, 2016). In fact, research has suggested that rebels in conflict areas such as the Democratic Republic of the Congo and Sierra Leone have historically funded their acts of violence through the TOC activities of trafficking gemstones (Duke, 2001). These so-called conflict diamonds have also been identified as funding resources for conflicts in areas of Zimbabwe and are recently of particular interest to Russian TOC groups working to establish roots in Africa within the diamond industry (MiaDonna, 2020). This is yet another instance where the trafficking of natural resources, which not only provides profits to TOC, has severe consequences for the environment and may also facilitate other criminal activities.

Illegal Wildlife Trade

The illegal trade in wildlife is another lucrative business for organized criminal groups—in particular, TOC—with, as demonstrated here, significant consequences to those wishing to prohibit the criminal action. Estimates suggest that wildlife-trafficking profits are approximately $23 billion annually across the globe, with poachers targeting animal skins and body parts for export to foreign markets. TOC groups, which focus on elephant ivory, rhino horns, and other animal parts, profit from **wildlife trafficking** and threaten the existence of some species. Specifically, in 2015, over 1,300 rhinos were poached throughout Africa and their horns transported across the globe, creating a profit of over $490 million for TOC (Mavrellis, 2016).

In 2016, American conservation investigator Esmond Bradley Martin, famed for his dangerous work uncovering illegal global trafficking of ivory and rhino horn, was stabbed to death at his home in Kenya. Martin's death continues the series of killings of high-profile environmental activists around the world (Dixon, 2018).

In addition, and to the detriment of animals not targeted for trafficking by TOC, wildlife trafficking allows the introduction of invasive species that compete with or prey upon the native species. TOC also results in the accidental killing of nontargeted species such as dolphins and seabirds during illegal fishing excursions, all for profit. In fact, based upon research on illegal fishing, it is suggested that illegal fishing depletes the waters, often utilizes forced labor, and discards much of the incidental and unwanted illegal catch (Chapsos, 2018). Unfortunately, even the effects of COVID-19 have not limited the efforts in wildlife trafficking.

In February 2020, in response to the COVID-19 pandemic, the Chinese government introduced multiple emergency measures (i.e., laws and enforcement) to limit the trade in wild animals for consumption (Wrigley & Duthie, 2020); however, given that wildlife trafficking is an illegal action, the effect of this government intervention is unclear. Hence, reducing wildlife trafficking or the illegal wildlife trade is beneficial to those targeted animals and ecology and for country development (Mavrellis, 2016). Lastly, TOC involvement in wildlife trafficking robs local communities of their resources, provides a foundation for violations of human rights and rule of law, and supports finance corruption, violence, and instability.

Fraudulent Medicines and Medical Information

With the cost of pharmaceuticals at a historical high and more people dependent upon these daily medications, the introduction of fake or **fraudulent medicines** affects more of the general population than drug trafficking, the weapons trade, or human trafficking. In particular, the sale of fraudulent medicines represents a potentially deadly trade for consumers, as instead of curing people it may result in increased harm, worsening addictions, and even death (United Nations Office on Drugs and Crime, 2021b).

The World Health Organization estimates that up to 10% of medicines available in developing countries and up to 30% in some countries of Asia, Africa, and Latin America are likely fraudulent. In addition, medicines purchased online are, in 50% of the cases, counterfeit (World Health Organization, 2006). TOC groups engage in these activities to profit (once again) from the demand of our current society norm of taking "a pill for every ill" (Mintzes, 2007). Through fictitious front companies, exploitations of border control agents, and fake documents to obtain pharmaceutical ingredients, approximately

$23 billion is added to the profits of TOC on an annual basis (United Nations Office on Drugs and Crime, 2021a). These profits are based upon a strong demand and are expected to increase annually.

Research suggests that both branded and generic drugs may be made fraudulently with medications for treating depression, schizophrenia, diabetes, blood pressure, and cholesterol among the most common (United Nations Office on Drugs and Crime, 2021a). With the current world focus on COVID-19, fraudulent medical information related to COVID-19 has been detected. Specifically, in December of 2020, Interpol issued a global alert to government agencies within its member countries, identifying the work of TOC networks (mainly originating in Russia) in producing and distributing fake COVID-19 vaccination certificates (Davis, 2021).

Fraudulent medical information includes fake COVID-19 vaccination certificates.

Given the new demand for proof of vaccine in order to travel, attend school, work, or attend social events, these falsified documents were not unexpected. Hence, fraudulent medicines trafficked through TOC, which target individuals in both developed and developing countries, can lead to major negative health implications for consumers.

Cybercrime

Cybercrime is one of the fastest growing areas of criminal activity today (McCabe, 2017). Through cybercrimes, individuals are often harassed, extorted, and made victims of identity theft, and, as demonstrated in the May 2021 case described here, cybercrimes produce significant profits for criminal groups. For TOC, cybercrime is yet another avenue for profit. Research suggests that cybercrime produces approximately $1.5 trillion annually for TOC (Greig, 2020). Cybercrime, which utilizes technology and the borderless environment of the internet, provides an even more difficult environment for authority controls and regulations. In crimes committed within the cyber environment, technology is either the target of the crime, such as financial accounts, or the tool

In May of 2021, the U.S. company Colonial Pipeline paid extortionists roughly 75 bitcoin (approximately $5 million) to recover its stolen data and clear the way for its gas lines to resume carrying fuel. The ransom was paid to the group DarkSide, which is believed to operate from Eastern Europe, possibly Russia (Shear et al., 2021).

for the crime, such as in facilitating trades in human-trafficking cases or identity theft.

Perpetrators of cybercrime and their victims can be located in different regions, which supports the transnational setting for TOC. There is no international definition of *cybercrime* or *cyberattack*; however, cybercrimes tend to be described as having cyber-dependent offenses, cyber-enabled offenses, and specific crime-type offenses. For clarity, a cyber-dependent crime requires an internet infrastructure and is often typified as creating, disseminating, and deploying malware, ransomware, attacks on critical national infrastructure (e.g., the cyber-takeover of an oil company by a TOC), or taking a website offline by overloading it with data (a "distributed denial of service," or DDoS, attack). Cyber-enabled crimes occur in the offline world but can also be facilitated by the internet, such as in drug trafficking and money laundering. Lastly, crime-specific types of offenses include crimes that are dependent upon technology, such as sextortion and child pornography (United Nations Office on Drugs and Crime, 2017).

For TOC, the anonymity of the online marketplace, which operates from hidden computers within multiple countries, creates significant problems for law enforcement in terms of technical requirements and the need for new investigative techniques. Hence, the profits from cybercrime activities continue to benefit TOC.

Smuggling of Goods

The **smuggling of goods** can be seen to constitute one of the most neglected aspects of illicit trade, as demonstrated in the May 2021 case above. Yet research suggests that this goods smuggling, of which tobacco and alcohol are among the most common goods, provides TOC over $1 billion annually (Lallerstedt et al., 2016). Specifically, the illicit trade in tobacco products is perhaps the most frequently identified sector in the shadow economy, as it refers to any practice prohibited by law that relates to shipment, receipt, possession, distribution, sale, or purchase of tobacco products (Ellis, 2017). Estimates suggest that, separate from the profits for

In May of 2021, French police and customs officers seized 250,000 counterfeit cigarettes and arrested five individuals (Europol, 2021). This TOC group received the illegal cigarettes from two criminal networks based abroad, arranged for their storage in various cities in France, and then managed their subsequent distribution through a number of criminal wholesalers on the black market. Investigations into the criminal network revealed questionable payments and financial flows, which were used to support TOC.

TOC, the trafficking of cigarettes costs tobacco-producing countries approximately $40.5 billion (approximately 9% in retail sales) in tax revenue (Ellis, 2017). Again, if cigarettes may be purchased in Serbia for 350 dinar (approximately $3.40) yet sold in Scotland for 10 pounds sterling ($13.40), then rational choice suggests that this is a product TOC will be motivated to provide and transport.

In 2020, Montenegrin police seized cigarettes estimated to be worth over $1 million that were intended for trafficking to Western Europe (Ljubas, 2020). In the United States, New York has the highest inbound trafficking activity, with an estimated 55% of the cigarettes consumed in the state originating in states other than New York (Boesen, 2020). The smuggling of cigarettes and tobacco not only profits TOC, but often provides those profits to the detriment of manufacturers and regional governments.

Alcohol, another identified sector, represents a significant percentage of worldwide consumption, with a sharp 26% of total world consumption in the form of unrecorded alcohol (Ellis, 2017). TOC involvement in the trafficking of alcohol is widespread, representing significant percentages of alcohol consumption worldwide and stripping governments of billions of dollars in tax revenues. In addition to the serious health risk for consumers, the illicit trade in alcohol (similar to the trade in tobacco) results in substantial losses in tax and duty revenue for governments (Transnational Alliance to Combat Illicit Trade, 2021).

Illicit trade in alcohol, or alcohol smuggling, encompasses a wide variety of illegal activities that are typically characterized as (1) alcohol with original branding that has been illegally imported or smuggled into a jurisdiction and sold, evading tariffs and customs duties; or (2) fraudulent imitations of legitimate branded products, including refilling, falsification, and tampering (Transnational Alliance to Combat Illicit Trade, 2021). TOC profits from alcohol are estimated to be over $3 billion annually (Lallerstedt et al., 2016). Thus, as the profits from the smuggling of goods continue to increase, the illegal actions continue be supported by the criminal activities of TOC.

Trafficking of Art and Antiquities

The **trafficking of art and antiquities**, often called the trafficking of cultural goods, refers to the import, export, and transfer of ownership of cultural property, which are items significant to archeology, prehistory, history, literature, art, or science (Ellis, 2017). According to the UN's Office on Drugs and Crime (United Nations, 2015), the trafficking of cultural goods provides $3.4 billion to $6.3 billion in annual profits—much of it through TOC. In many cases that are unique to the trafficking of art and antiquities, TOC must first be involved in obtaining the property. Specifically, the sources for these items are (1) theft of already identified treasures; (2) illicit excavation of artifacts, which involves local people for digging and various levels of local law enforcement for movement; and (3) counterfeiting, which often involves another group of experts producing the products and their provenance (i.e., history of origination and ownership). Given that provenance is required for the sale of most art and antiques, this area is especially relevant to TOC, as "legitimizing" a product increases its value.

Today, in addition to the growing awareness and evidence of the increasing involvement of TOC in "the looting, trafficking, and sale of cultural property," it is now acknowledged that these TOC groups "are also often involved in other types of crimes, such as illicit arms and drug trafficking, money-laundering, corruption and terrorism financing" (United Nations, 2015). Hence, within the trafficking of art and antiquities, other aspects of products trafficking and criminal activity are often central to TOC.

Counterfeiting

Counterfeiting, which is most often associated with the duplication of currency, is another aspect of TOC. However, although advances in technology, scanning, and printing have made the counterfeiting of currency more common and have cost countries millions of dollars annually (Cabitza, 2012), currency is not the only product counterfeited by TOC.

The manufacture and distribution of counterfeit of goods is another area for profit by TOC. As reported by the U.S. Department of Homeland Security (2020), the trafficking of counterfeit goods internationally reaches profits of up to $509 billion annually. Counterfeiting is no longer limited to the handbag items seen on the streets of cities such as New York; now it includes the counterfeiting of medicines (discussed earlier), clothing apparel, watches, and computer accessories, to name a few. In particular, research suggests that over 20% of counterfeit goods seized are footwear, with brands such as Nike and Adidas among the most common (Miloscia, 2019).

> The trafficking of counterfeit goods internationally reaches profits of up to $509 billion annually (U.S. Department of Homeland Security, 2020).

The ease of trafficking of counterfeit products is especially enticing to individuals involved in TOC, as the cost of set-up is relatively low (especially online) and maintaining an e-commerce website requires little work. This is especially the case in the counterfeiting of currency. From 2018 to 2020, during the COVID-19 pandemic, online sales in the United States increased over 50%, with TOC making significant profits from the sale of counterfeit goods (United Nations Conference on Trade and Development, 2022).

Money Laundering

Money laundering typically involves transferring money through several countries in order to obscure its origins. As the overwhelming majority of profits for TOC are cash, and it is difficult to keep large sums of cash from being undetected, TOC uses money laundering to hide those profits. In fact, the cross-border aspect of money laundering is an essential part of TOC. The United Nations Office on Drugs and Crime (2021a) suggests that between $800 billion and $2 trillion is laundered every year. Money laundering involves criminals and criminal organizations disguising the original source of money obtained through illegal activities so that it appears as though the profits were generated from legal sources (Layton & Curran, 2021).

Money laundering works by putting illicit money into the financial system by separating funds from the original source (often through shell companies) and then placing the returned money into a legitimate business, such as a construction company. Once the money is redistributed into the legitimate business (or cleaned), it is difficult to distinguish the illicit money from the company's legitimate financial resources. TOC is well versed in this process and therefore continues to utilize laundered money without detection (Global Financial Integrity, 2021).

Two newer aspects of money laundering are cryptocurrency and trade-based money laundering. *Cryptocurrency* is a digital currency that is secured electronically by cryptography (security codes); thus it is nearly impossible to counterfeit. In most cases, cryptocurrency is a form of digital asset based on a network that is distributed across a large number of computers, not banking systems; for that reason, it is outside the control of governments and central authorities.

Trade-based money laundering involves sending fraudulent invoices to companies for large quantities of legitimate goods for transfer among countries (Global Financial Integrity, 2021). By commingling the proceeds of crime with the proceeds of legitimate business, TOC networks are able to disguise the ultimate source of the illicit money. Obviously, money laundering remains a significant aspect of TOC.

Terrorism

TOC poses a significant and growing threat to national and international security—in particular, in facilitating acts of **violent extremism** and **terrorism** (National Security Council, 2011). Today, TOC is expanding its criminal actions as well as diversifying its activities, resulting in the convergence of threats that have dire consequences of fear, injury, and death for individuals and destabilizing effects within countries.

Research suggests that developing countries with weak rule of law can be particularly susceptible to TOC penetration and that TOC within states further weakens governance. One such example is the recent takeover of Afghanistan by the Taliban. As suggested by those who study the Taliban, this insurgency is funded not only by loyal outside sources with common philosophies, but also through the TOC activities of drug trafficking and weapons trafficking, the exploitation of precious minerals and mines, and the trafficking of people (Azami, 2021).

> Terrorists and insurgents are increasingly turning to TOC to generate funding and to acquire logistical support (National Security Council, 2011).

TOC networks imbed themselves into the political process in a variety of ways. In the majority of the cases it is through direct bribery, by infiltrating financial and security sectors, and by coercion or corruption (National Security Council, 2011). As TOC groups position themselves as alternate providers of governance, security, services, and livelihoods, they control the people of the state, the rule of law, the judicial systems, and the press. The result is that terrorists and insurgents are increasingly turning to TOC to generate funding and acquire logistical support to carry out their violent acts; hence, TOC helps to facilitate terrorism.

Sources of Data on TOC

In the study of TOC, questions about exact definitions make the task of identifying the proper data and assessing its availability for collection and analysis particularly complicated. There is no universally accepted definition of *transnational organized crime*, and the definitions that do exist focus on specific groups and often fail to capture what is commonly meant by the term—which can be either a particular type of criminal organization or a particular organized crime activity. This failure to arrive at a consistent definition makes it difficult to address legal aspects of TOC, as well as to make empirical attempts to examine data related to TOC. Some reliable sources of TOC data do exist, however, and are utilized in research into TOC and in various efforts that authorities have designed in order to prevent TOC. Sources of information and data include governmental and nongovernmental organizations, among them the International Organized Crime Intelligence and Operations Center, the United Nations Office on Drugs and Crime, Interpol, and the Corruption Perceptions Index.

International Organized Crime Intelligence and Operations Center

In 2009, the **International Organized Crime Intelligence and Operations Center (IOC-2)** was created. U.S. officials recognized that TOC poses a significant and growing threat to national and international security and has dire implications for public safety, public health, democratic institutions, and economic stability across the globe (Federal Bureau of Investigation, 2021). The IOC-2 combines the resources and information of multiple U.S. law enforcement agencies and federal prosecutors from across the country to collectively combat the threats that international criminal organizations pose to domestic safety and security.

The IOC-2 enables partner agencies to join together in a task-force setting, combine data, and produce actionable leads for investigators and prosecutors working nationwide to combat international organized crime and to coordinate the resulting multijurisdictional investigations and prosecutions. Those participating agencies are the Federal Bureau of Investigation (FBI); U.S. Immigration and Customs Enforcement (ICE); Drug Enforcement Administration (DEA); U.S. Internal Revenue Service (IRS); Bureau of Alcohol, Tobacco, Firearms and Explosives (ATF); U.S. Secret Service (USSS); U.S. Postal Inspection Service (USPIS); U.S. Department of State, Bureau of Diplomatic Security (DS); U.S. Department of Labor, Office of the Inspector General (DOL-OIG); and U.S. Department of Justice (DOJ), Criminal Division.

The goal of IOC-2 is to disrupt and dismantle TOC groups that pose threats to the United States by (1) providing de-confliction and coordination of multijurisdictional, multiagency, and multinational law enforcement operations, investigations, prosecutions, and forfeiture proceedings; (2) identifying and analyzing all source information and intelligence related to TOC; and (3) disseminating such information and intelligence to support member agency investigative efforts (Federal Bureau of Investigation, 2021). IOC-2 is an excellent source of information for those interested in TOC.

United Nations Office on Drugs and Crime

The mission of the United Nations Office on Drugs and Crime (UNODC) is to produce and disseminate high-quality statistics on drugs, crime, and criminal justice at the international level (United Nations Office on Drugs and Crime, 2020c). The UNODC regularly updates global statistical series on crime, criminal justice, drug trafficking and prices, drug production, and drug use to address TOC. In addition, UNODC has established joint centers with organizations around the globe to address TOC. One of these is the UNODC-INEGI Centre of Excellence in Statistical Information on Government, Crime, Victimization and Justice, which is a joint project run by UNODC and the Statistical Office of Mexico (INEGI) to develop best practices in the area of crime and criminal justice statistics in Latin America and the Caribbean. Another center, the UNODC-KOSTAT Centre of Excellence for Statistics on Crime and Criminal Justice in Asia and Pacific, is a joint project run by UNODC and the Statistical Office of the Republic of Korea (KOSTAT) that was established to provide technical assistance and training for countries in Asia and the Pacific (United Nations Office on Drugs and Crime, 2020c). Hence, UNODC may provide many sources of information on TOC.

Interpol

The International Criminal Police Organization, or **Interpol**, is an international law enforcement organization that facilitates worldwide police cooperation and crime control. Within Interpol is an Organized Crime unit with the goal of identifying major figures involved in transnational crime, their associated criminal networks, and the activities of those TOC. This Organized Crime unit conducts criminal analysis of data such as biometrics, images, and known associations—based on intelligence provided by member countries and partners. In addition, Interpol's Organized Crime unit conducts multiple projects focused on specific types of criminal networks.

Interpol—An international law enforcement organization that facilitates worldwide police cooperation and crime control.

These projects encourage national and international enforcement exchanges of operational data, and sharing of lessons learned; thus, Interpol provides a global picture of TOC for law enforcement throughout the world and links the various organizers, financers, recruiters, distributors, and corrupt officials as related to TOC (Interpol, 2021a). Interpol provides another data source for those interested in TOC.

World Factbook

The ***World Factbook***, also known as the *CIA World Factbook*, is a report produced by the U.S. Central Intelligence Agency (CIA). Its country-based reports on the 193 countries of the world include information such as country demographics (e.g., poverty, unemployment), geography, gender diversity (e.g., male and female literacy), and issues of security concern.

Unique to the *World Factbook* is its dedication to information on transnational issues for each country. For example, for a country such as Armenia, the *Factbook* documents an illicit cultivation in cannabis, a transit point for illicit drugs (opium and hashish) to move to Russia or Europe, and the current situation on human trafficking (the report suggests that Armenian women are exploited in sex trafficking and labor trafficking, often to countries such as Turkey and the United Arab Emirates).

The *World Factbook*, which has been produced since the 1960s and became available for public use in the 1970s, is frequently used as a resource for academic research papers, government and nongovernment efforts, and news articles. In addition, the information on countries is updated regularly, in some cases weekly, to provide the most recent accounts within the country.

Corruption Perceptions Index

One of the most commonly cited characteristics of TOC organizations is that they exist within areas of corruption. The **Corruption Perceptions Index (CPI)** is a measure of that corruption. Specifically, the CPI is an index that ranks countries by their perceived levels of public corruption, as determined by expert assessments and opinion surveys (Transparency International, 2021). In this report, *corruption* is defined generally as an abuse of entrusted public power for private gain. The index, published annually by the nongovernmental organization Transparency International, has existed since 1995. The 2020 CPI, published in January 2021, ranked 180 countries "on a scale from 100 (very clean) to 0 (highly corrupt)" based on the situation between May 2019 and May 2020 (Transparency International, 2021). Given that corruption is a large part of TOC, the Perceptions Corruption Index may provide insight into TOC.

Globalization Versus Hyperglobalization

Globalization is the word used to describe the growing interdependence of the world's economies through cross-border trade in goods and services. Use of the term became popular in the early 1990s with the beginning of the expansion of the internet. For the most part, globalization has been perceived as a positive aspect of today's culture, as it brings new ideas, exposes people to different cultures, and speeds up the retrieval of information, which can only come through the use of technology. **Hyperglobalization** is the term used to describe the dramatic increase in globalization that has occurred over the last two decades as technological advances and travel have expanded at a rate never before experienced by humankind. Unfortunately, just as with any form of new activity—especially illegal activities—rules, regulations, and the enforcement of those regulations appear later and often as a result of an action that society wishes to limit or prohibit. One particular example today is the involvement of TOC in actions related to COVID-19.

Hyperglobalization— A term used to describe the dramatic increase in globalization that has occurred over the last two decades.

Specifically, when an emergency response is needed and speed is essential, it is difficult to enforce procedures to ensure that public resources are spent appropriately; this is clearly a reason why the diversion of funds designed for health care, provisions of counterfeit vaccines, and the production and distribution of fake vaccine cards are all included within the criminal activities of TOC. People involved in TOC are well aware of the concept of hyperglobalization, as well as the lag in the enforcement efforts that are needed to address TOC's newly minted criminal activities.

Globalization, generally described as the removal of barriers to cross-national movement of goods and funds, has been extremely beneficial to TOC as it has created new markets for illicit goods and services (Forest, 2020). Hyperglobalization, which features the rise of multinational business and a surge in foreign investment to facilitate the flow of goods and services across borders, results in a decentralization of trade. A quick decentralization of trade often results in a large reduction in the time required for product delivery, which therefore means less time for the enforcement of trade regulations (Subramanian & Kessler, 2013). The result is more profit for TOC. Hyperglobalization is even better for TOC, as the speed of product demands and the expectation of instantaneous results have become the culture that supports the illegal actions of traffickers and TOC. More specific to TOC, in Europe and North America there is a high demand for drugs; in Africa and the Middle East the demand is for weapons; in Asia the demand is for wildlife and animal parts; and exploitable people are desired everywhere (Forest, 2020).

In addition, globalization and hyperglobalization support an environment that facilitates hate, violent extremism, and terrorism (McCabe, 2017). Through globalization, new opportunities exist for personal connections, and those groups interested in recruiting members for violent activities allow both transnational criminals and terrorists to be available via the internet. Today, through advances in technology, communications, and transport—all a consequence of hyperglobalization—loose networks of terrorists and organized criminal groups that operate internationally can easily connect and then significantly increase their capacity for violence (Forest, 2020). In a nutshell, TOC networks have benefited significantly from the globalization and hyperglobalization of new technologies and global markets.

Summary

TOC is one of the most profitable criminal activities in the world today, and yet it remains one of the most ambiguous areas to be addressed by law enforcement. Enforcement efforts are often minimal, and therefore individuals and countries continue to suffer the consequences of TOC. Some of the more common criminal activities associated with TOC are drug trafficking, human trafficking, weapons trafficking, and the illegal wildlife trade. For those interested in the study of TOC, multiple government sources exist, including IOC-2, UNODC, and Interpol. All of these sources provide unique perspectives on the information collected on TOC and should be considered as a whole for a picture of the most relevant information.

Unfortunately, TOC is no longer focused simply on profits from cross-border exchanges; it is also an essential strategy for armed groups around the world as well as a source of funding for terrorists. As demonstrated in this general introduction, countries have failed to combat the hyperglobalization of TOC, and profits through TOC are now at a historic high. By understanding the nature and dynamics of TOC, one may better address these criminal networks. This text provides the foundation for all who wish to help prevent TOC.

Questions for Further Thought

1. As TOC is emerging as one of the most profitable aspects of criminal activities, why is defining and enforcing the crime of TOC so difficult?
2. If TOC groups are often involved in multiple areas of criminal activity, why are only their crimes targeted and not the organizations themselves?
3. If hyperglobalization has increased the activities of TOC, will this increase continue as technology continues to evolve?

References

Abadinsky, H. (2017). *Organized crime* (11th ed). Cengage Group, 2–4.

Albanese, J. (2015). *Organized crime: From the mob to transnational organized crime.* Routledge.

Alexander, B. (2014). *Bad company and burnt power: Justice and injustice in the old southwest.* University of North Texas Press, 259–261.

Amadae, S. (2021, March 11). Rational choice theory. *Encyclopedia Britannica*. https://www.britannica.com/topic/rational-choice-theory

Anderson, E. (1999). *Code of the street: Decency, violence, and the moral life of the inner city*. W. W. Norton.

Azami, D. (2021, August 27). *Afghanistan: How do the Taliban make money?* BBC News. Retrieved August 28, 2021, from https://www.bbc.com/news/world-46554097

BBC News. (2021a, January 22). *Essex lorry deaths: Men jailed for killing 39 migrants in trailer*. Retrieved August 20, 2021, from https://www.bbc.com/news/uk-england-essex-55765213

BBC News. (2021b, July 15). *Peter R. de Vries: Dutch crime reporter dies after shooting*. Retrieved October 3, 2021, from https://www.bbc.com/news/world-europe-57853004

Boesen, U. (2020, November). *Cigarette taxes and cigarette smuggling by state, 2018*. Tax Foundation. Retrieved August 1, 2021, from https://taxfoundation.org/cigarette-taxes-cigarette-smuggling-2020/

Borst, A. (1992). *Medieval worlds: Barbarians, heretics, and artists in the Middle Ages*. University of Chicago Press, 3–4.

Broadhurst, K., Duffin, M., Owen, K., & Gill, M. (2005). *Research into the views and perceptions of drug dealers*. Perpetuity Research and Consultancy International. Retrieved from https://perpetuityresearch.com/wp-content/uploads/2017/12/2005-11-Research-into-the-views-and-perceptions-of-drug-dealers-Executive-Summary.pdf

Brzenchek, R. (2020). *Transnational organized crime and gangs: Intervention, prevention, and suppression of cybersecurity*. Rowman & Littlefield.

Cabitza, M. (2012, August 16). *Why fake dollars are big business in Peru*. BBC News. Retrieved August 20, 2021, from https://www.bbc.com/news/world-latin-america-19240999

Chandra, W. (2021, May 24). *Illegal loggers use pandemic as cover to ramp up activity in Sulawesi*. Mongabay News. Retrieved December 3, 2021, from https://news.mongabay.com/2021/05/illegal-loggers-use-pandemic-as-cover-to-ramp-up-activity-in-sulawesi/

Chapsos, I. (2018). Illegal fishing and fisheries crime as a transnational organized crime in Indonesia. *Trends in Organized Crime, 22*, 225–273.

Clough, C. (2017, March 27). *Transnational crime is a $1.6 trillion to $2.2 trillion annual "business."* Global Financial Integrity. Retrieved August 24, 2021, from https://gfintegrity.org/press-release/transnational-crime-is-a-1-6-trillion-to-2-2-trillion-annual-business-finds-new-gfi-report/

Davis, E. (2021, August 20). Black market for fake Covid-19 vaccination cards flourishing. *US News and World Report*. Retrieved August 24, 2021, from https://www.usnews.com/news/best-countries/articles/2021-08-20/global-black-market-for-fake-covid-19-vaccination-cards-flourishing

Dickens, Charles. (1838). *Oliver Twist*. Bentley's Miscellany.

Dixon, R. (2018, February 5). Renowned conservation investigator Esmond Bradley Martin killed at home in Kenya. Retrieved July 15, 2021, from https://www.latimes.com/world/africa/la-fg-kenya-conservationist-killed-20180205-story.html

Duarte, N. (2016, November 25). *Beyond blood diamonds: The violence behind the gold route*. Open Global Rights. Retrieved August 5, 2021, from https://www.opendemocracy.net/en/openglobalrights-openpage/beyond-blood-diamonds-violence-behind-gold-route/

Duke, L. (2001, April 29). Diamond trade's tragic flaw. *Washington Post*. Retrieved August 15, 2021, from https://www.washingtonpost.com/archive/business/2001/04/29/diamond-trades-tragic-flaw/b4c2c3c4-f5a8-4ba7-9d96-c9a8f80945a1/

Ellis, C. (2017). On tap Europe: Organised crime and illicit trade in tobacco, alcohol and pharmaceuticals. *RUSI Whitehall Report*, 2–17.

Europol. (2021, May 12). 12 Arrested in France in latest hit against tobacco smugglers. Retrieved August 22, 2021, from https://www.europol.europa.eu/newsroom/news/12-arrested-in-france-in-latest-hit-against-tobacco-smugglers

Federal Bureau of Investigation. (2021). *Transnational organized crime*. Retrieved August 1, 2021, from https://www.fbi.gov/investigate/organized-crime

Forest, J. (2020, September 16). *Globalization and transnational crime*. Retrieved August 15, 2021, from https://www.e-ir.info/2020/09/16/globalization-and-transnational-crime/

Free Dictionary. (2006). National criminal intelligence service. In *The free dictionary*. Retrieved November 5, 2021, from https://legal-dictionary.thefreedictionary.com/National+Criminal+Intelligence+Service

Global Financial Integrity. (2021). *Money laundering*. Retrieved July 30, 2021, from https://gfintegrity.org/issue/money-laundering/

Godson, R., & Olson, W. (1995). International organized crime. *Society, 1*, 18–29.

Greig, J. (2020, March 12). *Cybercriminal raking in $1.5 trillion every year*. Tech Republic. Retrieved July 30, 2021, from https://www.techrepublic.com/article/cybercriminals-raking-in-1-5-trillion-every-year/

Hobsbawn, E. (1985). *Bandits*. Penguin Press.

Hunter, M. (2018, April 18). *Tainted timber*. Global Initiative. Retrieved August 20, 2021, from https://globalinitiative.net/analysis/tainted_timber/

International Peace Institute. (2009). *Transnational organized crime*. Task Forces on Strengthening Multilateral Security Capacity [No. 2]. Retrieved January 3, 2022, from https://www.ipinst.org/wp-content/uploads/2015/06/toc_final.pdf

Interpol. (2021a). *Organized crime*. Retrieved August 20, 2021, from https://www.interpol.int/en/Crimes/Organized-crime

Interpol. (2021b, July 26). 286 *Arrested in global human trafficking and migrant smuggling operations*. Retrieved August 20, 2021, from https://www.interpol.int/en/News-and-Events/News/2021/286-arrested-in-global-human-trafficking-and-migrant-smuggling-operation

Klein, M. (1995). *The American street gang*. Oxford University Press.

Lallerstedt, K., Zhang, E., & Pauwelyn, J. (2016). *The world trade system must fight itself to fight illicit trade*. Global Initiative against Transnational Organized Crime. Retrieved July 30, 2021, from https://globalinitiative.net/wp-content/uploads/2016/08/illicittradeunderminingdevelopment-1.pdf

Layton, J., & Curran, O. (2021, April 19). *How money laundering works*. Retrieved August 2, 2021, from https://money.howstuffworks.com/money-laundering.htm

Ljubas, Z. (2020, August 11). *Montenegrin police bust cigarette smuggling ring.* Organized Crime and Corruption Reporting Project. Retrieved August 15, 2021, from https://www.occrp.org/en/daily/12928-montenegrin-police-bust-cigarette-smuggling-ring

Lunde, P. (2004). *Organized crime.* DK Publishing.

Mavrellis, C. (2017, March 27). *Transnational crime and the developing world.* Global Financial Integrity. Retrieved August 29, 2021, from https://gfintegrity.org/report/transnational-crime-and-the-developing-world/

Mavrellis, C. (2016, September 24). *Wildlife trafficking generates up to US $23 billion in illicit financial flows each year.* Global Financial Integrity. Retrieved August 1, 2021, from https://gfintegrity.org/press-release/wildlife-trafficking-generates-us23-billion-illicit-financial-flows-year/#:~:text=Wildlife%20Trafficking%20Generates%20Up%20to,Each%20Year%20%C2%AB%20Global%20Financial%20Integrity

McCabe, K. (2017). *Protecting your children online.* Rowman & Littlefield.

McCabe, K. (2008). *The trafficking of persons. National and international responses.* Peter Lang.

McCabe, K., & Murphy, D. (2016). *Child abuse: Today's issues.* CRC Press.

McMullan, T. (1982). Criminal organization in sixteenth and seventeenth century London. *Social Problems, 29*(3), 1–19. https://doi.org/10.2307/800162

MiaDonna. (2020, July 9). *Blood diamonds in 2020—What most jewelers don't want you to know.* Retrieved August 5, 2021, from https://www.miadonna.com/blogs/news/blood-diamonds-in-2020-what-most-jewelers-dont-want-you-to-know

Miloscia, J. (2019, October 9). *It's not just shoes: The world's most counterfeited products.* Retrieved August 5, 2021, from https://www.covectra.com/most-counterfeited-products/

Mintzes, Barbara. (2007). A pill for every ill—or an ill for every pill? *Visions Journal, 4*(2), 21–22. Retrieved July 11, 2022, from https://www.heretohelp.bc.ca/pill-every-ill-or-ill-every-pill

Müller, W. (1888). Notes on the people of the Serpentine. *Proceedings of the Society of Biblical Archaeology, 10*, 147–154.

National Security Council. (2011). *Transnational organized crime: A growing threat to national and international security.* Retrieved February 3, 2022, from https://obamawhitehouse.archives.gov/administration/eop/nsc/transnational-crime/threat

Pennell, C. (2001). The geography of piracy: Northern Morocco in the mid-nineteenth century. In C. Pennell (Ed.), *Bandits at sea: A pirates reader.* New York University Press.

Peters, G. (2011). The Taliban and organized crime. *Nacao e Defesa, 130*(5), 105–129.

Peterson Institute for International Economics (2012, August 24). *What is globalization?* Retrieved August 26, 2021, from https://www.piie.com/microsites/globalization/what-is-globalization

Schapiro, R. (2021, August 1). Plot thickens in Whitey Bulger murder case with transfer of two prisoners. *NBC News.* Retrieved May 15, 2022, from https://www.nbcnews.com/news/crime-courts/plot-thickens-whitey-bulger-murder-case-transfer-2-prisoners-n1275543

Shear, M., Perlroth, N., & Krauss, C. (2021, May 13). Colonial Pipeline paid roughly $5 million in ransom to hackers. *New York Times*. Retrieved August 20, 2021, from https://www.nytimes.com/2021/05/13/us/politics/biden-colonial-pipeline-ransomware.html

Sondhi, P. (2015). *Understanding organized crime* [Info 202 Case Study]. Retrieved November 2, 2021, from https://ischools.org/resources/Documents/Discipline%20of%20organizing/Case%20Studies/Organized-Crime-Sondhi2015.pdf

Stryker, A. (2019, December 17). *Rethinking the drug dealer.* We are the Drug Policy Alliance. Retrieved August 1, 2021, from https://drugpolicy.org/drugsellers

Subramanian, A., & Kessler, M. (2013, July 24). The hyperglobalization of trade and its future. In *Peterson Institute for International Economics* [Working Paper No. 13-6]. Retrieved July 15, 2021, from https://ssrn.com/abstract=2297994

Transnational Alliance to Combat Illicit Trade. (2021). *Illicit trade in alcohol.* Retrieved August 1, 2021, from https://www.tracit.org/alcohol.html

Transparency International (2021). *Corruption perceptions index, 2020.* Retrieved July 31, 2021, from https://www.transparency.org/en/what-we-do

United Nations. (2015, November 5). Trafficking in cultural property "source of enormous illicit profits" UN Official tells forum. *UN News*. Retrieved August 29, 2021, from https://news.un.org/en/story/2015/11/514712-trafficking-cultural-property-source-enormous-illicit-profits-un-official-tells

United Nations Conference on Trade and Development. (2022). *Impact of the COVID-19 pandemic on trade and development: Lessons learned*. https://unctad.org/system/files/official-document/osg2022d1_en.pdf

United Nations Office on Drugs and Crime. (2017). *Cybercrime: Global programme on cybercrime*. Retrieved July 30, 2021, from https://www.unodc.org/unodc/en/cybercrime/global-programme-cybercrime.html

United Nations Office on Drugs and Crime. (2018). *World drug report: Women and drugs: Drug use, drug supply, and their consequences* [UN Publication No. E.18.XI.9]. Retrieved June 1, 2021, from https://www.unodc.org/wdr2018/prelaunch/WDR18_Booklet_5_WOMEN.pdf

United Nations Office on Drugs and Crime. (2019). Module 3: Criminal justice responses to wildlife trafficking. Key issues: Criminalization of Wildlife Trafficking. *E4J University Module Series: Wildlife Crime*. Retrieved October 10, 2021, from https://www.unodc.org/e4j/en/wildlife-crime/module-3/key-issues/criminalization-of-wildlife-trafficking.html

United Nations Office on Drugs and Crime. (2020a). *Global study on firearms trafficking 2020*. https://www.unodc.org/unodc/en/firearms-protocol/firearms-study.html

United Nations Office on Drugs and Crime. (2020b, December). *Measuring organized crime in the Western Balkans*. Retrieved August 12, 2021, from https://www.unodc.org/documents/data-and-analysis/OC/Measuring-OC-in-WB.pdf

United Nations Office on Drugs and Crime. (2020c). *Statistical activities, survey and standards*. Retrieved August 20, 2021, from https://www.unodc.org/unodc/en/data-and-analysis/statistical-activities.html

United Nations Office on Drugs and Crime. (2020d, November 15). *United Nations convention against transnational organized crime and protocols thereto*. Retrieved

August 2, 2021, from https://www.unodc.org/unodc/en/organized-crime/intro/UNTOC.html

United Nations Office on Drugs and Crime. (2021a). *Money laundering, terrorist financing.* Retrieved August 20, 2021, from https://www.unodc.org/unodc/en/money-laundering/overview.html

United Nations Office on Drugs and Crime. (2021b, June 24). *World drug report 2021*. Retrieved August 20, 2021, from https://www.unodc.org/unodc/en/data-and-analysis/wdr2021.html

United Nations Security Council. (2016, December 20). Security Council condemns human trafficking in strongest terms, unanimously adopting resolution 2331 (2016). Accessed on August 19, 2022 at https://press.un.org/en/2016/sc12647.doc.htm

U.S. Department of Homeland Security. (2020, January 24). *Combating trafficking in counterfeit and pirated goods.* Retrieved August 5, 2021, from https://www.dhs.gov/sites/default/files/publications/20_0124_plcy_counterfeit-pirated-goods-report_01.pdf

U.S. Department of Justice. (2021, July 27). *Leader of a sophisticated drug trafficking organization and prolific ally of the Sinaloa cartel sentenced* [Press release]. Justice News. Retrieved August 22, 2021, from https://www.justice.gov/opa/pr/leader-sophisticated-drug-trafficking-organization-and-prolific-ally-sinaloa-cartel-sentenced

Valjak, D. (2017, March 13). *Bulla Felix was the Robin Hood of the Roman Empire who allegedly commanded a group of 600 bandits*. Vintage News. Retrieved May 15, 2022, from https://www.thevintagenews.com/2017/03/13/bulla-felix-was-the-robin-hood-of-the-roman-empire-who-allegedly-commanded-a-group-of-600-bandits/?chrome=1

World Health Organization. (2006). *Counterfeit medicines: An update on estimates.* Retrieved August 20, 2021, from https://www.who.int/medicines/services/counterfeit/impact/TheNewEstimatesCounterfeit.pdf

Wrigley, S., & Duthie, T. (2020, April 27). The illegal wildlife trade is still one of the most profitable criminal enterprises. *The FCPA Blog.* Retrieved July 30, 2021, from https://fcpablog.com/2020/04/27/the-illegal-wildlife-trade-is-still-one-of-the-most-profitable-criminal-enterprises/

Explaining Transnational Organized Crime

Key Terms

Alien conspiracy theory
Black's Law Dictionary
Cesare Beccaria
Civil law
Classical criminology
Common law
Corruption
Corruption Perceptions Index
Cultural deviance theory
Differential association theory
Free will
Illegal enterprise
Italian Mafia
Karl Marx
Organized crime
Positivism
Protection theory
Rule of law
Social conflict theory
Social disorganization theory
Social learning theory
Strain theory
Systems of law
Transnational organized crime (TOC)
Transparency International
United Nations Office of Counter-Terrorism

CHAPTER OBJECTIVES

Chapter 2 will enable readers to understand the following:

- issues related to explaining transnational organized crime (TOC)
- historical theories applied in explaining TOC
- contemporary theories applied in TOC
- how systems of law may facilitate TOC
- how structural failures such as border security and international laws may facilitate TOC
- the role of corruption in TOC
- the role of COVID-19 in explaining the increase in transnational crime activities

TRANSNATIONAL ORGANIZED CRIME (TOC) is criminal activities conducted for profit that involve actions that cross national or international borders. Research suggests that the largest five TOC groups receive over $30 billion annually from profits generated through the illegal drug trade, human trafficking, and other criminal activities (Matthews, 2014). For the most part, TOC operates without detection by law enforcement with little in terms of penalties for those who are identified.

The Federal Bureau of Investigation (FBI) has defined **organized crime** as any group with a formalized structure with the goals of obtaining money and power (Abadinsky, 2017). The concept of *transnational organized crime* generally refers to criminal activities by organized crime groups that cross police jurisdictions. In addition, contemporary definitions of *transnational organized crime* acknowledge globalization, trade liberations, and new technologies to discuss these criminal activities for the purpose of violence for political gains (Burns, 2018). However, whereas the goals of organized crime are profit and power within an area, the overarching goal of TOC is profit. Theories that offer multiple explanations for TOC must include the outcome of material gain; thus, this chapter provides theoretical as well as structural explanations for TOC with the assumption that the primary outcome goal for TOC is money (Ohr, 2001). Specifically, this chapter discusses the theories that guide research on TOC, the **systems of law** within countries that often experience TOC, the structural explanations of TOC that include limitations to border security and corruption, and the role of technology in facilitating TOC.

TOC often flourishes in countries with high levels of criminal activity and low levels of resistance against these activities (Global Initiative, 2021). Countries in this category tend to fall into two groups: those experiencing long-standing conflict and fragility (e.g., Ukraine) and those with more stable democracies but with compromised rule of law and an inability to address organized crime (e.g., Brazil and Sri Lanka). In these cases, conflict weakens social and economic abilities to provide goods and services, thus allowing for criminal groups to fill these voids (Global Initiative, 2021). In these cases, even countries that are characterized as strong and stable are unable to respond to the risk of TOC and criminal threats.

In the United States, TOC has been recognized to present with groups from many different countries. Specifically, African TOC groups have been identified to exist within the United States since the 1980s, with many major U.S. cities, such as Atlanta, Baltimore, and Chicago, identified as areas of criminal enterprise (Federal Bureau of Investigation, 2020). These African groups generally focus on the drug trade, human trafficking, and cybercrimes (McCabe, 2017). Asian TOC groups have been identified to exist within the United States since the 1900s, with the majority of the members of Asian criminal enterprises emerging from the South Pacific (Federal Bureau of Investigation, 2020). These groups often focus on drugs and sexual exploitation (McCabe, 2017). Balkan TOC groups in the United States, unlike other groups that operate under a hierarchy structure, utilize ethnic associations and friendships in their U.S. operations, with a focus on fraud, drug trafficking, and human trafficking and smuggling. Middle Eastern TOC groups in the United States are typically involved in financial fraud, auto theft, and stolen property crimes (Federal Bureau of Investigation, 2020). However, as is the case in the United States, in every country where groups involved in TOC are present, there are factors that facilitate the criminal activities, researchers attempting to explain TOC, and justice officials attempting to address TOC.

Classical Criminology, Positivism, and Social Perspectives of TOC

During the mid-1800s, social philosophers proposed that the relationship between crime and punishment should be balanced and fair (Siegel, 1998). This proposal was based on the idea that the punishment should "fit the crime" and that those who commit crimes such as vandalism or larceny should not receive the same punishment as those who commit assault or murder. Before this **classical criminology** time period, one of the most famous of these philosophers, was Cesare Beccaria (1738–1794), who suggested that in explaining criminal behavior and punishment, one must assume (1) that in every society, people have *free will* to choose criminal or lawful actions; (2) that criminal solutions may be more attractive than lawful solutions, as they require less work for greater reward; and (3) that a person's choice of a solution may be controlled by their fear of punishment.

Cesare Beccaria— Considered the father of modern criminal law and the father of criminal justice, as he condemned torture as a form of punishment.

Hence, when these assumptions are applied to TOC, the concept of *free will* simply suggests that those involved in TOC will continue their criminal actions if the reward is significant and the punishment is minimal or unlikely.

During the 19th century, as the concept of **free will** dominated the philosophies of law and justice, another movement, **positivism**, emerged, with the concept of *other forces* dominating the explanations of criminal behavior. The first explanation of "other forces," which helped found the discipline of sociology, was the belief that human behaviors were a function of external forces (such as poverty) that are beyond the individual's control. The second explanation of "other forces," which was more person- and psychology-based, found that the mental ability or mental health of the individual drives the criminal behavior. Finally, some contemporary research on TOC motivations suggests that the nationality or ethnicity of a criminal organization, with histories and cultures specific to a region, supports these criminal groups by providing social bonds and trust within the organization (Allum & Sands, 2004). Therefore, in addition to economic want or needs, a highly adaptable cultural, political, and transnational phenomenon exists.

Today, the four main perspectives utilized to explain criminal behavior are individual factors, social factors, political and economic influences, and a combination of perspectives or an integrated perspective (Siegel, 1998). Given that the general perceptions or explanations for TOC come from an economic perspective, this chapter focuses on the social (structural and process) perspectives to explain the criminal actions of those engaged in TOC.

The social perspectives used to explain criminal behavior and TOC include the *structural* perspective, which essentially acknowledges the ecological forces that are related to crime, and the *process* perspective, which acknowledges the forces of socialization as an influence on criminal behaviors. In other words, within the structural perspective, crime rates are a function of a community's cultural forces and conditions, while within the process perspective, crime is a function of learning. The specific theories that explain TOC from the historical *structural* perspective are social disorganization, strain, and cultural deviance. The specific theories that explain TOC from the historical *process* perspective discussed in this chapter are differential association and labeling.

Structural Perspectives of Crime

Social structure perspectives of criminology emphasize the conditions of the social structure and their relationship to the individual and the individual's propensity for criminal behavior. This perspective emphasizes poor economic conditions, the limitation of education and marketable skills, and negative cultural values as related to criminal behavior. This section discusses the social structural perspective of criminal behaviors as applied to members within TOC groups.

Social Disorganization Theory

Social disorganization theory links criminal behaviors to community conditions. Based upon this theory, neighborhoods that are experiencing deterioration and poverty in conjunction with inadequate law enforcement and limited informal forms of social control often facilitate the formation of gangs and criminal groups—with law-violating actions seen as norms of behavior.

Shaw and McKay (1972) explained crime and criminal behavior as related to the ecological developments of urban areas. Specifically, they suggested that these transitional neighborhoods experience high rates of population turnover and therefore a lack of neighborhood investment in the activities of the areas. In addition, within these transitional neighborhoods, as diversity increases with newly arrived immigrants, informal social controls that limited inappropriate behaviors in "home countries" were diminished and replaced with slum areas that are perceived to be the breeding grounds for criminal activities (Siegel, 1998). The criminal values that are developed in these neighborhoods are passed down through cultural transmission and are reinforced through the rewards (i.e., profits) obtained through criminal activities. Hence, explanations of organized crime and TOC actions are supported through social disorganization theory.

As criminal subgroups such as those with members in TOC emerge within an area, the norms of behavior, including criminal actions, become the norms of the subgroup. Without the consistency of cultural members demonstrating and supporting noncriminal behaviors, the criminal subgroup is able to attract and retain memberships with the purpose of profit through organized criminal actions.

Strain Theory

Strain theory links criminal behavior to the conflict between the goals of a community and the means to reach those goals. Based on this theory, the unequal distribution of wealth, power, and income leads to many members of disadvantaged groups becoming frustrated. These group members, working together or independently, utilize alternative and often illicit or illegal means to obtain their objectives or goals.

Merton (1968) suggested that in countries where legitimate means to acquire wealth are stratified across social status lines, those with little education and few job skills are denied the ability to access the skills required to be successful in obtaining wealth. Consequently, those who are unable to achieve wealth or other objectives such as a nice car may develop criminal solutions to the problem of obtaining the objective. Inhabitants in a disorganized or strained community often feel frustrated, left out of the economic mainstream, and hopeless. From this perspective, strain results when individuals attempt to become successful through socially accepted, legitimate means but, because of limited resources and/or blocked social opportunities, are unable to reach success. Membership in a TOC group provides the member the financial resources as well as the opportunities to be successful within the society through a different but illegal avenue. To relieve the stresses of legitimate community life, these individuals may turn to TOC criminal activities such as theft or drug trafficking to achieve their goals (Siegel, 1998).

Cultural Deviance Theory

The theory of cultural deviance links criminal behaviors with the conditions of the surrounding community or culture (Bevier, 2015). In particular, **cultural deviance theory** combines social disorganization theory and strain theory to suggest that subcultures develop as a response to community characteristics and the inability of individuals to successfully achieve the societal goals of wealth and power. Within the cultural deviance perspective, subgroups form with sets of values that are in opposition to the conventional values of the main culture.

Miller (1958) suggested that a subculture's deviation from the norms of the dominant culture does not necessarily represent a rebellion against middle-class values, but rather that a revised set of values has emerged within the subculture. Regarding the activities of TOC and membership within the group, the individual member of the group is not as responsible for their criminal behaviors as is the society in which they live. Specifically, as gang-related criminal behaviors increase within a community, the formation of new gangs and gang memberships also increases. Hence, members of a subculture may display the ability to navigate and survive within a street setting, or they may display perceived commonsense approaches to living, or they may display that fortune is based upon luck at a gambling casino; therefore, membership in a criminal group or TOC is a rational choice given the criminal conditions of society.

Process Perspectives on Crime

Process perspectives of criminology emphasize the socialization forces of society and their relationship to the individual and the individual's propensity for criminal behavior. This perspective suggests that crime is a function of learning and that peers, parents, and societal members influence behaviors—including criminal behaviors. This section discusses the process perspective of criminal behaviors as applied to TOC and crime activities.

Social Learning Theory

Social learning theory suggests that crime is a product of learning the norms and behaviors of criminal actions (Siegel, 1998). In other words, criminal actions are learned and rewarded through human interactions, and thus the criminal actions continue. For many researchers attempting to explain membership in TOC groups, social learning is applied in the intergenerational continuity of the criminal organization. Specifically, research suggests that children of TOC members are more likely to join TOC groups than are children of non-TOC members (van Dijk, Kleemans, and Eichelsheim, 2019). In particular, children of TOC members, often not exposed to poverty or repression, may view the actions or community-recognized reputations of their parents as positive and strive to also be successful within the organizational structure of a TOC group (van Dijk, Kleemans, and Eichelsheim, 2019). In particular, social learning theory acknowledges that crimes such as producing fraudulent documents, picking locks for unauthorized entry into structures, and producing methamphetamines are learned behaviors and that criminals learn these behaviors/skills from other criminals. Social learning theory, as applied to the criminal behaviors of TOC group members, suggests that group members are motivated to continue their criminal actions when they receive positive reinforcement for the criminal behaviors from other TOC members and from the community at large.

In the introduction of aspirants into TOC, the role of social learning must be acknowledged. In many areas, associating with members of criminal groups on a daily basis is common; hence, "wannabes" seek to imitate such members. As suggested by Pileggi (1985), power is obtained by membership in criminal organizations and by learning from those members of the organization. These criminal behaviors offer the options of wealth and status within the community. Hence, members of a TOC group learn or refine their criminal behaviors by observing other TOC members and by participating in the actions with those members.

Differential Association Theory

In discussions on gangs and criminal organizations, one of the most commonly discussed forms of social learning theory is differential association. Sutherland's (1939) research on white-collar crime and professional criminals led him to suggest that criminal behavior is a result of more than simply poverty and low socioeconomic status.

According to Sutherland's principles of **differential association theory**, criminal behavior is learned through interactions with others; learning criminal behavior includes learning the specific techniques for committing crimes; the motives for criminal activities are learned from the perception of various laws as favorable or unfavorable; and the process of association with criminal groups is related to the frequency, duration, priority, and intensity of the interactions. Thus, differential association suggests that criminal behavior will occur when the ideas that support or justify crime—such as that the criminal activity is okay and the end justifies the means—outweigh the ideas that prohibit the crime—such as that honest is the best policy and evil is always punished (Siegel, 1998).

In research on criminal gangs of young offenders, Brownfield (2003) suggested that differential association explains a young person's drift toward criminal groups in that the values favorable to violations of law and to peer involvement in organized crime were both significantly related to membership in an organized criminal gang. In TOC, where social relationships are important and illicit relationships are built over time, differential association provides an explanation for membership within the criminal organization.

Social Conflict Theory

Social conflict theory explains crime as a reaction to the economic and social context of a society. In particular, conflict theory views crime as a part of class struggle, where conflict promotes criminal behaviors as a reaction to the conditions of a community. Karl Marx (1857/1973) suggested that all human relations are controlled by economic structures. In other words, conflict theory suggests that the ruling class determines appropriate behaviors and utilizes the criminal justice system to protect their interests and to control the inferior class.

Karl Marx (1818–1883)—Known for his theories regarding capitalism, communism, and conflict.

In Marx's (1857/1973) view, all stratified societies consist of two groups: the ruling class and the working class, with the ruling class using their power to exploit the working class. Organized crime groups are individuals joined together by a shared interest or situation with the only mode for acquiring power within the social structure being membership in an organized criminal organization. In fragile states today, TOC has emerged as a major characteristic. In fact, criminal networks, such as those associations with TOC groups, fuel violent conflict, finance terrorists, and complicate conflict resolution all in attempts to gain power and control within a society (De Boer & Bosett, 2015).

Contemporary Theory to Explain TOC

Based upon the historical perspectives of crime and criminal behavior, additional theories have emerged to address organized crime and, for the purpose of this text, transnational organized crime. Specifically, three such contemporary models are alien conspiracy, illegal enterprise, and protection.

Alien Conspiracy

A common definition of the term *alien* refers to science fiction accounts of space and spacecrafts and beings from another planet. However, a more accurate definition of the term refers to a person who is not a legal citizen of the country where they live; this definition of *alien* is applied in the phrase "alien conspiracy theory."

> In October of 2021, the U.S. District Court for the Southern District of California sentenced a Sinaloa Cartel money launderer to 10 years in prison. The convicted was extradited from Mexico to San Diego. According to court documents, the launderer, a Mexican national, along with her brother and seven other Mexican nationals pleaded guilty to conspiracy to commit money laundering (Justice News, 2021b).

Alien conspiracy theory, developed not by social scientists but by policy makers, resulted when specific immigrant groups were blamed for the problems of organized crime in their areas (Kleemans, 2013). Alien conspiracy sees organized crime and TOC as bureaucratic in structure, with criminal actions supported and monitored by unified leadership and a shared value system (Siegel, 1998). These "crime syndicates" communicate regularly; make decisions on production, manufacturing, and distribution of products; and settle disputes among parties. The October 2021 case noted here presented the ethnic background of the launderer as pertinent to the criminal activity.

The alien conspiracy model of organized crime emerged in the United States in an attempt to explain the **Italian Mafia**, which were relatively locally controlled groups involved in organized crime (Arsovska & Temple, 2016). Research into current TOC groups supports alien conspiracy theory in that in Greek TOC groups, Greek nationals were heavily involved in the different phases and levels of the illicit activities (Antonopoulos, 2009).

In addition, in the United States, it is suggested that certain ethnic groups remain associated with specific products, such as Jamaican immigrants and the drug trade (Williams & Roth, 2011). In the United Kingdom, experts suggest that Moroccans are associated with the trade of cannabis and heroin, Columbians with cocaine, and Albanians with human trafficking (McLean et al., 2020). However, others examining Albanian criminal organizations suggest that there is no single ethnic-type organization (Arsovska & Temple, 2016) and that current groups engaged in TOC are organized around the nature of the product supplied within the illegal market.

Illegal Enterprise

As demonstrated in the October 2021 case of selling exotic cats, illegal enterprises operate in the same manner as legitimate enterprises. The sale of illegal or illicit goods to those who are willing to purchase them is an illegal enterprise. For the most part, the purchase of an illegal

In October of 2021, a New York man was sentenced to 18 months in prison for trafficking exotic African cats. The trafficker advertised and sold the cats on a webpage, then imported and sold the animals, claiming that he operated a big cat rescue organization (Justice News, 2021a).

product is a rare—maybe one-time—event. However, for those involved in TOC, this practice provides a never-ending revenue stream. Research suggests that three factors explain **illegal enterprise**: systematic corruption, partnership in which entrepreneurs design and implement an illegal business, and the internal economic characteristics of illegal businesses (Haller, 1990). Within this theory, the business of TOC is the focus, not ethnicity. Specifically, this spectrum-based theory has been identified as productive in explaining TOC (Woodiwiss, 2014). The illegal enterprise model views criminal organizations as bureaucracies with specific organizational structures and views the recruitment of members through demonstrated altruistic acts, such as not revealing the identities of other TOC members but instead taking the penalty themselves (Kleemans, 2013).

The theory of illegal enterprise views criminal behavior as a reflection of specific structural factors. Under this theory, TOC exists because legitimate markets leave a gap in the supply of demanded products, and criminal organizations, aware of the profits to be made from hard-to-obtain products, engage in the distribution of such products (Albanese, 2008).

Protection Theory

As demonstrated in the October 2020 case above, by protecting the criminal behaviors of others, protectors profit. Economists and political science researchers have used **protection theory** explain the concentrated protection of product manufacturing and distribution. In applying protection theory to organized crime, links between government officials and criminal groups are examined. Specifically, the key element of protection theory is the association between those who commit the crimes and those who allow the criminal behaviors to continue (Shortland & Varese, 2014).

In October of 2020, the mayor of Scranton, Pennsylvania, was sentenced to seven years in prison for public corruption. While mayor, the convicted man had engaged in multiyear conspiracies and received cash payments from vendors seeking various city contracts (U.S. Department of Justice, 2020).

Research on Chinese organized crime documents the support of the criminal activities by political officials (Wang, 2011). The criminal activity of pirating in Somalia also suggests that some political officials protect the actions of piracy within certain areas because they are financially supported by these organized criminals (Shortland & Varese, 2014). Finally, research in the United States suggests that the role of government authorities cannot be underestimated when it comes to bids for work and the construction industry (Jasper, 2018). Hence, in states where financial and economic interests are supported by specific businesses, the protection of one by the other is likely to exist, especially in areas with TOC groups.

Systems of Law

Every country in the world has some system of justice. Systems of justice or systems of law represent the rules and principles that govern the communities and are enforced by the legal representatives of the country's justice system. These systems of law are enforced by the individuals employed within the three general categories of law enforcement, courts, and corrections. Law enforcement fulfills the responsibilities of enforcing laws, maintaining public order, and managing public safety (Banks & Baker, 2016). Courts apply the laws to specific actions in support of justice, resolve disputes, and in some cases, further the investigation into criminal actions. Corrections enhances social order and public safety by separating those convicted of a crime from society (Banks & Baker, 2016).

The legal codes or laws are critical to justice systems around the world. A prominent reference for legal terms, ***Black's Law Dictionary***, describes *law* as a body of rules of action or conduct prescribed by controlling authority, and having binding legal force, which must be obeyed and followed by citizens subject to sanctions or legal consequence (Law Dictionary, 2018). In essence, the legal codes outline what behaviors a society has decided to prohibit. Laws identify the behaviors that society has deemed to be criminal, not the behaviors that society has deemed noncriminal. Laws tell citizens what they cannot do.

Black's Law Dictionary—The most widely used law dictionary in the United States for over 100 years.

Rule of law, embraced by democratic institutions around the world, embodies the concept that no person is above the law—and also that no person is below it. The concept requires that laws are clear, publicized, and applied evenly. Through rule of law, established standards of behavior are identified, with the consensus by citizens that their

Rule of law—A principle under which all persons and entities are accountable to laws that are publicly promulgated, equally enforced, and independently adjudicated in support of international human rights principles.

government will take necessary actions against behavior that has been deemed illegal. Rule of law stipulates what actions may be employed against those committing violations of the legal code. Rule of law provides formal mechanisms to resolve disputes. Rule of law protects persons and society as a whole and the person as an individual. Of course, laws may be applied by unjust regimes or unscrupulous people to support a specific political, social, or economic agenda; in the same way, laws may be applied by TOC to discriminate or marginalize a targeted group; however, these applications jeopardize the rule of law.

Having laws "on the books" or in practice should make a system transparent and fair. However, it is important to look beyond the codified laws or practices and examine what actually occurs in the community and in the justice system—in other words, what is the "ground truth" for the system. Specifically, some nations may have just or equitable laws within their legal codes, but the experiences of offenders in the courts suggest that these laws are not always applied as written. Just as some nations will eagerly sign an international treaty only to regularly violate the said conditions of that agreement, governments may ignore the just dispensation of laws completely or they may use the legal codes in accordance with their statutes only when the situation benefits those in power. For those involved in TOC, the differences between law and practice may facilitate criminal activities.

Research suggests that essentially there are six categories of legal systems: (1) common law, (2) civil or inquisitorial law, (3) socialist law, (4) islamic law, (5) mixed systems or hybrid law, and (6) indigenous, customary, or informal law. It is acknowledged that even within these categories of systems of law there can be many variations, influenced by a variety of historical and societal factors unique to each country, and while there may be similarities between places, there are probably no two nations whose legal systems work exactly the same in all aspects of their approaches to limit criminal behaviors and their administrations of justice. For the purpose of this discussion, the two most common systems—common law and civil law—are presented as related to TOC and their efforts to address TOC.

Common law—One of the most widespread systems of law in the world, and it is the system of law associated with the United States.

Common Law

Common law is one of the most widespread systems of law in the world and it is the system of law associated with the United States.

Approximately one third of all of the world's legal systems is based on common law (Hang & Jacobson, 2017). Around the globe, countries following common law systems were often linked historically or economically to England, where the concept of common law was developed. Approximately 80 countries in the world practice common law, where case law or the published judicial opinions on a case are of primary importance to the system (Washington University, 2014). The concept of common law was essentially developed on a case-by-case basis from judicial decisions and is historically viewed as the "English system."

Common law continued to evolve over time, as England, and later Great Britain, established colonies and economic ties across the world. Even as countries became independent of English rule, their legal systems often remained "English." For a recent example, on November 30, 2021, the country of Barbados transitioned to a fully sovereign republic by replacing the British monarch with a newly elected president as its head of state (Aljazeera, 2021). Though now an independent country, Barbados has chosen to remain within the Commonwealth (a group of over 50 countries across Africa, Asia, Europe, and the Americas) and will remain active under a legal system of common law. Today, countries in the Americas, the Caribbean, Africa, the Middle East, and Asia all have legal systems that are based primarily upon concepts of common law.

Although based predominantly on precedent, common law provides for some flexibility and creativity, allowing adjustments for unique situations. Unfortunately, that same flexibility may also allow for the oppression of targeted populations or for delivery of verdicts that unjustly support a ruling elite or criminal groups of influence. For most countries, following what had been done in the past (that is, following precedent) in similar cases would ensure a sense of fairness and consistency in judicial decisions; however, this may not always be the case. This concept of basing current judicial decisions upon past decisions became known as the "stare decisis" system. *Stare decisis*, which is Latin for "to stand by things decided" (Cornell Law School, 2018), is the idea of following precedent. Cases that bring about changes in precedent are known as "landmark cases," and they allow the law and the courts to evolve over time and reflect the changes in a society's sense of decency. Therefore, landmark cases become the primary source of law within common law systems. However, historical case law or precedent may not apply to current TOC cases or to TOC cases involving the use of technology.

As common law countries evolve, the trend is often toward an ever-increasing codification of laws and penalties within these systems. In addition to the domestic legal system is the application of international law to common law. Most *civil law* countries are considered "monist": Typically, international law is imposed on a nation by its having signed a treaty; that law becomes part of the nation's domestic law as well. However, *common law* countries are often "dualist," meaning that international law is separate from domestic law (Hang & Jacobson, 2017). Thus, even if a nation joins a treaty, the international law becomes part of the nation's laws only when it is converted into the domestic codes by legislative action. International law may be referred to in common law countries, but the precedents or case law is not binding unless the law has been specifically adopted domestically (O'Connor, 2012).

The roles of law enforcement officers and prosecutors are different in common law countries than that in other legal systems, and those in TOC are aware of these roles. In common law systems, law enforcement enjoys significant independent investigative powers and may choose whether or not to investigate or arrest. Also, in common law prosecutors exercise a powerful control over investigations through their power of prosecutorial discretion, as they have the decision to file charges or not file charges in a case. Specifically, prosecutors may refuse to file charges on weak investigations or may decline to charge on unjust investigations. In a common law court the *burden of proof* at trial falls on the prosecutor; thus, prosecutors may choose not to take a case to trial if they are unable or unwilling to present sufficient and credible evidence that meets or exceeds the "beyond a reasonable doubt" standard for a jury (or a judge in a bench trial) to find the defendant guilty (O'Connor, 2012).

In common law systems judges, who are not part of the law enforcement or the investigative process, are responsible for indirect oversight of investigations. Judges decide whether to issue search, seizure, and arrest warrants to law enforcement, and they preside over the trials of cases brought by the prosecutors. Another independent and non-governmental entity in the common law system is the jury. The manner in which juries are selected, who is eligible to serve, and the number of people who sit on the jury may vary by country, but all are determined based upon tradition. Jurors, who are members of the community, hold the fate of many court outcomes in their hands.

Finally, in common law systems the participants are guided by historical actions, and they hold an enormous amount of power with regard to prosecution and conviction. In common law systems, the flexibility of action provides flexibility in reacting to the criminal behaviors and criminal actions of TOC.

In October of 2020, Transparency International (a global organization for identifying corruption) stated that Australia had taken no steps to enforce or punish foreign aid contractors for bribing foreign officials (Knaus, 2020).

Civil Law

Unlike common law, which grew from the legal system of essentially one country, the foundation of **civil law** or inquisitorial law is the result of varied influences from different countries. While both civil law and common law have evolved from Western-based societies, civil law can be found primarily in Central and South America, Africa, Asia, the Middle East, and Oceania. Approximately 150 countries practice some form of civil law (Washington University, 2014). Many researchers on civil law consider the common law system to be chaotic, whereas the civil law system is perceived to be a more careful or systematic way to discover the truth (O'Connor, 2012). This perception may be due to the adversarial approach of common law system, which is a much more confrontational method of determining the truth. Civil law involves the active participation of civil law judges in the search for the truth; this is why some refer to civil law systems as "inquisitorial" systems (O'Connor, 2012).

In discussions on the legal origins of civil law, scholars suggest that French Civil Law is identified in countries such as France, Italy, and Spain; German Civil Law is identified in countries such as Germany, Austria, Switzerland, and Turkey; and Scandinavian Civil Law is identified in countries such as Denmark, Norway, and Sweden (Franklin, 1951).

For countries with civil law systems, the written code is of primary importance. Beyond legal codes, there is a hierarchy of documents that includes many of the nations' constitutions and governmental regulations, along with regional and local ordinances. Hence, the importance of what is actually written is also demonstrated. A civil law criminal proceeding relies more on the investigative file or dossier than on the oral testimony of witnesses, the latter being more typical in common law criminal trials (O'Connor, 2012). Civil systems rest upon the notion that codification ensures a rational, logical, and systematic approach to law, resulting in a fair, or more just, application of criminal law. Judges' decisions are not about past rulings but about the specific case before the judge and the existing legal codes. The legal statutes, typically established by legislators, are to be applied by the judge in a specific case.

In the practice of civil law, there are a variety of players in the courtroom, and their specific roles may vary from country to country; generally, however, the courts are presided upon by a *panel* of judges, meaning more than one "sitting judge." Civil law system court proceedings focus on clarifying or expanding on the evidence outlined in the dossier; therefore, civil law trials may be shorter than comparable common law proceedings for similar cases. In this system, both the prosecution and the defense may assist the judges in finding clarity, but they do not have the burden of presenting all of their evidence as in a common law criminal trial (O'Connor, 2012).

Judges in civil law systems may also participate outside the courtroom; for example, in some nations there are judges who are part of the investigative process and are referred to as "investigative judges." Investigative judges may be involved in all aspects of the case, including interviewing suspects, witnesses, and the victim. In addition to the judge, there may be legal representatives for the people or the state, such as a prosecutor along with those assisting the accused. The roles of these prosecutors vary with the country; in some nations they are seen as part of the judiciary, often sitting at a level equal with judges or at least higher than the defense attorney. In countries where there is no investigative judge, the prosecutor may be in charge of the investigation; however, a prosecutor's degree of investigative control varies by nation—from truly leading the investigation to primarily "advising" the lead police entity in charge of the case. In addition, in some countries the prosecutor is focused on discovering the truth and weighing the evidence, rather than just proving the case. Specifically, in Germany, the prosecutor may request that a defendant be acquitted and also may appeal a wrongful conviction (Banks & Baker, 2016). Thus, in many civil law systems the prosecutor enjoys the power of "prosecutorial discretion" and can decide to not charge an offender or to dismiss a case entirely.

In countries such as Italy, under the concept of "compulsory prosecution" the prosecutor cannot dismiss cases. However, prosecutors have been known to allow a case to linger, not taking additional steps until the case dies an administrative death due to exceeding legal time requirements such as the statute of limitations (Banks & Baker, 2016).

In the civil law system, attorneys for the defendant may be referred to as defense attorneys or legal advocates and are just like the prosecutors in civil law systems; however, the participation of the defense attorney varies with each civil law country, and, in general, attorneys are there to advise the defendant or to bring certain matters to the attention of the court. In some countries the defense counsel's role is to be impartial to the defendant; these defense lawyers basically are there just to make sure the proceedings follow the law and procedure. As the process continues, the judges ask the questions of witnesses and the defendant. Typically, the defense council does not present evidence and the defense attorney may be limited to just being present during investigative interviews in order to ensure that the defendant is treated humanely (O'Connor, 2012).

In civil law systems, participants are guided by written documentation that gives specific guidelines regarding prosecution, convictions, and sentencing. In some cases, however, systems that are perceived to be over-authoritative, with rules on every action, may result in the perception that some laws or rules are less critical. This perception of selective obedience opens the window for criminal actions of TOC and for the sense that some laws are less significant than others.

> In March of 2021, an ex-president in France was sentenced to one year in jail after being convicted of corruption in attempting to obtain confidential information from a judge in exchange for helping the judge obtain a new job (Breeden, 2021).

Structural Failures and TOC

We would be remiss to explain TOC without identifying the structural conditions that are often associated with the criminal actions. For clarity, the structural approach to explaining organized crime focuses less on individual behaviors and more the role played by broader systemic factors, such as sociological, legal, economic, and political attributes of the international system (United Nations Office on Drugs and Crime, 2018). While it is acknowledged that these factors may not necessarily cause crime, research suggests that they are associated with organized crime activity (McCabe, 2017). Specifically, as shown below, the worst countries for human trafficking are also those with some of the worst border security. For the purpose of this section, structural failures are related to border security, legal efforts, and corruption.

WORST COUNTRIES FOR HUMAN TRAFFICKING

1. Belarus
2. Central African Republic
3. China
4. Eritrea
5. Iran
6. North Korea
7. Russia
8. Sudan
9. Syria
10. Venezuela

(Borgen Project, 2017)

The capacity of countries to control their borders is related to TOC. In particular, there are numerous reasons why it is difficult to control corruption and TOC within areas, including extreme violence against informants and witnesses, ethnic solidarity, violence against members of the criminal justice system, corruption, blackmail, and safe places to hide (Democracy Russia, 1999).

In particular, TOC members often support political candidates through financial contributions. If TOC members are perceived as having "friends in high places," law enforcement may be willing to avoid investigating their activities. In addition, if a politician is blackmailed by a TOC member, then the TOC group can use this information and the threat of exposure to compel the politician to support their criminal activities (Democracy Russia, 1999). Further, TOC groups are able to employ accountants as well as lawyers, identify safe havens for locations, and disguise the fact that money has been derived from illegal activities, especially if a crime network stretches across a number of different countries. Specifically, there is often a large advantage for crime syndicates to corrupt the politicians of a small town or a small country, as this disparity of wealth between a relatively poor, small country and an international syndicate with huge resources will make it relatively easy for criminals to bribe the top politicians, remain safely in the area, and take effective control of the government (Democracy Russia, 1999). In the United States, there have been some notorious safe haven towns from which organized criminals have operated with impunity, as criminals controlled the mayor and the police and the town became a safe center for criminal operations covering several surrounding states (Democracy Russia, 1999).

Impoverished areas are also more susceptible to organized criminal activities (Abadinsky, 2019). Unfortunately, the conditions that impede economic development also support TOC. In addition, corruption emerges and supports shadow economies, black markets, and TOC. Lastly, the failure of a country to provide for its residents often results in high unemployment, a low standard of living, and a reliance on criminal organizations to supply goods, services, and jobs (United Nations Office on Drugs and Crime, 2018). Specifically, TOC supports the presence of economic failures as well as the existence of black-market activities (Sung, 2004); TOC is perceived to be strongest in countries that fail to provide for their populations (Kostakos, 2018). TOC groups continue to cross land and sea borders to traffic drugs, weapons, and other goods as well as to facilitate terrorist attacks; thus, border security is essential for addressing TOC as well as providing security.

In particular, as reported by the **United Nations Office of Counter-Terrorism (UNOCT)**, effective surveillance of remote border areas and border zones adjacent to any port of entry is necessary to prevent persons from bypassing official checks, smuggling commodities, infiltrating an area in advance of conducting a terrorist attack, or attempting to enter or leave a state's territory illegally. In particular, UNOCT suggests that a broad and consistent presence of border officers in a given area deters terrorists, prevents other cross-border criminal activities, and builds resilience in border communities against the influence of terrorist groups and criminal enterprises. A consistent security presence can increase border communities' awareness

United Nations Office of Counter-Terrorism (UNOCT)—Approved in 2017 by the UN Council; office leads and coordinates an all-of-UN approach to countering and preventing terrorism.

of terrorist threats and build an understanding of the local and personal impacts of terrorist activities of as well as TOC groups (United Nations Office of Counter-Terrorism, 2018).

Strict border control measures often play a part in the development of formal agreements or understandings of procedures between states. These agency cooperative actions support not only border security but also standard operational procedures, reporting and communication related to security, and methods of data collection and analysis.

In addition to the conditions of the country, the structure of the international system is also associated with TOC (United Nations Office on Drugs and Crime, 2018). From this perspective, if one country views a behavior as legal but another government has criminalized it, TOC will likely take advantage of the discrepancies between the competing legal jurisdictions (Block & Chambliss, 1981). Currently, there are still countries whose laws are poorly enforced; such countries offer a safe place for those involved in criminal behaviors to operate and avoid detection. *Jurisdictional arbitrage*, which refers to criminals initiating their crimes from jurisdictions that have few or no laws against the crimes, is facilitated by these vulnerabilities (Walterbach, 2007). Those involved in TOC benefit from the increasing use of communications technology and lower trade barriers to commit crimes, knowing that the risk of detection and punishment is low.

The structural factors assumed to create opportunities for TOC are (1) the differences between countries in their ability to implement border controls; (2) the disparity in the distribution of natural, human, and economic resources; (3) the discrepancies in countries' ability to prevent other types of crimes; and (4) the disharmonization of legal systems within an area (United Nations Office on Drugs and Crime, 2018).

Another of the more commonly discussed structural factors related to criminal behaviors and TOC is corruption. For clarity, **corruption** is the act of unfairly or illegally influencing a decision-making process by giving a benefit to a third party or receiving a benefit that is connected to the decision maker. In general, corruption is thought of as illegal activities that are deliberately hidden and that come to light only through scandals, investigations, or prosecutions.

One of the best measures of corruption within a country is the Corruption Perceptions Index, calculated annually by Transparency International.

Transparency International is a global movement, registered as a German voluntary association, which was founded in the 1990s by former employees of the World Bank. The focus of Transparency International is advocacy and research to expose systems and networks that facilitate corruption (Transparency International, 2021). The most recognized aspect of Transparency International is its annually calculated **Corruption Perceptions Index (CPI)**. The CPI scores and ranks countries/territories based on how corrupt a country's public sector is perceived to be by experts and business executives. Specifically, the CPI is a composite index, a combination of 13 surveys and assessments of corruption; collected by a variety of reputable institutions, it is the most widely used indicator of corruption worldwide. The 2020 CPI ranked 180 countries on a scale of 0 to 100. As displayed below, Somalia and South Sudan were tied for first place among the countries identified as most corrupt (World Population Review, 2021).

Transparency International—A global movement best known for its annually calculated Corruption Perceptions Index (CPI), which scores and ranks countries based on perceived corruption.

MOST CORRUPT COUNTRIES IN 2020

1. Somalia and South Sudan
2. Syria
3. Venezuela and Yemen
4. Equatorial Guinea and Sudan
5. Libya
6. Democratic Republic of the Congo and Haiti and North Korea

(*World Population Review, 2021*)

Role of Technology in TOC

Modern-day technologies such as the internet, social media, and mobile applications have accelerated the activities of TOC. Specifically, in the trafficking of products, including drugs, weapons, and humans, technology has given members of TOC increased anonymity as they identify, advertise, and facilitate transactions for such products. In addition, as criminal organizations capitalize on the increase in e-commerce and on legislative limits to the regulation of cyberworld transactions, the use of technology has increased TOC's profits (Homeland Security Today, 2020).

TOC and the trafficking of products such as drugs exists within a market-based society, with the illicit markets generally categorized either as open, in the case of the street-corner purchase of drugs, or as closed, where sellers sell only to those individuals known to them. Of course, in these cases, the more open the market area, the higher the risk to the perpetrators. With technology such as the mobile applications used today, sellers are now able to be more open regarding their products but closed regarding their distribution (Berry, 2018). Sellers are now able to arrange more closed-market sales of their products and avoid detection by authorities (Wainwright, 2016).

TOC and the trafficking of humans also exist within a market-based economy; however, where are drugs are products to be used once and replaced, human may be exploited over and over again. TOC understands that this investment in a human will provide revenue beyond the first sale. In the cases of human exploitation by TOC, direct and indirect victimization occurs for profit (McCabe, 2017). Individuals and members of TOC utilize the internet and technology to produce and distribute pornography as well as to arrange for the sale of human victims of sex trafficking (McCabe & Johnston, 2014). In addition, sex rings, particularly child sex rings—involve multiple offenders, often members of organized crime or TOC, and multiple perpetrators. Through this form of sexual exploitation, there is sexual activity among multiple child victims and multiple adult perpetrators. Arrangements for a sex-ring encounter typically are made online among the offenders; the desired characteristics of the children (i.e., age, gender) are "ordered," and those within the TOC deliver the children, who are products for consumption or victimization (McCabe, 2017).

In addition, TOC utilizes technology to facilitate the illicit flow of financial gains, illicit funds from tax evasion, and a variety of illegal activities. Cryptocurrency, the most common of which is Bitcoin, allows criminal to move funds without the regulations of traditional banking systems. For law enforcement, determining the original source of Bitcoin is difficult and is often obscured by a blending of services where Bitcoin is utilized to fund "legitimate" enterprises and is retrieved once it has been "washed." For example, illicit gambling websites may be prohibited from accepting credit cards due to their inability to access a merchant account; however, the number of bitcoins being accepted is undetected (Marker, 2018). As TOC groups understand the limitations in current banking systems and the lack of regulations with cryptocurrency, funds such as Bitcoin are providing even more revenue for TOC.

Specifically, through online and mobile banking, electronic payments through unregulated intermediaries, digital currencies, online gambling, and e-commerce or online manipulation of supply goods, TOC profits are increased through the use of technology and their risks for apprehension are minimized (Tropina, 2016).

Lastly, research continues to support the risk in favor of TOC within countries that are experiencing political instability, as was demonstrated in the 1990s with the end of Yugoslavia and the formation of the Western Balkan countries of Serbia, Croatia, Montenegro, Slovenia, Macedonia, and Bosnia and Herzegovina. These new countries were and continue to be more susceptible to organized crime activities (Djordjevic & Dobovsek, 2020). However, the COVID-19 pandemic further weakened these countries.

For all countries, COVID-19 forced changes in governmental and police priorities. One consequence of the pandemic was the lockdown of countries and borders; the movement of people within and into countries was restricted. Police efforts were shifted from fighting crime to monitoring curfews and enforcing safety measures related to public health. Members of TOC, seeking to limit their profit losses related to border transportations, sought ways to take advantage of the new conditions and viewed them as opportunities. In particular, with the trade of drugs across international jurisdictions reduced, TOC supported the manufacturing and/or cultivation of "homegrown" drugs (Djordjevic & Dobovsek, 2020). As the pandemic continued, many of the TOC groups' opportunities for profit also continued.

During COVID-19, not only did countries with already weakened economic development and rule of law experience an increase in intracountry drug trafficking by TOC, but also these countries experienced supply shortages related to public health and vulnerabilities related to online day-to-day operations. Specifically, research suggests that TOC groups capitalized on the shortages of medical equipment,

> In December of 2020, Interpol issued a global alert to law enforcement across its 194 member countries, warning them to prepare for TOC networks targeting COVID-19 vaccines both physically and online. These efforts by TOC groups have included the falsification, theft, and illegal advertising of COVID-19 and flu vaccines, with examples of crimes where individuals have been advertising, selling, and administering fake vaccines (Interpol, 2020).

personal protective equipment (such as face masks), and sanitation supplies. TOC members who had the ability to meet the supply of demands profited by price-gouging counterfeit products and by providing products that had been obtained through illicit processes (i.e., theft). In addition, as daily operations shifted to online, TOC members were able to increase their profits in online fraud through mobile and online scams that were focused on people who had less experience operating within cybercommunities (Djordjevic & Dobovsek, 2020). Hence, along with specific country demographics, corruption, and technology, COVID-19 facilitated the activities and profits of TOC groups.

Summary

The motivation behind TOC is relatively simple: profit. However, regarding the dynamics that support TOC, academics and practitioners offer a wide variety of explanations. Just as the reach of TOC is broad, so are the explanations for the criminal behaviors. This chapter provided theoretical explanations from a structural perspective as well as from a process perspective to include historical theories and contemporary theories on TOC. In particular, in this chapter the social perspectives of bond, disorganization, and conflict were presented in an attempt to explain organized crime historically. With hyperglobalization of today's world, the expanded theories of alien conspiracy, protection, and illegal enterprise were utilized to explain TOC.

In addition, this chapter discussed systems of law (common and civil) in terms of foundations and support for the structure and the activities of TOC. Finally, this chapter discussed structural explanations of the activities of TOC groups as related to structural limitations such as border vulnerabilities and security, corruption of criminal justice and of government representatives, the role of technology and the cybercommunity, and the role of the COVID-19 pandemic in facilitating TOC.

Questions for Further Thought

1. Although TOC is emerging as one of the most profitable aspects of criminal activities, the dynamics that facilitate TOC are still difficult to explain. Why?
2. If people who attempt to address TOC know that national border vulnerabilities and gaps in international law provide advantages to TOC, why do they not simply address these risk factors?
3. If technology supports the actions of TOC, what can those in the justice system plan in response?

References

Abadinsky, A. (2017). *Organized crime* (11th ed). Cengage Group.

Albanese, J. (2008). Risk assessments in organized crime developing a market and product-based model to determine threat levels. *Journal of Contemporary Criminal Justice, 24*(3), 263–273.

Aljazeera. (2021, November 29). *Barbados becomes a republic, renouncing British queen*. Retrieved November 15, 2021, from https://www.aljazeera.com/news/2021/11/29/barbados-set-to-become-a-republic-ditching-british-queen

Allum, F., & Sands, J. (2004). Explaining organized crime in Europe: Are economics always right? *Crime, Law, and Social Change, 41*(1), 133–160.

Antonopoulos, G. A. (2009). Are the "others" coming? Evidence on 'alien conspiracy' from three illegal markets in Greece. *Crime, Law and Social Change, 52*(5), 475–493.

Arsovska, J., & Temple, M. (2016). Adaption, rationality, and advancement: Ethnic Albanian organized crime in New York City. *Crime Law Society Change, 66*, 1–20.

Banks, C., & Baker, J. (2016). *Comparative, international, and global justice*. SAGE.

Berry, M. (2018, October 29). Technology and organized crime in the smart city: An ethnographic study of the illicit drug trade. *City, Territory, and Architecture, 16*, 1–8.

Bevier, L. (2015). The meaning of cultural criminology: A theoretical and methodological lineage. *Journal of Theoretical and Philosophical Criminology, 7*(2), 34–48.

Block, A., & Chambliss, W. (1981). *Organising crime*. Elsevier.

Borgen Project. (2017, October 23). *2017's Worst countries for human trafficking*. Retrieved November 3, 2021, from https://borgenproject.org/tag/worst-countries-for-human-trafficking/

Breeden, A. (2021, March 2). Ex-president Sarkozy gets jail sentence for corruption in France. *New York Times*. Retrieved November 3, 2021, from https://www.nytimes.com/search?query=https%3A%2F%2Fwww.nytimes.com%2F2021%2F03%2F01%2Fworld%2Feurope%2Ffrance-sarkozy-trial-guilty.html

Brownfield, D. (2003). Differential association and gang membership. *Journal of Gang Research, 11*(1), 1–12.

Burns, M. (2018). Participating operational and security assessment on homeland security risks: An empirical research method for improving security beyond the border through public/private partnership. *Journal of Transportation Security, 11*, 85–100.

Cornell Law School. (2018). *Legal Information Institute*. Retrieved November 3, 2021, from https://www.law.cornell.edu/

De Boer, J., & Bosett, L. (2015, September 18). *Examining the interactions between conflict and organized crime*. Retrieved November 7, 2021, from https://ourworld.unu.edu/en/examining-the-interactions-between-conflict-and-organized-crime

Democracy Russia. (1999). *Why is it so difficult to control and eliminate corruption which stems from organized crime?* Retrieved January 10, 2022, from http://www.democracy.ru/english/library/international/eng_1999-6/page2.html

Djordjevic, S., & Dobovsek, B. (2020). Organised crime in Western Balkans six at the onset of coronavirus. *International Journal of Sociology and Social Policy, 40*(9/10), 807–820. https://doi.org/10.1108/IJSSP-06-2020-0229

Federal Bureau of Investigation. (2020). *What we investigate. Transnational organized crime*. Retrieved October 3, 2021, from https://www.fbi.gov/investigate/organized-crime

Franklin, M. (1951). On the legal method of the uniform commercial code. *Law and Contemporary Problems, 16*(2), 330–343.

Global Initiative. (2021). *Global organized crime index 2021*. Retrieved December 3, 2021, from https://globalinitiative.net/wp-content/uploads/2021/09/GITOC-Global-Organized-Crime-Index-2021.pdf

Haller, M. (1990). Illegal enterprise: A theoretical and historical interpretation. *Criminology, 28*(2), 201–236.

Hang, K., & Jacobson, B. (2017). How global is the common law? A comparative study of Asian common law systems—Hong Kong, Malaysia, and Singapore. *Asian Journal of Comparative Law, 21*(1), 209–232.

Homeland Security Today. (2020, October 19). *How modern technologies help organized crime groups traffic people across borders*. Retrieved November 8, 2021, from https://www.hstoday.us/subject-matter-areas/border-security/how-modern-technologies-help-organized-crime-groups-traffic-people-across-borders/

Interpol. (2020, December 2). *Interpol warns of organized crime threat to Covid-19 vaccines*. Retrieved January 3, 2022, from https://www.interpol.int/en/News-and-Events/News/2020/INTERPOL-warns-of-organized-crime-threat-to-COVID-19-vaccines

Jasper, J. (2018). Business cartels and organised crime: Exclusive and inclusive systems of collusion. *Trends in Organized Crime, 10*(1), 107–117.

Justice News. (2021a). *New York man sentenced to 18 months in prison for trafficking exotic African cats* [Press release]. Office of Public Affairs. Department of Justice. Retrieved November 8, 2021, from https://www.justice.gov/opa/pr/new-york-man-sentenced-18-months-prison-trafficking-exotic-african-cats

Justice News. (2021b). *Sinaloa cartel money launderer sentenced to 10 years in prison* [Press release]. Justice News. Office of Public Affairs. Department of Justice. Retrieved November 8, 2021, from https://www.justice.gov/opa/pr/sinaloa-cartel-money-launderer-sentenced-10-years-prison

Kleemans, E. (2013). Theoretical perspectives on organized crime. In L. Paoli (Ed.), *Oxford handbook on organized crime*. Oxford University Press.

Knaus, C. (2020, October 13). Australia ignored OECD over failure to punish foreign bribery, report finds. *The Guardian*. Retrieved November 3, 2021, from https://www.theguardian.com/australia-news/2020/oct/13/australia-ignored-oecd-over-failure-to-punish-foreign-bribery-report-finds

Kostakos, P. (2018). Public perceptions on organized crime, mafia, and terrorism: A big data analysis based on Twitter and Google trends. *International Journal of Cyber Criminology, 12*(1), 282–299.

Law Dictionary. (2018). *Law definition and legal meaning*. Retrieved August 19, 2022, from https://thelawdictionary.org/law/

Matthews, C. (2014, September 14). *Fortune 5: The biggest organized crime groups in the world*. Retrieved January 12, 2022, from https://finance.yahoo.com/news/fortune-5-biggest-organized-crime-100022359.html

Marker, M. (2018). Organized crime has gone high tech. *Police Chief*. Retrieved November 3, 2021, from https://www.policechiefmagazine.org/organized-crime-has-gone-high-tech/

Marx, Karl. (1973). *Grundrisse: Introduction to the critique of political economy* (M. Nicolaus, Trans.). Vintage. (Original work published 1857)

McCabe, K. (2017). *Protecting your children online*. Rowman & Littlefield.

McCabe, K., and Johnston, O. (2014). Perceptions on the legality of sexting: A report. *Social Science Computer Review, 32*(6), 765–68.

McLean, R., Holligan, C., & Riaz, N. (2020). Alien conspiracy theory? Exploring ethnicity and drug supplies in Scotland. *Deviant Behavior, 41*(1), 1244–1257.

Merton, R. (1968). *Social theory and social structure*. Free Press.

Miller, W. B. (1958). Lower-class culture as a generating milieu of gang delinquency. *Journal of Social Issues, XIV*, 5–9.

O'Connor, V. (2012, February 17). *Common law and civil law traditions*. Retrieved November 3, 2021, from https://dx.doi.org/10.2139/ssrn.2665675

Ohr, B. G. (2001). Effective methods to combat transnational organized crime in criminal justice processes. *Resource Material Series, 58*, 40–60.

Pileggi, N. (1985). *Wise guy: Life in the mafia family*. Pocket Books.

Shaw, C., & McKay, H. (1972). *Juvenile delinquency and urban areas*. University of Chicago Press.

Shortland, A., & Varese, F. (2014). The protector's choice: An application of protection theory to Somali piracy. *British Journal of Criminology, 54*(3), 741–764.

Siegel, L. (1998). *Criminology: Theories, patterns, and typologies* (6th ed). Wadsworth.

Sung, H. (2004). State failure, economic failure, and predatory organized crime: A comparative analysis. *Journal of Research in Crime and Delinquency, 41*(2), 111–129.

Sutherland, E. (1939). *Principles of criminology*. Lippincott.

Transparency International. (2021). *About Transparency International*. Retrieved November 9, 2021, from https://www.transparency.org/en/about

Tropina, T. (2016). *Do digital technologies facilitate illicit financial flows?* World Development Report. Retrieved November 3, 2021, from https://www.worldbank.org/en/publication/wdr2016

United Nations Office of Counter-Terrorism. (2018). *Good practices in the area of border security and management in the context of counterterrorism and stemming the flow of foreign terrorist fighters.* Retrieved November 3, 2021, from https://www.un.org/counterterrorism/sites/www.un.org.counterterrorism/files/goodpractices_bsm_english_2018_0.pdf

United Nations Office on Drugs and Crime. (2018). Module 6: Causes and facilitating factors of organized crime. Key issues: Structural factors. *E4J University Module Series: Organized crime.* Retrieved November 9, 2021, from https://www.unodc.org/e4j/en/organized-crime/module-6/key-issues/structural-factors.html

U.S. Department of Justice. (2020). *Public corruption prosecutions.* U.S. Attorney's Office. Middle District of Pennsylvania. Retrieved November 8, 2021, from https://www.justice.gov/usao-mdpa/public-corruption-prosecutions

van Dijk, M., Kleemans, E. & Eichelsheim, V. (2019). Children of organized crime offenders: Like father, like child? An explorative and qualitative study into mechanisms of intergenerational (dis)continuity in organized crime families. *European Journal of Criminal Policy Research, 25*, 345–363. https://doi.org/10.1007/s10610-018-9381-6

Wainwright, T. (2016). *Narconomics: How to run a drug cartel.* PublicAffairs.

Walterbach, M. (2007). International illicit convergence: The growing problem of transnational organized crime groups' involvement in intellectual property rights violations. *Florida State University Law Review, 34*(2), 10. Retrieved June 20, 2021, from https://doc-0s-74-apps-viewer.googleusercontent.com/viewer/secure/pdf/d8fentl8eo13kufbl2dgbn8o2hrkdr7p/higqa3erl9880fgor9c3ns5pa7cgvha8/1640624400000/gmail/14900144076219756676/ACFrOgAG1Vwmi85VCzxLn8lChga1pG0UfOApv6q6SF1w62-CbfQc-jVRVkEUVDX7TvWnVNwWJ04W79xa0dNzYm8GmYjHbzP39A259hVOgxY-FQvwpSyr5SsDFwRv3e-kE=?print=true&nonce=qnm74t3rv25g4&user=14900144076219756676&hash=s7bs0710spom3n03d2sdr6hvmnmepgfj

Wang, P. (2011). The Chinese Mafia: Private protection in a socialist market economy. *Global Crime, 12*(1), 290–311.

Washington University. (2014). *What is the difference between common law and civil law?* Retrieved August 19, 2022, from https://onlinelaw.wustl.edu/blog/common-law-vs-civil-law/

Williams, C., & Roth, M. (2011). The importation and re-exportation of organized crime: Explaining the rise and fall of the Jamaican posses in the United States. *Trends in Organized Crime, 14*, 298–313.

World Population Review. (2021). *Most corrupt countries 2020.* Retrieved August 3, 2021, from https://worldpopulationreview.com/country-rankings/most-corrupt-countries

Woodiwiss, M. (2014). Enterprise not ethnicity: An interview with Dwight C. Smith Jr. *Trends in Organized Crime, 18*(1), 41–55. https://doi.org/10.1007/s12117-014-9216-x

CHAPTER 3

The Structure of Transnational Organized Crime

Key Terms

- Al Capone
- Autocratic leadership
- Camorra
- Charmaine Roman
- Core group
- Criminal network
- Cryptocurrency
- Cyberspace
- Democratic leadership
- Griselda Blanco
- Joseph "Crazy Joe" Gallo
- Laissez-faire leadership
- Mafia
- Organizational structure
- Participative leadership
- Regional hierarchy
- Rosetta Cutolo
- Russian Bratva
- Social network
- Standard hierarchy

CHAPTER OBJECTIVES

Chapter 3 will enable readers to understand the following:

- the various structures of transnational organized crime (TOC) organizations
- the differences in the structures of TOC organizations
- factors that facilitate structural changes for TOC organizations
- factors related to leadership within a TOC group
- differences in male and female leaders of TOC groups
- the influence of technology and cyberspace on the structure of a TOC organization
- TOC structures that exist within the United States

RESEARCH SUGGESTS THAT TOC is a distinct area of crime, one in which the criminal behaviors of those involved are controlled by some unit of command (Edwards & Gill, 2002). Therefore, the crimes of those involved in TOC are not random and not impulsive but well planned and executed for the benefit of some criminal group. Given the businesslike model of TOC groups, for clarity of discussion on the functions of the group, one must also understand the structure of the organization—an organization with the business of crime.

Weber (1947) suggested that all businesses or bureaucracies are made up of two parts: a division of labor and a hierarchy of structure. These components are not only interrelated but also dependent upon each other. When one component is successful, the other component is also successful. When conflicts occur, then the systems break. These breaks produce vulnerabilities.

As social conditions change or as market demands change, the successful business organization must also change. Hence, if one considers TOC as a business with a unit of command, a specialization and a span of control over a profit, the main objective of profit, and rules that govern the organization, then examining structures that facilitate the success of TOC provides explanations and insights into the organization as well as the successes or failures of the group.

In other words, the interactions between the structure of an organization and the members of the organization are directly related to either the success or the failure of the organization's efforts. This is especially true for TOC, as success leads to profit and failure leads to detection and, potentially, incarceration for TOC members. Research on leadership suggests that the effectiveness of an organization is affected more by situational factors and organizational elements than by the control its leadership exerts (DuBrin, 2016); however, without strong leadership within a TOC group, structures are weakened and sustainability is jeopardized.

History suggests that tomb raiding was one of the earliest forms of profit-driven organized crime for an early world of traveling criminals and an **organizational structure** of leaders and workers with an international market in crime (Tupman, 2015). However, even within this earliest of crime networks, some members' roles involved only the identification of targets while other members' roles involved the distribution of goods. Later, the pirates who looted merchant vessels

Organizational structure—How tasks are allocated, coordinated, and supervised for the success of the organization's goals.

in the 17th century were also organized groups of criminals, as they not only received information on the merchandise aboard a ship but also knew of land-based contacts who would pay for the consumption of such illicitly gained merchandise (JRank, 2022). Hence, for organized criminal groups to operate across international boundaries is not a new phenomenon. This chapter discusses the structure of TOC from historical, present-day, and predicted future perspectives. In addition, because the actions of group members are critical in the various criminal activities of TOC, this chapter discusses leadership as it relates to TOC groups and the composition and recruitment of group members in order to better explain their criminal outcomes. Lastly, acknowledging that the membership and leadership of a TOC group are generally male-dominated positions, this chapter discusses the role of women in contemporary TOC groups as well as how gender relates to TOC structural characteristics.

Organizational Structure

The organized crime model of "alien conspiracy" (discussed in Chapter 2), which emerged in North America with the fear of newly arriving immigrants, led to the depiction of TOC groups as bureaucracies with connections that cross borders and threaten the safety of Americans (Arsovska and Temple, 2016). In reality, in many cases the members of TOC groups are members of immigrant populations within a society. In the early 18th century, criminal activity was the path to upward social mobility for immigrant communities (Bell, 1960). Today as well, many members of new immigrant populations fill positions within TOC groups. Specifically, just as new immigrants often fill positions within a society that are legitimate but typically are poorly paid, dangerous, and seen by local populations as undesirable (such as taxi driving in New York City), it seems reasonable to assume that some of these populations will choose membership in a TOC with similar degrees of danger but more opportunity for significant payments and elevated social strata (Becucci, 2004). Some suggest that recruitment of new members of TOC groups often occurs online, with leaders and/or recruiters targeting the young or economically vulnerable (McCabe, 2017). Leaders of TOC groups are able to recognize vulnerabilities in countries and in individuals from these countries.

COUNTRY VULNERABILITIES TO TOC

- Emerging from conflict or other major crises
- High rates or rise of violent crime
- Proximity to trafficking routes and destination markets
- Favorable international security conditions
- Institutional fragmentation
- High levels of inequality (Briscoe, 2011)

History suggests that organized crime groups were most often under the control of one strong leader. In these cases, sufficient internal cohesion leads to positions of authority within TOC groups (Becucci, 2004). Early research on Mafia groups within the United States and Italy suggests a hierarchal organizational structure, consisting of bosses, lieutenants, and foot soldiers, who control land territories and operate profitable criminal enterprises based upon product demand and corruption (Maas, 1968). In these cases, the clear lines of responsibility lead to profitable endeavors for all involved. In a fundamental way, the conditions of concentrated populations of varying ethnic backgrounds, within limited geographical areas, facilitated the establishment of organized crimes in the United States (JRank, 2022). These individuals formed ties within their new areas while retaining a connection to their home areas, thus facilitating cross-border connections. In official reports that are used to characterize organized crime, this hierarchal identification of TOC groups remains the most frequently adopted structural formation (Albanese, 1996). However, this structure has been jeopardized over the years through focused and directed law enforcement operations—and through globalization of the world, with foreign nations becoming involved in anti-TOC efforts (Becucci, 2004). As a result, the structure of hierarchy for TOC groups may have evolved. Current research suggests that the structure of original organized crime groups has changed based upon the conditions of society and the fluidity of today's market demands for illicit products (McCabe, 2008).

Camorra—An Italian secret society of criminals, thought to have originated in 15th-century Spain and moved to Italy, whose operations include smuggling, blackmail, and extortion (Britannica, The Editors of Encyclopaedia, 2011).

The **Camorra**, starting in 17th-century Italy, is one of the oldest known criminal organizations to operate without the triangular-shaped structure of leadership and control that is assumed to have existed in early groups of organized crime. Specifically, the Camorra divided its power into individual groups, known as clans, based upon their areas of specialty (Santino, 2012). In other words, clans that specialized in drugs were involved within the drug trade, while clans skilled in the financial sector were involved in banking and money laundering. However, in an organization with insufficient internal cohesion, there is a risk of structural destruction or marginalization (Becucci, 2004). As time passed, the clans failed to focus exclusively on their assigned specific areas or products; thus, conflicts emerged within the groups as they chose to compete with each other for goods and consumers. As a result, these feuds between the various clans led to a more formalized structure of organized crime. Historically, this more formal and strict structure is often recognized as the most prolific structure for organized crime groups (Abadinsky, 2017), as demonstrated in the operations of TOC groups such as the Bratva within the Russian Federation. For clarity, the **Bratva** is identified as the largest criminal organization to ever exist, with roots in Russia and an estimated membership of over 300,000 individuals involved in the major activities of sex trafficking, the drug trade, arms dealing, and white-collar crimes such as black-market businesses and cybercrime (Levin, 2019). Recently, it has been suggested that these organized crime groups have been used by Russia's Kremlin for intelligence-gathering and political influence (Galeotti, 2017).

Mafia—An organized international body of criminals, originally in operation in Sicily and now well known in Italy and the United States for operating highly profitable illicit business and demonstrating violent and ruthless behaviors.

RUSSIA'S BRATVA

Russia's Bratva has been compared with many TOC groups, including the U.S. Sicilian **Mafia** and the Italian Mafia; however, the Bratva, in addition to visible crimes such as human trafficking and drug smuggling, is also involved with the less-visible crimes of counterfeiting of goods and tax evasion on an industrial scale (Grant, 2012). Unlike many other TOC groups, Russian TOC enjoys significant levels of state protection. In fact, research suggests that in Russia big business is TOC and that no big business in Russia can operate without government approval. As a result, Russian law enforcement structures offer international agencies only very limited cooperation related to TOC investigations, and evidence often suggests that there is state protection for criminal agents of the state who carry out serious crimes outside Russia (Grant, 2012).

In the 1980s and 1990s as the Soviet Union collapsed, with the reductions in trade restrictions and the increased mobility across jurisdictional boundaries, both new TOC groups and criminal organizations that already existed within the area were able to expand their operations within a global market. Cities with a historical presence of crime families changed as new crime clans moved into their areas (Becucci, 2004). In 2000, the United Nations Office on Drugs and Crime (UNODC) analyzed 40 TOC groups within 16 countries to identify the structures within these groups that facilitated criminal activities. Later research supports the claim that the majority of organized crime groups reflect similar typologies (Le, 2012). This chapter focuses on four of the most common structures or typologies that have been identified as facilitating the criminal activities of TOC: (1) standard hierarchy, (2) regional hierarchy, (3) core group, and, (4) criminal network. These structures, and changes in these structures, are often relative to time and market demands for products and services (McCabe, 2008).

Standard Hierarchy

A **standard hierarchy** is structured through clear levels of command and connections related to position and power within the organization. Historically, research supports the notion that organized crime operates through a formal hierarchy of command with written rules and extensive divisions of labor, as well as positions assigned on the basis of expertise and communications among members following strict chains of command (Abadinsky, 2017). This structure, with the advantages of clearly identified positions of power and decision-making, operates in many legitimate business organizations as well as the military and police structures throughout the world. In this structure, a small number of members determine the actions of the groups.

As illustrated by Figure 3.1, this structure is similar to the structure within bureaucracies of legitimate businesses. As with any structure, the standard hierarchy also has inherent weaknesses, which may not be revealed until the structure has been engaged in multiple aspects of criminal activity. In particular, in single actions, communications through chains of command may be successful; however, as the secret activities continue and the communications increase, in some cases these communications become vulnerable to interception by law enforcement and/or result in miscommunications. This supports research in penology, which concludes that first-time offenders are rarely incarcerated (Cuthbertson, 2017). In addition, with written rules of operations and records of criminal activities, which are inherently included within the standard hierarchy, the TOC group's activities are documented; thus, the TOC group is often vulnerable to further risk of exposure.

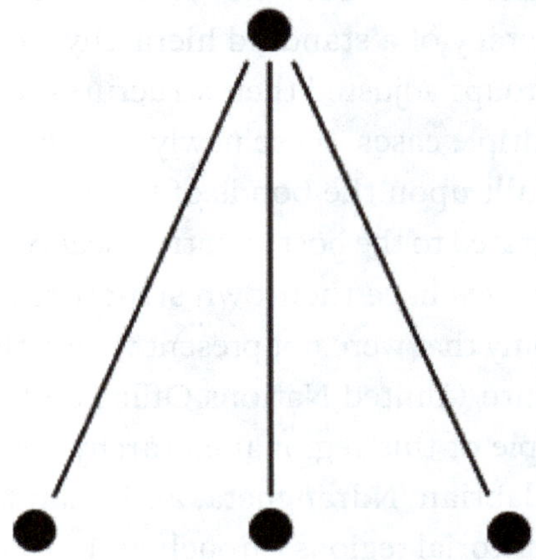

FIGURE 3.1 Standard Hierarchy

By design, the standard hierarchy relies on the expertise of certain members, such as their ability to provide realistic fraudulent documents. Unfortunately, expertise, by definition, is not a skill for every member of the TOC group. Hence, the removal of an expert, through either an arrest or a death, exposes the group to the vulnerability of individuals with subpar skills or knowledge attempting to assume an expert position. Unfortunately, violence often erupts when the structure of TOC changes (Thoumi, 2003). Lastly, as the traditional hierarchy assumes a dedication to the leadership and the chain of command, betrayal by members within the TOC group further exposes the criminal organization to risk of detection and ultimately arrest, prosecution, and conviction. In fact, internal threats to TOC groups are often the result of in-group betrayals (Edwards & Gill, 2002). As described in the 1972 account here, betrayal within the organization may have severe consequences.

In April of 1972, the Mafia figure **Joseph Gallo**, known as Crazy Joe, was assassinated at a restaurant in the Little Italy neighborhood of New York City as he celebrated his 43rd birthday. Sources report that the killing was a result of wars between family factions within the TOC group (Stevens & Mervosh, 2019).

Regional Hierarchy

Specific structures (regional) and markets such as drugs exhibit high levels of violence (Reuter, 2009). As organized crime moved from local territorial controls to global TOC, the tension of one structure control resulted in vulnerabilities in terms of detection and product provisions (Edwards & Gill, 2002). Over time, the vulnerabilities of the strict bureaucracy of a standard hierarchy were acknowledged and many TOC groups adjusted their structures to a more **regional hierarchy**. In multiple cases, these newly established transnational networks were built upon the bonds of trust with associates who have newly immigrated to the host country (Becucci, 2004). However, these new hierarchies have their own structure and operate with degrees of autonomy that were not present within the standard organizational structure (United Nations Office on Drugs and Crime, 2018a). An example of this regional hierarchy structure is demonstrated in the Calabrian 'Ndrangheta, an Italian Mafia–style TOC syndicate with territorial regions throughout Europe, including Germany, Switzerland, and France, as well as Australia, Canada, and the United States (The Local, 2019). In these cases, the functionality of new foreign communities supports the sustainability of the TOC group (Becucci, 2004). As illustrated by Figure 3.2, this local or regional organized crime structure operates in smaller regions or territories with control over specific criminal activities. For example, in the United States in rural areas, a criminal organization may produce marijuana or methamphetamines for distribution while in an urban area another criminal organization might focus on the receipt and distribution of cocaine and heroin. Therefore, the overall structural focus of the TOC group is the illegal drug trade with regional

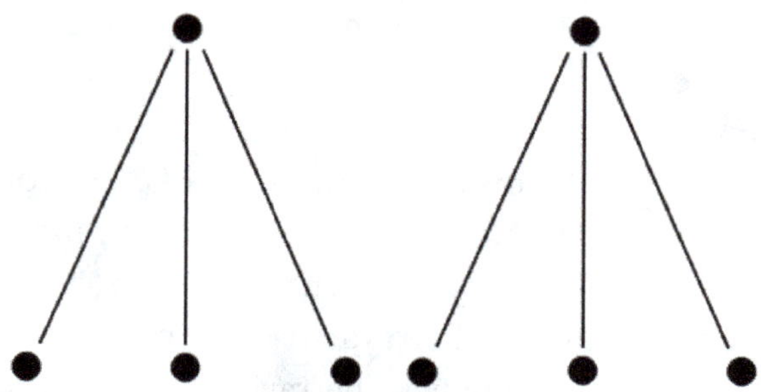

FIGURE 3.2 Regional Hierarchy

hierarchies specializing in specific drug typologies. In other examples of regional hierarchies, new structures may exist with members in management positions from one ethnic group, members in production from another ethnic group, and members in distribution from another ethnic group (Becucci, 2004).

Studies suggest that the TOC groups within these regional hierarchies operate with little large-scale supervision of their daily activities; however, as with similar types of criminal activities, as they exploit the illicit markets for goods and services, they are components of a larger organization (Smith & Papachristos, 2016). As with any TOC activity, where there is demand for a product, there will be a group willing to supply it (Thoumi, 2003). In some cases, as demonstrated in the 2021 account here, conflicts may occur between regional groups.

> In November of 2021, two suspected drug dealers were shot and killed at a resort on Mexico's Caribbean coast. This action was part of a conflict between two organized crime groups that both wished to dominate the lucrative market of selling drugs to tourists (Rojas, 2021).

Core Group

By themselves, variables such as poverty, income, economic crisis, and corruption do not explain crime and violence (Thoumi, 2003). In many cases, violence by TOC groups is facilitated within the structure. The core criminal group, different from the hierarchical structure, consists of a horizontal structure of core individuals with membership in the same TOC organization. This organizational structure is often identified as existing to support the criminal activity of human trafficking (Kangaspunta, 2006). An example of this **core group** structure of TOC is Australia's McLean Syndicate (United Nations Interregional Crime and Justice Research Institute, 2021). Specifically, within the McLean Syndicate, the recruitment of members is based on resources, skills, and the changing demand market. In these cases, members are recruited on an ad hoc basis as required by the product (United Nations Office on Drugs and Crime, 2002). For example, in the case of trafficking children for adoption, caretakers are recruited to ensure the health and safety of the children prior to reaching their destination (McCabe, 2008). Because a core group uses some of its members only temporarily to complete the criminal activity, their detection by law enforcement is rare (Le, 2012). In this organizational structure, a small number of individuals form a relatively tight structure, or a core group. As shown in Figure 3.3, around this small core group is a larger group of associated individuals, and around the group of associated individuals is a larger number of peripheral TOC group members (McCabe, 2008).

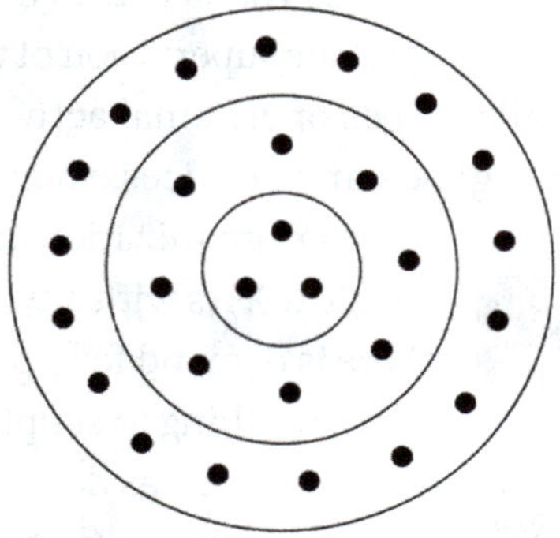

FIGURE 3.3 Core Group

In the United States, this core criminal group emerged in the late 1990s when the vulnerabilities of the hierarchical structures were demonstrated in the federal arrests of the Lucchese and Gambino crime families (Arsovska & Temple, 2016). Albania's TOC group in New York City also adopted this core structure of members working with specific bosses and peripheral positions being assumed within the larger criminal network (Arsovska & Temple, 2016).

In many of the Dutch organized crime networks, women working as prostitutes are in the peripheral positions to recruit and control girls for sex trafficking (Kleemans et al., 2014). This supports work by Zhang et al. (2007) on the roles of Chinese women in human smuggling as a form of TOC.

Criminal Network

The **criminal network** structure, sometimes appearing disorganized, is actually organized around the need of the specific criminal action at the time (McCabe, 2017). A current example is found in the exit of women and children during the 2022 Russia–Ukraine war: TOC members involved in human trafficking and organ trafficking assembled at border crossings in an attempt to attract these vulnerable individuals into their criminal organizations. In these structural networks, some members integrate in general society in areas such as construction or real estate sites to facilitate criminal activities and to legitimize the illegal profits, while others continue the victimization of persons (Becucci, 2004).

As shown in Figure 3.4, this criminal network structure is characterized by strong connections between actors as well as weak or temporary connections between actors. Specifically, within this organization, the criminal network exists to provide the actors or members required for the specific product. In other words, the solid line connections depicted in Figure 3.4 represent the more permanent actors within the network, such as would exist in the transportation of a product across borders using a transporter and a border agent. In the transportation of people, an additional connection may be required to provide required documentation for individuals crossing a border; this is depicted by the broken line in Figure 3.4. However, as documentation is not required in the illicit drug trade, the connection is not required for this criminal network.

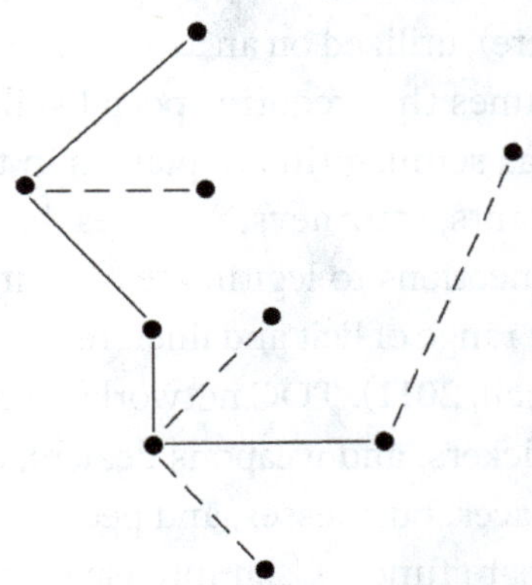

FIGURE 3.4 Criminal Network Structure

Social network—A social structure or organization made up of actors (e.g., people or countries) and links to illustrate the relationships between actors. The social network perspective, founded in sociology but often utilized by criminologists, provides a set of methods for analyzing the structure of an entire social entity.

While there are relatively few individuals currently exploring TOC groups through network analysis, in fact network analysis may lead to a better understanding of today's TOC groups. For clarity, *social network analysis* is an approach to understanding network structures and the behaviors of actors within those networks (United Nations Interregional Crime and Justice Research Institute, 2021). A fundamental step for analyzing **social networks** is to use a set of nodes to represent individual elements (or actors) within the network and a set of links or connections to represent relationships or ties. Researchers studying social networks have identified the concept of centrality to identify actors who have numerous ties or connections within the network and serve as significant members of the criminal network, as well as the concept of "betweenness" to identify those central and significant members of TOC who facilitate the activities of the criminal network (Meyers, 2017). An example of these connection characteristics is demonstrated daily for criminal networks and those individuals in a position to either facilitate the flow of information or products or end the flow of information or products.

Today, this centrality of TOC members has been identified in multiple crime groups, including many of the Albanian criminal groups in the United States. Those members no longer operate on the periphery as enforcers or drug mules but now occupy central positions for distribution (Arsovska & Temple, 2016). In these cases, new criminal actors enter the network to fill any void in the trafficking of the product. In addition to centrality in today's criminal networks, one cannot discount the critical roles of peripheral members of TOC groups (similar to those in the core group structure), utilized on an as-needed basis, who make possible many of the crimes that require special skills. Specifically, these facilitators serve as semilegitimate players in the "legitimate world," such as accountants, attorneys, notaries, bankers, and real estate brokers, with connections to legitimate customers, criminals, and terrorists alike; their range of licit and illicit relationships is broad (National Security Council, 2011). TOC networks, such as organized crime groups, drug traffickers, and weapons dealers, often share the convergence points of places, businesses, and people to convert their illicit profits into legitimate funds. Cash-intensive and high-volume businesses such as casinos are especially attractive, particularly those in jurisdictions that lack the political will and oversight to regulate casino operations. As a result, TOC groups utilize some of the same front companies, with officials receiving either revenues from the criminal businesses or ownership stakes in the legitimate-appearing commercial entity (National Security Council, 2011).

Cyberspace Structure

Research has suggested that the organizational structure of a group may change with the incorporation of technology (Etzioni, 2005).

Specifically, as technology use increases, the flexibility within the organization for completing tasks increases and a more decentralized structure will emerge (Boubour, 1997). Hence, technology usage within an organization often results in a decrease in control for those directing the structure (Bensghir, 1996). These changes in structure, resulting from the incorporation of technology, do not occur only in legitimate business enterprises; they are experienced in today's TOC structures as well. Of course, based on purpose and product, structures vary in the ways that technology affects them (Crowston & Malone, 1994). This changing and new structure of TOC is a result of criminal activities within the virtual world of cyberspace.

Cyberspace, for clarity, is the electronic marketplace utilized by TOC groups to sell illicit goods and services without physical contact between buyers and sellers. These cyber-related crimes, or cybercrimes, allow TOC members to be physically disconnected from the activities, customers, and victims (United Nations Office on Drugs and Crime, 2018b). Europol (2017) suggests that approximately 20% of the criminal actions by TOC groups within the regions of the European Union are completed through temporary or short-term criminal schemes. These more fluid structures have emerged from the increased opportunities to provide illicit goods and services through the globalization of commerce and technological advances (e.g., remote banking). These structures, often made up of the more educated, more trained, and more intelligent criminal members (Schiks et al., 2022), have provided TOC groups a more refined way to ensure success.

Lastly, and as related to cybercrimes, over the years TOC groups have used money laundering to distribute billions of dollars across the globe (Schneider, 2008). With the formation of Bitcoin, the most recognized brand of cryptocurrency, TOC members can now utilize technology and cryptocurrency to launder their profits. Specifically, **cryptocurrency**, which is a recorded string of computer code, allows for direct person-to-person financial exchanges without the middle entity of a banking system. Since the owner of the cryptocurrency is unidentified, the financial transactions that are being made (as illustrated next) are nearly impossible to track. For this reason, TOC groups are using cryptocurrency and black markets to continue supporting their criminal activities (Deepika, 2017). In other words, because cryptocurrency does not involve the use of a traditional banking system, with its many regulations, money can be deposited in accounts and withdrawn from them without detection (Albrecht et al., 2019).

ITEMS PURCHASED WITH BITCOIN

- Luxury Cars
- Real Estate
- Works of Art
- Airplanes
- Tickets to Sporting Events
- Education Tuition
- Club Memberships
- Citizenship in Antigua or Barbuda (Stormgain, 2020)

Therefore, the structure of the TOC group is related to the product and the mode of distribution that will support the profits of the group. In many cases, the structure of TOC is related not only to the illicit markets but also to the legal markets within the society (Edwards & Gill, 2002). As there is currently no decrease in the demand for illegal goods and services, the structure of TOC will continue to evolve to the benefit of the organization.

Leadership of a TOC Group

A *leadership style* refers to a leader's characteristics and style of communicating when directing, motivating, guiding, and managing groups of people (Cherry, 2021). Great leaders can inspire political movements, increase employee work efforts, and produce social change. Hence, the leadership within a TOC group is critical not only for producing profitable returns, but also for avoiding criminal justice officials' detection of the group's criminal activities. In the late 1930s, leadership styles as related to bureaucracies were found to exist within TOC organizations. As most research on the topic suggests that TOC organizations often follow business models, their leadership styles are applied in this text as discussions on leadership within TOC organizations.

The three styles of leadership most often identified within current business models are autocratic, democratic, and laissez-faire (Lewin et al., 1939). Authoritarian leaders, also known as autocratic leaders, provide clear expectations for what needs to be done, when it should be done, and how it should be done. This style of leadership is strongly focused on both command by the leader and control of the followers, with a clear division between the leader and the members of the organization; it is often demonstrated in historical accounts of hierarchical organized crime structures. Research suggests that under this category of leadership decision-making was less creative, and leaders who used this style of leadership were usually viewed as controlling, bossy, and dictatorial (Lewin et al., 1939). However, considering the secretive structure of TOC organizations as well as the requirement for quick and decisive actions, the autocratic style of leadership is seen most often within organized crime (McCabe, 2008).

Al Capone was probably the most famous crime boss in U.S. history (Davidson, 2021b). Before moving to Chicago, Capone was a member of the Five Points Gang in New York City. In Chicago he started a bootlegging business, which later expanded to include smuggling and sex work. His method of leadership included extreme violence, along with bribery of police, judges, and the mayor of Chicago. He was identified as the FBI's Public Enemy Number One after he publicly murdered seven members of a rival gang during the infamous Saint Valentine's Day Massacre (Davidson, 2021b).

Democratic leadership, also known as **participative leadership**, is typically most effective if the goal of the organization is to guide and nurture members (Lewin et al., 1939). This style of leadership is rare within a TOC organization, however. Democratic leaders focus their time on the nurturing and motivation of followers, whereas in TOC organizations the focus is on profit and rarely on mentoring (McCabe & Manian, 2010).

Laissez-faire leadership involves leaders offering little or no guidance and leaving the decision-making to the group members (Lewin et al., 1939). Therefore, the laissez-faire style of leadership does not exist in TOC organizations, where the focus is on profit at all costs regardless of consequences. However, TOC groups do exist within the other models.

Within TOC organizations, **autocratic leadership** prevails. The typical leader is male, with strong ties or connections to the organization, usually through family or through longevity in the organization. This person usually is involved in criminal activities, and many members joined the organization as juveniles. Historically, membership was restricted based on criteria such as ethnicity, kinship, race, and criminal background (Finckenauer, 2005). In Abadinsky's (2017) discussion on the patrimonial model, the autocratic leadership position includes a network model that focuses on the relationships between families, friends, and patrons, with the assumption that a group's members are of similar ethnicities due to the organization's emphasis on recruiting members from among family and friends (Halstead, 1998). This model places a strong emphasis on relationships of trust and on emotional ties (Paoli, 2002). In addition, loyalty and allegiance to the crime organization are maintained through penalties for defections, and violence is a mechanism used to enforce internal order (Williams & Godson, 2002). Thus, in these cases, individuals controlled their own activities and recruited partners as needed. The historical structure of organized crime groups incorporates elements from both a standard hierarchy and a criminal network, with essential characteristics—including fluidity in relationships; informal exchange networks; and the importance of contacts, ties, and loyalty—forming the basis, all within a male-headed organization.

Three categories of leadership: autocratic, democratic, and laissez-faire.

Historically, TOC leadership was the role for male members of the group; today, however, females are increasing not just their memberships in TOC groups but also their positions of leadership. In fact, research in recent decades has suggested that women now see the transnational and fluid opportunities embedded in TOC as attractive means to gain money and power (Siegel, 2014). This window of opportunity for women, often as a result of policing efforts against male leaders or through kinship with the leaders, has started to create a culture of women bosses in TOC groups. In particular, the majority of the women involved with Cosa Nostra activities are related by kin or marriage to male members of those groups (Siegel, 2014). In one example, Maria Licciardi, alias La Piccolina, the daughter and sister of two of the male leaders of La Cosa Nostra, heads an alliance of 20 criminal clans of the Camorra.

Women as Leaders

Historically, there has been an ongoing gender gap in organized crime, with women occupying structural positions that are generally associated with a lack of power (Diviak et al., 2020). It has been acknowledged that women are less present in the TOC networks and that those who are involved in TOC tend to collaborate with other women rather than with men, in more of a democratic model of leadership. However, this may not always be the case.

Research on the leadership styles of women in the business world suggest that women are more task-focused, preferring to concentrate on the daily activities of operating the company, whereas men prefer to focus on outcomes and performance (Krinzman, 2021). In addition, women tend to prefer a flat organization that allows for collegial input, whereas men prefer the more standard hierarchy. Lastly, women prefer indirect communications, in order to allow the organization's members to complete tasks as they choose; men in leadership prefer direct communications for task completion (Krinzman, 2021). However, while there are differences between the typical leadership styles of men and women, TOC organizations tend to find a place for both styles in continuing to profit from criminal activities.

For the most part, TOC organizations have been under the leadership of men, often called "mob bosses." However, in the 1980s, with police focusing their efforts on addressing the leaders within organized crime organizations, the woman mob boss began to emerge. Specifically, in countries such as the United States and Italy, criminal convictions of the male leaders and their sons led to assets going to their wives and daughters (Davidson, 2021a). This control of TOC by women continues. In fact, as related to TOC today, it is thought that women control about a third of all of the Mafia's financial resources (Davidson, 2021a). The cases of three particular women in leadership positions of TOC groups, all of whom operated within similar time periods, are provided below.

Griselda Blanco (1943–2012), also called the "Godmother of Cocaine," grew up in poverty in Colombia, with a life of crime beginning before her teen years when she helped kidnap a boy; after his wealthy family refused to pay the ransom, she fatally shot him. While still a teenager, she married a small-time criminal, and the couple had three children. However, Blanco was believed to have ordered his murder several years later when she began a relationship with Alberto Bravo, a drug trafficker whom she ultimately married. Blanco went on to have her second and third husbands killed, while at the same time she built a drug empire. Through violence and planning, Blanco became one of the world's wealthiest drug traffickers, with estimated earnings of some $80 million per month. Blanco was finally arrested, convicted, and sentenced to 15 years in prison in the United States for drug trafficking. She also was implicated in more than 200 murders. Blanco was killed in 2012 (Tikkanen, 2022).

(continued)

In 1993, Italian police arrested **Rosetta Cutolo**, the leader of the Naples Mafia, after she'd been on the run for 13 years. Cutolo, known as "Rosetta Ice-Eyes" for her steely gaze and alleged management of a multimillion-dollar criminal empire, is said to have headed the New Camorra Organization after her brother Raffaele, its founder, was incarcerated. Her toughness and sharp business brain became legendary; investigators say they suspect her of having ordered the assassinations of several rivals—one of them the deputy chief of Naples's Poggioreale prison, where her brother and other family members had served time. Already sentenced in absentia to almost 10 years in jail for organized crime activities, Rosetta Cutolo was wanted for a variety of offenses, among them murder, armed robbery, and extortion. Police say she presided directly over the clan's finances, acting as treasurer and planning strategies for drug trafficking, money laundering, prostitution, and protection rackets (Pedrick, 1993).

In 2013, an Orlando woman, **Charmaine Roman**, was arrested for serving as the head of a violent Jamaican drug-trafficking ring that brought thousands of pounds of marijuana into Central Florida and for committing a host of violent crimes herself (Pavuk, 2013). Police, who have been investigating Roman for years, say the 42-year-old was in charge of the group's finances and the laundering of their money in amounts over $3 million.

Membership Within a TOC Group

In the 1970s, research on criminal networks identified members of organized crime groups as existing within craft organizations, project organizations, or business organizations. For clarity, *craft organizations* consisted of a small number of people with separate specialists' roles and equal profit-sharing. *Project organizations* were special teams of organized criminals brought together for specific criminal jobs. *Business criminal organizations* were thought of today as dealing with large-scale extortion and transnational supply of illegal goods, with corruption a key element of their operation (McIntosh, 1975). It is this business criminal organization that has the focus of the global community today.

Other research on members of an organization views the most dedicated members as either participants or diehards. The *participant* members of TOC groups often invest their own time to gain knowledge and learn new skills (such as technology) to better support the profits of the group. The *diehard* members of a TOC group are heavily invested in the organization to the point that they may lobby to commit other serious crimes to attain a leadership position of (DuBrin, 2016).

In an attempt to control TOC, countries across the globe have adopted laws and policies that include harsher penalties, the protection of witnesses, and asset forfeiture programs (Calderoni et al.,

2021). However, they've had little success. In fact, most large TOC organizations have existed for decades, with their continuity assured based upon steady recruitment of new members (Paoli, 2020). This section of the chapter discusses the recruitment of TOC members, while acknowledging the lack of attention often paid to these personal investments (La Spina, 2004).

Like any organization, to ensure survival TOC groups must recruit new members. The recruitment process for TOC groups is crucial in that members must not only continue the criminal activities but also withstand interventions by criminal justice officials (Reuter, 1983). Researchers who focus on recruitment as an aspect of TOC suggest that the process of TOC recruitment is not only embedded within the social environment but also is an outcome of social interactions.

Research on those individuals involved in transnational crime cites a variety of reasons for membership, including social ties and identity, criminal backgrounds, economic condition, age, ethnicity, and gender (Calderoni et al., 2020). This section of the chapter provides a discussion on factors related to recruitment and membership within TOC.

Social relationships or social ties are the factors most frequently reported as leading to recruitment into organized criminal groups (Kleemans & de Poot, 2008). These social relationships include parental, family, kinships, friendships, and acquaintances. This generational effect of "parent then child" involvement in TOC has been recognized through the centuries, as stereotypically in the United States one common notion about an Italian family in the New York area is that they are "members of the mafia." Historical research suggests that social, professional, and criminal connections are frequently interrelated and mutually reinforcing, and often create opportunities for criminal activities; in other words, social ties are an important driver for recruitment into TOC groups (Arlacchi, 1983). More recent research shows that the importance of the family extends even beyond the more traditional and family-based criminal organizations to the modern blended-family concept as increasing the probability that an individual will become a gang member (Kissner & Pyrooz, 2009). Lastly, TOC groups provide members an identity or a sense of belonging; for many, the desire to be a part of a group fuels memberships in TOC (Albini, 1971).

A history of criminal behavior is also associated with membership in a TOC group. Specifically, research suggests that members of TOC groups report having had long, violent, and prolific criminal careers before joining the criminal group (Requena et al., 2014). These individuals not only are within their norm of criminal activity, but also usually maintain criminal contact to further facilitate the profits of the group (Behan, 1996).

Economic conditions are also identified as related to membership in TOC groups. In particular, poor economic conditions and low socioeconomic status are often identified as facilitating recruitment into TOC groups. However, individuals with higher socioeconomic status may also become involved in criminal organizations, as they are attracted to the profit-making opportunities of TOC (Van Koppen, 2013).

Age and gender are also related to recruitment into TOC (McCabe, 2017). In particular, some suggest that many of the individuals who choose to join a TOC group are young (Arlacchi, 1983). Recruitment into organized criminal groups at a young age may include appeals to access to money, drugs, and sex (Carvalho & Soares, 2016). Oftentimes, individuals who are a bit older but still considered young adults join TOC groups for work opportunities (Blokland et al., 2019). As discussed in more detail in other sections of this chapter, TOC membership is dominated by men; however, several studies have focused on women's involvement in criminal organizations and their sometimes significant roles (Van San & Sikkens, 2017).

Finally, longevity is also related to membership in a TOC group. Specifically, leaders and founders of an organization are more influenced by short-term criminal opportunities and economic considerations, while simple members of a TOC group often are impacted more by long-term social dynamics that arise from ties and exposure to criminal activities (Kemp et al., 2020). Those with a history of exposure to TOC groups are more likely to join and maintain membership within these groups.

These characteristics of members of TOC, as well as the characteristics of leaders within TOC groups, apply across the globe to international groups engaged in criminal activities. These characteristics are also common in TOC groups operating in the United States.

TOC in the United States

The structural factors that exist to support the activities of TOC around the world also exist to support the activities of TOC within the boundaries of the United States. The size of the continent, the coastlines on the east and west boundaries, and the nonregulated access across state boundaries provide TOC groups ready avenues for access to products and trade of those products. In addition, because of the ethnic and racial diversity within the United States, both foreign and domestic crime networks are able to assimilate into the population without detection (Federation of American Scientists, 2000).

ORGANIZED CYBERCRIME

TOC groups that participate in cybercrime typically commit acts such as the following:

- Stolen data
- Stolen identities
- Malware releases
- Phishing schemes
- Digital denial of services
- Production and release of information on vulnerabilities (Espinosa, 2022)

TOC groups in the United States are led by men and women who have histories of involvement in criminal activities. In addition, socioeconomic status in the United States provides the opportunity for numerous lucrative criminal ventures to exist without other people being aware of any sudden influx of wealth for TOC members. Technology, telecommunications, and financial systems in the United States also support the structure of TOC, as cybercommunity policies promote the exchange of ideas and products through quick and often unregulated communications. Finally, the decentralized system of policing in the United States (discussed further in Chapter 11) may also facilitate TOC, as in these common law systems of law, priorities are based upon individual rights and local police support; hence, the interstate communications that might detect similar illicit markets and illegal trades are less likely to occur in the United States.

Summary

TOC is a response to the demands within society for illicit services, and it indicates the limitations of states in exercising sovereign authority over their domestic populations (Edwards & Gill, 2002). The structure of TOC facilitates the criminal activities of the group. In most cases, a sound structure and dedicated members of an organization will result in the success of the organization; the same outcomes of success are expected with dedicated members and a sound structure of a TOC group.

Most research identifies the standard hierarchy, the regional hierarchy, the core group, and the criminal network as the most common criminal structures for TOC organizations. Members of these groups, regardless of structure, are dedicated to financial profits, and leaders of TOC demand loyalty from their members within the group.

For some societies and in some cases, crime as enterprise emerges and provides short-term financial support and employment opportunities. However, the effects of TOC actions within a society expose vulnerabilities in law and democracy. By understanding the strengths as well as the weaknesses of the structure of TOC groups, one can also understand the modes of criminal activity. By understanding these structures, one can identify product or service and delivery through TOC groups. Hence, identifying the structure of TOC can help explain the vulnerabilities of these organizations and their criminal activities.

Questions for Further Thought

1. What are the common structures for TOC, and what are their vulnerabilities?
2. How is the structure of TOC related to their products and/ or services?
3. How are technology and cybercrime related to the structures of TOC?

References

Abadinsky, H. (2017). *Organized crime* (11th ed.). Cengage Group.

Albanese, J. (1996). *Organized crime in America* (3rd ed.). Routledge.

Albini, J. (1971). *The American mafia: Genesis of a legend* (Sociology series). Appleton-Century-Crofts.

Albrecht, C., Duffin, K., Hawkins, S., Rocha, M., & Manuel, V. (2019). The use of cryptocurrency in the money laundering process. *Journal of Money Laundering Control, 22*(2), 210–216.

Arlacchi, P. (1983). *La mafia imprenditrice: L'etica mafiosa e lo spirito del capitalismo.* Il Mulino.

Arsovska, J., & Temple, M. (2016). Adaption, rationality, and advancement: Ethnic Albanian organized crime in New York City. *Crime, Law, and Social Change, 66*(1), 1–20.

Becucci, S. (2004). Old and new actors in the Italian drug trade: Ethnic succession or functional specialization? *European Journal of Criminal Policy and Research, 10*(4), 257–283.

Behan, T. (1996). *The Camorra*. Routledge.

Bell, D. (1960). *The end of ideology.* Free Press.

Bensghir, T. (1996). *Information technology and organizational change.* TODAIE Publishing.

Blokland, A., van Hout, L., van der Leest, W., & Soudijn, M. (2019). Not your average biker: Criminal careers of members of Dutch outlaw motorcycle gangs. *Trends in Organized Crime 22*(1), 10–33.

Boubour, L. (1997). Computers transforming the work setting. In M. Ermann, M. Williams, & M. Shauf (Eds.), *Computers, Ethics and Society* (2nd ed.) (pp. 169–173). Oxford University Press.

Briscoe, I. (2011, September). *What makes countries vulnerable to transnational organized crime.* Norwegian Peacebuilding Resource Centre. Retrieved March 20, 2022, from https://www.files.ethz.ch/isn/137502/What%20makes%20countries%20vulnerable.pdf

Britannica, The Editors of Encyclopaedia. (2021, December 9). Cocaine. *Encyclopedia Britannica*. Retrieved February 28, 2022, from https://www.britannica.com/science/cocaine

Britannica, The Editors of Encyclopaedia. (2011, November 8). Camorra. *Encyclopedia Britannica*. Retrieved February 26, 2022, from https://www.britannica.com/topic/Camorra

Calderoni, F., Campedelli, G., Comunale, T., Marchesi, M., & Savona, E. (2020, January). Recruitment into organized criminal groups: A systematic review. *Trends and Issues in Crime and Criminal Justice, 583*. Australian Institute of Criminology. Retrieved February 22, 2022, from https://www.aic.gov.au/sites/default/files/2020-05/ti583_recruitment_into_organised_criminal_groups.pdf

Calderoni, F., Campedelli, G., Szekely, A., Paolucci, M., & Andrighetto, G. (2021). Recruitment into organized crime: An agent-based approach testing the impact of different policies. *Journal of Quantitative Criminology*, 38, 197–237. Retrieved February 20, 2022, from https://link.springer.com/content/pdf/10.1007/s10940-020-09489-z.pdf

Carvalho, L., & Soares, R. (2016). Living on the edge: Youth entry, career and exit in drug-selling gangs. *Journal of Economic Behavior & Organization 121*, 77–98.

Cherry, K. (2021, August 11). *Leadership styles and frameworks you should know.* VeryWellMind. Retrieved February 21, 2022, from https://www.verywellmind.com/leadership-styles-2795312

Crowston, K., & Malone, T. (1994). Information technology and work organizations. In T. Allen & M. Scott Morton, *Information Technology and the Corporation of the 1990s* (pp. 250–252). Oxford University Press.

Cuthbertson, P. (2017, December). *Who goes to prison? An overview of the prison population of England and Wales.* CIVITAS. Retrieved March 17, 2022, from https://civitas.org.uk/content/files/whogoestoprison.pdf

Davidson, L. (2021a, October 13). *6 of the most notorious female mobsters in history.* Retrieved February 21, 2022, from https://www.historyhit.com/the-most-notorious-female-mobsters-in-history/

Davidson, L. (2021b, October 12). *10 of the most infamous mob bosses in history.* Retrieved February 24, 2022, from https://www.historyhit.com/the-most-infamous-mob-bosses-in-history/

Decker, S., & Pyrooz, D. (2015). Street gangs, terrorists, drug smugglers, and organized crime: What's the difference? In S. H. Decker & D. C. Pyrooz (Eds.), *The handbook of gangs* (pp. 294–308). Wiley.

Deepika, P. (2017). Cryptocurrency: Trends, perspectives, and challenges. *International Journal of Trends in Research and Development, 4*, 4–6.

Diviak, T., Coutinho, J., & Stivala, A. (2020). A man's world? Comparing the structural positions of men and women in organized criminal networks. *Crime, Law, and Social Change, 74*, 547–569. Retrieved February 20, 2022, from https://pure.rug.nl/ws/portalfiles/portal/144254533/Divi_k2020_Article_AManSWorldComparingTheStructur.pdf

DuBrin, A. (2016). *Leadership: Research findings, practice, and skills* (8th ed.). Cengage Group.

Edwards, A., & Gill, P. (2002). Crime as enterprise? The case of "transnational organized crime." *Crime, Law, and Social Change, 37*, 203–223. https://doi.org/10.1023/A:1015025509582

Espinosa, C. (2022). *Top 10 organized crime syndicates.* Retrieved March 17, 2022, from https://christianespinosa.com/blog/top-10-organized-cybercrime-syndicates/

Etzioni, A. (2005). Authority structure and organizational effectiveness. *Administrative Science Quarterly, 4*(1), 43–67.

Europol. (2017). *European Union serious and organized crime threat assessment.* https://www.europol.europa.eu/publications-events/main-reports/european-union-serious-and-organised-crime-threat-assessment-2017

Federation of American Scientists. (2000). *International crime threat assessment (Chapter 3).* Retrieved February 3, 2022, from https://irp.fas.org/threat/pub45270chap3.html

Finckenauer, J. (2005). Problems of definition: What is organized crime? *Trends in Organized Crime* 8(3), 63–83.

Galeotti, M. (2017, April 18). *Crimintern: How the Kremlin uses Russia's crime networks in Europe.* European Council on Foreign Relations. Retrieved March 18, 2022, from https://ecfr.eu/publication/crimintern_how_the_kremlin_uses_russias_criminal_networks_in_europe/

Grant, E. (2012, October 12). *The Russia mafia and organized crime. How can this global force be tamed?* Open Democracy. Retrieved March 17, 2022, from https://www.opendemocracy.net/en/odr/russian-mafia-and-organised-crime-how-can-this-global-force-be-tamed/

Halstead, B. (1998). The use of models in the analysis of organized crime and development of policy. *Transnational Organized Crime* 4(1), 1–24.

JRank. (2022). *Organized crime: History.* Retrieved March 3, 2022, from https://law.jrank.org/pages/1624/Organized-Crime-History.html

Kangaspunta, K. (2006, April). *Trafficking in persons: Global patterns.* United Nations Office on Drugs and Crime.

Kemp. L., Zolghadriha, S., & Gill, P. (2020). Pathways into organized crime: Comparing founders and joiners. *Trends in Organized Crime, 23*(1), 203–226.

Kissner, J., & Pyrooz, D. (2009). Self-control, differential association, and gang membership: A theoretical and empirical extension of the literature. *Journal of Criminal Justice 37*(5), 478–487.

Kleemans, E., & de Poot, C. (2008). Criminal careers in organized crime and social opportunity structure. *European Journal of Criminology 5*(1), 69–98.

Kleemans, E., Kruisbergen, E., & Kouwenberg, R. (2014). Women, brokerage, and transnational organized crime. Empirical results from the Dutch Organized Crime Monitor. *Trends in Organized Crime, 17*(1), 16–30.

Krinzman, B. (2021, February 12). *A review of workplace leadership styles: Men vs. women.* Retrieved February 27, 2022, from https://www.helioshr.com/blog/2015/06/a-review-of-gender-leadership-styles-common-traits-in-men-vs-women/

La Spina, A. (2004). The paradox of effectiveness: Growth, institutionalisation and evaluation of anti-Mafia policies in Italy. In C. Fijnaut & L. Paoli (Eds.), *Organised crime in Europe: Concepts, patterns and control policies in the European Union and beyond: Studies of organized crime* (pp. 641–675). Springer. Retrieved February 20, 2022, from https://doi.org/10.1007/978-1-4020-2765-9_24

Le, V. (2012). Organised crime typologies: Structure, activities, and conditions. *International Journal of Criminology and Sociology, 1*, 121–131.

Levin, N. (2019). *10 Largest criminal organizations to ever exist.* Retrieved February 12, 2022, from https://largest.org/people/criminal-organizations/.

Lewin, K., Lippitt, R., & White, K. (1939). Patterns of aggressive behavior in experimentally created "social climates." *Journal of Social Psychology, 10*(2), 271–301.

The Local. (2019, July 9). *Meet the 'Ndrangheta: It's time to bust some myths about the Calabrian mafia.* Retrieved February 26, 2022, from https://www.thelocal.it/20190709/meet-the-ndrangheta-its-time-to-bust-some-myths-about-the-calabrian-mafia/

Maas, P. (1968). *The Valachi papers.* Putnam.

McCabe, K. (2008). *The Trafficking of persons: National and international responses.* Peter Lang.

McCabe, K. (2017). *Protecting your children online.* Rowman & Littlefield.

McCabe, K., & Manian, S. (2010). *Sex trafficking. A global perspective.* Rowman & Littlefield.

McIntosh, M. (1975). *The organization of crime.* MacMillan.

Meyers, T. (2017). Examining the network components of a Medicare fraud scheme: The Mirzoyan-Terdjonian organization. *Crime, Law, and Social Change, 68*(1), 251–279.

National Security Council. (2011). *Transnational organized crime: A growing threat to national and international security.* Retrieved February 3, 2022, from https://obamawhitehouse.archives.gov/administration/eop/nsc/transnational-crime/threat

Paoli, L. (2002). The paradoxes of organized crime. *Crime, Law and Social Change 37,* 51–97.

Paoli, L. (2020). What makes Mafias different? *Crime and Justice, 49.* Retrieved February 20, 2022, from https://doi.org/10.1086/708826

Pavuk, A. (2013, October 25). Local woman is crime kingpin, cops say. *Orlando Sentinel.* Retrieved February 3, 2022, from https://www.orlandosentinel.com/news/os-xpm-2013-10-26-os-jamaican-drug-ring-leader-charmaine-roman-20131026-story.html

Pedrick, C. (1993, February 9). Italian police arrest woman said to head Naples Mafia. *Washington Post.* Retrieved February 3, 2022, from https://www.washingtonpost.com/archive/politics/1993/02/09/italian-police-arrest-woman-said-to-head-naples-mafia/ea791a2e-bc24-42e6-a228-0dfde5c84176/

Requena, L., de Juan, M., Giménez-Salinas, A., & de la Corte, L. (2014). A psychosocial study on crime and gender: Position, role and status of women in a sample of Spanish criminal organizations. *International Journal of Social Psychology, 29*(1), 121–149.

Reuter, P. (1983). *Disorganized crime: The economics of the visible hand.* MIT Press.

Reuter, P. (2009). Systemic violence in drug markets. *Crime, Law, and Social Change, 52*(1), 275–284.

Rojas, D. (2021, November 5). A dozen drug gangs are fighting for tourist market in Mexico's Caribbean, official says. *Los Angeles Times.* Retrieved February 20, 2022, from https://www.latimes.com/world-nation/story/2021-11-05/a-dozen-drug-gangs-fighting-for-tourist-market-in-mexicos-caribbean-says-official

Santino, U. (2012). Mafia and mafia-type organizations in Italy. In J. Albanese, D. Das, & A. Vermas (Eds.), *Organized Crime: World Perspectives* (pp. 82–100). Prentice Hall.

Schiks, S., van de Weijer, S., & Leukfeldt, E. (2022). High tech crime, high intellectual crime? Comparing the intellectual capabilities of cybercriminal, traditional criminals, and non-criminals. *Computers in Human Behavior, 126.* Retrieved May 4, 2022, from https://www.sciencedirect.com/science/article/pii/S0747563221003083?via%3Dihub

Schneider, F. (2008). Money laundering and financial means of organized crime: Some preliminary empirical findings. *Global Business and Economics, 19*(3), 309–330.

Siegel, L. (2014). *Criminology: The core* (4th ed). CA: Cengage.

Smith, C., & Papachristos, A. (2016). Trust thy crooked neighbor: Multiplexity in Chicago organized crime networks. *American Sociological Review, 156*(1), 1–24.

Stevens, M., & Mervosh, S. (2019, March 14). A look at 5 high-profile mob hits before the Frank Cali slaying. *The New York Times.* Retrieved February 20, 2022, from https://www.nytimes.com/2019/03/14/nyregion/famous-mob-hits.html.

Stormgain. (2020, February 5). *The 10 most expensive things ever bought with cryptocurrency*. Retrieved May 26, 2022, from https://stormgain.com/news/10-most-expensive-things-ever-bought-cryptocurrency

Thoumi, F. (2003). *Illegal drugs, economy, and society in the Andes*. Johns Hopkins University Press.

Tikkanen, A. (2022, February 11). Griselda Blanco. *Encyclopedia Britannica*. https://www.britannica.com/biography/Griselda-Blanco

Tupman, B. (2015). What does the way crime was organized yesterday tell us about the way crime is organized today and will be tomorrow? *Journal of Money Laundering, 18*(2), 220–233.

United Nations Interregional Crime and Justice Research Institute. (2021). *Countering terrorism online with artificial intelligence*. Retrieved February 3, 2022, from http://213.254.5.198/sites/default/files/2021-06/Countering%20Terrorism%20Online%20with%20AI%20-%20UNCCT-UNICRI%20Report.pdf

United Nations Office on Drugs and Crime. (2002). *Results of a pilot survey of 40 selected organized criminal groups in 16 countries*. UNODC.

United Nations Office on Drugs and Crime. (2018a). Module 7: Models of organized criminal groups. Key issues: Local, cultural model of organized crime. *E4J University Module Series: Organized crime*. Retrieved February 20, 2022, from https://www.unodc.org/e4j/en/organized-crime/module-7/key-issues/local-cultural-model.html

United Nations Office on Drugs and Crime. (2018b). Module 7: Models of organized criminal groups. Key issues: New forms of organized crime: Network structure. *E4J University Module Series: Organized crime*. Retrieved May 2, 2022, from https://www.unodc.org/e4j/en/organized-crime/module-7/key-issues/networked-structure.html

Van Koppen, M. (2013). Involvement mechanisms for organized crime. *Crime, Law and Social Change 59*(1), 1–20.

Van San, M., & Sikkens, E. (2017). Families, lovers, and friends: Women, social networks, and transnational cocaine smuggling from Curaçao and Peru. *Howard Journal of Crime and Justice 56*(3), 343–57.

Weber, M. (1947). *The theory of social and economic organization*. Free Press.

Williams, P., & Godson, P. (2002). Anticipating organized and transnational crime. *Crime, Law and Social Change 37*(4), 311–355.

Zhang, S., Chin, K., & Miller, J. (2007). Women's participation in Chinese transnational human smuggling: A gendered market perspective. *Criminology, 45*(3), 699–733.

PART II

Issues and Consequences

CHAPTER 4

Risk Factors and Vulnerable Groups

Key Terms

Amnesty International
Antislavery International
Child trafficking
Conscription
Crimes against humanity
Criminogenic asymmetries
Environmental crimes
Europol
Gangs
Gender-based crimes
Ghislaine Maxwell
Global Organized Crime Index (GOCI)
Green criminology
Human Rights Watch
Internally displaced person (IDP)
Interpol
Jeffrey Epstein
LGBTQ
Save the Children
Sex ring
Sex tourism
Sex trafficking
Sexual exploitation
Social contract
Stateless person (SP)
Structural risk factors
Vulnerable populations

CHAPTER OBJECTIVES

Chapter 4 will enable readers to understand the following:

- the problem of defining a vulnerable population
- the risk factors for transnational organized crime (TOC)
- the consequences of COVID-19 for transnational organized crime
- the consequences of environmental crimes
- the phrase "green criminology"
- the connection between environmental crimes, TOC, and government regulations
- the importance of advocacy groups

MOST INDIVIDUALS SEE TOC as having little effect on them and as posing minimal risk to their being victimized, as they see TOC as related to drug-dealing, weapons possession, and gang-related violence. For the most part, this perception is true; however, whenever any vulnerable group within a society is targeted, then stability, democracy, and the protections of basic human rights are also in jeopardy. Thus, the portrayal in the media of these "Mafia groups" with blood relatives targeting each other and other crime families for control over a geographic territory is often not the reality of TOC groups.

Research suggests that TOC flourishes in communities that are disadvantaged and fractured (Hamilton-Smith, 2018). Weak and failing countries as well as conflict regions within countries have traditionally been considered to be crime-facilitative environments. In these settings, TOC emerges from the power vacuum that is created by the absence of enforcement and good governance (United Nations Office on Drugs and Crime, 2018c). In particular, failed states have weak institutions and high levels of corruption, which can not only be a consequence of TOC but also facilitate the criminal activities of TOC. In these cases, TOC capitalizes on the weak order of these governments as well as the lack of law and order (United Nations Office on Drugs and Crime, 2018c). Thus, to examine risk for TOC within an area, one must consider the structure of the community as well as the victims at risk. Although, even in cases where communities may not be the power bases for TOC, they often provide the victims. Communities that are flush with individuals who have mental health issues, substance abuse issues, debt, family disfunction, and runaway children are all vulnerable to profit-seeking by TOC groups (Hamilton-Smith, 2018). In particular, loan sharks, drug distributors, and sex workers may all be in the subsets of members of vulnerable communities utilized by TOC for profit.

This chapter discusses the risk factors for TOC, including community-level and individual-level variables. While the following chapters focus on the specific products targeted by TOC (i.e., drugs, people), this chapter sets the stage by discussing such vulnerabilities in terms of structural risk, potential harm to individuals, and risk to environments and societies as a whole. The chapter provides an overview of TOC's role in crimes against humanity, crimes against vulnerable groups such as women and children, crimes against internally displaced and/or stateless persons, crimes against LGBTQ individuals, and crimes against the environment. Also noted in this chapter is the Global Organized Crime Index and the recent effects of COVID-19 on the risk for TOC.

Structural Risk Factors

Structural risk factors within communities that are assumed to create opportunities for TOC are classified as asymmetry of controls, asymmetry of resources, asymmetry of prices, asymmetry of investments, and legal asymmetries (United Nations Office on Drugs and Crime, 2018c). As asymmetry indicates a lack of equality between parts, these differences or disparities can facilitate the activities of TOC as the strengths and weaknesses of countries are realized. According to research conducted through cooperation with the European Union, there are currently approximately 5,000 TOC groups operating with Europe with 180 nationalities involved (Hurdubaie, 2017). This reflects an increase of over 30% since 2013, with most of the suspected members of TOC also identified as citizens of the EU (Hurdubaie, 2017). Therefore, country conditions that facilitate TOC are continuing to support involvement in TOC and may even encourage more of it. In particular, the incapacity of countries to control national borders is also closely connected to the ability of the government to ensure its presence in remote areas of the country, as abandoned, economically marginal, and sparsely populated areas are often more at risk for becoming a safe haven for TOC members. For example, Osama bin Laden was born and raised in Saudi Arabia; however, he chose the unstable country of Afghanistan to seek refuge after the 9-11 attacks on the United States.

To facilitate TOC, country failure and states of economic and political transition can result in the inability of the government to deliver key political goods and services (United Nations Office on Drugs and Crime, 2018c). As suggested in Chapter 2, economic failures, such as high unemployment, low standard of living, and reliance on underground markets, will stimulate TOC to supply goods and services. From this perspective, TOC groups can accumulate political capital and broad public support, which allows them to assume a quasicountry role. Hence, the conditions that impede economic development—and diminish the country's incentives to develop the infrastructure necessary to maintain a robust presence—lead to the emergence of shadow economies, black markets, and TOC groups (United Nations Office on Drugs and Crime, 2018c).

With regard to the structure of TOC, research suggests that between 30% and 40% of TOC groups do not have the historically perceived authoritarian, formal lines of control and structured networks, as many operate only during the time required to complete their specific criminal activity (Hurdubaie, 2017). In addition, the majority of the TOC groups operate with six or more members and are active in four or more countries (Hurdubaie, 2017). In these cases, the structure of the international system also contributes to the formation of TOC opportunities. From this perspective, inequalities of various kinds, along with the so-called **criminogenic asymmetries** embedded in the international system, create circumstances that criminal organizations are able to capitalize on (Zabyelina, 2014). In these cases, when one country identifies an activity as illegal while another country does not, TOC utilizes the discrepancies between competing legal jurisdictions for their advantage. Therefore, the international or cross-border aspect of TOC is also a structural risk factor.

As discussed in Chapter 2, the positivist perspective in criminology examines internal or external influences on individuals as the primary cause of their criminal behavior. For the most part, research has examined social factors as the cause of crime (McCabe, 2008); overwhelmingly, however, the most commonly associated structural risk for TOC is the criminal subculture (McCabe, 2008). Factors that facilitate an individual's decision to join a gang (or criminal subculture) support the outcomes of safety, security, and a sense of belonging for the gang member. In particular, research on women and their recent trend of increasing membership with TOC suggests that factors facilitating the joining of **gangs** include (1) feelings of belonging and family, (2) protection, (3) financial resources, (4) a path of least resistance and immediate rewards, (5) under- and unemployment in the licit economy, and (6) substance abuse as their addictions made it difficult to find steady and licit employment (United Nations Office on Drugs and Crime, 2018a). Also, but in no way insignificant, is the current status of the world's quality of life. Specifically, the outbreak of the global COVID-19 pandemic created dire consequences for victimization by TOC groups. Specifically, as more than 90 million people were infected, and nearly 2 million people lost their lives, the race for personal protective equipment (or PPE) and vaccines created a void that TOC was happy to address. In particular, the emergency response to the COVID-19 pandemic revealed enormous cracks in health systems and democratic institutions, with those in power or holding the government purse strings often serving their own interests rather than addressing the needs of the most vulnerable (Transparency International, 2021). As a result, countries with higher levels of corruption and the highest prevalence of TOC activities were the worst perpetrators of democratic and rule-of-law breaches during COVID-19.

Although the pandemic may have dominated the headlines, it was not the only event to have an impact on TOC and the illicit economy (Global Initiative, 2021). In early 2020, criminal justice authorities uncovered a large-scale subsidies fraud, whereby clans of the Sicilian Mafia were found to have siphoned off millions of euros of agricultural funds from the European Union (Global Initiative, 2021); in other words, instead of protecting the environment, they supported even more damage. In addition, the Taliban in Afghanistan benefited from the opportunities presented during troop withdrawals to continue their drug trade, to seize precious military equipment and ammunition, and to resume their control of the country. In the United States and other developed countries such as the United Kingdom, the Black Lives Matter movement fueled debates on issues of power, race, and inequality, as well as the relationship between law enforcement and marginalized communities, which further left these vulnerable communities more at risk for victimization and recruitment by criminal groups (Global Initiative, 2021).

Global Organized Crime Index (GOCI)— A ranking of over 190 countries to assess the scale and impact of organized crime within their borders.

In summary, as indicated by the **Global Organized Crime Index (GOCI)**, more than 75% of the world's population live in countries with high levels of criminal behaviors and low levels of resistance to organized crime (Global Initiative, 2021). Thus, while TOC groups will target the most vulnerable of the communities, countries with little resistance are at risk for TOC. For clarity, the GOCI, just introduced, is the first tool of its kind designed to assess levels of organized crime and resilience to organized criminal activity (Global Initiative, 2021). The GOCI ranks all 193 member states of the United Nations to provide a comprehensive data set, informed by experts worldwide, in order to assess the scale and impact of organized crime. The GOCI highlights a country's involvement in criminality and helps to identify the TOC group or groups that have influence over state authorities. As criminal networks, often driven by economics and politics, have significantly increased in size and influence over the last two decades, the GOCI provides the most comprehensive assessment to date of the pervasiveness of criminal markets, the dynamics of criminal actors, and countries' effectiveness in addressing TOC. The GOCI metrics are based on three constituent parts: the scope, scale, and impact of specific criminal markets; the structure and influence of criminal actors; and the extent and effectiveness of countries' resilience measures (Global Initiative, 2021). These three domains are used to assign each country a criminality score and a resilience score (using a scale of 1 to 10) and to identify the indicators affecting a country's criminality and resilience. As this is the first iteration of the GOCI and it will be updated every two years, longitudinal measurements will be available for future examinations of organized crime (Global Initiative, 2021).

TOC and Crimes Against Humanity

Central to the mission of the United Nations is the maintenance of international peace and the protection of human rights, with a focus on **crimes against humanity** (United Nations, 2019). Included in this mission is the protection of vulnerable people and **vulnerable populations** in approximately 195 countries. This section of the chapter discusses these populations, as well as the structural factors within countries that facilitate risk by TOC groups. Vulnerable populations to be covered here include women and girls, children, internally displaced persons, stateless persons, and LGBTQ individuals, and *risk* is defined as a situation of danger.

When individuals read historical accounts of genocide, terrorist attacks, sexual exploitation, or forcible labor, they frequently experience shock and outrage that these events could have ever occurred. Unfortunately, what many individuals do not realize is that often these incidents are not simply events of the past. These intentional acts of destruction, committed against vulnerable groups of people, occur on a daily basis throughout the world and are repeatedly

Crimes against humanity—Murder, extermination, enslavement, torture, forcible transfers of populations, imprisonment, rape, persecution, enforced disappearance, and apartheid, among others. In other words, crimes that are a part of a widespread or systematic attack directed against any civilian population (Vernon, 2017).

Vulnerable populations—The economically disadvantaged, racial and ethnic minorities, the uninsured, low-income children, the elderly and the homeless (*American Journal of Managed Care,* 2006).

identified as "crimes against humanity" (McCabe, 2017). Unfortunately, these victimizations do not receive the reaction that one would assume a crime against humanity would provoke—and some crimes, depending upon the population of their victims, are never acknowledged. In this chapter, crimes against humanity as well as crimes against vulnerable populations are discussed in terms of the role of TOC and their consequences within the global arena.

> In August of 2021, Amnesty International reported evidence that Afghanistan's Taliban had massacred 13 ethnic Hazara people in the province of Daykundi. These victims, some of whom were former government soldiers who had surrendered to the Taliban, were members of Afghanistan's third largest ethnic group and have faced long-term discrimination and persecution in predominantly Sunni Afghanistan and Pakistan (BBC News, 2021).

In many cases, the phrase *crimes against humanity* has been used interchangeably with the phrase *war crimes*, as some crimes against humanity occur during times of war. However, crimes against vulnerable populations also often occur in times of peace (Luben, 2004).

Some of the first identified and detailed cases of crimes against vulnerable populations occurred prior to the 1800s in the forcible transfer of African Americans to the United States and in the 19th-century occupancy of the Congo by King Leopold II of Belgium, where natives were tortured, killed, and forced to work for the profits of the slave master or the king (Hochschild, 1999). In these cases, thousands of Africans were forcibly transported by TOC groups within their counties to the United States and Europe. Estimates of the number of deaths from King Leopold's orders ranged from 10 million to 15 million people (Luben, 2004b).

Social Contract— First promulgated by the French philosopher Jean-Jacques Rousseau (1712–1778), an understanding formed when free and equal persons come together and agree to create themselves anew as a single body, directed to the good of all considered together. This general will, once formed, is directed toward the common good, understood and agreed to collectively (Internet Encyclopedia of Philosophy, 2018).

Just as today, these crimes against vulnerable populations rarely occur when the populations are economically and socially strong. These crimes, which are often the outcome of TOC's efforts to capitalize on social vulnerabilities and cultural biases, affect those individuals who are unable to defend themselves and are dependent upon the strengths of others or the strengths of governments for protection. Hence, without these necessary protections by society, as suggested by Jean-Jacques Rousseau's **social contract** theory, the victimization of individuals and groups is an outcome of their vulnerability in a society and is capitalized upon by those involved in TOC. Most often included within the discussions of vulnerable populations are women and children (McCabe, 2017).

Women and TOC

By the 1950s, efforts to explain criminal behaviors shifted toward the perspective of the victim, as criminology began to develop victim typologies to include victimization of women, children, and other populations. In particular, based upon von Hentig's (1948) typology categories, psychological, social, and biological factors were used to explain the victimization of certain groups. Specifically, von Hentig highlighted the victimization of women as a consequence of their limited physical strength. Later, another criminologist, Mendelsohn (1974), asserted that victimization, including the victimization of women, occurs as a result of the functional interplay among social elements. Finally, feminist criminology, which emerged in the 1980s, explored violence against women through a gender-based lens on power, relationships, and the legal rights of women (Regehr & Glancy, 1995).

In discussions on the victimizations of women by members within TOC groups, the primary focus is on sex crimes and particularly the commercial sex trade. Although TOC involvement in the sex business has changed over time (McCabe, 2017), TOC members still organize, finance, or connect with proprietors of commercial sex establishments, which victimize women and children.

Transnational crime presents intricate problems of victimization for all vulnerable people, but it has had a disproportionately adverse impact on women (Erez, 2007). In particular, it is well documented that migration exacerbates the gender-linked vulnerability of women as they are oftentimes dependent upon their husbands, male sponsors, or male employers for safety (Erez, 2000). Furthermore, the rapid globalization of the world's economies has ensured that the number of migrants has increased substantially in all of the world's major geographical regions (Teitelbaum & Russel, 1994). Unfortunately, the victimization of women by the actions of TOC is one of the most difficult issues to address, as it is often associated with historic gender ideologies that tolerate, and in some instances may even encourage,

> In May of 2020, a teenage girl in Afghanistan who is believed to have broken a particular social norm paid the ultimate price this week when her brother reportedly killed her after she ran away from home with her boyfriend. Historically, girls and women in Afghanistan who have relationships with men outside marriage are often the target of brutal punishments such as public floggings, prison, and even death (Ahmadi & Bezhan, 2020).

the victimization of women. In particular, sexual exploitation commonly refers to trafficking and a large part of TOC profits through the international sex industry—prostitution, entertainment, and pornography—and is now increasingly understood to encompass domestic help, forced or arranged marriages, "mail order" brides, temporary wives, and marriages of convenience.

Research on victimization suggests that factors of lifestyle often contribute to risk (Burgess, 2019). Specifically, factors related to demographics and culture provide varying degrees of victimization risk and varying degrees of vulnerability of these individuals to the actions of TOC. For example, drug mules are often women utilized by TOC to transport from Mexico into the United States (Hicks, 2021).

TOC results in intricate problems for all vulnerable populations, with disproportionately adverse outcomes for women and girls (Erez, 2001). Unfortunately, even the identification of cases against women and girls is difficult given the ideologies that present women as inferior to men, who often tolerate and participate in their victimization (Daly, 1994). Hence, crime against women and girls, or gender-based violence, is a phenomenon deeply rooted in gender inequality, and it continues to be one of the most significant human rights violations in the world. "Gender-based violence," a relatively new phrase in the research community, is violence directed against a person because of their gender, and, although both women and men experience gender-based violence, the majority of victims are women and girls (European Institute of Gender Equality, 2019).

Sex trafficking, a crime discussed in a later chapter, affects individuals across the globe, and particularly women and girls. Research suggests that over 90% of the victims of sex trafficking are women and that nearly 50% of those victims are under the age of 18 (McCabe & Murphy, 2016). For many of these women and girls, the victimization occurs repeatedly. From London to Lusaka and from Mumbai to Mombasa, sex trafficking flourishes (McCabe & Manian, 2010), and in many cases, women and members of TOC groups are the perpetrators.

As there are numerous crimes under the category of **gender-based crimes**, including intimate partner violence and sexual violence (Asian Pacific Institute on Gender-Based Violence, 2018), and as human trafficking is discussed later in this text, this section focuses on victimization as related to TOC.

Although TOC was originally involved in drug trafficking, today human trafficking is one of the most common of TOC's criminal activities—involving women as both victims and perpetrators (Shelley, 2010). In terms of women and their roles in facilitating these crimes by TOC, researchers categorize their tasks and responsibilities into three divisions: supporters, partners-in-crime, and madams (Hicks, 2021).

First, the role of supporter indicates a position that is subordinate to that of the leading traffickers, and it is within these supporter positions that women are either under threat or "willing" to execute the leader's orders. Second, the role of partner-in-crime indicates a partnership in principle on the basis of equal roles and responsibilities. Lastly, madams are female offenders who fulfill a leadership role in the TOC group with the responsibilities of coordinating the trafficking activities.

In December of 2021, a jury convicted **Ghislaine Maxwell**, the longtime associate of serial sex offender **Jeffrey Epstein**, on five of six counts related to the abuse and trafficking of underage girls. In the indictment, Maxwell faced charges for conspiring with and aiding Epstein in his sexual abuse of underage girls between 1994 and 2004 (Hill et al., 2021).

The most commonly identified supportive role for women involved in human trafficking with TOC groups is the recruiter or trainer. In these cases, research suggests that the recruitment of victims, or "happy trafficking," involves women recruiting other women to victimization and this occurs in approximately 40% of the cases (Aronowitz, 2009). Women offenders will also serve in a training role to manage the brothel and maintain control over their victims (Shelley, 2010. Finally, the leadership role fulfilled by women who are members of TOC groups is the position of *madam* (Zhang et al., 2007).

TOC and Crimes Against Children

In von Hentig's (1948) victim category typology, it is asserted that children or the young are viewed by criminals as weak, inexperienced, and vulnerable to attack. Whereas historically children were not the victims of crime for profit, today they are products for profit. Specifically, children provide profits for TOC either through various forms of exploitation—including child sexual exploitation and in some cases as victims of kidnapping for profit—or through use by criminal organizations to commit other crimes such as the smuggling of drugs.

Thus, children are yet another vulnerable population for the criminal activities of TOC.

Children, by nature, depend upon others for their safety and security, and while the child is never the reason for the abuse, there are factors inherent in childhood that lower children's defenses against abuse and cause them to be less able to protect themselves or less able to receive the help they need (Stop It Now, 2019). This section focuses upon the following crimes against children: (1) **conscription** (sometimes referred to as "the draft"), enlistment, and the use of children in hostilities; (2) **child trafficking**; (3) attacks against education and health care; and (4) sexual exploitation.

Conscription—The orderly selection of people for required military service.

Conscription and Enlistment

Conscription is the orderly selection of people for required military service, and although conscription is usually used in the selection of male soldiers, it may also be used to select child soldiers. Unfortunately, conscription, enlistment, and the use of children in hostilities occur daily around the world (de Silva, Hobbs, & Hanks, 2001).

> South Korea's government has stated that during the Korean War, it conscripted more than 30,000 soldiers between the ages of 14 and 17, with an estimated 3,000 of them killed in the war (Kuhn, 2020).

In today's world, child soldiers are used as snipers, fighters, suicide bombers, spies, and messengers, and in some cases the children are "recruited and enlisted" for these services through TOC connections (Keene, 2018). Specifically, the term *silent partner* has been used by U.S. government officials to describe the collaborations between TOC and nation-states (Keene, 2018). These relationships, although only rarely acknowledged by host countries, are generally perceived as necessary for state interventions to accomplish tasks quickly (Keene, 2018). In other cases, children are conscripted or drafted through mandated military service laws in their state. Unfortunately, there also exists a precedent of kidnapping where some children are kidnapped and forced into participation in these military efforts (McCabe, 2008). For the male children, their lives often include

> In Russia, the first day of the annual spring military conscription is April 1, with dates for registration continuing until July 15 (Petrova, 2022). In 2022, the government assured the population that conscripts would not be sent to any "hot spots"—a euphemism for the war in Ukraine. However, a Russian senator has reported that at least 100 young soldiers, mostly conscripts, were forced to sign contracts to serve in Ukraine, and of those soldiers, only four are now alive (Petrova, 2022).

harsh conditions, violence, and death; for the females, their lives often include harsh conditions, sexual servitude, and death. However, as discussed below, if the need arises, children may also be vulnerable for actual combat within military conflicts.

The United Nations suggests not only that children have been utilized as soldiers in the past but that there are thousands of children serving as soldiers in areas of conflict today, with aftereffects that last a lifetime (WarChild, 2018). In many of these countries, children are considered adults by the time they are age 15, and given that extreme poverty exists throughout these regions, recruiting children is an easy task for members of TOC. Thus, TOC may be involved in providing children to be trained and used as soldiers in areas of conflict.

Unfortunately, for many of these children, if they are able to survive the harsh realities of soldiering, their futures include no family, physical limitations that prevent them from finding gainful employment, and limited amounts of the educational and social skills necessary to

TEN FACTS ABOUT CHILD SOLDIERS

1. Tens of thousands of children are estimated to be recruited, in some cases by members of TOC, and used by armed groups.
2. The Democratic Republic of the Congo, Somalia, Syria, and Yemen currently have the largest number of child soldiers.
3. Children are not only recruited by armed forces and groups as fighters but also used as informants, looters, messengers, and spies.
4. The forced recruitment of children for use in armed conflict is considered one of the worst forms of child labor.
5. Not all child soldiers are boys holding guns, as many girls are also used by armed forces in countries such as Afghanistan, Colombia, the Central African Republic, Nigeria, South Sudan, Syria, and Yemen.
6. The recruitment and use of children as soldiers is a violation of UN policy.
7. Many children are forcibly recruited.
8. Armed conflicts have damaging effects on children directly involved in violence and atrocities.
9. If former child soldiers are not successfully reintegrated into society, there is a high risk that they will be recruited again.
10. A total of 170 countries have ratified the Optional Protocol to the Convention on the Rights of the Child on the involvement of children in armed conflict (OPAC); however, the practice continues in more than a dozen nations. (Wuilbercq, 2021)

exist outside of armed conflict. In addition, children who have served as soldiers often carry emotional scars and anxieties similar to those of adults with post-traumatic stress disorder (McCabe and Murphy, 2016). Hence, child conscription and enlistment are a concern for children who are vulnerable to this form of victimization, which is often facilitated by TOC.

Child Trafficking

Human trafficking involves an act of recruiting, transporting, transferring, harboring, or receiving a person through a use of force, coercion, or other means for the purpose of exploiting them (United Nations Office on Drugs and Crime, 2019). Unfortunately, estimates suggest that as many as 50% of all trafficking victims are under the age of 18; these victims are children, and international estimates suggest that approximately 5.5 million children are trafficked annually (Their World, 2018). Children are trafficked for labor, adoption, drug smuggling, **sexual exploitation**, removal of their healthy internal organs, and soldiering and camel jockeying (McCabe, 2008).

> In June of 2021, a leader of a criminal enterprise (the "Organization") involved in various criminal acts, including drug distribution and sex trafficking, was convicted of sex trafficking and sentenced to prison for more than 27 years as a result of specialized investigative work by the FBI-NYPD New York Child Exploitation and Human Trafficking Task Force and the Special Agents of the U.S. Attorney's Office for the Southern District of New York (U.S. Department of Justice, 2021).

Research indicates that many individuals subjected to the crime of forced labor, including children, have given their consent (McCabe & Murphy, 2016). Children, however, because of their age, are considered by law to be unable to give such consent. Children are often placed in positions of forced labor by TOC, with cooperative agreements from their parents or caregivers (Melrose, 2002). In these cases, child victims continue to work under deployable conditions without complaint and without ever attempting to leave their work environment.

Children are also trafficked for sex, and some of the obstacles these victims face are similar to forced labor. The sex trafficking of children includes child pornography, child prostitution, sex rings, molestation, supporting the sex tourism industry, and nude dancing (Dalton, 2013). Unfortunately, as sex involving children is supported by secret human desires for gratification, profit, and fulfillment, it is neither easily identified nor easily remedied. In addition, the sex trafficking

TRAFFICKING INVOLVES THREE MAIN ELEMENTS

- The act: Recruitment, transportation, transfer, harboring, or receipt of persons
- The means: Threat or use of force, coercion, abduction, fraud, deception, abuse of power or vulnerability, or giving payments or benefits to a person in control of the victim
- The purpose: For the purpose of exploitation, which includes exploiting the prostitution of others, sexual exploitation, forced labor, slavery or similar practices, and the removal of organs (Save the Children, 2021)

of children provides income for many individuals involved in the enterprise, including individuals involved in TOC. In fact, recent work by the United Nations Office of Drugs and Crime (UNODC) suggests a strong link between child sex trafficking and TOC, which continues to gain in prevalence and profit.

In December of 2020, after he was indicted for running a human-trafficking operation in three states. a U.S. man pleaded guilty and was sentenced to over six years in prison for illegally arranging for pregnant women from the Marshall Islands to come to the United States to give up their babies for adoption. In this case, the convicted man, through connections with citizens of the Marshall Islands (a Pacific island nation), smuggled as many as 12 pregnant women at a time in order for them to give birth in the United States (Thompson, 2020).

Children are also trafficked for adoption, and in some cases of child adoption, government officials are again recognizing the involvement of organized crime (McCabe & Murphy, 2016). Specifically, in international cases revealed over the past few years, there have been a number of organized child-trafficking rings involved in the criminal activity (Vu Ngoc Binh, 2006). TOC provides infants to individuals or couples seeking to adopt a child with traffickers typically purchasing desired babies from the poorest of families, from orphanages, or from single mothers (McCabe & Murphy, 2016).

Children are also used in drug smuggling, where they may serve as "drug mules" to transport illegal narcotics into the United States from other countries (Estes & Weiner, 2001). At one time, adult women who appeared to be pregnant were used to transport drugs; however, as security measures have increased and the searching of baggage and persons has become more prevalent in airports and at land-border crossings, children are now being used to transport drugs across borders (McCabe, 2008). Since children often are not closely scrutinized by Customs or Immigration officials as they enter the country accompanied by an adult, and because TOC will provide fraudulent paperwork if necessary, the use of children by TOC for drug trafficking produces even more profit.

Another reason to traffick individuals, and specifically children, is to harvest their healthy internal organs. With healthy organs needed for transplantation in the United States and other developed countries, and a fear of contracting AIDS from adult donors, a healthy child is the perfect victim for human trafficking of internal organs. TOC groups that can facilitate the international transportation and delivery of these organs within a timely manner are regularly involved in this type of child victimization.

Lastly, the growth of child pornography is another explanation for the increase in child trafficking (McCabe & Johnston, 2014). Online child pornography fuels the demand for child victims, and child pornography and TOC involved in sex trafficking are often involved in this type of sexual exploitation. As it becomes easier to identify and contact children via the internet, it becomes easier for traffickers and those interested in the exploitation of children to identify potential victims for child trafficking; therefore, children are once again vulnerable for abuse and exploitation.

Sexual Exploitation

Child abuse, for the most part, is a crime that is intimate and personal; however, child abuse through sexual exploitation is considered cold, calculated, revenue-generating, and global (Chawai, 2015). Unfortunately, with the ease of movement across and within countries, the mobility that facilitates the likelihood of an individual's involvement in the illegal trades of sex rings, sex tourism, and child trafficking facilitated by TOC is also easier.

For clarity, a child **sex ring** (hereafter, sex ring) involves one or more offenders, usually adult males, who are simultaneously sexually involved with several child victims at one time (McCabe, 2003). These children can be either male or female, and from a variety of ethnic and racial backgrounds. Further, while most are teens or preteens, many are as young as preschoolers or infants (McCabe & Murphy, 2016). **Sex tourism**, another avenue in the sex trade, entails adult individuals engaging in both national and international travel to participate in sexual activities considered illegal and unethical in those individuals' respective countries of residence (McCabe & Murphy, 2016). In these cases, typically adult males visit other countries to engage in sex with very young girls or boys. Specifically, in sex tourism the constant travel by offenders and child victims (the latter are moved throughout an area to provide variety for their clients) results in illegal activities that are extremely difficult for law enforcement and other governmental officials to detect.

The child sex trade does not affect most children, and the majority of the affected children are from outside of the United States. In fact, it has been suggested that only a fraction of approximately 1% of the children in the world are victims; however, cases of child sexual exploitation through sex rings, sex tourism, and child trafficking are often identified in reports of human trafficking (McCabe, 2017). Specific information on the young victims is limited; however, most child victims were provided an avenue into the criminal victimization through someone who is known to them and is connected to a TOC group. To explain these categories of victimization and the role of TOC, one must first consider the dynamics of the actions.

In child sex rings, multiple children and multiple abusers are involved, usually within the category of extrafamilial (outside the family) abuse. Traditionally, in child sex rings, there are communications among the offenders in terms of the desired demographic characteristic(s) of a child, such as age and/or gender, and the TOC member's ability to locate and obtain a sought-after child. Historically, this line of communication involved either a phone or email; today, however, these conversations are more likely to occur online in private chat rooms, via instant apps, and on websites operated as "discussion-only" forums within the online community, without the enforcement of legal restrictions (Dalton, 2013). These forums, often operated by members associated with TOC and self-identified as discussion-only for individuals to share their thoughts on sexual activity, often lead to members moving to more private venues for sharing images and videos of child pornography as well as their plans for participation in a sex ring to abuse children (McCabe, 2003).

In considering the child victims of sex tourism (or as some governments define it, the extraterritorial sexual exploitation of children), U.S. law as well as laws in other countries prohibit citizens from traveling to a foreign country with intent to engage in any form of sexual conduct with a minor or to help organize such travel or assist another person in traveling for this purpose (McCabe, 2017). Each year individuals are convicted of this crime; however, TOC continues to profit from the criminal activity (Protect.org, 2015).

Internally Displaced and Stateless Persons

Von Hentig's (1948) victim typology places immigrants and minorities in two distinct categories, with each identified as vulnerable because of their assimilation into a new culture as well as the economic and social difficulties of poverty and rejection by native inhabitants. In the case of immigrants, members of TOC are aware of the immigrant's situation, and they act to benefit from it. Von Hentig describes minority populations, who may also find themselves internally displaced or stateless, as similar to immigrants in their lack of social equity and their experience of prejudices against them, thus increasing their risk for victimization by members of TOC.

Internally displaced person (IDP)—Someone who is forced to leave their home but remains a resident within their country's borders.

Stateless person (SP)—An individual who is not considered a citizen under the operations of the laws of the country where they reside.

Both **internally displaced persons** (IDP) and **stateless persons** (SP) are vulnerable to victimization by TOC groups. For clarity, an IDP is someone who, because of war or population victimization, is forced to leave their home but remains a resident within their country's borders. Although IDPs are often referred to as refugees, they are technically not refugees as they have not crossed an international border (Brav & Bouchet-Saulnier, 2002). In 2020, it is estimated that there were approximately 55 million IDPs globally (Internal Displacement Monitoring Center, 2021).

By definition, a *stateless person* (SP) is an individual who is not considered a citizen under the operations of the laws of the country where they reside. In most cases, stateless persons are also refugees, as they have crossed an international border. In some cases, however, individuals may be born stateless or may become stateless within their own country. In most of these cases, statelessness occurs with the emergence of a new country, the transfer of territories between countries, or gaps in nationality laws. According to the Institute on Statelessness and Inclusion (2021), in 2019 there were an estimated 15 million stateless persons globally.

IDPs often include women, children, and families facing either economic hardship or political hardship. A November 2021 report by the media company CNN identified the specific risk to IDP in its story of a nine-year-old girl sold by her father to a 55-year-old man to serve as his child bride (Coren et al., 2021). With fathers desperate for money to feed their families, TOC members will soon recognize this new source of product.

Unfortunately, although IDPs are legally entitled to the same rights and freedoms of those persons who are not displaced within a country, they seldom receive these benefits due to their transient status. Essentially, it is a result of their current living status that these groups are most vulnerable for crimes against them by TOC. In response, the UN's *Guiding Principles on Internal Displacement* describes the rights of IDPs and the obligations of national authorities in the protection of and services to IDPs (United Nations High Commissioner for Refugees , 2004). However, time after time, the victimization of IDPs is documented across the globe, with one example of these inequalities occurring in Tokyo in 2020, where homeless people were pressured to move their camp away from the area hosting the Olympic Games (Siripala, 2020).

Reports from the United Kingdom suggest that IDPs, who are sleeping on the streets, are nearly 17 times more likely to be victims of violence, with approximately one third of these individuals being hit or kicked while on the streets (Crisis, 2019) In California, reports suggest that nearly one half of adults living on the streets have been victims of a violent attack and more than one half have witnessed attacks on other IDPs (Shortt, 2018). In Australia, IDPs were 13 times more likely to experience violence and 47 times more likely than non-IDPs to be victims of theft (Australian Institute for Criminology, 2008). Members of TOC recognize the vulnerabilities of IDP and will often offer these individuals a "better quality of life" that actually includes more violent victimizations, exploitations, and perhaps death, all while TOC makes a profit from the use of these IDP products. Similar to the vulnerabilities of IDP by TOC, stateless persons are also victimized by the criminal activities of TOC.

Research suggests that statelessness that discriminates against particular ethnic or religious groups occurs for many reasons. Some of those reasons are gaps in nationality laws, which establish the circumstances under which someone acquires nationality or can have nationality withdrawn. In addition, a child born in a foreign country can become stateless if that country does not permit nationality based on birth alone or if the country of origin does not allow a parent to pass on nationality through family ties (United Nations High Commissioner for Refugees, 2019).

Lastly, research on the stateless population of the Rohingya (Myanmar), Lumad (Philippines), and Roma (Europe) suggests that both the children and the adults in these groups are highly vulnerable to human trafficking and other forms of exploitation by TOC—specifically, sex trafficking and labor trafficking (Herring, 2019). Recognizing that these population have little or no protection or intervention afforded to them, TOC members capitalize on these risk factors.

LGBTQ Individuals

Although LGBTQ individuals are not specifically discussed in von Hentig's (1949) historical research on victims, von Hentig did identify the category typology of "the blocked" as victims who have been so enmeshed in disadvantaged situations that their defense is nearly impossible. For those within the LGBTQ community, their lifestyle (often a secret) leads to possible victimization not only by violent actions but also through blackmail, and with the inability to seek help from law enforcement, they are vulnerable to exploitation by TOC members. ***LGBTQ*** is an acronym for "lesbian, gay, bisexual, transgender and queer or questioning," terms that are used to describe a person's sexual orientation or gender identity. Unfortunately, for individuals identifying with the LGBTQ community, the risk of victimization is high throughout the majority of the countries in the world. For clarity within this section, the following definitions will be utilized (The Center, 2019):

> *Lesbian*—A woman whose enduring physical, romantic, and/or emotional attraction is to other women. Some lesbians may prefer to identify as gay or as gay women.
>
> *Gay*—The adjective used to describe people whose enduring physical, romantic, and/or emotional attractions are to people of the same sex.
>
> *Bisexual*—A person who has the capacity to form enduring physical, romantic, and/or emotional attractions to those of the same gender or to those of another gender.

Transgender—An umbrella term for people whose gender identity and/or gender expression differs from what is typically associated with the sex they were assigned at birth.

Queer—An adjective used by some people, particularly younger people, whose sexual orientation is not exclusively heterosexual or is Questioning. Sometimes, when the Q is seen at the end of *LGBT*, it can also mean *questioning.* This term describes someone who is questioning their sexual orientation or gender identity.

Members of organized crime groups have a history of associations with LGBTQ communities. Specifically, in the 1960s in the United States, organized crime families owned the majority of the cities' gay bars and clubs (Maurice, 2021). As TOC is based upon profit, and as many gay clubs operated in secrecy, members of TOC would provide these clubs the alcohol and drugs desired by their patrons in an unmonitored and unregulated mode of distribution. Hence, TOC groups operated with these clubs and were able to provide subpar products, all with maximized profits. Today, LGBTQ communities continue to be victimized by TOC members. Specifically, LGBTQ members are often victims of sex trafficking by TOC, and in most cases they are overlooked by researchers in the study of human trafficking. Examples of documented cases include Caribbean and Latin American LGBTs moved from Western Europe and African LGBT victims of Arab Gulf–based trafficking rings ending up as sex slaves for the wealthy United Arab Emirates, Qatar, and Saudi Arabia (Martinez & Kelle, 2013).

From an international perspective, LGBTQ communities are also at risk for victimization by TOC members, as in many countries same-sex prostitution is illegal and hidden (Simon, 2014). Specifically, the trafficking of gay men is a serious issue with its own particular set of difficulties, as sexual violence against males is considered taboo in most societies; for this reason, many male victims are constrained by societal barriers from reporting their ordeals (Martinez & Kelle, 2013). Due to the nature of this business, the trafficking of LGBTQ victims is less likely to be reported. TOC members are not only aware of the demand for same-sex sexual relations but also aware of the limited detection, and so TOC profits from the victimization of the LBGTQ communities nationally and internationally (Martinez & Kelle, 2013).

Environmental Crimes and TOC

One of the most overlooked but also very profitable areas of TOC is **environmental crime** (studied by researchers under the name "**green criminology**"). Since 2020, issues of environmental crime have begun to be recognized as a major concern due to the theory that a trafficked wild animal, perhaps a pangolin, was the vector for the coronavirus (COVID-19) making the leap from animal species to humans (Global Initiative, 2021). Green criminology is a branch of criminology that involves the study of crimes against the environment, including environmental law and policy; however, for the purpose of this section, green criminology will be discussed only around the outcome of environmental harm. As proposed by researchers for decades, environmental crime is transnational in nature (White, 2011). Unfortunately, although much attention is currently focused on China as the largest consumer of wildlife and wildlife parts (particularly ivory and pangolins, discussed later in this text), the European Union is also significant to these crimes, as the region has one of the highest demands for wildlife products and is a processing point for much of the wildlife product distributed across the globe (Arroyo-Quiroz & Wyatt, 2019). Although wildlife trafficking and illegal logging are discussed in Chapter 8, the impact that the actions of TOC have on the environment should not be ignored. Specifically, TOC's involvement in the trafficking of species, the trafficking of substances, and the trafficking of illicit waste is significant.

Europol spotlighted TOC's involvement in the trafficking of endangered species as a highly specialized action that serves an elite market of consumer (del Castillo, 2015). Estimates suggest that the revenues generated by trade in endangered species amount from 18 billion to 26 billion euros (20 billion to 30 billion U.S. dollars) per year and that the trade is principally coordinated by well-organized networks based throughout Europe. Historically, perpetrators of wildlife trafficking traveled personally to collect animals; today, however, couriers, air mail orders, and technology facilitate the illegal enterprise. Animals from several destinations are often located within one location, which eases transportation from the common source area. Some of the most profitable assets are the ivory and rhino horns poached in Africa and sold and distributed from Europe to Asia. The TOC groups participating in these criminal activities are characterized as being small in size with just a few members and as exclusively focused on this activity, unlike the TOC involved in drug trafficking (del Castillo, 2015).

As in the drug trade, smaller animal specimens trafficked by TOC have been found concealed within sculptures or disguised as other goods (del Castillo, 2015). There have also been reports of endangered species packed in concealed containers for transport by couriers, and there is also evidence that trade in endangered species is of increasing interest to poly-criminal groups. Thus, TOC groups involved in high-level drug trafficking in Brazil, Colombia, and Mexico have established a notable role in the illegal supply of endangered species to the EU and U.S. markets (del Castillo, 2015).

In November of 2021, an investigation by **Interpol** documented the involvement of TOC in the trafficking of millions of tons of discarded plastic from the United States, Europe, and Australia to countries in Southeast Asia and Africa (Phillips, 2021).

In the case of illegal logging, another environmental crime, Europol has noted that the modus operandi for transporting bulk commodities involves faked and forged documents and permits (del Castillo, 2015). Frequently, border guards or customs personnel lack the expertise required to distinguish protected tropical woods from unprotected woods, and TOC groups are well aware of these limitations.

Interpol—An international law enforcement organization that facilitates worldwide police cooperation and crime control.

In addition, **Europol** has identified the illicit waste-trafficking activities of TOC, which has expanded exponentially during the economic crisis (del Castillo, 2015). This illicit enterprise is a high-profit, low-risk activity that goes underreported and underinvestigated. In addition, since the illicit waste trafficking involves both TOC and legal companies, TOC groups profit from the loopholes in the European open-market regulations and from the absence of standardized modes of control and required enforcement mechanisms. Environmental crime, especially the dumping of illegal waste through TOC, is exploiting a wide legislative vacuum and a lack of law enforcement, with much of the trafficking in hazardous waste focused on storage, which produces even more of a threat to environmental sustainability. In particular, in many countries a continuous growth of the economy is taking place and

Europol—The law enforcement agency of the European Union; handles criminal intelligence and fights serious international organized crime and terrorism.

Europol has suggested that profits from environmental crimes can equal profits from drug trafficking, and of course TOC is attracted to these profits. In 2015, the UN estimated that that 60% to 90% of the world's electronic waste, or e-waste, valued at some $2 billion to $19 billion annually, is traded or disposed of illegally, often with the involvement of TOC (Sigursteinsson, 2021).

the amount of waste produced is also growing, thus, in-country disposal systems are often unable to meet these growing demands. As well, environmental crimes are increasingly recognized as a specialized area of TOC within a globalized society of trade, and also as a significant threat to many plant and animal species (Arroyo-Quiroz and Wyatt, 2019).

As a result, the most vulnerable regions are at risk for this form of victimization. Also, over a decade ago, Interpol undertook a project to identify links between TOC and pollution crime (Interpol, 2009). In particular, as the electronics industry is the world's largest and fastest growing manufacturing industry, it provides much of the e-waste product for TOC (Grossman, 2006). Specifically, in e-waste disposal, the opportunities for criminal involvement are many. Regulations on e-waste are often limited and confusing to most manufacturers; therefore, TOC exploits those weaknesses in the system, particularly where e-waste can be disguised or mislabeled, and naturally TOC profits from those complications (Interpol, 2009).

Waste trafficking has become so widespread that the phrase "waste tourists" is used to describe individuals who visit countries such as the United Kingdom as tourists with the intention of organizing the purchase and export of waste. These arrangements are a highly profitable business; with the volume of waste involved, the trade is estimated to have an annual turnover of approximately $3 million (Interpol, 2009). Since historically many of the traditional crime families had some level of involvement in the waste industry, it is reasonable that TOC today is also involved in the hazardous waste industry. Thus, under the umbrella of legitimate business, TOC groups use property rights, predatory pricing, and threats of violence to profit from the waste industry as well as all environment crimes.

Addressing Vulnerable Persons

Although there are many organizations that provide support for vulnerable persons through funds dedicated by an agency's mission, governmental organizations operate within specific criteria and guidelines. For example, the UN's World Food Programme, founded in 1961, operates under the mission of delivering food assistance to individuals living in emergency situations such as military conflicts or famine (United Nations World Food Programme, 2022). In addition, the World Health Organization, or WHO, founded in 1948, promotes health and safety within vulnerable areas across 194 member states (World Health Organization, 2022). Lastly, UNICEF, founded in 1946 as the United Nations International Children's Emergency Fund (now called the United Nations Children's Fund), provides for child protections across 194 member states, focusing on child survival, child education, social policy, and child health (United Nations International Children's Emergency Fund, 2022a). However, the role of nongovernment organizations, or NGOs, is critical in addressing those vulnerable to risks.

> In April of 2022, UNICEF documented an increase in measles cases affecting millions of children and suggested that pandemic-related disruptions have increased inequalities in access to vaccines, leaving children (especially in Ukraine, Ethiopia, Somalia, and Afghanistan) without protection against measles and other vaccine-preventable diseases (United Nations International Children's Emergency Fund, 2022b).

By definition, *a non-government organization* (NGO) is an organization that seeks to address some element of risk but is not part of a state government action. For most NGOs, the primary purpose is to defend or promote a specific action; thus, NGOs essentially serve as organizations for advocacy to the benefit of some at-risk or vulnerable group. NGOs also often raise awareness and knowledge on certain actions through efforts of presswork, events, and lobbying activities (Nonprofit Expert, 2017). Four of the more commonly recognized advocacy groups that are NGOs, dedicated to addressing the vulnerable populations identified in this chapter, are Amnesty International, Human Rights Watch, Save the Children, and Antislavery International.

Amnesty International, established in the United Kingdom in 1961 after a British attorney wrote a news article about two students in Portugal jailed for toasting to freedom, is now an NGO recognized in over 150 countries (Amnesty International, 2022b). Amnesty International addresses the vulnerabilities of children and adults, focusing on victims of armed conflicts, children's rights, discrimination, indigenous people, refugees, asylum seekers, and immigrants. With over 10 million supporters across the

> In February of 2020, Amnesty International published research indicating that three companies based in the European Union had sold digital surveillance technologies, such as facial recognition technology, to the Chinese government (Amnesty International, 2022a). In these cases, none of the companies had conducted adequate human rights due diligence on the investigated transactions.

globe, Amnesty International is one of the leading NGOs in campaigns to end abuses related to human rights.

Human Rights Watch, originally called Helsinki Watch when it was established in New York in 1978, focuses on investigations, exposures, and changes affecting human rights in approximately 100 countries (Human Rights Watch, 2022a). Human Rights Watch was formed to support citizen groups throughout the Soviet Union and was later expanded to Asia, Africa, and the Middle East. The foci of Human Rights Watch include children's rights, disability rights, LGBT rights, women's rights, and refugee and migrant rights. Today, as reported below, Human Rights Watch continues to defend vulnerable populations, seeking justice for victims and for perpetrators.

> In March of 2022, Human Rights Watch reported rising poverty and economic inequalities fueled by COVID-19 in Kenya, Nigeria, Ghana, Uganda, and Cameroon (Human Rights Watch, 2022b). In addition, research in Kenya and South Africa highlighted the need for infrastructure to protect women and girls from ever-present gender-based violence, as seen in elevated levels of sexual and physical domestic violence against women and girls.

When **Save the Children**, actually called Save the Children Fund, was established in the United Kingdom in 1999, its mission was to improve the lives of children through education, health care, and economic opportunities (Save the Children, 2022b). Today, Save the Children operates in approximately 120 countries, and it is one of the most recognized NGOs within the global arena that specifically focuses on children and the risks associated with childhood. Based on annual reports, in 2020 nearly 45 million children were directly supported by the efforts of Save the Children working across 117 countries. As noted below, these risks to children continue today.

> As reported in February of 2022, approximately 100,000 people, including at least 40,000 children, were displaced from Eastern Ukraine due to the Russian conflict (Save the Children, 2022a). In addition, over 150 children have been killed, and an estimated 7,000 have been injured.

Antislavery International is one of the oldest NGOs, founded in 1839 as a British and foreign antislavery society (Antislavery International, 2022b). Antislavery International focuses on human trafficking, forced labor, child slavery, child and forced marriage, and slavery in supply chains, with operations in Europe, Africa, Asia, and the

> As reported in 2022 by Antislavery International, by failing to provide for basic needs, governments severely limit the recovery of survivors of the COVID pandemic. Survivors are vulnerable to increases in cost of living and increased debt—just a few of the things that can heighten the risk of being re-trafficked (Antislavery International, 2022a).

Middle East. In 2021, Antislavery International supported 21 projects in 10 countries, including Mali and Niger. In addition, Antislavery International provides plans, as reported below, to help those victimized by slavery.

Summary

TOC is aware of the vulnerabilities of countries and populations and their risk for victimization, as well as their propensity to generate profits. In particular, TOC is well equipped for crimes against the vulnerable as it is facilitated by violence, forgery, corruption, and limited governmental interventions. Unfortunately, because of structural biases in their societies, some individuals and/or groups are more at risk for victimization by TOC. These vulnerable populations exist in every country, and they include women, children, internally displaced persons, stateless persons, and LGBTQ individuals—with current conditions and COVID-19 only exacerbating the problems.

For many of these individuals, victimization is a daily occurrence that is instilled in the social and economic biases of their country, and is supported by a lack of government intervention and by the presence of TOC. As indicated by the Global Organized Crime Index, the majority of the countries in the world are experiencing high rates of criminality and the presence of TOC. From the perspective of the United Nations, these crimes against the vulnerable are often crimes that generate profits for TOC. Advocacy groups across the globe attempt to assist these at-risk populations, but unfortunately, not all of these victimizations receive the reaction that a crime against humanity deserves and often receives. Some crimes, depending upon the population of the victims, are never acknowledged; in fact, members of TOC utilize these "invisible" populations without detection. Thus, if an attempt to reduce TOC is to be successful, both the vulnerabilities and TOC's role in them must be acknowledged, identified, and addressed at both the national level and the international level.

Questions for Further Thought

1. Why are some populations more vulnerable to TOC than others?
2. Why are environmental crimes becoming a focus for TOC?
3. How is the GOCI attempting to provide a foundation for studying TOC?

References

Ahmadi, N., & Bezhan, F. (2020, May 7). *Horrific murder of teenage girl again puts spotlight on Afghanistan's honor killings.* Radio Free Europe. Retrieved June 30, 2021, from https://www.rferl.org/a/horrific-killing-of-teenage-girl-puts-spotlight-on-afghanistan-s-honor-killings/30599545.html

American Journal of Managed Care. (2006, November 1). *Vulnerable populations: Who are they?* Retrieved August 3, 2021, from https://www.ajmc.com/view/nov06-2390ps348-s352

Amnesty International. (2022a, February 28). *The practical application of the guiding principles on business and human rights in the tech sector.* Retrieved May 5, 2022, from https://www.ohchr.org/sites/default/files/2022-03/Amnesty-International.pdf

Amnesty International. (2022b). *Who we are.* Retrieved May 5, 2022, from https://www.amnesty.org/en/who-we-are/

Antislavery International, (2022a, April 25). *How the RNA process created yet another hostile environment.* Retrieved May 25, 2022, from https://www.antislavery.org/how-the-rna-process-created-yet-another-hostile-environment/

Antislavery International. (2022b). *2021 in action.* Retrieved May 5, 2022, from https://www.antislavery.org/2021-in-action/

Aronowitz, A. (2009). *Human trafficking, human misery: The global trade in human beings.* Praeger Press.

Arroyo-Quiroz, I., and Wyatt, T. (2019). Wildlife trafficking between the European Union and Mexico. *International Journal for Crime, Justice, and Social Democracy, 8*(3), 23–37.

Asian Pacific Institute on Gender-Based Violence. (2018). *Types of gender-based violence.* Retrieved January 16, 2020, from https://www.api-gbv.org/about-gbv/types-of-gbv/

Australian Institute for Criminology. (2008, April 15). *Homeless people: Their risk of victimization.* Australian Government. Retrieved February 18, 2020, from https://www.aic.gov.au/sites/default/files/2020-05/crm066.pdf

BBC News. (2021, October 5). *Afghanistan: Taliban unlawfully killed 13 Hazara people, Amnesty says.* Retrieved November 3, 2021, from https://www.bbc.com/news/world-asia-58807734

Brav, L., & Bouchet-Saulnier, F. (2002). *The practical guide to humanitarian law.* Rowman & Littlefield.

Burgess, A. (2019). *Victimology theories and applications* (3rd ed). Jones and Bartlett Learning.

Chawai, A. (December 18, 2015). The disturbing reality of human trafficking and children. *Huffington Post.* Retrieved October 19, 2016, from http://www.huffingtonpost.com/

Coren, A., Yeung, J., & Bina, A. (2021, November 1). She was sold to a stranger so her family could eat as Afghanistan crumbles. *CNN.* Retrieved November 1, 2021, from https://www.cnn.com/2021/11/01/asia/afghanistan-child-marriage-crisis-taliban-intl-hnk-dst/index.html

Crisis. (2019). *About homelessness.* Retrieved September 2, 2021, from https://www.crisis.org.uk/ending-homelessness/about-homelessness/

Dalton, R. (2013). Abolishing child sex trafficking on the internet: Imposing criminal culpability on digital facilitators. *University of Memphis Law Review, 43,* 1097–1144.

Daly, K. (1994). *Gender, crime, and punishment.* Yale University Press.

del Castillo, T. (2015). *Organized crime and environmental crime: Analysis of EU legal instruments.* Retrieved June 30, 2021, from https://efface.eu/sites/default/files/EFFACE_Organised%20Crime%20and%20Environmental%20Crime_EU%20Level/index.pdf

de Silva, H., Hobbs, C. and Hanks, H. (2001). Conscription of children in armed conflict—a form of child abuse. A study of 19 former child soldiers. *Child Abuse Review, 10*(2), 125-134.

Erez, E. (2000). Immigration, culture conflict and domestic violence/woman battering. *Crime Prevention and Community Safety: An International Journal 2*(2): 17–21.

Erez, E. (2001). The victimization of women in the context of transnational crime. In N. Ollus & S. Nevalas (Eds.), *Women in the criminal justice system: International examples and national response: Proceedings of the workshop held at the Tenth United Nations Congress on the Prevention of Crime and the Treatment of Offenders, Vienna, Austria, April 2000* (pp. 136–146). European Institute for Crime Prevention and Control.

Erez, E. (2007). *Women as victims and survivors in the context of transnational crime.* Retrieved June 30, 2021, from https://www.ojp.gov/pdffiles1/nij/220775.pdf

Estes, R. and Weiner, N. (2001, September 18). The commercial sexual exploitation of children in the US, Canada, and Mexico. Accessed on August 19, 2022 at https://abolitionistmom.org/wp-content/uploads/2014/05/Complete_CSEC_0estes-weiner.pdf

European Institute for Gender Equality. (2019). *What is gender-based violence?* Retrieved January 16, 2020, from https://eige.europa.eu/gender-based-violence/what-is-gender-based-violence

Global Initiative. (2021). *Global organized crime index, 2021.* Retrieved November 3, 2021, from https://globalinitiative.net/wp-content/uploads/2021/09/GITOC-Global-Organized-Crime-Index-2021.pdf

Grossman, E. (2006). *High tech trash: Digital devices, hidden taxes, and human health.* Island Press.

Hamilton-Smith, N. (2018, June 13). *How organized crime affects the most vulnerable communities. The conversation.* Retrieved November 5, 2021, from https://theconversation.com/how-organised-crime-affects-the-most-vulnerable-communities-98262

Herring, T. (2019). Prevention and protection. Interventions for stateless non-refugees and forced displaced children. *New England Journal of Public Policy,* 31(2), 1–26.

Hicks, J. (2021, March). *The Role of gender in serious and organised/transnational crime.* K4D. Retrieved November 5, 2021, from https://opendocs.ids.ac.uk/opendocs/bitstream/handle/20.500.12413/16554/984_Gender_and_Serious_Organised_Crime.pdf?sequence=1

Hill, J., Katersky, A., & Dukakis, A. (2021, December 30). *Jeffrey Epstein associate Ghislaine Maxwell convicted in sex trafficking trial.* Retrieved December 31, 2021, from https://abc7chicago.com/ghislaine-maxwell-jeffrey-epstein-verdict-trial/11406235/

Hochschild, A. (1999). *King Leopold's ghost: A story of greed, terror, and heroism in colonial Africa* (pp. 95–105). Houghton Mifflin Harcourt.

Human Rights Watch. (2022a). *About us.* Retrieved May 5, 2022, from https://www.hrw.org/about/about-us

Human Rights Watch. (2022b, March). *Policy brief for the African Union.* Retrieved May 25, 2022, from https://www.hrw.org/news/2022/03/09/policy-brief-african-union

Hurdubaie, I. (2017). Organized crime risk factors for the European Union. *Romanian Journal of Forensic Science, 18*(111), 2624–2627.

Institute on Statelessness and Inclusion. (2021, August). *Statelessness in numbers: 2020.* Retrieved November 1, 2021, from https://files.institutesi.org/ISI_statistics_analysis_2020.pdf

Internal Displacement Monitoring Center. (2021). *Global report on internally displacement, 2021.* Retrieved November 1, 2021, from https://www.internal-displacement.org/publications/2021-global-report-on-internal-displacement

Internet Encyclopedia of Philosophy. (2018). *Social contract.* Retrieved June 30, 2021, from https://iep.utm.edu/soc-cont/

Interpol. (2009). Electronic waste and organized crime—Assessing the links. *Trends in Organized Crime, 12,* 352–278.

Keene, S. (2018, October). *Silent partners: Organized crime, irregular groups, and nation-states.* U.S. Army War College Press. https://press.armywarcollege.edu/monographs/389

Kuhn, A. (2020, June 22). Thousands of child soldiers died in the Korean War. Survivors want more recognition. *NPR.* Retrieved November 3, 2021, from https://www.npr.org/2020/06/25/882046201/thousands-of-child-soldiers-died-in-the-korean-war-survivors-want-more-recogniti

Luben, D. (2004). A theory of crimes against humanity. *The Yale Journal of International Law, 29*(1), 85–167.

Martinez, O., & Kelle, G. (2013). Sex trafficking of LGBT individuals. *International Law News, 42*(4), 1.

Maurice, E. (2021, June 27). *The Italian mafia played a pivotal role in the 1969 Stonewall Uprising—but don't call them allies.* Pink News. Retrieved November 2, 2021, from https://www.pinknews.co.uk/2021/06/27/mafia-stonewall-inn-riots-lgbt-rights-pride-new-york-gay-bars/

McCabe, K. (2003). *Child abuse and the criminal justice system.* Peter Lang.

McCabe, K. (2008). *Human trafficking: National and international responses.* Peter Lang.

McCabe, K. (2017). *Protecting your children online.* Rowman & Littlefield.

McCabe, K., & Johnston, O. (2014). Perceptions on the legality of sexting. *Social Science Computer Review, 32*(6), 765–768.

McCabe, K., & Manian, S. (2010). *Sex trafficking. A global perspective.* Lexington Books.

McCabe, K., & Murphy, D. (2016). *Child abuse—Today's issues.* Taylor & Francis.

Melrose, M. (2002). Labour pains: Some considerations of the difficulties of researching juvenile prostitution. *International Journal of Social Research Methodology, Theory, and Practice,* 5(4), 333–351.

Mendelsohn, B. (1974). The origins of the doctrine of victimology. In L. Drapkin & E. Viano (Eds). *Victimology.* Lexington Books.

Nonprofit Expert. (2017, June 16). *NGOs—Non governmental organizations*. Retrieved May 5, 2022, from https://www.nonprofitexpert.com/ngos-non-govermental-organizations/

Petrova, S. (2022, May 5). Explainer: How does conscription work in Russia? *Aljazeera*. Accessed May 27, 2022, from https://www.aljazeera.com/news/2022/5/5/are-russian-conscripts-fighting-in-ukraine

Phillips, A. (2021, November 8). Trafficking of plastic waste is on the rise and criminal groups are profiting, report says. *Los Angeles Times*. Retrieved November 30, 2021, from https://www.latimes.com/environment/story/2021-11-08/report-trafficking-of-plastic-waste-is-on-the-rise-and-criminal-groups-are-profiting

Protect.org. (2015). *What is the magnitude of child exploitation?* Retrieved November 23, 2016, from http://www.protect.org/articles/what-is-the-magnitude-of-child-exploitation

Regehr, C., & Glancy, G. (1995). Battered women syndrome defense in the Canadian courts. *Canadian Journal of Psychiatry, 40*(3), 130–135.

Save the Children. (2021). *Child trafficking: Myth vs. fact*. Retrieved June 30, 2021, from https://www.savethechildren.org/us/charity-stories/child-trafficking-myths-vs-facts

Save the Children. (2022a, February 22). *Ukraine: Don't give up on diplomacy—because more violence will destroy generations of children*. Retrieved May 23, 2022, from https://www.savethechildren.net/news/ukraine-don-t-give-diplomacy-because-more-violence-will-destroy-generation-children

Save the Children. (2022b). *What we do*. Retrieved May 5, 2022, from https://www.savethechildren.org.uk/what-we-do

Shelley, L. (2010). *Human trafficking: A global perspective*. Cambridge University Press.

Shortt, S. (2018, October 15). We don't need protection from the homeless. They need protection from us. *Los Angeles Times*. Retrieved February 18, 2020, from https://www.latimes.com/opinion/op-ed/la-oe-shortt-homeless-victims-20181015-story.html

Sigursteinsson, B. (2021, April 6). *Environmental protection creates opportunities for organized crime*. Open Think. Retrieved November 3, 2021, from https://blogs.dal.ca/openthink/environmental-protection-creates-opportunities-for-organized-crime/

Simon, P. (2014, November 19). *Popular tourist destinations that are surprisingly anti-gay*. Retrieved November 1, 2021, from https://www.destinationtips.com/advice/12-popular-tourist-destinations-anti-gay/4/

Siripala, T. (2020, February 7). *Tokyo's homeless pressured to disappear ahead of Olympics*. The Diplomat. Retrieved November 1, 2021, from https://thediplomat.com/2020/02/tokyos-homeless-pressured-to-disappear-ahead-of-olympics/

Stop it Now. (2019). *Understanding what makes kids vulnerable to being sexually abused*. Retrieved February 17, 2020, from https://www.stopitnow.org/ohc-content/understanding-what-makes-kids-vulnerable-to-being-sexually-abused

Surtees, R. (2008). Trafficked men as unwilling victims. *St. Anthony's International Review, 4*(1), 16–36.

Teitelbaum, M., & Russell, S. (1994). Fertility, international migration, and development. In R. Cassen (Ed.), *Population and development: Old debates, new conclusions* (pp. 229–252). Transaction Publishers.

The Center. (2019). *What is LGBTQ?* Retrieved February 18, 2020, from https://gaycenter.org/about/lgbtq/

Their World. (2018). *Child Trafficking.* Retrieved August 19, 2022, from https://theirworld.org/resources/child-trafficking/

Thompson, D. (2020, December 1). Petersen sentenced to 6 years, 2 months in human trafficking case involving Marshallese adoptions. *Arkansas Online.* Retrieved November 3, 2021, from https://www.arkansasonline.com/news/2020/dec/01/sentencing-underway-in-human-trafficking-case/

Transparency International. (2021). *Corruption perceptions index, 2020.* Retrieved June 30, 2021, from https://images.transparencycdn.org/images/CPI2020_Report_EN_0802-WEB-1_2021-02-08-103053.pdf

United Nations. (2019). *Shaping our future. What we do.* Retrieved February 17, 2020, from https://www.un.org/en/sections/what-we-do/

United Nations High Commissioner for Refugees. (2004, September). *Guiding principles of internal displacement.* Retrieved July 18, 2021, from https://www.unhcr.org/en-us/protection/idps/43ce1cff2/guiding-principles-internal-displacement.html

United Nations High Commissioner for Refugees. (2019). *Ending statelessness.* Retrieved February 18, 2020, from https://www.unhcr.org/en-us/ending-statelessness.html

United Nations International Children's Emergency Fund. (2022a, April 22). *UNICEF and WHO warn of perfect storm of conditions for measles outbreaks, affecting children.* Retrieved May 23, 2022, from https://www.unicef.org.uk/press-releases/unicef-and-who-warn-of-perfect-storm-of-conditions-for-measles-outbreaks-affecting-children/

United Nations International Children's Emergency Fund. (2022b). *Where we work.* Retrieved May 5, 2022, from https://www.unicef.org/where-we-work

United Nations Office on Drugs and Crime. (2018a). Module 6: Perspectives on crime causes and facilitating factors. *E4J University Module Series: Organized crime.* Retrieved June 30, 2021, from https://www.unodc.org/e4j/en/organized-crime/module-6/key-issues/perspectives-on-crime-causes.html

United Nations Office on Drugs and Crime. (2018b). Module 6: Perspectives on crime causes and facilitating factors. Positivism—Environmental influences. *E4J University Module Series: Organized crime.* Retrieved June 30, 2021, from https://www.unodc.org/e4j/en/organized-crime/module-6/key-issues/positivism-environmental-influences.html

United Nations Office on Drugs and Crime. (2018c). *Structural factors and organized crime.* Retrieved June 30, 2021, from https://www.unodc.org/e4j/en/organized-crime/module-6/key-issues/structural-factors.html

United Nations Office on Drugs and Crime. (2019). *Human trafficking.* Retrieved January 16, 2020, from https://www.unodc.org/nigeria/en/human-trafficking.html

United Nations World Food Program. (2022). *Saving lives, changing lives.* Retrieved May 4, 2022, from https://www.wfp.org/overview

U.S. Department of Justice. (2021, June 30). *Manhattan man sentenced to more than 27 years in prison for sex trafficking* [Press release]. U.S. Attorney's Office. Southern District of New York. Retrieved November 3, 2021, from https://www.justice.gov/usao-sdny/pr/manhattan-man-sentenced-more-27-years-prison-sex-trafficking

Vernon, R. (2017, June 2). Crime against humanity. *Encyclopedia Britannica.* Retrieved December 31, 2021, from https://www.britannica.com/topic/crime-against-humanity.

Von Hentig, H. (1948). *The criminal and his victims: Studies in the sociobiology of crime.* Yale University Press.

Vu Ngoc Binh. (2006). Trafficking of women and children in Vietnam: Current issues and problems. In K. Beaks & D. Amir (Eds.), *Trafficking and the global sex industry* (pp. 33–45). Lexington Books.

WarChild. (2018, April 4). *The effects of being a child soldier can last a lifetime.* Retrieved November 5, 2021, from https://www.warchild.org.uk/what-we-do/protection/risks-for-child-soldiers-are-huge-and-the-effects-can-last-a-lifetime

White, R. (2011). *Transnational environmental crime: Toward an eco-global criminology.* Routledge.

World Health Organization. (2022). *About WHO.* Retrieved May 4, 2022, from https://www.who.int/about

Wuilbercq, E. (2021, February 12). *Factbox: Ten facts about child soldiers around the world.* Reuters. Retrieved November 3, 2021, from https://www.reuters.com/article/us-global-childsoldiers-factbox-trfn-idUSKBN2AC0CB

Zabyelina, Y. (2014). The "fishy" business: A qualitative analysis of the illicit market in black caviar. *Trends in Organized Crime, 17*(3), 181–198.

Zhang, S., Chin, K., & Miller, J. (2007). Women's participation in Chinese transnational human smuggling: A gendered market perspective. *Criminology, 54*(3), 699–733.

CHAPTER 5

Drug Trafficking

Key Terms

Cannabis
Cartel
Cocaine
Counternarcotics
Darknet
Drug market
Drug mule
Drug trafficking
Ecstasy
Free trade
Heroin
Illicit drug trade
Marijuana
Methamphetamine
Money laundering
Syndicate
Synthetic drugs

CHAPTER OBJECTIVES

Chapter 5 will enable readers to understand the following:

- the roles that drug trafficking has played in the criminal activities of transnational organized crime (TOC) groups
- the most common drugs trafficked by TOC in the illicit drug trade, and the role of drug addiction in the success for this trafficking
- efforts by law enforcement to counter drug trafficking
- the role of globalization in facilitating the trafficking of illicit drugs by TOC groups
- factors that facilitate TOC activities within the illicit drug trade
- the role of the darknet in the trafficking of drugs
- the role of free trade in drug trafficking

ON AN ANNUAL basis, drug trafficking by TOC groups provides over $400 billion in profits (United Nations Office on Drugs and Crime, 2009). TOC is a business and, as a business, it operates for profit. Drug trafficking, or the illegal drug trade, is often considered the original crime for TOC groups. Drug trafficking is one of the most profitable aspects of this business, it is one of the crimes that receives the most attention by police and legal systems throughout the world, and it is one of the criminal activities expected to continue and increase over time (Williams & Felbab-Brown, 2012).

Drug trafficking is defined as the cultivation, manufacture, distribution, and sale of substances that are subject to prohibitive or regulated drug laws (May, 2017). Drug trafficking and TOC groups' involvement in it affects all citizens throughout the world, as there is no country on earth without issues related to the illegal trade of drugs or the consequences of drug trafficking. In particular, drug trafficking has been tied to corruption, addiction, and violent crime. Whether it is the manufacturing, the distribution, or the consumption of illegal drugs, most individuals know at least one person who is affected by the **illicit drug trade**. As with the majority of TOC activities, drug trafficking has a destabilizing effect on all countries involved. These criminal activities result in community violence, public health threats, and economic distortions that threaten the ability of developing countries to devote meaningful resources to their citizens and to domestic resource mobilization (May, 2017). The illicit drug trade is one of the major criminal activities of TOC groups; it produces profits that most individuals find to be beyond belief, and its illegal activity continues to occur on a daily basis.

Historically, the trafficking of drugs is one of the most common topics in research of the criminal activities of organized crime. In many accounts, the illicit drug trade is discussed in terms of its engagement in **money laundering** and its results of financial instability. Rarely a day goes by when a story about a drug crime or about violence related to drug trafficking is not reported through the mainstream media, with some research suggesting that the media coverage of drug crimes shapes not only individuals' perceptions of the drug trade but also legal responsibilities (Forsyth, 2005).

Money laundering— A process by which illegally obtained money is concealed, usually by transfers of funds through foreign banks or legitimate businesses.

Estimates suggest that the global market in drug trafficking produces annual profits for TOC groups ranging from $426 billion to

In 2017, the World's GDP (gross domestic product) was $80,934,771,028,340 (Worldometer, 2017).

$652 billion, which accounts for nearly 1% of the global gross domestic product, or GDP (May, 2017). In addition, drug-related proceeds, utilized in money laundering through the financial systems, account for an estimated 0.5% of the GDP (Organization of American States, 2013).

For clarity, GDP is a comprehensive monetary measure of a country's well-being; *GDP* stands for "gross domestic product," which is the value of finished goods and services produced minus the value of the goods and services used in production, and it is a measure utilized to determine the economic stability of a country. Countries with a large GDP are often considered financially stable, whereas those with low GDP are considered by some as being more at risk for financial vulnerabilities. In relation to the economic state of the world, the United States and China hold approximately 40% of the world's GDP, which indicates a large share of the global economy (Worldometer, 2017). For some countries, the illicit drug trade contributes significantly to their overall economies. In countries such as Afghanistan, Myanmar, and Laos, which produce approximately 95% of the opium poppies in the world (Thoumi, 2019), the drug trade supports the livelihood of many citizens. Hence, in some cases, states are often passive bystanders in the trade (Williams & Felbab-Brown, 2012).

Attempts to Control Drug Trafficking

Early drug trafficking in the United States traces back to the activities of bootlegging during the Prohibition era of the 1920s (Abadinsky, 2017). Bootlegging in the United States involved the manufacture and distribution of alcoholic beverages, which were prohibited for sale during the time. Critical to the bootlegging business was the transporting of these beverages to their final destinations of bars, nightclubs, or gathering places called "speakeasies." Successful bootleggers required a network of criminal partners, fast cars, and modifications to the interiors of those vehicles in order to conceal the products (Washington State University, 2014). Today, this notion of product concealment is continued in the trafficking of drugs and antiquities; it is a concern for police as discussed further in this text and it was notably relevant to the illicit drug trade during the COVID-19 pandemic restrictions.

COMMON CONCEALMENT AREAS FOR DRUGS ON SHIPS

- Anchor
- Containers
- Fishing Nets
- Fuel Tanks
- Propellers
- Vents (Jones, 2021)

Although the Prohibition era brought the subject of organized criminal activities to the attention of Americans in the 1920s, crimes committed through maritime piracy are actually even earlier demonstrations of criminal activities by TOC groups. In fact, piracy has been a feature of humanity since ancient times, as goods that were being transported around the globe have always fallen prey to groups of sea-based thieves with global networks for the distribution and sale of their stolen possessions (Nowakowska-Krystman, 2016). Research suggests that the maritime domain has the potential for the greatest impact on drug smuggling both historically and today (Eski, 2022). In these early cases, sea piracy groups, similar to TOC groups today, were well-organized, often resorted to violence, and had a hierarchy structure similar to a small army (Nowakowska-Krystman, 2016). The ancient drugs of choice for pirates were alcohol and cocaine. As illustrated in the 2018 case described here, the UN Security Council recognizes the continued sophistication of maritime TOC groups, as they still provide challenges to maritime safety and still exploit the jurisdictional boundaries of the sea for profit (United Nations, 2019).

In October 2018, eight Guyanese fishermen had their boat hijacked by a TOC group of suspected Venezuelan nationals on the Waini River in Guyana on the border with Venezuela. The fishermen were forced to abandon their ship, demonstrating the current vulnerabilities to fishermen and larger commercial vessels. In South America and the Caribbean, piracy increased 163% between 2016 and 2017 (Fevrier, 2018).

For years, nations across the world have attempted to address drug trafficking. In the early 1900s the International Opium Commission, consisting of 12 countries across the globe, met in Shanghai, China, to discuss options for international controls on the opium trade (Jelsma, 2011) and to lay the foundation for global efforts to address the illicit drug trade of the day. Even in these early meetings, the damage from drugs to both individuals and society was recognized.

Although the first Hague International Opium Convention and the treaties negotiated subsequently in the League of Nations era—which included the U.S. Harrison Narcotics Act of 1914—focused more on regulations than on prohibitions, the issues of illicit drug trade were identified as limitations; as a result, restrictions on the distribution of drugs were imposed on exports to many countries (Jelsma, 2011). These early conventions, in effect, established administrative import and export regulations for opiates, cocaine, and cannabis.

> The U.S. Congress passed the Harrison Narcotics Act of 1914 with the intent of suppressing drug dealing by requiring persons in the business of providing drugs (opium, cocaine, etc.) to register annually with the Commissioner of Internal Revenue (now the Internal Revenue Service, or IRS) before they could dispense these drugs. The penalties for not registering with the IRS were fines up to $2,000 or up to five years in prison.

This earliest "war or drugs" in the early 18th century specifically addressed opium, an analgesic used to dull pain by depressing the central nervous system; opium had become a commonly used drug for soldiers and those with chronic pain (Terry & Pellens, 1928). In the United States, within the first year of the Harrison Act, over 200,000 medical professionals were registered as legitimized distributors of opiates, but with little oversight of their prescription records (Musto, 1973). As a result, those with registered authority became the gatekeepers for supplying drugs. The legislative action designed to regulate opium, in essence, gave free and unsupervised control to those in the position of profiting from its distribution.

After the federal law prohibiting alcohol was repealed in 1933, the United States continued its international drive to restrict other drugs. For example, at the Convention of 1936 for the Suppression of the Illicit Traffic in Dangerous Drugs, U.S. representatives worked with the UN to begin prohibiting the distribution of certain narcotics, through agreements that identified their distribution as not only illegal but also an international crime (Jelsma, 2011). Over the decades, through legislative efforts, **counternarcotics**, and policy, the international community has continued to attempt to address the illicit drug trade facilitated by TOC groups. However, international drug trafficking continued to expand into an annual multibillion-dollar business.

Counternarcotics— Measures or activities by criminal justice officials that are designed to prevent the use or distribution of illegal narcotic drugs.

During the 1980s in the United States, which was experiencing the most rapidly growing illicit drugs market, the political response was to declare war on the foreign providers. The phrase "War on Drugs" was adopted to identify drug abuse as Public Enemy No. 1 (Jelsma, 2011). From that point through today, drug manufacturers and growers in multiple countries have been the targets of antidrug enforcement by the United States and other countries. These counternarcotic efforts in the United States are applied through a comprehensive five-pillar program. As detailed below, this five-pillar effort includes law enforcement, interdiction, eradication, alternative livelihood projects, and public information campaigns. However, the trafficking of illicit drugs by TOC groups continues.

FIVE PILLARS OF COUNTERNARCOTIC EFFORTS

Law Enforcement—The immediate concern in any attempt at counternarcotics is law enforcement. Police training and supports of critically needed infrastructure and equipment are required to ensure that the police have all the skills and tools they need to perform effectively and professionally. Included under this pillar are programs to strengthen the criminal justice and corrections sectors to improve their capacities to enforce laws, including drug laws.

Interdiction—In addition to addressing the needs of law enforcement, interdiction is required. Through expanding the capacity of special forces police, interdiction teams have identified and destroyed multiple tons of cultivated drugs, precursor chemicals, and multiple conversion labs.

Eradication—Although eradication is a major disincentive to many countries, such as the opium poppy growers in Afghanistan, an alternative to the cultivation of some drugs has been implemented. These efforts coordinate delivery of public information antidrug messages to facilitate coordinated delivery of alternative livelihood programs.

Alternative Livelihoods—In order to provide viable and sustainable legitimate income streams for the Afghan rural sector, alternative livelihood programs are essential for the success of a counternarcotic strategy. This pillar includes the training of farmers in technologies and techniques for the production of alternative high-value crops.

Public Information—The goal of our public information efforts is to change attitudes in a culture where drug production and distribution is a norm. In these efforts, emphasis is placed on the danger and immorality of the drug trade. These efforts include the broadcasting of anti-drug messages that link the drug trade to conflict, crime, and corruption. (U.S. Department of State, 2005)

Public health attempts to address the drug trade target not only the sources and manufacturers of illegal drugs but also those individuals involved in the drug trade; in most cases, however, police efforts generally focus on eliminating specific drug dealers, not on eliminating the organization (Thoumi, 2003). These efforts by police to remove the drug dealers from the streets have the effect of momentarily removing the drug dealers from the community; however, these individuals are soon replaced by other street dealers, with the individuals who occupy the control positions within the TOC structure rarely being apprehended. Hence, most police efforts produce only a minimal effect. In particular, the arrest records from across the globe identify domestic males from destination countries as the main perpetrators of TOC groups involved in drug trafficking.

In the United States, nearly 90% of those convicted for drug trafficking are male and 75% are citizens (U.S. Sentencing Commission, 2021). Across the globe, the most common drugs found within the land-based illegal drug trade are heroin, methamphetamine, cocaine/crack, and marijuana (Villa, 2022) with estimates of all drugs increasing since 2020 and major source countries identified (U.S. Customs and Border Protection, 2022). Today, on the seas, the drugs of cocaine, marijuana, and heroin are often seized (Eski, 2022). Specifically, as discussed later in this chapter, Afghanistan is identified as one of the largest source countries for global opium production, with increases of over 65% from 2016 to 2017 (World Drug Report, 2018). Colombia has been identified as the largest source country for cocaine, increasing its manufacture and distribution by over 33% from 2015 to 2016 (World Drug Report, 2018). Further, with the legalization of marijuana in many U.S. states and in Europe, multiple countries have been identified as significant contributors to the trafficking of marijuana.

Common Drugs for TOC Groups

Research suggests that in countries such as the United States, approximately 8% of citizens are users of illicit drugs (Nordstrom & Dackis, 2011); hence, the market for drugs is strong. Globally, it is suggested that illicit drug use is related to over 750,000 deaths per year and that approximately 1% of the world has a drug-use disorder (Ritchie & Roser, 2019). Among the most common of the illicit drugs trafficked by TOC groups and utilized on a regular basis are heroin, cocaine, methamphetamine, cannabis, and synthetic drugs such as ecstasy.

WORLD DRUG USE FACTS

Cannabis

In 2019, approximately 200 million people used cannabis, which represents approximately 4% of the global population. Over the last decade, the number of cannabis users has increased by nearly 18%.

Cocaine

In 2019, approximately 20 million people used cocaine, which represents approximately 0.4% of the global population. Over the last decade, the number of cocaine users has increased by 22%.

Opioids

In 2019, approximately 62 million people used opioids for nonmedical purposes, which represents approximately 1.2% of the global population. Over the last decade, the number of opioid users worldwide has nearly doubled.

Methamphetamine

In 2019, approximately 27 million people used methamphetamine, which represents approximately 0.5% of the global population. Over the last year, the number of methamphetamine users has increased by over 30%.

Synthetic Drugs

Although there are no statistics on the number of people who used a synthetic drug in 2019, synthetic drugs continue to be used by marginalized population groups, with general suggestions of an increase in use within low- and middle-income countries. (United Nations Office on Drugs and Crime, 2021)

To understand the dynamics for illicit drugs, one most understand not only the factors that facilitate the manufacture and distribution of the drugs but also the market demand and desire for specific drugs. Research has suggested that TOC and drug trafficking are related to poverty and inequality; however, for drug trafficking to exist there must be a demand for the illegal production and supply of the product (Thoumi, 2019). Each drug provides users with some desirable outcome, and as these desired outcomes continue, so too will TOC groups' distribution of these drugs.

Heroin

Heroin is one of the most profitable drugs sold on the illicit drug market (Mob Museum, 2022). The United States and countries in the Middle East, Europe, and the Russian Federation are all major destinations for the product. **Heroin** is a drug that can be sniffed, snorted, smoked, or injected into a vein within the body (MyHealth.Alberta.ca, 2022). For some individuals, heroin begins as a recreational drug but its use quickly leads to addiction, especially for those who inject the drug. The pleasurable sensation from heroin is called a rush. Soon after the rush, the person feels drowsy and very relaxed. Breathing and heart rate slow, thinking becomes cloudy, and the person may fall into a trancelike state that can last four to six hours (MyHealth.Alberta.ca, 2022). Annual estimates suggest that illicit heroin provides over $60 billion in profits to TOC groups (United Nations Office on Drugs and Crime, 2009).

With repeated use, heroin can cause the person using it to need higher and higher doses of the drug to get the same effect (tolerance). As suggested earlier, use of heroin often results in addiction, which results in the person's body requiring the drug in order to function (physical dependence). This dependence leads to withdrawal symptoms within a few hours, and if the person stops using the drug, addiction can develop within a few weeks. As illustrated in the 2022 case here, the demand for heroin fuels TOC efforts. TOC groups are not only aware of the profits produced by heroin, they are also aware of the probability of addiction to the drug. Heroin is often sold on the streets by local drug dealers (Abele, 2003); however, the distribution of heroin to those street dealers is generally the results of efforts by TOC groups.

> In March of 2022, a Pennsylvania man was sentenced in federal court to 70 months imprisonment followed by four years of supervised release upon his conviction for conspiracy to distribute and possess with intent to distribute 100 grams or more of heroin (U.S. Department of Justice, 2022). The convicted, working through a heroin-trafficking organization of which he was a member, orchestrated and directed the movement of heroin from Philadelphia to Pittsburgh for distribution throughout Pittsburgh by various members of the organization. In addition to the heroin, firearms were also seized.

Cocaine

Europe is a major destination for cocaine trafficking (Mob Museum, 2022). **Cocaine** is a powerful stimulant that is used legally as a local anesthetic for some surgeries; however, much of its use by global populations begins as recreational. Cocaine is also called coke, C, snow, flake, or blow (MyHealth.Alberta.ca, 2022). The two common forms of cocaine are (1) the white crystalline powdered form that is sniffed through the nose or dissolved in water then taken through a vein and (2) the freebase form, which is heated and smoked. Crack is the most commonly identified form of freebase cocaine, with associations to lower socioeconomic groups. Annual estimates suggest that the illicit drug market for cocaine provides over $85 billion in profits for TOC groups (United Nations Office on Drugs and Crime, 2009). As illustrated in the 2022 case here, cocaine trafficking may involve multiple countries.

> In February of 2022, police in Brussels and Spain arrested 45 people involved in a TOC group operating in seven countries with the goal of trafficking cocaine (Associated Press, 2022). This operation involved one of the most active Albanian TOC groups in Europe, importing cocaine from Latin America to a number of European ports.

Initial amounts of cocaine produce feelings of euphoria and energetic or talkative behavior. Research suggests that of all the illicit drugs, cocaine is among the top choices for women. For many female users of cocaine, the initial use is as a means to suppress their appetite and to lose weight. Cocaine also decreases the need for sleep, so college students wishing to stay awake for an exam or individuals with employment that requires long hours of wakefulness may utilize cocaine. When large amounts of cocaine are taken, the high is more intense; however, large doses can cause strange or violent behaviors in which the individual may exhibit tremors or verbalize thoughts of paranoia. Some individuals who use cocaine may develop a stimulant use disorder and an addiction.

Although men generally engage in criminal behaviors earlier than women (Nordstrom & Dackis, 2011), research suggests that women are more likely to select stimulants—and cocaine is such a stimulant. Those involved in the trafficking of cocaine are aware of this bias, and in many cases those TOC groups involved in the illicit drug trade are also involved in sex trafficking (McCabe, 2008). From a practical perspective, those TOC groups provide cocaine for the general demand as well as the women they force into engaging in sex trafficking. Hence, the trafficking of cocaine by TOC is not just directly profitable; it is also indirectly profitable as the distribution of cocaine not only helps to finance the activities of TOC groups but also often provides the victims of the sex trade with a stimulant (McCabe, 2008).

Methamphetamine

Mexico is one of the major producers of methamphetamine for the Americas (Congressional Research Service, 2020). **Methamphetamine** is a powerful stimulant and also an amphetamine, which doctors often prescribe to treat sleep problems (narcolepsy), attention deficit hyperactivity disorder (ADHD), and severe cases of obesity in adults (MyHealth.Alberta.ca, 2022). The illegal form of methamphetamine, often trafficked through TOC groups, is a white, odorless, bitter-tasting, crystalline powder that can be dissolved in water or alcohol.

Methamphetamines are often referred to as speed, meth, ice, crystal, glass, or chalk. The smoked form of methamphetamine is often called ice, crystal, or crank. People who use methamphetamine may become anxious, confused, and violent (MyHealth.Alberta.ca, 2022). Many users of methamphetamine gradually develop serious psychological effects such as paranoia, seeing or hearing things that are not present (hallucinations) and believing things that are not true (delusions) (MyHealth.Alberta.ca, 2022).

Methamphetamine, often in tablet form, is trafficking by TOC groups through numerous modes. Much of this product is transported via private vehicles; however, some is trafficked through commercial vehicles, mail services, or aboard commercial flights and ships (U.S. Department of Justice, 2005). As illustrated in the 2021 case here, profits for the sale of methamphetamine are significant for TOC groups. As methamphetamine can be transported in tablets, purchased on the darknet, and shipped through mail services, methamphetamine provides profits for TOC groups as well as reduced risks for detection by law enforcement or customs officials.

> In November of 2021, Australian police charged three members of a TOC group for attempting to import 140 kilograms of methamphetamine into Melbourne from Canada (Australian Federal Police, 2021). The drugs, if they had been sold, were estimated to be worth more than $88 million.

Cannabis

The United States is a major source and destination country for cannabis. Of various drugs produced by the cannabis plant, marijuana is referred to most commonly. **Cannabis** is a drug made up of the leaves, flowers, and buds of the cannabis plant and may be used for medical purposes and nonmedical purposes (MyHealth.Alberta.ca, 2022). Although there are more than 100 different chemical compounds, or cannabinoids, in the cannabis plant, the two most common are tetrahydrocannabinol (THC) and cannabidiol (CBD). Results from using **marijuana** are changes in actions and feelings of relaxation.

Marijuana is sold on the street, and also in some shops as it is now governmentally regulated in many states.

While use of marijuana often results in an immediate feeling relaxation for the user, the short-term effects of marijuana include problems with memory and learning, distorted perception, difficulty in thinking and problem-solving, and loss of coordination (U.S. Department of Justice, 2020). In addition, the effect of marijuana on perception and coordination is responsible for serious impairments in learning and psychomotor behaviors. The long-term effects of marijuana are physical dependence and withdrawal following discontinuation, as well as psychological addiction or dependence (U.S. Department of Justice, 2020). Marijuana is often referred to as a "gateway drug," as generally it is the first illicit drug a person uses and, in some cases, provides the sense of security that allows the user to attempt another drug. As illustrated in the 2021 case here, the trafficking of marijuana often involves other crimes of a violent nature. Many first-time users are young, school-aged persons. TOC groups are aware of the populations of users of marijuana as well as the age limitation for purchasing marijuana legally. Hence, TOC groups engage in the trafficking of marijuana for profit and under the existing umbrella of secrecy.

In December 2021, a federal jury convicted a Virginia man of murdering another man in retaliation for robbing him of an ounce of marijuana. The convicted man, an alleged marijuana dealer with ties to organized criminal gangs, carried firearms for protection while dealing drugs (U.S. Department of Justice, 2020). The man was convicted of murder by firearm in relation to drug trafficking.

Ecstasy

Detecting the trafficking of drugs cultivated from plants within certain regions provides law enforcement with many challenges. In the cases of transportation by sea, interventions rarely occur (Eski, 2016). TOC groups are fully aware of these limited risks. Detecting human-made **synthetic drugs** is an even greater challenge, and police efforts against synthetic drugs are more often unsuccessful (Abele, 2003). Multiple countries are involved in the production and distribution of synthetic drugs, with ecstasy identified as one of the more common varieties. **Ecstasy** is both a stimulant (amphetamine-like) and a mild calming (tranquillizing) substance (MyHealth.Alberta.ca, 2022). Synthetic drugs like ecstasy are mostly sold among relatives, friends, and acquaintances in private settings.

They are also frequently referred to as "dance drugs," as they are linked with dance clubs and nightclub settings, where they are used as a recreational drug (Abele, 2003).

Ecstasy is also called Adam, XTC, X, hug, beans, and the love drug, with many ecstasy pills often having logos, such as cartoon characters, stamped on them (MyHealth.Alberta.ca, 2022). The drug is most often taken as a pill, but it can be snorted or injected into a vein within the body. Ecstasy is said to enhance the sense of pleasure and boost self-confidence; its hallucinogenic effects include feelings of peacefulness, acceptance, and empathy (MyHealth.Alberta.ca, 2022).

However, ecstasy can also cause nausea, blurred vision, rapid eye movement, faintness, and chills or sweating (MyHealth.Alberta.ca, 2022). In high doses, ecstasy can cause a sharp increase in body temperature, leading to dehydration, muscle breakdown, kidney failure, or heart failure and death. Over time, use of ecstasy can lead to thought and memory problems. As police efforts are often focused on nonsynthetic drugs, the use and market demand for synthetic drugs has increased. As illustrated in the 2019 case here, TOC groups, often protected through the private sales of synthetic drugs, engage in the criminal activity of trafficking with little risk of incurring penalties; thus, TOC groups are able to manufacture and distribute these drugs fairly easily, with profits (as indicated below) increasing annually.

In 2019, a Canadian, who trafficked ecstasy into the United States by hiking across rugged areas of the northern border, was sentenced to seven years in prison (U.S. Department of Justice, 2019). The convicted, a member of a TOC with other members identified previously, will be deported back to Canada once his sentenced is served.

PURCHASING DRUGS ON THE STREET (U.S. AND U.K.)

In the United States, one ounce of marijuana typically provides for 42 cigarettes (joints), so a person smoking four joints per day would spend between $4,800 and $13,905 a year on marijuana. Heroin costs approximately $150 per gram; a single Vicodin tablet costs approximately $5 on the street; and according to the World Drug Report, cocaine in the United States costs between $25 and $200 a gram (Bezrutczyk & Parisi, 2022).

In the United Kingdom, marijuana sells for $45 to $70 per ounce. Heroin costs approximately $140 per gram, a single methamphetamine tablet costs approximately $14 on the street, and cocaine costs between $40 and $70 a gram (Drugwise, 2021).

Profits from marijuana trafficking continue to be consistent sources of revenue for TOC groups. In addition, in many of these cases, the illegal drug markets are relatively peaceful (Reuter, 2009). Thus, for many cases of drug trafficking, police tend not to focus their efforts on any nonviolent actions by TOC groups.

TOC and Drugs

Drug trafficking has always been a significant part of TOC activities, as the prohibition of alcohol led to the development of crime syndicates that added drugs such as heroin to their products (Abadinsky, 2017). To continue their criminal activities, TOC groups involved in drug trafficking or drug-trafficking organizations use bribery to handle government and police officials, and violence to handle employees and competitors (Congressional Research Service, 2020). In the drug trade, TOC may be in the form of a crime syndicate or a drug cartel. For clarity, the term ***cartel*** applies to a criminal network whose structure resembles a holding company with a collection of groups designed to control a market (Glenny, 2008). Crime **syndicates** often engage in violence to settle disputes and to serve as a credible threat to suppliers, creditors, and clients (Congressional Research Service, 2020). Cartels, on the other hand, prefer bribery to violence (Brooke, 1991). Occasionally, however, cartels do exhibit high levels of violence in specific **drug markets** if necessary (Reuter, 2009). In cases of drug trafficking where violence does occur, the violence tends to be between competing groups (Thoumi, 2003). In these circumstances, violence is usually a consequence of territorial conflicts. However, in some countries the drug trade has been linked not only to TOC but also to violent instabilities (Williams & Felbab-Brown, 2012).

Cartel—A group of individuals working together to limit competition and monopolize a certain product. A *syndicate* is a group of individuals formed to operate a specific business.

It should be acknowledged that a strong presence of TOC groups does not necessarily indicate a high level of violence within an area (Thoumi, 2019). Historically, foreign criminal groups were limited to pursuing their drug-trafficking efforts on a large scale because they had less access to judicial representatives. In these cases, indigenous criminal group members with connections to individuals from the legal sphere had an advantage (Becucci, 2004). TOC groups involved in the illicit drug trade operated within limited regions where substance farmers in the countries were dependent upon the sale of their

Drug mule—The phrase used to refer to an individual who smuggles drugs across an international border. Such individuals often swallow balloons containing illicit drugs, and once the drug mule has reached their destination, these balloons are retrieved from their body. Some research suggests that victims of human trafficking are also used as drug mules.

products (i.e., poppies or coca) for their livelihoods (Abadinsky, 2017). As many TOC group members were limited in their upward mobility, those who cultivated the products or sold the products on the street maximized their efforts to maximize their profits (Becucci, 2004).

Today, exporters, who are typically located outside of the destination country, have little or no risk of arrest (Abadinsky, 2017). In fact, arrest data suggest that as the price of illicit drugs increases in Europe, the risk of detection for those operating these drug rings in the Americans decreases (DW.com, 2021) Thus, drug trafficking by TOC groups now operates through international connections, with members of TOC located across the globe; further, research suggests that drug trafficking or the illicit drug trade increases corruption, increases cases of extortion, increases violence, and increases the prevalence of other crimes within societies (United Nations Office on Drugs and Crime, 2009).

Why TOC Continues Its Involvement in the Drug Trade

Governments continue to spend trillions on measures to reduce the illicit drug trade; specifically, between 2010 and 2015 the U.S. government spent over $5 billion to address drug trafficking (Galindo, 2018). From 2018 to 2021, Germany significantly increased its cocaine seizures (DW.com, 2021). The United Kingdom has also achieved success against TOC and drug trafficking (Bolt, 2009). As demonstrated in the 2021 Interpol report mentioned here, law enforcement efforts continue; however, drug trafficking and illicit profits to TOC groups continue as well.

> In 2021, Interpol's Operation Lionfish arrested 287 individuals and seized illicit drugs estimated to be worth approximately 100 million euros (Interpol, 2021). This operation, with the goal of disrupting drug trafficking in Africa and the Middle East, involves law enforcement officers in over 40 countries.

> Fake carrots, doughnuts, catapults, drones, and submarines are just some of the media that traffickers have used to smuggle drugs (Woody, 2017).

As the trafficking of illicit drugs continues and evolves, many governments must approach drug trafficking with tools in addition to legalities. The United States has attempted to employ authorized intelligence and operational capabilities in an integrated manner to target, disrupt, and degrade criminal networks, especially those in the drug trade that pose the greatest threat to national security (White House, 2021). In addition, through fostering collaboration with private entities and international, multilateral, and bilateral organizations, governments have the potential to combat drug trafficking through TOC. Finally, estimates suggest that 70% of drug-trafficking profits are laundered through financial systems. Only about 1% are detected by authorities (United Nations Office on Drugs and Crime, 2009), and much of the illicit profits are re-invested in other, nonillicit businesses.

SECTORS WHERE ORGANIZED CRIME INVESTS PROFITS

- Businesses that use cash
- Low-tech, labor-intensive, and not export-oriented sectors
- Sectors with a high involvement of public administration and/or public subsidies
- Sectors with weak or developing regulation, which may imply weaker monitoring or more infiltration opportunities (for example, renewable energy or gaming) (United Nations Office on Drugs and Crime, 2017)

By expanding tools and capabilities to combat illicit finance and by developing new technologies to identify and disrupt existing and newly emerging transnational organized criminal threats, the illicit drug trade by TOC may be reduced (White House, 2021). In many cases, however, police knowledge about TOC groups is limited to only particular visible groups with no clear links to supply chains or ideas regarding drug markets or the scope of drugs within an area (Bolt, 2009). As a result, drug enforcement by police remains focused on maintaining public order and reducing street-level dealing (Abele, 2003).

HOW IS DRUG MONEY LAUNDERED?

- Cash, including smuggling and stockpiling
- Hawala, an informal system of money transfer
- Purchases of real estate and related construction activities
- Investments in cash-generating activities such as restaurants, casinos, red-light entertainment, and gas stations
- Purchases of luxury items such as villas yachts, and jewels
- Investments in offshore centers (United Nations Office on Drugs and Crime, 2017)

The trafficking of illicit drugs continues to represent a major source of revenue for TOC groups. However, as discussed in Chapter 3, business models and organizational structures are changing along with changes in mobility and technology. In particular, synthetic drug markets have been characterized as disorganized, with small groups and loosely connected networks (Abele, 2003). Today, criminals are exploiting new technologies and networks, such as the **darknet** (i.e., an encrypted virtual network), that are altering the nature of the illicit drug trade and the types of players involved (United Nations Office on Drugs and Crime, 2020). In addition, some researchers have suggested that the legal efforts of free trade actually, although unintentionally, facilitate the illicit drug trade (Bartilow & Eom, 2009).

For clarity, **free trade** as applied to products indicates that countries can import and export goods without tariff barriers that generally exist in product distribution across international boundaries. A free trade agreement exists within the countries of the European Union, which facilitates the movement of goods across over 25 countries in Europe. Unfortunately, although free trade can open new markets for products, it also provides TOC groups the opportunity to move drugs with more opportunities to launder money and invest in other criminal and noncriminal actions within the trading countries (Bartilow & Eom, 2009).

As suggested in Chapter 3, current TOC, utilizing technology, tends to have the flexibility of temporary connections. In addition, as related to specific drugs, legal efforts in some cases offer support—as in the case of cannabis, which continues to be the most widely produced drug worldwide; however, this market is undergoing transition and diversification in countries that allow nonmedical use of cannabis. This blurring of legalities has actually helped to support TOC involvement in the criminal activity (United Nations Office on Drugs and Crime, 2020a).

In most regions across the globe, the drug market is the largest criminal market on the darknet (Europol, 2017). Some estimates suggest that the profits made by cyber-facilitated illicit drug trades are at least equivalent to the profits of the legitimate drug trades. Throughout Europe, the monthly revenues of the main darknet markets are estimated to be approximately 19 million euros, or 20 million U.S. dollars. Research suggests that the main advantage of darknet markets is their perceived anonymity as related to the physical anonymity of those who do business on such markets (United Nations Office on Drugs and Crime, 2020b). On the darknet, the purchasing of drugs does not require physical contact, which may reduce the inhibitions of customers who might otherwise be reticent to interact personally with drug dealers. Darknet purchases overcome the challenge of sellers and buyers having to be in the same location and do not need a mass of customers to sustain a local market (United Nations Office on Drugs and Crime, 2020b). In most cases, goods bought on the various darknet marketplaces are then typically paid for in cryptocurrencies, which can be exchanged for various national currencies. In general, the cyber-facilitated crimes can occur offline or online, with both providing profits (Europol, 2017). Bought online, and thus avoiding detection, the drugs purchased on the darknet are delivered by public or private postal services, presumably without the services' knowledge (United Nations Office on Drugs and Crime, 2020b).

> Research from analyses of email addresses linked to drug listings found on eight major darknet markets in 2016 revealed that most could be linked to the United States (34%) and Europe (32%), with China accounting for 9% of the market and India for 3% of the market (United Nations Office on Drugs and Crime, 2020b).

The global synthetic drugs market, another newer area for TOC groups, is also helping to support TOC activities, as synthetic drugs can be manufactured anywhere, with a process that does not involve the extraction of active constituents from plants that have to be cultivated in certain conditions for them to grow. The relative ease of manufacturing is appealing to TOC groups with the desire of maximizing profits. Hence, North America's synthetic opioid overdose crisis reached new heights, and West, Central, and North Africa are currently experiencing a crisis of abuse of tramadol, another synthetic opioid (United Nations Office on Drugs and Crime, 2020a).

Strategies to reduce the drug trade have largely ignored any TOC crime activity that is not limited strictly to drug trafficking. This not only risks strengthening the structures required in the trafficking of drugs but also fails to address the cause and effect of current TOC activities and TOC's propensity to enter the illicit drug trade (Galindo, 2018). Research suggests that the largest parts of the illegal drug trade originate in less-developed counties and are moved to the more developed countries by TOC groups for higher

CURRENT ILLICIT DRUG CHALLENGES

Marijuana
Engineered cannabis products have become more potent, and an increase in marijuana use has been observed in many countries.

Cocaine
Manufacturing was disrupted during the initial stages of the COVID-19 pandemic; but it returned to its typical level shortly afterward, with greater competition between traffickers increasing the quality of the products and reducing prices.

Opioids
Roughly 50,000 people died from opioid overdoses in the United States in 2019, indicating an increase of nearly 100% in the last decade. As the result of the economic downturn triggered by the COVID-19 pandemic, fragile communities in areas of illicit cultivation of drugs are now increasing.

Methamphetamine
Seizures of methamphetamine have strongly declined in the past decade, while injecting and use of stimulants is driving HIV outbreaks among people who use the drugs.

Synthetics
The limited capacity of forensic, law enforcement, and health experts to identify different synthetic drugs is adding to the challenges for countries that are attempting to address these new products for the drug trade. (United Nations Office on Drugs and Crime, 2021)

profits. These moves involve various routes and modes of transportations. As a result, over the last decade new gangs have emerged as older gangs have splintered (Congressional Research Service, 2020). However, most forms of illegal drugs that originate overseas and are trafficked into the United Kingdom for further distribution are delivered via container ships, yachts and small boats, light aircraft, and vehicle traffic from continental Europe; by airline passengers; and in post and fast parcels (National Crime Agency, 2022). The workers on these ships, often from low-cost countries, continue the efforts (Liang, 2011). In the United States, the majority of

In March of 2021, U.S. Customs and Border Protection (CBP) officers stationed at the port of Cincinnati seized four shipments containing cocaine, methamphetamine, marijuana, and undeclared U.S. currency. In these seizures, cocaine was packed inside compartments in the bottom of the kitchen pans, liquid methamphetamine was found in a shipment of injectable equine medication, and $15,000 of undeclared U.S. currency was found secured behind an action figure (U.S. Customs and Border Protection, 2021).

the illegal drugs are trafficked over land borders, with commercial airlines transporting less (Drug Enforcement Administration, 2021); however, drug trafficking continues to increase, with concealment of drugs changing as illustrated in the report on the previous page. Specifically, maritime drug trades flourish, with inspections rarely occurring (Eski, 2022).

TOC undermines human rights standards and increases insecurity within regions. What many individuals attempting to address the drug trade do not realize is that illicit drug trafficking remains one of the most complex and dire issues facing the modern world (United Nations Office on Drugs and Crime, 2014). In some cases, profits from the drug trade support legitimate earning to further the TOC groups' influence (Interpol, 2020b). The secretive nature of drug trafficking has always tied it to TOC, with consequences in terms of money laundering, political corruption, and terrorism. Today, the problem is even more dire, as the fight against illicit drug trafficking is often now digital. An increasing number of countries and organizations around the world have noted a dramatic rise in the online trade of drugs and precursor chemicals (United Nations Office on Drugs and Crime, 2014). These advances in technology and the use of the darknet to conceal origination provide more challenges to law enforcement and to those attempting to address TOC and the drug trade.

Today, many family-tied TOC groups are being replaced with looser-connected members (Congressional Research Service, 2020). It is estimated that between 2000 and 2011 cannabis seizures obtained through the postal service increased 300% (United Nations Office on Drugs and Crime, 2014). With technology providing the avenue for sale and with shipping authorities providing delivery, it is difficult if not impossible to identify the prevalence of the drug trade via cybercommunities. As illustrated in the 2022 case reported here, this new age of drug trafficking further provides support for TOC and their criminal activities.

In February of 2022, European police forces arrested 45 members of an Albanian TOC group, operating in Belgium and Spain, that was attempting to traffick cocaine from Latin America into Europe using technology, planes, and shipping containers (Euronews, 2022).

Since 2020 as the world has suffered with the COVID-19 pandemic, TOC groups have taken advantage of the opportunities presented to further profit within the illicit drug trade. Specifically, as other legitimate businesses have plummeted, drug trafficking activities have continued to increase (Interpol, 2020b). With the restrictions on travel, the focus of police on enforcing public health measures, and restrictions on face-to-face interactions, drug traffickers have found new ways to conceal and transport their products. In particular, illicit drugs have been detected in shipments of pandemic supplies that easily pass through customs (Global Initiative, 2021). In addition, TOC groups have used food service delivery containers such as pizza boxes and home-delivery packages to hide their illicit products, with often-ignorant delivery persons or unwilling drug mules (Interpol, 2020a). Finally, drugs hidden in other products, such as housewares or sculptures, continue to be transported across borders with less risk of detection (Interpol, 2021).

Summary

Drug trafficking is one of the oldest and most profitable of the criminal activities of TOC groups. As demonstrated in the report here, these actions continue today.

Drug trafficking organizations are among the most significant and well-resourced transnational criminal threats facing governments. These trafficking organizations, often within TOC groups, operate like international businesses, with their growing infiltration of commercial and economic activity fundamentally threatening free markets and financial systems that are critical to the stability and efficiency of the global economy (White House, 2021). The activities of these TOC groups include corruption, violence, and the undermining of democracies.

The effects of globalization, hyperglobalization, free trade, and the darknet are apparent in the drug trade and the activities of TOC groups. Large-scale drug

In May of 2022, U.S. law enforcement arrested six individuals and identified a tunnel, which was the length of six football fields, between Mexico and California that was being used to transport drugs into the United States (CBS News, 2022). It was unclear how long the tunnel has been used for drug trafficking.

The Global Drug Survey, which is based on a nonrepresentative convenience sample of roughly 100,000 to 500,000 self-selected people from more than 50 countries, indicated that in 2014 approximately 5% of drugs were purchased over the darknet and just six years later, in 2020, 15% of drugs were purchased over the darknet (United Nations Office on Drugs and Crime, 2020b).

organizations now resemble corporate organizations, with division of labor, applications of technology, and huge cash reserves designed to keep their operations moving smoothly (Zill & Bergman, 2014). To better facilitate the profits of TOC groups, many organizations have diversified into the crimes of human trafficking, oil theft, and other criminal activities while maintaining their hold on the illicit drug trade (Congressional Research Service, 2020). In these cases, both major and minor TOC groups continue to profit. For some groups, their profits are facilitated through their contacts with multiple suppliers to increase business volume (Becucci, 2004). For other TOC groups, a division of labor and product markets facilitates profits. For example, Mexico's Los Zetas, a well-known drug-trafficking group operating in the United States, has expanded its operations to arms trafficking and fuel products. Mexico's Gulf Cartel has split into separate drug-trafficking operations based upon product and regions (Congressional Research Service, 2020). Profit margins are critical to TOC groups, and in the drug trade those margins are significant. Specially, producing drugs is generally a very cheap process, and once the product is delivered the profits are large. In addition, losses in the narcotics business through seizures or theft are rare; the United Nations estimates that current drug interdiction efforts intercept only about 13% of heroin shipments and 28% to 40% of cocaine shipments (Zill & Bergman, 2014).

TOC groups are aware of the limited risks and the large profits. Like any cash business organization, TOC organizations often invest in the legitimate economy of their own country and use investment advisors who handle financial instruments available in the international marketplace (Zill & Bergman, 2014). For example, during the 1980s, while other Latin American nations faced major recessions, the influx of billions of dollars in drug proceeds helped keep Colombia's economy operating (Zill & Bergman, 2014). Drug money, which helped to support the economy, became the foundation for power by TOC groups, which later continued in the forms of extortion, corruption, and violence. That is, some TOC groups have combined the business of selling illegal drugs with the elements of selling legal products (Abadinsky, 2017). TOC, historically exclusively involved in criminal activity of drug trafficking, continues to profit from the illicit drug trade.

Questions for Further Thought

1. What drugs are more commonly trafficked by TOC groups, and what are the challenges to addressing this trafficking of drugs?
2. How has the illicit drug trade supported societies over time?
3. How have technology and the darknet facilitated the activities of TOC as related to the illicit drug trade?

References

Abadinsky, H. (2017). *Organized crime* (11th ed). Cengage Group.

Abele, G. (2003). *Synthetic drugs trafficking in three European cities: Major trends and involvement of organized crime.* Retrieved March 3, 2022, from http://www.organized-crime.de/revgru01.htm

Associated Press. (2022, February 15). *45 arrested in major cocaine network bust in Belgium, Spain.* Retrieved March 3, 2022, from https://apnews.com/article/europe-arrests-germany-spain-netherlands-a253e40cfa0c8ab91c-8844d2eb663345

Australian Federal Police. (2021, November 21). *Joint agency operation charges three people in 140kg meth importation.* Retrieved March 1, 2022, from https://www.afp.gov.au/news-media/media-releases/joint-agency-operation-charges-three-people-140kg-meth-importation

Bartilow, H., & Eom, K. (2009). Free traders and drug smugglers: The effects of trade openness of states' ability to combat drug trafficking. *Latin American Politics and Society, 51*(2), 117–145.

Becucci, S. (2004). Old and new actors in the Italian drug trade: Ethnic succession or functional specialization. *European Journal on Criminal Policy and Research, 10*(4), 257–283.

Bezrutczyk, D., & Parisi, T. (2022, January 31). *How much do drugs cost?* Addiction Center. Retrieved March 20, 2022, from https://www.addictioncenter.com/drugs/how-much-do-drugs-cost/

Bolt, D. (2009). Tackling serious organized crime drug harms. *Safer Communities, 8*(1), 24–28.

Brooke, J. (1991, April 21). Colombia's rising export: Fake U.S. money. *The New York Times.* Retrieved March 3, 2022, from https://www.nytimes.com/1991/04/21/world/colombia-s-rising-export-fake-us-money.html

CBS News. (2022, May 17). Authorities find massive drug-smuggling tunnel between Tijuana and San Diego. Retrieved May 20, 2022, from http://www.cbsnews.com/news/drug-tunnel-tijuana-san-diego/

Congressional Research Service. (2020, July 28). *Mexico: Organized crime and drug trafficking organizations.* Retrieved June 3, 2021, from https://crsreports.congress.gov/product/pdf/R/R41576/38

Drug Enforcement Administration. (2021, March). *2020 national drug threat assessment.* Retrieved March 3, 2022, from https://www.dea.gov/sites/default/files/2021-02/DIR-008-21%202020%20National%20Drug%20Threat%20Assessment_WEB.pdf

Drugwise. (2021). *How much do drugs cost?* Retrieved March 20, 2022, from https://www.drugwise.org.uk/how-much-do-drugs-cost/

DW.com. (2021, March 7). *Cocaine: The drug pipeline in Europe*. Retrieved March 3, 2022, from https://www.dw.com/en/cocaine-the-drug-pipeline-to-europe/a-56782666

Eski, Y. (2016). *Policing, port security and crime control: An ethnography of the port securityscape*. Routledge.

Eski, Y. (2022). Diving for dope: Identifying in submarine drug policing at the maritime gateway to Europe. *European Journal of Criminology, 19*(1), 139–159.

Euronews. (2022, February 15). 45 arrests in crackdown on Albanian-speaking criminals flooding Europe with cocaine. Accessed on August 19, 2022 at https://www.europol.europa.eu/media-press/newsroom/news/45-arrests-in-crackdown-albanian-speaking-criminals-flooding-europe-cocaine

Europol. (2017). *Serious and organized crime threat assessment*. Retrieved May 12, 2022, from www.europol.euopa.eu

Fevrier, V. (2018, October 15). *Maritime threats in South America: Piracy and drug trafficking*. Intelligence Fusion. Retrieved March 2, 2022, from https://www.intelligencefusion.co.uk/insights/resources/intelligence-reports/maritime-threats-in-south-america-piracy-and-drug-trafficking/

Forsyth, A. (2005). Drug scares: The really long term effects. *Criminal Justice Matters, 18*(1), 18–19.

Galindo, J. (2018). *An improved strategy to fight drug trafficking, organized crime, and corruption in the hemisphere*. Global Americans. Retrieved March 3, 2022, from https://theglobalamericans.org/reports/improved-strategy-fight-drug-trafficking-organized-crime-corruption-hemisphere/

Glenny, M. (2008). *McMafia: A journey through the global criminal underworld*. Knopf.

Global Initiative. (2021). *Global organized crime index*. Retrieved March 3, 2022, from https://globalinitiative.net/wp-content/uploads/2021/09/GITOC-Global-Organized-Crime-Index-2021.pdf

Interpol. (2020a, April 30). *Dealers using food delivery services to transport drugs during Covid-19 lockdowns*. Retrieved January 3, 2022, from https://www.interpol.int/en/News-and-Events/News/2020/Dealers-using-food-delivery-services-to-transport-drugs-during-COVID-19-lockdowns

Interpol. (2020b, June 26). *On global anti-drug trafficking day Interpol and WCO highlight the pandemic's multiplying effect on illicit activities*. Retrieved January 3, 2022, from https://www.interpol.int/en/News-and-Events/News/2020/On-global-anti-drug-trafficking-day-INTERPOL-and-WCO-highlight-the-pandemic-s-multiplying-effect-on-illicit-activities

Interpol. (2021, May 17). *Massive drug seizures in twin operations across Africa and Middle East*. Retrieved February 20, 2022, from https://www.interpol.int/en/News-and-Events/News/2021/Massive-drug-seizures-in-twin-operations-across-Africa-and-Middle-East

Jelsma, M. (2011, January). *The development of international drug control: Lessons learned and strategic challenges for the future*. Global Commission on Drug Policies. Retrieved March 5, 2022, from http://www.globalcommissionondrugs.org/wp-content/themes/gcdp_v1/pdf/Global_Com_Martin_Jelsma.pdf

Jones, K. (2021, February 20). *Hide and seek: How drug traffickers get creative at sea.* Insight Crime. Retrieved March 20, 2022, from https://insightcrime.org/news/hide-and-seek-drug-traffickers-creative-at-sea/

Liang, A. (2011). Sailing on a neoliberal sea: Multinational seafarers on container ships. *Hong Kong Anthropologist, 5*(1), 1–20.

May, C. (2017, March). *Transnational crime and the developing world.* Global Financial Integrity. Retrieved February 20, 2022, from https://secureservercdn.net/50.62.198.97/34n.8bd.myftpupload.com/wp-content/uploads/2017/03/Transnational_Crime-final.pdf

McCabe, K. (2008). *The trafficking of persons: National and international responses.* Peter Lang.

Mob Museum. (2022). *The world's top five organized crime rackets.* Retrieved February 23, 2022, from https://themobmuseum.org/blog/the-worlds-top-five-organized-crime-rackets/

Musto, D. (1973). *The American disease: Origins of narcotic control.* Yale University Press.

MyHealth.Alberta.ca. (2022). Heroin. My health Alberta. Retrieved August 19, 2022, from https://myhealth.alberta.ca/health/pages/conditions.aspx?hwId=uq2454

National Crime Agency. (2022, January). *Drug trafficking.* Retrieved March 4, 2022, from https://www.nationalcrimeagency.gov.uk/what-we-do/crime-threats/drug-trafficking

Nordstrom, B., & Dackis, C. (2011). Drugs and crime. *Journal of Psychiatry and Law, 39*(4), 530–531.

Nowakowska-Krystman, A. (2016). Maritime piracy as a form of organized crime: A strategic management approach. *Connections: The Quarterly Journal, 3*, 41–53.

Organization of American States. (2013). *The drug problem in the Americas. Studies: Chapter 4—The economics of drug trafficking.* Retrieved March 3, 2022, from http://www.cicad.oas.org/drogas/elinforme/informedrogas2013/laeconomicanarcotrafico_eng.pdf

Reuter, P. (2009). Systemic violence in drug markets. *Crime, Law and Social Change, 52*(1), 275–284.

Ritchie, H., & Rose, M. (2019, December). *Opioids, cocaine, cannabis and illicit drugs.* Our World Data. Retrieved January 3, 2022, from https://ourworldindata.org/illicit-drug-use

Terry, C., & Pellens, M. (1928). *The opium problem.* Committee on Drug Addictions in Collaboration with the Bureau of Social Hygiene, Inc. *Journal of Mental Science, 75*(309), 322–323. https://doi:10.1192/bjp.75.309.322

Thoumi, F. (2003). *Illegal drugs, economy, and society in the Andes.* Johns Hopkins University Press.

Thoumi, F. (2019, May 16). *The relationship between illegal drugs and violence: Is there a cause and effect?* Retrieved March 23, 2022, from https://franciscothoumi.com/2019/05/06/the-relationship-between-illegal-drugs-and-violence-is-there-a-cause-and-effect/

United Nations. (2019, February 5). Piracy and high seas crime growing, becoming more sophisticated, UN Security Council told. *UN News.* Retrieved March 5, 2022, from https://news.un.org/en/story/2019/02/1032011

United Nations Office on Drugs and Crime. (2009). *Transnational organized crime. The globalized illegal economy.* Retrieved March 1, 2022, from https://www.unodc.org/toc/en/crimes/organized-crime.html

United Nations Office on Drugs and Crime. (2014). *Princeton Model United Nations Conference (PMUNC) 2014.* Retrieved March 3, 2022, from https://irc.princeton.edu/pmunc/docs/UNODC%20BG%20formatted.pdfUnited Nations Office on Drugs and Crime. (2017, May). *The drug problem and organized crime, illicit financial flows, corruption, and terrorism.* Retrieved March 3, 2022, from https://www.unodc.org/wdr2017/field/Booklet_5_NEXUS.pdf

United Nations Office on Drugs and Crime. (2020a, February). Module 3:Organized crime markets. Key issues: Drug trafficking. *E4J University Module Series: Organized crime.* Retrieved March 3, 2022, from https://www.unodc.org/e4j/en/organized-crime/module-3/key-issues/drug-trafficking.html

United Nations Office on Drugs and Crime. (2020b). *Trafficking over the darknet.* Retrieved March 20, 2022, from https://www.unodc.org/documents/Focus/WDR20_Booklet_4_Darknet_web.pdf

United Nations Office on Drugs and Crime. (2021, June). *World drug report, 2021.* Retrieved March 20, 2022, from https://www.unodc.org/res/wdr2021/field/WDR21_Booklet_1.pdf

U.S. Customs and Border Protection. (2021, March 8). *The concealment methods criminals use to peddle their drugs.* U.S. Department of Homeland Security. Retrieved March 21, 2022, from https://www.cbp.gov/newsroom/local-media-release/concealment-methods-criminals-use-peddle-their-drugs

U.S. Customs and Border Protection. (2022, January 3). *CBP releases operational fiscal year 2021 statistics* [Press release]. U.S. Department of Homeland Security. Retrieved March 4, 2022, from https://www.cbp.gov/newsroom/national-media-release/cbp-releases-operational-fiscal-year-2021-statistics

U.S. Department of Justice. (2005, March). *Methamphetamine drug threat assessment—Transportation.* National Drug Intelligence Center. Retrieved March 3, 2022, from https://www.justice.gov/archive/ndic/pubs13/13853/trans.htm

U.S. Department of Justice. (2019, February 22). *Canadian drug trafficker sentenced to 7 years in prison for ecstasy smuggling conspiracy* [Press release]. Retrieved March 3, 2022, from https://www.justice.gov/usao-wdwa/pr/canadian-drug-trafficker-sentenced-7-years-prison-ecstasy-smuggling-conspiracy

U.S. Department of Justice. (2020, April). *Drug fact sheet: Marijuana/cannabis* [Fact sheet]. Retrieved March 3, 2022, from https://www.dea.gov/sites/default/files/2020-06/Marijuana-Cannabis-2020_0.pdf

U.S. Department of Justice. (2021, December 17). *Jury convicts marijuana trafficker of drug-related murder* [Press release]. Retrieved March 3, 2022, from https://www.justice.gov/usao-edva/pr/jury-convicts-marijuana-trafficker-drug-related-murder

U.S. Department of Justice. (2022, March 10). *Pittsburgh man sentenced to prison for role in heroin distribution scheme* [Press release]. Retrieved March 13, 2022, from https://www.justice.gov/usao-wdpa/pr/pittsburgh-man-sentenced-prison-role-heroin-distribution-scheme

U.S. Department of State. (2005, July 12). *Counternarcotics programs* [Archive]. Retrieved March 3, 2022, from https://2001-2009.state.gov/p/inl/rls/rm/51065.htm

United States Sentencing Commission. (2021, June). *Drug trafficking offenses: Quick facts*. Retrieved January 23, 2022, from https://www.ussc.gov/sites/default/files/pdf/research-and-publications/quick-facts/Drug_Trafficking_FY20.pdf

Villa, L. (2022, January 4). *Trafficking statistics: American addiction centers*. Retrieved March 3, 2022, from https://drugabuse.com/statistics-data/drug-trafficking/

Washington State University. (2014). *Bootlegging during Prohibition*. Retrieved March 3, 2022, from http://digitalexhibits.wsulibs.wsu.edu/exhibits/show/prohibition-in-the-u-s/bootlegging-during-prohibition

White House. (2021, December 15). *The Biden administration launches new efforts to counter transnational criminal organizations and illicit drugs* [Fact Sheet]. Retrieved March 5, 2022, from https://www.whitehouse.gov/briefing-room/statements-releases/2021/12/15/fact-sheet-the-biden-administration-launches-new-efforts-to-counter-transnational-criminal-organizations-and-illicit-drugs/

Williams, P., & Felbab-Brown, V. (2012). *Drug trafficking, violence, and instability*. Bibliogov Publishing.

Woody, C. (2017, April 2). Fake vegetables, frozen sharks, and an Xbox—here are some of drugs smugglers' most bizarre methods. *Insider*. Retrieved March 20, 2022, from https://www.businessinsider.com/drug-smugglers-methods-hiding-places-2017-4

World Drug Report. (2018, June). World drug report 2018. *Executive summary conclusions and policy implications* [United Nations publication E.18.XI.9]. United Nations Office on Drugs and Crime. Retrieved January 4, 2022, from https://www.unodc.org/wdr2018/prelaunch/WDR18_Booklet_1_EXSUM.pdf

Worldometer. (2017). *GDP by country*. Retrieved March 4, 2022, from https://www.worldometers.info/gdp/gdp-by-country/

Zill, O., & Bergman, L. (2014). Do the math: Why the illegal drug business is thriving. *PBS*. Retrieved March 4, 2022, from https://www.pbs.org/wgbh/pages/frontline/shows/drugs/special/math.html

Weapons Trafficking

Key Terms

1968 Firearms Act (U.K.)
3D printer
AK-47
Ammunition
Ant trade
Arms Trade Treaty (ATT)
Arms trafficking
Broker
Bureau of Alcohol, Tobacco, Firearms, and Explosives (ATF)
Firearms trafficking
Ghost gun
Gunrunning
International Court of Justice (ICJ)
Light weapons
Pistol
Small arms
Straw purchaser
Weapons trafficking
World Court

CHAPTER OBJECTIVES

Chapter 6 will enable readers to understand the following:

- the products included in the category of weapons trafficking
- the role of transnational organized crime (TOC) groups in the trafficking of weapons
- the different markets that provide weapons for illicit trade by TOC groups
- the link between postconflict zones and the availability of weapons
- common weapons trafficked by TOC groups
- the phrase "ghost gun" as applied to the weapons trade
- the links between weapons trafficking, technology, and 3D printers by TOC groups in the illicit trade of weapons

THE TRAFFICKING OF guns and weapons, or the illicit arms trade, is one of the most common forms of criminal activity committed by members of TOC networks. **Weapons trafficking**, a natural trade for TOC groups, supports other forms of illicit trade, as most are enforced through coercion and violence—with violence often demonstrated by TOC groups through the use of firearms. Those who benefit from weapons trafficking by TOC groups include guerrilla groups, paramilitary organizations, criminal groups, and ordinary citizens within consumer countries (Cragin & Hoffman, 2003). At one time, weapons trafficking was followed only by drug trafficking in profits for TOC. Today, profits from weapons trafficking are still significant as this illicit action follows the profits made in human trafficking, the drug trade, and wildlife trafficking, with weapons trafficking, unlike other aspects of TOC crimes, often accompanying the illicit trade of other products. In addition, the illicit trafficking of firearms is often linked to human trafficking, drug trafficking, violent extremism, and terrorism (Abadinsky, 2017).

The trafficking of weapons by TOC groups provides billions in profits on an annual basis (United Nations Office on Drugs and Crime, 2009). In addition, Interpol (2017) suggests that approximately 250,000 lives are lost each year by the use of illegal firearms. Just as the trafficking of drugs includes a variety of drugs, **arms trafficking** includes a variety of weapons and various components necessary for the operations of those weapons. In particular, the trafficking of arms includes not only firearms but also the trade of ammunition, which is necessary for the proper use of all firearms. Arms trafficking also includes arms components and parts, which account for approximately 5% of all arms seizures by governing authorities (United Nations Office on Drugs and Crime, 2020).

In this chapter, the terms *arms trafficking*, *weapons trafficking*, *gun trafficking*, and **firearms trafficking** will be used to discuss the illicit practices of the gun trade by TOC groups. One unique aspect to the trade of weapons, as compared to the illicit trade of drugs or exotic meat, is the fact that weapons are not consumable. Specifically, firearms are durable goods that can exist for decades once introduced to society for use (United Nations Office on Drugs and Crime, 2020). Therefore, given the longevity trafficked weapons, their impact on society may have longer consequences than other consumable products.

The Stockholm International Peace Research Institute (SIPRI) estimates that the total value of the global arms trade is nearly $100 billion annually, with the United States, Russia, France, China, and Germany accounting for the majority of the arms exported (Wezeman et al., 2022). Demand for weapons is dependent upon violence within an area as well as hot spots of conflict within countries (Kartha, 2000). Research suggests that in addition to the violence and profits, the trafficking of weapons is often a major concern for many global citizens (Doody et al., 2021). The United States is by far the world's biggest exporter of arms, and Saudi Arabia receives over 20% of the U.S. exports (Amnesty International, 2019). Unfortunately, the volume of international arms transfers has grown steadily since 2003 to reach its highest level since the end of the Cold War. The largest arms importers, in addition to Saudi Arabia, are India, Egypt, Australia, and Algeria (Amnesty International, 2019). In addition, the movement of guns into Pakistan, Russia, and China facilitates ethnic and criminal conflicts and military conflicts in Kyrgyzstan and Tajikistan (Kartha, 2000). As illustrated in the 2021 case here, these illicit trades often involve multiple weapons, multiple traffickers, and multiple locations.

> In April of 2021, police in South America arrested nearly 4,000 suspects and confiscated some 200,000 illicit firearms, ammunition, explosives, and components in a massive operation targeting arms trafficking (Pineda, 2021). This international operation, which included authorities from 13 countries, also seized more than 21 tons of cocaine, marijuana, and other chemicals.

Arms trafficking, which includes the import, export, acquisition, sale, movement, and transfer of firearms, their components, and ammunition, affects all societies across the globe (May, 2017). In Middle Eastern countries such as Afghanistan, weapons are often trafficked from European countries such as Ukraine, Albania, and Bulgaria (Kartha, 2000).

Arms trafficking and its involvement by TOC groups affects everyone, as there is no country on earth without issues related to gun violence or the illegal sale of guns. Like the majority of TOC activities, arms trafficking has a destabilizing effect on all countries involved. In fact, it is suggested that weapons trafficking is not simply a rational choice by TOC group members but that the decision to trade illicit arms is also linked with the intimacy of one's own personal network with TOC groups as well as their perceptions of risk (Arsovska & Kostakos, 2008). Today, it is acknowledged that narcoterrorism, which usually refers to the link between drug trafficking and terrorism, now recognizes the role of weapons trafficking as related to violence (Chouvy, 2004). In particular, terrorist groups are often dependent upon illicit arms in support of their violent actions. Arms trafficking is often associated with the exercise of power by a TOC group within a region (Arsovska & Kostakos, 2008).

Research suggests that arms trafficking provides significant profits to members of TOC groups and that the illicit trade of arms accounts for at least 10% of the arms market as a whole (Arsovska, 2014). Unfortunately, the distinction between legal trade in arms and illegal trade in arms is not always clear, as laws regulating the legal trade vary by state or country and enforcement is limited. Specifically, with firearms provided from three different market types, their supply is abundant and regulation of their distribution are limited. In particular, firearms are provided through legal, illicit, and illegal markets (United Nations Office on Drugs and Crime, 2019). The legal or regulated transfer market is regulated through state and international laws. The illicit grey-market transfers include the transfers of firearms made by government-circumventing police as well as transfers of unregistered firearms such as antiques and souvenirs that may have been utilized in historical battles and are still capable of live fire (United Nations Office on Drugs and Crime, 2019). These antique guns help to support the demand for ammunition within the firearms trade. In fact, this market is utilized often, as many armed conflicts are supported by external powers that supply weapons and ammunition to fighters (Suchanek & Zubrzycki, 2013). Lastly, the illegal black-market transfers include firearms that are purchased illegally or are trafficked into extremist groups with the intent of commit violence.

> In November of 2021, police in Israel arrested 65 suspects from various countries involved in arms trafficking (Breiner, 2021). The arrest included a seizure of over 60 weapons that included M16 rifles, guns, an antitank missile, a machine gun, and explosives.

As illustrated in the 2021 account above, the trafficking of arms includes a variety of weapons. Of course, licensed firearms dealers play a significant role in fostering illicit trafficking (NABIS, 2018). In addition, the use of straw purchasers, someone who purchases a handgun for a person who is not eligible for ownership, is also common (Schroeder, 2013). Lastly, brokers, who are often linked with the TOC group, bring together all relevant parties to facilitate the transactions

Broker—A person who arranges transactions between a buyer and a seller for a fee.

Straw purchaser—An individual who purchases a handgun for another individual who, because of legal requirements, is not eligible for gun ownership.

in the illicit trade of arms (United Nations Office on Drugs and Crime, 2018). Hence, these criminal activities result in violence, threats to public safety, and economic instabilities that threaten developing countries. Sources of these illicit firearms include illicit manufacturers, theft, diversion, and the recycling or reactivation of older guns (Schroeder, 2013).

Firearms are often manufactured or trafficked illicitly. The factors that facilitate the illicit trafficking of firearms include existing demand, existing supply, and expertise (such as private military contractors or mercenaries who use such weapons) (Griffiths & Wilkinson, 2007). For clarity, *illicit manufacturing* refers to the manufacture or assembly of firearms, their parts and components, or ammunition from parts and components that are trafficked illegally—that is, without a license or authorization from a competent authority of the state party where the manufacture or assembly takes place (United Nations Office on Drugs and Crime, 2019). *Illicit trafficking* refers to the import, export, acquisition, sale, delivery, movement, or transfer of firearms, their parts and components, and ammunition from or across the territory of one state party to that of another country (United Nations Office on Drugs and Crime, 2019).

In most cases, firearms are manufactured for legal markets by licensed manufactures but may be diverted into illegal markets at any point in their life cycle (United Nations Office on Drugs and Crime, 2020). It is these points of diversion that cause concern for regulating authorities and provide members of TOC groups the avenues to serve in the capacity for theft of a newly manufactured weapon, the theft of the weapon during transport to a legitimate or licensed dealer, or the position for acquiring the weapon from corrupt officials once the weapon has been confiscated.

Distinguishing these actions of illicit manufacturing and licit manufacturing is based upon the legislative measures taken by states and the international community. Differences in regulation among parties result in vulnerabilities in legal venue, and TOC groups view this vulnerability as an opportunity for profit. In addition, many TOC groups involved in the trafficking of arms avoid detection due to the lack of legal consistencies and lack of cooperation between nations. Because the infusion of specific weapons is usually based upon demand (Kartha, 2000), and because there are a variety of modes for supply of these weapons, TOC groups seize upon the opportunity to provide arms for profit.

Arms trafficking includes the movement of a variety of weapons most commonly identified as firearms. It seems natural for members of TOC groups to be involved in the trafficking of firearms (Abadinsky, 2017). Since TOC groups already have routes established for trafficking other products, and since the use of firearms by TOC members is common, the illicit trade of arms requires little additional effort and produces exceedingly increasing profits. These firearms are generally classified as either small arms or light weapons. **Small arms**, which are the subject of much of the research on gun trafficking, include revolvers and self-loading pistols, rifles, submachine guns, assault rifles, and light machine guns (Greene, 2000). Small arms are designed to be used by one person for personal use such as for hunting or self-protection. The most commonly seized type of firearm across the globe is the **pistol** (United Nations Office on Drugs and Crime, 2020), also classified as a small arm.

Light weapons include heavy machine guns, handheld grenade launchers, portable antiaircraft or antitank guns, and portable launchers, which are designed for use by several persons in combative actions (Greene, 2000). As illustrated in the 2022 case here, the smuggling of weapons can involve hundreds of guns. In this chapter, firearms trafficking or arms trafficking includes the supply of illegal small arms, light weapons, weapons components, and **ammunition.** Estimates suggest that over one million small arms and light weapons are trafficked annually by TOC groups (United Nations Office on Drugs and Crime, 2018).

> In April of 2022, individuals within the United States were indicted for illegally selling guns from southern states to people in a northern state. Specifically, these 14 individuals face gun-trafficking charges and conspiracy charges in connection with nearly 400 firearms purchased in Georgia and South Carolina and brought to Philadelphia (Fox 29 Staff, 2022).

Globally, 50% of all homicides are committed with the use of a firearm (United Nations Office on Drugs and Crime, 2020). Research suggests that there are more than one billion firearms in the world and that the vast majority of these weapons are in the hands of ordinary citizens (Amnesty International, 2019). In addition, there are about 21 firearms for every 100 residents in the United States, 53 in Yemen, 39 in Montenegro and Serbia, and 35 in Canada and Uruguay (United Nations Office on Drugs and Crime, 2019). On an annual basis, over 500,000 firearms are seized by law enforcement and regulating authorities across the globe (United Nations Office on Drugs and Crime, 2020). Lastly, covert operations by government militaries often utilize the illicit trade (Kartha, 2000). It is suggested that within 50 years, the production of military assault rifles, carbines, pistols, and light and heavy machine guns will exceed 36 million units (Amnesty International, 2019).

A History of Arms Trafficking

The history of weapons trafficking dates back to the beginning of the manufacture of weapons. The trade of firearms, the products most associated with arms trafficking, dates back to the beginning of civilizations and the wars that helped to establish those civilizations (Cooper, 2018). Research suggests that in the 1500s, European traders were trafficking firearms into Africa, the Americas, and Asia (Grant, 2015). In these cases, these exchanges were often to gain favor or to gain territory. Hence, the last six centuries of arms trafficking is inherent to today's current societal conditions—and where the demand exists, the product is supplied.

Research suggests that the industrialization of nations in the 1800s led to a dramatic expansion in manufacturing of firearms and in the distribution and exchange of these firearms. The end of World War II in the 1940s resulted in thousands of former military-designed weapons being available on the common market (Grant, 2015). The illegal possession of firearms and ammunition continues to be a concern in postconflict zones (Suchanek & Zubrzycki, 2013). The demand for this supply of weapons continues today in countries with military conflicts and high levels of violence, and with citizens wishing to express their desire to "bear arms." In fact, today's rise of fundamentalist groups has resulted in an increase in the demand for weapons (Kartha, 2000). It has also been suggested by many globally based agencies that governments in nonconflicted countries may encourage security firms to supply arms and ammunition to the legal forces of another government (Schabas, 2004). Unless a country is embargoed or sanctioned, arms trading between nations is a largely private affair with little in the way of checks and balances (Sharife, 2021). Generally, arms trafficking at the government level proceeds as follows: (1) an importing government typically advertises, tenders, or privately solicits suppliers; (2) the exporting government then authorizes the international sale of weapons, as well as services and technological systems, to the importing party; and, (3) the weapons are manufactured and sold by private companies or government-owned or controlled entities (Sharife, 2021). A described in the case below, these countries include the United States. TOC groups are aware of this global demand for firearms, and they often direct and/or facilitate the exchange of such weapons in situations commonly referred to as arms trafficking.

INTERNATIONAL COURT OF JUSTICE (1986)

Nicaragua v. United States of America was a 1986 case in which the International Court of Justice (ICJ) concluded that the United States had violated international law by supporting the Contras (the armed opposition to the government of Nicaragua) and their rebellion against the Sandinistas (a socialist political party that controlled the government of Nicaragua). The case was decided in favor of the country of Nicaragua and against the United States. Specifically, the ICJ ruled that the United States was "in breach of its obligations under customary international law not to use force against another State," "not to intervene in its affairs," "not to violate its sovereignty," "not to interrupt peaceful maritime commerce," and "in breach of its obligations under Article XIX of the Treaty of Friendship, Commerce and Navigation between the Parties signed at Managua on 21 January 1956." In addition, the ICJ stated that the United States had encouraged human rights violations by the Contras.

As displayed in the table below, there are many guns in the hands of civilians across the globe. Most illegal firearms are seized within a country's borders (United Nations Office on Drugs and Crime, 2020). However, those weapons seized upon entering a territory are seized at land boundaries or in airports (May, 2017). TOC groups are also utilizing mail centers and various techniques for concealing their products and their identities. For example, TOC groups utilizing mail services will often use fictitious or intermediary addresses and employ fake invoice schemes, such as misidentifying the arms as objects of similar shape (May, 2017). In addition, since firearms trafficking is rarely a focus for policing efforts, many TOC groups engage in the criminal action, as they are less likely to fail. Specifically, in the United States, biker groups, which historically were involved in drugs and prostitution, have shifted their focus to arms trafficking (Piano, 2018).

International Court of Justice (ICJ)—Also known as the **World Court**, one of the six principal organs of the United Nations, with the responsibility of setting disputes between countries.

These organizations, with ample storage space for guns and ammunition (Thachuk & Saunders, 2014) and connections already established for the smuggling of illicit products, are rarely detected. In many cases, countries involved in the legal trade of arms are involved in the illicit trade as well, with many of their citizens (as displayed below) owning firearms.

COUNTRIES WITH THE MOST FIREARMS IN CIVILIAN HANDS DURING 2017	
Country	**Total Firearms**
United States	393,300,000
India	71,100,000
China	49,700,000
Pakistan	43,900,000
Russia	17,600,000
Mexico	16,800,000
Germany	15,800,000
Yemen	14,900,000
Saudi Arabia	5,500,000

Source: Small Arms Survey, 2020

Today's research on arms trafficking suggests that the top clients are in the Middle East and Saudi Arabia-Yemen (Amnesty International, 2019). As displayed below, some countries are common clients. In addition, many of these countries work together in the arms trade. In particular, in India weapons are generally trafficked from Pakistan, and Nepal is often the transit point for weapons en route to the Middle

TOP COUNTRIES (AND CLIENTS) FOR ARMS TRAFFICKING BY SOURCE COUNTRY
United States: Saudi Arabia (22% of total exports), Australia (7.7%), UAE (6.7%)
Russia: India (27%), China (14%), Algeria (14%)
France: Egypt (28%), India (9.8%), Saudi Arabia (7.4%)
Germany: South Korea (19%), Greece (10%), Israel (8.3%)
China: Pakistan (37%), Bangladesh (16%), Algeria (11%)

(Amnesty International, 2019)

East (Kartha, 2000). In addition, arms trafficking includes (this is often not acknowledged) the trafficking of grenades and other forms of explosives, which are also in demand in countries seeking illicit trades.

Common Items for Weapons Trafficking

Given the less-often-regulated trade of firearms and the privatization of gun sales that often exist across regions, the value of the legal arms trade is likely underestimated, and likewise the profits from the illegal arms trade are undervalued (May, 2017). In the United States and in other developed countries, TOC group members involved in firearms trafficking opt for handguns rather than rifles (Arnett & Reidy, 2014). Of those handguns, the majority are semiautomatic pistols, which are easily trafficked as they are easily concealed and transported, thus providing a lucrative business for TOC groups (Interpol, 2022). However, the **AK-47**, a type of assault rifle that is easily produced, is one of the most universally popular weapons, particularly in conflict zones (Arsovska, 2014).

Destination countries for trafficked weapons depend upon the type of weapon. Specifically, regions in Africa and Asia generally prefer shotguns, while regions in Oceania and Europe prefer shotguns, rifles, and pistols (United Nations Office on Drugs and Crime, 2020). As suggested by conflict-area research, terrorist organization often select AK-47s, sniper rifles, and Belgian-made pistols called "cop killers," as their ammunition can pierce a bulletproof vest (Andru & Esposito, 2008). The price of an AK-47 varies by country of source and destination but may cost $2,000 per firearm. For child soldiers, as reported here, explosives are common weapons.

> Throughout history, child soldiers have been used in armed conflicts across the globe. Many of these children, trafficked and forced into military duty, are not only victims of their traffickers but also victims of the conflicts (McCabe, 2008). It is suggested that thousands of children are forced into soldier roles every year and that some of these children are as young as six (Hubbard, 2021). Many of them are used in association with explosive devices. Research suggests that child labor is used for fighting and to create explosive devices (McCabe, 2008). In addition, and relevant to this chapter, the illicit trade of explosives directly affects these children, as they are also used as suicide bombers; improvised explosive devices (IEDs) are the most well-documented explosive weapon used by child soldiers (Hubbard, 2021).

Many determinants affect a weapon's price, some of them related to the market environment and others related to the type of weapon. In addition to the condition of the weapon and market demand for it, there are other factors that are related to the price of the weapon (Schroeder & Lamb, 2006). In some regions, such as Latin America, illicit weapons are often less expensive than licit weapons (United Nations Office on Drugs and Crime, 2020).

First, political instability is one of the strongest drivers of both sales volume and price: the greater the level of conflict, the higher the price of the weapon (Schroeder & Lamb, 2006). In addition, the price of a weapon generally increases the further it is smuggled, and these costs are reflected in the price. Also, countries with high levels of drug trafficking tend to have high levels of arms trafficking (United Nations Office on Drugs and Crime, 2020). Lastly, the risk of detection/interdiction ordinarily increases according to the distance the weapon must travel to market, particularly when crossing borders; this is also reflected in the price of the weapon (Schroeder & Lamb, 2006).

The life cycle of a weapon begins with its production and continues with its sale or trade, then its use, possible trade, or resale. Its life cycle ends with either destruction or deactivation (European Commission, 2020). A weapon can be used for many years. For clarity, a firearm is deactivated by several means, including plugging the barrel, removing the firing pin or bolt from the chamber, or eliminating the type of ammunition it uses. Members of TOC groups are aware of the various ways to reactivate a weapon, as well as the modes to reverse the deactivation to provide a renewed and workable weapon.

> In January of 2022, six men were indicted on federal charges for allegedly being part of an organized crime group with plans to smuggle weapons and ammunition from the United States to a violent Mexican cartel (Von Quednow, 2022).

Finally, as illustrated in the case here, the market for ammunition is also profitable for members of TOC groups engaged in arms trafficking. In the case of antique weapons or retired weapons, oftentimes they are still usable if they have the proper ammunition. In these cases, TOC groups arrange for the manufacturing and distribution of the "retired" ammunition for these historic battle guns, and they provide these products through illicit trades.

As illustrated below, the demand may not be for the weapon itself but rather for the ammunition required for the weapon. Most recently, the market for ammunition has led to increases in demand and increases in price. In some cases, this illicit trade produces three times the profit for the legal trade, with TOC groups providing the much-needed ammunition (Suciu, 2021).

AMMUNITION IN DEMAND (TOP FIVE)

Rank	Caliber	Weapon of Use
1	9 mm (9 × 19)	Handgun
2	30-30	Rifle
3	.388	Rifle
4	.40	Handgun
5	.233	AR-15

Source: Suciu, 2021

The same holds true for ammunition that is in short supply, such as bullets for 38-caliber pistols in the United States. The ammunition is rare, yet it is available through TOC groups and the black market.

> Antique guns are being used more and more often in violent crimes in the United Kingdom due to a lack of control around the sale, transfer, and ownership of firearms made before 1939 (Williamson, 2018). In the United Kingdom, antique weapons are exempt from the 1968 Firearms Act, as banning them would supposedly make it impossible to find suitable ammunition for them. TOC groups, with members able to modify and reactivate these firearms, are profiting from the trafficking. In addition, the ammunition, which is not easily available, can be modified relatively easily by milling down the length of the casing, or rim, of available ammunition. TOC are aware of these procedures, and thus are profiting from the sale of the ammunition as well as the firearms (Williamson, 2018).

Sources of Illicit Firearms

Illicit firearms exist throughout the world, and although most firearms violence involves members of conflicting TOC groups (Longmire & Longmire, 2008), gun violence is still a concern across the globe. In addition, terrorist groups around the world require arms (Abadinsky, 2017). The guns involved in these violent actions are made by either legitimate manufacturers or illegitimate manufacturers, as is the case of "ghost guns." These **ghost guns** may be produced on 3D printers (Coble, 2015). Similar to the theft of art and antiquities, the dynamics of arms trafficking have been distorted by popular culture to suggest that the trade is made up of large-scale transactions (May, 2017). Of course, some large-scale transactions or **gunrunning** operations do take place; however, they are only one conduit through which arms are trafficked (May, 2017).

Ghost gun—A gun that is privately made without serial numbers or identifying marks (Winton, 2022).

Gunrunning—Another phrase to describe arms trafficking, often associated with TOC groups.

Specifically, arms dealers often cater to governments as well as rebel groups, while providing anonymity and protection between buyers and sellers (May, 2017). In many cases, members of TOC groups use their global financial systems to mask their involvement in the actions, which helps to facilitate the sales. In particular, much of the arms trafficking is accomplished through numerous small-scale transfers, often referred to as the **"ant trade"**—in other words, by individuals who are loosely affiliated with the criminal network (May, 2017). Hence, there is no one model, or even several models, employed by members of TOC groups involved in the illicit weapons trade.

In April of 2022, seven men were arrested and charged with multiple federal firearms- and drug-related offenses as part of a federal investigation that recovered seven automatic weapons and many ghost guns (Winton, 2022). Through this operation more than 30 firearms, including several fully automatic guns that were not legally owned, were recovered.

Ant trade—The use of individuals loosely connected with a TOC group to purchase guns for the illicit arms trade.

Lastly, one cannot dismiss the role of technology in the sourcing of illicit weapons. Specifically, black markets and other online platforms facilitate the identification of customers and the sale of weapons. In addition, the manufacturing technology of **3D printers** cannot be ignored. These printers are capable of producing items from clay, plastic, and metal—including handguns, gun magazines, and other arms components (Europol, 2017).

Through the use of 3D printers, weapons that generally require days to manufacture can now be produced within hours (Europol, 2017). This technology can be used to provide criminal groups and extremists with lighter-weight weapons on demand (Saunders, 2017). A 3D printer works by creating a three-dimensional solid object from a digital file. Once an object is scanned or the manufacturing plans for the objects are loaded onto the software, a graphic model of the object is printed in a layered approach that produced a physical three-dimensional duplicate of the original object, in the materials (often plastic) provided. Through this process, a 3D printer can essentially build a weapons system (Saunders, 2017). These weapons can include handguns, grenade launchers, and thermonuclear bombs (Coble, 2015). As reported below, many of these newly created products act in the same manner as the original weapon.

3D printer—Hardware utilized to create three-dimensional solid objects from digital files (Saunders, 2017).

In March of 2017, the U.S. Army successfully tested the outcome results of a 3D-printed grenade launcher and 3D-printed grenades

(Saunders, 2017). Both the weapons test and the ammunition tests were successful.

In many cases, supplying arms is relatively easy for those members of TOC groups who seek to profit from the illicit arms trade. From source countries, to manufacturers, to reproduction through 3D printers, the products in demand are easily supplied to consumers.

Factors Facilitating Arms Trafficking

The problem of arms trafficking is multidimensional as weapons are manufactured both legally and illegally. In addition, some legally manufactured guns are diverted to illicit markets (United Nations Office on Drugs and Crime, 2018). These illicit markets and the criminal actions of TOC groups within these markets only increase the profits and power of members of TOC groups. Just as in the case for drug trafficking, weapons trafficking through online sales and purchases has grown with the development and spread of the internet. Encrypted networks are increasingly being used to trade firearms (United Nations Office on Drugs and Crime, 2018). Weapons that are illegally sold to individuals are often difficult to detect some are ghost guns and some are sold as components, which are frequently disassembled and mailed separately (May, 2017). In addition, the use of the dark web further hides these criminal activities.

> Research by the U.S. Department of Justice suggests that 43% of criminals purchase their firearms on the black market, 6% get their guns through theft, and 10% acquire them through a legitimate retail purchase; lastly, 11% of criminals acquire their guns through a straw purchase (McKay, 2020).

Specifically, individuals in the United States who are involved in weapons trafficking will purchase arms from online dealers or classified ads, have them delivered to an intermediary address, then repackage the weapons and illegally export them via post (May, 2017). Of course, this scenario is not unique to the United States, as research suggests that weapons were obtained in a similar manner to support the November 2015 attacks in Paris and the July 2016 shooting at the Olympia shopping center in Munich (May, 2017).

As with any product, demand dictates price. In addition, central locations such as the United States or the United Kingdom are often critical for accessibility and for supporting the trade (Thachuk & Saunders, 2014). As related to illegal firearms, demand includes high levels of crime or violence in an area, large-scale armed conflicts within an area, weak security forces, citizens' lack of trust in their state's ability to maintain their safety, and an absence of the rule of law (Saferworld, 2012). In addition, gang culture, civil conflict, and terrorist radicalization accelerate the demand for firearms, and TOC groups are quite familiar with these demands (Saferworld, 2012). In most cases, large-scale trafficking is associated with supplies to groups involved in armed conflicts or shipments to embargoed or banned destinations (United Nations Office on Drugs and Crime, 2015).

Addressing Arms Trafficking

Many countries have attempted to address the trade of illicit weapons; however, their efforts are successful in only some cases, as TOC groups involved in the trade know of the legislative and enforcement efforts and often utilize the vulnerabilities in these areas as opportunities. For example, the **1968 Firearms Act** in the United Kingdom banned the ownership of all guns, except for certain hunting rifles and antique weapons (Elkin, 2020). TOC groups, well aware of the ban, continue to provide weapons on the black market and have now increased their offerings to include the illicit trade of antique ammunition. The result is a continued increase in the use of handguns—a 5% increase in criminal violence from 2018 to 2019 alone (Elkin, 2020). In addition, international cooperative efforts continue, with groups such as Interpol and Europol as well as cross-national efforts. As reported below, some of these efforts target specific regions.

In April of 2022, the U.S. Navy reported the establishment of a task force to address arms trafficking in the waters around Yemen (Arab Weekly, 2022). This task force will target the waters between Somalia, Djibouti, and Yemen, which are well-known trafficking routes for weapons.

Unfortunately, the violence associated with drug trafficking often involves weapons obtained through the illicit weapons trade (Longmire & Longmire, 2008). Strategies to reduce the illicit arms trade have largely focused on drug trafficking and human trafficking, with arms trafficking noted as an existing condition of the TOC group; however, as demonstrated in the report above, governments are beginning to address arms trafficking on its own.

At this point, criminal justice systems' focus on firearms trafficking applies to only a small percentage of trafficking cases

(United Nations Office on Drugs and Crime, 2020). These efforts often fail to address the cause and effect of current TOC activities and TOC's propensity to enter the illicit arms trade (Galindo, 2018). In fact, although the United States, Russia, France, Germany, and China are recognized as the five largest source countries for unauthorized arms, and Saudi Arabia, India, Egypt, Australia, and Algeria are identified as the most common countries of destination (Amnesty International, 2019), research on the factors that facilitate arms trafficking is limited. In addition, without the exchange of currency, which sometimes does not exist in the illicit trade, financial institutions are unable to assist in the detection of such activities. Specifically, research suggests that firearms may be exchanged for drugs, for people, or for other products such as blood diamonds (Schabas, 2004).

In the United States, the **Bureau of Alcohol, Tobacco, Firearms and Explosives (ATF)** is the law enforcement agency most involved in fighting arms trafficking. Another attempt to address the trafficking of weapons, the **Arms Trade Treaty**, or ATT, is an international treaty signed in 2014 that regulates the international trade in conventional arms and seeks to prevent and eradicate illicit trade and diversion of conventional arms by establishing international standards to govern arms transfers (Arms Trade Treaty, 2022). The global ATT seeks to stop the international transfer of weapons, ammunition, and related items when those items are known to have been used to commit or facilitate genocide, crimes against humanity, or war crimes (Amnesty International, 2019). Unfortunately, existing arms regulation under the ATT suffers from serious limitations related to responsibility, jurisdiction, and defense (Hamilton, 2021).

Bureau of Alcohol, Tobacco, Firearms and Explosives (ATF)—U.S. law enforcement agency, founded in 1961, that seeks to protect communities from violent criminals, criminal organizations, the illegal use and trafficking of firearms, the illegal use and storage of explosives, acts of arson and bombings, acts of terrorism, and the illegal diversion of alcohol and tobacco products (Bureau of Alcohol, Tobacco, Firearms and Explosives, 2022).

Specifically, since the legal basis for the treaty was related to protection, one must consider (1) the responsibility of individual executives for a corporation's decision to carry out an arms export, (2) the challenges to the jurisdictional boundaries where arms regulations may differ, and (3) the potential relevant defenses for such actions, such as to address conflict (Hamilton, 2021). However, despite their commitment to regulating irresponsible arms trade, many key states and parties continue to sell arms to governments that commit serious human rights abuses. Oftentimes, nations are associated with arms trafficking by TOC groups and arms dealers.

VIKTOR BOUT

The Russian entrepreneur Viktor Bout (born in 1967), who has been called the world's biggest arms trafficker, is known for delivering all types of cargo, but especially illicit weapons. His client list for arms includes the leader of the Northern Alliance in Afghanistan, the government of Angola, the despotic ruler of Zaire, the Revolutionary Armed Forces of Colombia (FARC), and a Libyan. His business has included hundreds of trips for the UN and other humanitarian organizations. He has worked with multiple Western governments, including the United Kingdom and the United States. The U.S. Pentagon and its contractors have paid him millions of dollars to support postwar reconstruction efforts (Sharife, 2021).

Unfortunately, most methods of trafficking firearms evolve continuously and adapt very quickly to law enforcement response (United Nations Office on Drugs and Crime, 2019). The use of the internet has opened a new dimension in matching demand with supply as the darknet has increased opportunities for TOC groups to engage in illegal online trade of firearms and to adopt a crime-as-a-service (CaaS) model as a key distribution channel (Europol, 2014). Specifically, the CaaS model involves criminals developing advanced tools and then offering the tools for sale (Europol). With firearms, this entails providing guidelines on the manufacture of firearms through assembly of parts, or through distribution of blueprints for printing 3D firearms. It includes instructions on how to convert signal or gas pistols (also known as flare guns), as well as offering functioning firearms, components, and ammunition. This model has a powerful effect on firearms trafficking, because it lowers the bar for inexperienced actors to gain access to information on manufacturing firearms and purchasing illicit firearms.

The online trade of firearms takes place at specific marketplaces that have a regional language platform; therefore, the illegal trade of firearms—as well as discussions on the methods for purchasing and selling firearms, parts, components, and ammunition, along with the size, scope, and value of the illegal trade, the main shipping routes, and the most common shipping techniques—may occur without detection by law enforcement (Paoli et al., 2017). Compared to other forms of firearms trafficking, estimates on the scale of trafficking online are limited (Paoli, 2018).

Summary

The trafficking of weapons is a criminal activity long associated with the actions of TOC groups. These guns, gun components, ammunition, and other weapons continue to be in great demand by paramilitary forces, those involved in criminal activities, terrorists—and ordinary citizens. For many of these individuals, it is easier to obtain a weapon illegally than legally.

TOC groups are aware of the demand for these products, and the groups often use the opportunity to supply these products to further their profits and other criminal actions. The rare focus on arms trafficking by law enforcement and other regulating authorities only fuels the problem and increases the profits for TOC groups.

Recently, TOC groups have begun using technology and mail delivery services to support their criminal trade. In particular, through no-contact online requests, members of TOC groups are able to identify customers and deliver products to them with little risk. Legislative efforts to reduce arms trafficking, although in place at national and international levels, receive little financial support for enforcement; arms trafficking is rarely acknowledged as a priority unless it has a direct association with another form of criminal activity, such as drug trafficking. In addition, cross-border efforts are only as strong as their weakest laws. In the end, weapons trafficking supports violent conflicts across the globe, weakens democracies and the rule of law, and increases the overall rate of homicides by firearms. For these reasons, weapons trafficking is considered to be among the most notorious forms of trafficking (Wagner et al., 2019). This problem continues despite national action from governments or international agreements such as the Arms Trade Treaty. Specifically, global arms trading is still on the rise (Amnesty International, 2019).

Questions for Further Thought

1. What are the markets that facilitate weapons trafficking?
2. How do legal trades in weapons facilitate the illicit trade of weapons, particularly small arms?
3. How have TOC groups seized upon opportunities in the current culture to engage in the criminal activity of weapons trafficking?

References

Abadinsky, H. (2017). *Organized crime* (11th ed). Cengage Group.

Amnesty International. (2019). *Killer facts 2019: The scale of the global arms trade.* Retrieved April 3, 2022, from https://www.amnesty.org/en/latest/news/2019/08/killer-facts-2019-the-scale-of-the-global-arms-trade/

Andru, R., & Esposito, M. (2008). *Get Lost.* Hermes. Hermes Press. (Originally published in 1954.)

Arab Weekly. (2022, April 14). *US sets up new Mideast naval task force to target Yemen smuggling.* Retrieved April 30, 2022, from https://thearabweekly.com/us-sets-new-mideast-naval-task-force-target-yemen-smuggling

Arms Trade Treaty. (2022). *Arms trade treaty.* Retrieved April 20, 2022, from https://thearmstradetreaty.org/

Arnett, G., & Reidy, T. (2014, June 25). US gun traffickers opt for handguns rather than rifles. *The Guardian.* Retrieved April 3, 2022, from https://www.theguardian.com/news/datablog/2014/jun/25/us-gun-traffickers-handguns-rifles

Arsovska, J. (2014). Introduction: Illicit Firearms market in Europe and beyond. *European Journal on Criminal Policy and Research, 20*(3), 295–305.

Arsovska, J., & Kostakos, P. (2008). Illicit arms trafficking and the limits of rational choice theory: The case of the Balkans. *Trends in Organized Crime, 11*(4), 352–378. https://doi.org/10.1007/s12117-008-9052-y

Breiner, J. (2021, November 9). *Israel police arrest 65 suspects in biggest ever weapons bust in Arab community.* Haaretz.com. Retrieved March 30, 2022, from https://www.haaretz.com/israel-news/.premium-israel-police-arrests-65-suspects-in-biggest-ever-arms-trafficking-operation-in-the-1.10366995

Bureau of Alcohol, Tobacco, Firearms and Explosives. (2022). *About the Bureau of Alcohol, Tobacco, Firearms and Explosives.* U.S. Department of Justice. Retrieved March 3, 2022, from https://www.atf.gov/

Chouvy, P. (2004). Narco-terrorism in Afghanistan. *Terrorism Monitor, 2*(6), 305–324.

Coble, C. (2015, October 8). *Three things that are illegal to 3D print.* FindLaw. Retrieved May 6, 2022, from http://www.findlaw.com/legalblogs/law-and-life/3-things-that-are-illegal-to-3d-print/

Cooper, N. (2018). Race, sovereignty, and free trade: Arms trade regulations and humanitarian arms control in the age of the empire. *Journal of Global Studies, 3*, 444–462.

Cragin, K., & Hoffman, B. (2003). *Arms trafficking and Colombia.* RAND Corporation. National Defense Research Institute.

Doody, J., Reid, J., Bilali, K., Diaz, J., & Mattheus, N. (2021). In the post Covid-19 era, is the illegal wildlife trade the most serious form of trafficking? *Crime Science, 10*(19), 1–12.

Elkin, M. (2020, February 13). *Offenders involved in the use of firearms: Year ending March 2019.* UK Office of National Statistics.

European Commission. (2020, July 27). *Communication from the commission to the European Parliament, the Council, the European Economic and Social Committee, and the Committee of the Regions.* Retrieved April 3, 2022, from https://ec.europa.eu/home-affairs/system/files/2020-07/20200724_com-2020-608-commission-communication_en.pdf

Europol. (2014). *The internet organized crime threat assessment. Chapter 3: Crime areas.* Retrieved April 20, 2022, from https://www.europol.europa.eu/iocta/2014/chap-3-1-view1.html

Europol. (2017). *IOCTA 2017 internet organised threat assessment.* Retrieved April 20, 2022, from https://www.europol.europa.eu/cms/sites/default/files/documents/iocta2017.pdf

Fox 29 Staff. (2022, April 11). *Iron pipeline: 14 charged for allegedly trafficking nearly 400 guns to the Philadelphia area from south.* Fox 29 Philadelphia. Retrieved April 20, 2022, from https://www.fox29.com/news/officials-announce-charges-in-connection-with-illegal-trafficking-of-nearly-400-guns-to-the-philadelphia-area

Galindo, J. (2018). *An improved strategy to fight drug trafficking, organized crime, and corruption in the hemisphere.* Global Americans. Retrieved March 3, 2022, from https://theglobalamericans.org/reports/improved-strategy-fight-drug-trafficking-organized-crime-corruption-hemisphere/

Grant, J. (2015). The arms trafficking in world history. In G. Bruinsma (Ed.), *Histories of transnational crime.* Springer.

Greene, O. (2000). Examining international responses to illicit arms trafficking. *Crime, Law and Social Change, 33*(1), 151–190.

Griffiths, H., & Wilkinson, A. (2007). *Planes and ships: Identification and disruption of clandestine arms transfers.* SEESAC.

Hamilton, T. (2021, September 23). *An arms trade case at the International Criminal Court: Would the Article 25(3)(c) purpose requirement really matter?* Rethinking SLIC. Retrieved April 20, 2022, from https://rethinkingslic.org/blog/criminal-law/93-an-arms-trade-case-at-the-international-criminal-court-would-the-article-25-3-c-purpose-requirement-really-matter

Hubbard, V. (2021, April 6). *Explosive violence and child soldiers.* Relief Web. United Nations Office for the Coordination of Humanitarian Affairs. Retrieved April 3, 2022, from https://reliefweb.int/report/world/explosive-violence-and-child-soldiers#:~:text=IEDs%20are%20the%20most%20well,intercepted%20on%20suicide%20bomb%20missions

International Court of Justice. (1986). *Case concerning military and paramilitary activities in and against Nicaragua.* Retrieved April 10, 2022, from https://www.icj-cij.org/public/files/case-related/70/070-19860627-JUD-01-00-EN.pdf

Interpol. (2022). *Firearms trafficking.* Retrieved March 30, 2022, from https://www.interpol.int/en/Crimes/Firearms-trafficking

Interpol. (2017). *Illicit arms records and tracing management system.* Retrieved March 30, 2022, from https://www.interpol.int/en/Crimes/Firearms-trafficking/Illicit-Arms-Records-and-tracing-Management-System-iARMS

Kartha, T. (2000, May). Organized crime and the illegal market in weapons in Southern Asia. *Strategic Analysis, 24*(2). Retrieved May 20, 2022, from https://ciaotest.cc.columbia.edu/olj/sa/sa_may00kat01.html

Longmire, S., & Longmire, J. (2008). Redefining terrorism: Why Mexican drug trafficking is more than just organized crime. *Journal of Strategic Security, 1*(1), 35–52.

May, C. (2017, March). *Transnational crime and the developing world.* Global Financial Integrity. Retrieved February 20, 2022, from https://secureservercdn.

net/50.62.198.97/34n.8bd.myftpupload.com/wp-content/uploads/2017/03/Transnational_Crime-final.pdf

McCabe, K. (2008). *Human trafficking: National and international responses*. Peter Lang.

McKay, H. (2020, February 19). *Where do criminals really get their guns?* Fox-News.com. Retrieved March 5, 2022, from https://www.foxnews.com/us/where-do-criminals-get-guns

National Ballistics Intelligence Service (NABIS). (2018). Annual report. Accessed on August 19, 2022 at https://www.nabis.police.uk/SysSiteAssets/media/downloads/annual-reports/nabis-annual-report-2018.pdf

Paoli, G. (2018). *The trade in small arms and light weapons on the dark web*. UNODA Occasional papers, No. 32. UN Office for Disarmament Affairs.

Paoli, G., Aldridge, J., Ryan, N., & Warnes, R. (2017). *Behind the curtain: The illicit trade of firearms, explosives, and ammunition on the Dark Web*. RAND Corporation. https://www.rand.org/pubs/research_reports/RR2091.html.

Piano, E. (2018). Outlaws and economies: Biker gangs and club goods. *Rationality and Society, 30*(3), 350–376.

Pineda, J. (2021). South American authorities arrest thousands of arms trafficking suspects. Organized Crime and Corruption Reporting Project. Accessed on August 19, 2022 at https://www.occrp.org/en/daily/14184-south-american-authorities-arrest-thousands-of-arms-trafficking-suspects

Saferworld. (2012). *Small arms and light weapons control*. Retrieved March 30, 2022, from https://www.saferworld.org.uk/resources/publications/713-small-arms-and-light-weapons-control

Saunders, S. (2017, March 10). *US Army successfully tests 3D printed grenade launcher with 3D printed grenades*. Retrieved May 8, 2022, from https://3dprint.com/167567/3d-printed-grenade-launcher.

Schabas, W. (2004). A synergistic relationship: The Sierra Leone truth and reconciliation commission and the special court of Sierra Leone. In W. Schabas & S. Darcy (Eds.), *Truth Commission and Courts*. Springer.

Schroeder, M. (2013). Captured and counted: Illicit weapons in Mexico and the Philippines. In *Small Arms Survey 2013* (pp. 283–311). Cambridge University Press.

Schroeder, M., & Lamb, G. (2006). The illicit gun trade in Africa: A global enterprise. *African Analyst Quarterly, 1*(3), 69–78.

Sharife, K. (2021, October 4). *Investigating arms trafficking*. Global Investigative Journalism Network. Retrieved March 23, 2022, from https://gijn.org/2021/10/04/investigating-arms-trafficking/

Small Arms Survey. (2020). *Global firearms holding*. Retrieved March 3, 2022, from https://www.smallarmssurvey.org/database/global-firearms-holdings

Suchanek, P. and Zubrycki, W. (2013, July-December). Republic of Kosovo regulations on the marking of weapons, parts of weapons and ammunition from the perspective of international standards. *Internal Security, 5*(2), 51–62. U.S. Department of Justice, Office of Justice Programs.

Suciu, P. (2021). Ammo shortage: The five hardest to find common calibers. *The National Interest*. Retrieved May 8, 2022, from http://nationalinterest.org/blog/buzz/ammo-shortage-five-hardest-find-common-calibers-178822

Thachuk, K., & Saunders, K. (2014). Under the radar: Airborne arms trafficking operations in Africa. *European Journal on Crime Policy and Research, 20*(3), 350–376.

United Nations Office on Drugs and Crime. (2009). *Transnational organized crime. The globalized illegal economy.* Retrieved March 1, 2022, from https://www.unodc.org/toc/en/crimes/organized-crime.html

United Nations Office in Drugs and Crime. (2015). *Study on firearms, 2015.* Retrieved March 15, 2022, from https://www.unodc.org/unodc/en/firearms-protocol/firearms-study-2015-new.html

United Nations Office on Drugs and Crime. (2018). Module 3: Organized crime markets. Key issues: Firearms trafficking. *E4J University Module Series: Organized crime.* Retrieved April 3, 2022, from https://www.unodc.org/e4j/en/organized-crime/module-3/key-issues/firearms-trafficking.html

United Nations Office on Drugs and Crime. (2019). Module 4: The illicit market in firearms. *E4J University Module Series: Organized crime.* Retrieved March 30, 2022, from https://www.unodc.org/documents/e4j/Module_04_-_The_Illicit_Market_in_Firearms_FINAL.pdf

United Nations Office on Drugs and Crime. (2020, March). *Global study on firearms trafficking.* Retrieved April 3, 2022, from https://www.unodc.org/documents/data-and-analysis/Firearms/2020_REPORT_Global_Study_on_Firearms_Trafficking_2020_web.pdf

Wagner, K., Owen, S., & Burke, T. (2019). Not wild about wildlife protection? The perceived harmfulness, wrongfulness, and seriousness of wildlife crimes. *Society and Animals, 27*(4), 383–402.

Wezeman, P., Kuimova, A., & Wezeman, S. (2022, March). *Trends in international arms transfers, 2021.* Stockholm International Peace Research Institute.

Williamson, H. (2018, September 21). *Criminals are using antique weapons due to a loophole in UK law.* The Conversation. Retrieved March 3, 2022, from https://theconversation.com/criminals-are-using-antique-weapons-due-to-a-loophole-in-uk-law-102666

Winton, R. (2022, April 13). Seven men charged with gun trafficking in Inland Empire, "ghost guns" among 30 firearms seized. *LA Times.* Retrieved April 20, 2022, from https://www.latimes.com/california/story/2022-04-13/gun-trafficking-charges-inland-empire-ghost-guns-seized

Von Quednow, C. (2022, January 24). Six men accused of smuggling weapons, ammunition for violent Mexican cartel. *KTLA 75 News.* Retrieved April 3, 2022, from https://ktla.com/news/local-news/6-men-accused-of-smuggling-weapons-ammunition-for-violent-mexican-gang/

Human Trafficking

Key Terms

Cartel
Consent
Cybercommunity
Debt bondage
Forced labor
Gang
Human trafficking
Labor trafficking
Mail-order bride
Organ trafficking
People smuggling
Pornography
Prostitution
Push-pull theory of migration
Recruiter
Sex industry
Sex ring
Sex trafficking
Trafficker
Trafficking Victims Protection Act
Trafficking Victims Protection Reauthorization Act (TVPRA)
UN's Protocol to Prevent, Suppress and Punish Trafficking in Persons
Victim

CHAPTER OBJECTIVES

Chapter 7 will enable readers to understand the following:

- the definition of *human trafficking*
- the difference between human trafficking and human smuggling
- the role of transnational organized crime (TOC) in human trafficking
- the structure of TOC as related to human trafficking
- how country conditions may facilitate human trafficking
- U.S. efforts to address human trafficking
- international efforts to address human trafficking

OFTENTIMES, WHEN INDIVIDUALS think of organized crime or crimes across borders, the first criminal action that comes to mind is human trafficking. In fact, with current awareness efforts across the globe focused on human trafficking, it may be hard to find individuals who have not heard about human trafficking and its effect on its victims. This chapter is dedicated to discussion on human trafficking and the role of organized crime.

In August of 2020, 11 members of the gang MS-13 in Virginia and Maryland were arrested for the sex trafficking of a 13-year-old minor (U.S. Department of Justice, 2020). The victim, trafficked in exchange for cash and drugs, was a runaway from a youth home in northern Virginia.

Human trafficking is one of the most profitable aspects of TOC to date, with profits estimated to be over $150 billion annually (United Nations Office on Drugs and Crime, 2021). Every year, millions of men, women, and children are trafficked from source countries, through transit countries, and into destination countries for victimization and profits to traffickers (McCabe, 2008). As demonstrated in the August 2020 report above, estimates suggest that the majority of the victims of human trafficking are women and that approximately one half of the victims are under the age of 18 (in other words, children) (McCabe & Murphy, 2016). For many cases of human trafficking, the traffickers and the involvement of TOC go unnoticed, with most efforts to reduce the criminal activity aimed at prevention through awareness campaigns or through assistance to victims' services (McCabe, 2017). Traffickers, through TOC, utilize a variety of techniques to deliver their products (i.e., persons) to consumers. These techniques include in-person recruitment, victim-to-victim recruitment, the use of technology, and the identification of routes of travel. In particular, common travel routes from multiple countries into Europe and then into the United States by way of Canada have been identified (McCabe, 2008). Unfortunately, once law enforcement authorities identify these routes, TOC members simply adjust the lines of travel and the venues across borders to continue their enterprises. As a result, human trafficking, once viewed as a "less significant" component of profit for TOC, now follows only drug trafficking in terms of TOC involvement and profits (McCabe, 2017).

Human trafficking— A crime that involves the exploitation of a person for labor, services, or commercial sex (U.S. Department of Justice, 2021b).

Unfortunately, even though the phrase *human trafficking* is widely recognized from television dramas, documentaries, and movies, the clarity of its definition, the profile and recruitment of victims, the demographics and motivations for traffickers, and the dynamics behind human trafficking still often remain without clarity of action or conditions. Research suggests that today's influence of technology and the physical-distancing mandates of COVID-19 have only increased the problem of human trafficking, as traffickers may now capitalize on losses of income and increases in online time to lure victims and satisfy consumer demand (United Nations Office on Drugs and Crime, 2021).

In the United States and across the globe, individuals are victimized through the criminal action of human trafficking every day. In fact, in 2019, in the United States over 10,000 cases of human trafficking were reported to police (World Population Review, 2020), which research suggests is only a fraction of the cases actually occurring within the United States (McCabe & Manian, 2010). Internationally, current estimates include 25 million victims of human trafficking on an annual basis (Niethammer, 2020). These victims of human trafficking originate from a variety of countries and a variety of cultures, with factors such as poverty, gender inequality, and corruption often accompanying the victimization (McCabe, 2018). In many cases, victims of human trafficking are deceived, coerced, and abused—all for profits to their perpetrators or traffickers. This chapter recognizes human trafficking as a significant part of the criminal activities of TOC, reaching far beyond geographic boundaries and flourishing with the victimization of a seemingly endless supply of potential victims.

This chapter is organized to provide an overview of human trafficking; to discuss some of the causes, victims, and offenders of human trafficking; and to explain some of the reasons why human trafficking continues to thrive, with the role of TOC highlighted. In addition, the chapter discusses the common structures of TOC as related to human trafficking, introduces the role of technology in the trafficking of adults and children, and discusses international policing efforts and international laws to address human trafficking. In a nutshell, this chapter provides readers with clarity on the terms associated with human trafficking and, in particular, the issues surrounding sex trafficking, which is the most commonly discussed category of human trafficking related to TOC (McCabe & Manian, 2010).

The Business of Human Trafficking

There are many false notions regarding human trafficking. Historically, human trafficking has been referred to as *White slavery*; however, not all of the victims are White (McCabe, 2007). In addition, human trafficking is not a choice by the victim but rather a situation based upon force and coercion. Lastly, victims of human trafficking are not satisfied with their role in the criminal enterprise, and, as many are victimized on multiple occasions daily, victims rarely choose to protect their traffickers or continue participating in trafficking rings if identified by or through law enforcement efforts.

> Human Trafficking Victims: 66% Women (age 18+); 12% Men (age 18+); 13% Girls (under age 18); and 9% Boys (under age 18) (United Nations Office on Drugs and Crime, 2009).

The United Nations has defined *human trafficking* as follows: Human Trafficking is the recruitment, transportation, transfer, harboring or receipt of people through force, fraud or deception, with the aim of exploiting them for profit. The U.S. State Department's Trafficking Protection Act (2000), in an attempt to provide a consistent definition across countries, further identified severe forms of human trafficking: "(1) sex trafficking in which a commercial sex act is induced by force, fraud, or coercion, or in which the person induced to perform such an act has not attained 18 years of age; or (2) the recruitment, harboring, transportation, provision, or obtaining of a person for labor or services through the use of force, fraud, or coercion for the purpose of subjection to involuntary servitude, peonage, debt bondage, or slavery." Although neither definition of *human trafficking* includes the dynamic of TOC, the movement of individuals across boundaries for profit to satisfy a demand for product is the essence of TOC. *Human trafficking*, by definition, deprives its victims of the freedom of **consent** and control over their actions and locations and is often a significant part of TOC.

> Reasons for Human Trafficking: 79% Sexual Exploitation, 18% Labor Trafficking, 3% Other (United Nations Office on Drugs and Crime, 2009).

Perpetrators of human trafficking, who frequently come from a variety of backgrounds and demographics similar to their victims, are referred to as **traffickers**. Individuals are victims of human trafficking for a variety of reasons, including prostitution, domestic work, pornography, farm labor, and organ transplants; however, the two main reasons for human trafficking are sex and labor, and the most common form of human trafficking involving TOC is classified as sex trafficking. This chapter focuses on sex trafficking, although other aspects of human trafficking are discussed. For clarity, the structure of the trafficking routes through which individuals are identified, acquired, and moved is referred to as the "trafficking network" or simply "the network." *Sex trafficking* is defined as "human trafficking for the purpose of sexual exploitation to include forced prostitution, pornography, and, for children, sexual corruption and child sex rings." TOC, which operates by illegal means and often without respect for geographic lines (Federal Bureau of Investigation, 2020), is a major facilitating element in sex trafficking; this chapter discusses TOC in terms of its structure and role.

To begin to identify victims of human trafficking and understand human trafficking and the role of TOC, one most first recognize the uniqueness of the criminal activity and the rationale behind the trafficking of persons. Human trafficking may occur in many forms as individuals are forcibly moved within countries or across borders. Although the international community began increasing its cooperative efforts in the late 1990s to improve and coordinate responses, the criminal activity of TOCs and sex trafficking often goes undetected as there is a tendency to conflate sex trafficking with all forms of sex work (Cockbain & Bowers, 2019). In other cases, human trafficking is misidentified as **people smuggling** (McCabe, 2018). Whereas *people smuggling* implies enabling passage into a region (i.e., across a border) where the person is not a resident (Americans commonly recognize people smuggling as one way that illegal immigrants cross the border between the United States and Mexico), *human trafficking* does not, and the element of consent often found initially in cases of human smuggling does not exist in cases of human trafficking.

In January of 2022, a Belgium court convicted 18 people in a people-smuggling case tied to U.K. truck deaths. This act of smuggling resulted in the deaths of 39 Vietnamese migrants in 2019 (Pronczuk, 2022).

It should be noted that some cases of human smuggling (as demonstrated just above) may become cases of human trafficking if the initial consent from the victim to leave one country for another was achieved through deception or coercion (McCabe, 2008). These source countries provide the product (i.e., humans) for consumption within the destination countries.

TRAFFICKING IN PERSONS REPORT—COMMON COUNTRIES

Source Countries for Human Trafficking: Pakistan, Thailand, China, India, and Bangladesh
Transit Countries for Human Trafficking: Canada, United Kingdom
Destination Countries for Human Trafficking: United States, United Kingdom, and the Middle East

U.S. Department of State (2020)

TOC Structures

Research done in the United States—but applicable to all regions of the world—suggests five distinct typologies of organized crime that facilitate human trafficking and specifically sex trafficking (Bouche, 2017). TOC may also be identified in some of these typologies. These typologies, classified on the basis of size, scope, structure, and sophistication, often operate without detection and result in countless individual victims and unlimited profits.

The first typology, which encompasses approximately one third of organized crime networks, is the small "Mom and Pop" category. These organized crime groups usually engage only in sex trafficking, although some may support labor trafficking, with the venues for sex trafficking being massage parlors, brothels, and the **cybercommunity** (Bouche, 2017). On average, this category exploits between 15 and 20 victims, with the majority of their movements being across state borders within the United States. However, based upon the organizations' location in proximity to an international border, this classification of organized crime will function as TOC when victims are moved from the United States to either Mexico or Canada, often to participate in sex rings (McCabe & Murphy, 2016).

The second typology of organized crime, which also consists of approximately one third of the cases, is the crime ring (Bouche, 2017). In this typology, sex trafficking is the focus and commercial sexual exploitation is the goal, with the cybercommunity and technology playing a large role in recruiting both victims and consumers. On average, this category exploits between 5 and 10 victims (Bouche, 2017). With a reach in the virtual community and with little risk in terms of regulation or detection, this typology may also be engaged in TOC (McCabe, 2017).

The third typology of organized crime is the **gang** (Bouche, 2017). Research suggests that 100% of the cases in this classification involve trafficking for commercial sexual exploitation (Bouche, 2017). Specifically, street prostitutes and young people identified through online sites (such as in the cases where teens engage in online chats with potential traffickers) are the victims. On average, this category exploits between five and ten victims; however, in contrast to the Mom and Pop or crime ring classification, this category, through its use of technology, often involves more perpetrators; also, as the online market for victims is global, TOC is engaged to receive the profits.

The fourth typology of organized crime is the **cartels**, mafias, or crime syndicates, which are often portrayed in the movies but are rarely prosecuted by federal authorities; for this reason, the degree of their presence in the United States is unknown (Bouche, 2017). This typology is made up almost exclusively of TOC groups, as they work to facilitate all of the operations of human trafficking, including identifying victims, transporting them, and providing false travel documents. As these cases are rarely detected, the number of victims and the number of perpetrators remains unknown.

The last typology of organized crime, which encompasses approximately 25% of the cases in the United States, is the category of illegal enterprise (Bouche, 2017). Although all of the typologies are technically illegal enterprises, this classification, often involving TOC, is diverse in its criminal actions and may include sex trafficking and labor trafficking. Research suggests that the number of victims in this classification ranges from 50 to 100 (Bouche, 2017) and that the reach of TOC in this category—through its in-country presence and its use of technology range—is limitless (McCabe, 2017).

Sex Trafficking and TOC Networks

TOC groups are made up of individuals who operate by illegal means and often without concern for geography or jurisdictional laws. These groups seek profit and power without concern for laws, policies, or victims. As discussed previously, research suggests that there is no single structure for organized crime, such groups vary from hierarchies to networks, and the groups are characteristically insular and operate through corruption and violence (Federal Bureau of Investigation, 2020). However, the link between TOC and human trafficking cannot be dismissed. Again, as suggested by the UN's Office on Drugs and Crime, sex trafficking through TOC continues to be one of the most profitable industries in the world (McCabe, 2017).

Researchers who study **sex trafficking** and TOC suggest that the movement of these victims may be on a group basis or an individual basis. These movements are generally based upon the relationship between the traffickers and the brothel owners, the size of the traffickers' networks, and the need for a certain type of victim. In Central Asia, for example, a blonde female from Sweden is very profitable for her trafficker. Those trafficked within TOC networks are aware of these preferences, and they capitalize on the knowledge.

Some of the original crime networks that have existed over the years have more than 50 individuals involved in the delivery of product (Raymond & Hughes, 2001). Discussion on crime networks and human trafficking today suggests that most sex-trafficking organizations are small networks of one to five persons, which may connect with other similar-sized TOC groups (McCabe, 2008). The United Nations Office on Drugs and Crime also suggests that these small criminal organizations maintain very high levels of secrecy, often more because of fear of community reactions than fear of police reactions, and that these small units continue to exist for long periods of time by keeping flexible structures and simply changing their products based upon demands of the market (e.g., changing from drugs to people). These smaller TOC groups are involved in the identification, transportation, housing, and victimization of the victims; thus, the criminal process is essentially invisible to observers.

Today these smaller networks are supported as group members by incorporating cyber techniques and web pages to facilitate their illicit activities. Technology is enabling these networks to engage in traditional criminal activities such as sex trafficking with a greater reach to expand their global impact (Federal Bureau of Investigation, 2020). Thus, regardless of the size of the network and the use or non-use of technology, TOC networks are involved in much of the sex-trafficking business.

Victims

It is impossible to document the first time that sex trafficking occurred. In the 1980s, however, globalization and technology was first identified in facilitating the movements of individuals across international borders—what we now call human trafficking (McCabe & Murphy, 2016). Often, **victims** of sex trafficking are subjected to more than one form of exploitation, including not only forced **prostitution** but also the forced production of **pornography**. Unfortunately, in many cases, victims of sex trafficking are viewed simply as individuals involved in prostitution, with rarely an acknowledgment of the role of TOC. This is particularly the case in the U.S. state of Nevada, which has legalized prostitution and the highest rate of sex trafficking (World Population Review, 2020). In response, police efforts and nonprofit organizations that help victims of sex trafficking have existed there for over three decades (Guinn & Steglich, 2003).

Research suggests that on an annual basis there are over 5 million victims of sex trafficking globally, with at least 20% of these victims under the age of 18 (Toney-Butler et al., 2020). In fact, in research conducted by Internet Watch Foundation (2020), approximately 30% of the pornography was from children who were groomed, deceived, or extorted into producing sexual images or videos of themselves. Thus, the popularity of the internet has increased the popularity of sex trafficking, and the victimization of minors by TOC has profited from this popularity.

Historically, the general demographic characteristics of the victims of sex trafficking are that they are young and female (McCabe, 2008). Current research supports these general demographics, as further explorations suggest that victims of sex trafficking are twice as likely to be female and are significantly younger (median age of 22.8 years) than victims of labor trafficking (median age of 29.2 years) and domestic servitude (median age of 25.2) (Cockbain & Bowers, 2019). However, with many different types of human trafficking, this means that there is no single, typical victim profile. Thus, cases are seen in all parts of the world and victims are targeted irrespective of gender, age, or background. Children, for example, might be trafficked from Eastern Europe to Western Europe for the purpose of begging or as pickpockets; or young girls from Africa could be deceived with promises of fashion modeling or au pair jobs, only to find themselves trapped in a world of sexual and pornographic exploitation (United Nations Office on Drugs and Crime, 2012). Boys from states in that are in wartime conflicts may find themselves trafficked into child soldiering.

Since sexual exploitation is the goal of sex trafficking, the more "attractive" the product, the higher the sale price. Although specific ages of sex-trafficking victims are not known, research suggests that the average age of a sex slave in the United States is around 20 years old while the average age outside of the United States is approximately 12 years old (McCabe & Murphy, 2016). TOC is aware of the market for younger victims and facilitates this demand for product (McCabe, 2016).

In January of 2022, a Madison, Wisconsin, man was sentenced to four years in prison for conspiring to sex-traffic a minor. The victim, originally from Utah, was transported to Wisconsin by an associate of the man (U.S. Department of Justice, 2022).

Unfortunately, the estimates on child victims of sex trafficking may be conservative, as the prostitution of children is not always recognized (Clawson et al., 2009). Given that sex trafficking is the most prevalent aspect of human trafficking and by far receives the most publicity, discussions on victimization are often provided from both a personal or individual perspective and an environmental or structural perspective. As demonstrated in the 2022 case above, young victims are often trafficked across jurisdictional boundaries. For those who are interested in combating human trafficking, these perspectives of explanation provide the baseline of information required to establish evidence-based efforts for prevention and law enforcement.

Researchers, attempting to provide generalizations about sex trafficking from an individual perspective, suggest that many adult victims are aware of their potential involvement in the **sex industry** prior to their commitment to the work (McCabe, 2018). This is not the case for child victims (McCabe & Murphy, 2016). Unfortunately, often the long-term consequences are that these consenting adults become unable to control their activities or provide consent to sexual encounters for profit, and therefore become a victim of sex trafficking—with TOC once again profiting from their victimizations (McCabe & Murphy, 2016). In the majority of the cases of sex trafficking in the United States, traffickers prostitute their victims by force, and the victims do not have the choice to decide to work or not (McCabe & Manian,

2010). In many cases, these adults are willing participants of smuggling efforts or willing participants in the sex industry with a desire to relocate; however, they become victims of sex trafficking when their authority over their free will is removed. Unfortunately, in the cases of victims who have agreed to prostitution but are then trafficked, assistance from law enforcement is extremely difficult to obtain. The victims have willingly agreed to participate in an illegal activity (prostitution) and are unlikely to report their victimization for fear of being arrested. It is also these victims who often are perceived by the public as unworthy of legal assistance because they participated in the criminal activities voluntarily.

In addition, regardless the degree of victim involvement in sex trafficking, the destinations for most of the trafficking victims are cities with large commercial trade centers or areas with large military bases, and TOC help to facilitate these destinations. It is within these densely populated areas that victims of sex trafficking and their traffickers easily blend in and function. Therefore, just as the criminal activity of prostitution occupies a central position in the development of national and international capitalism, sex trafficking flourishes within the same governmental structure (McCabe, 2018).

Child victims of sex trafficking, who by law do not have the authority of consent, are common in the United States, and even more common outside the United States (Kangaspunta, 2006). For many of these child victims of sex trafficking, consent has been provided by their families (McCabe and Manian, 2010). In other instances, the child has participated in their sexual exploitation because of their attempt to satisfy another person (McCabe, 2017). In these cases, the child victims may not perceive themselves as victims. In fact, often the child victim views their trafficker as their boyfriend and everyone else as an enemy; hence the child, isolated and controlled, is a victim of sexual exploitation through sex trafficking (Tennis, 2020). The U.S. government estimates that approximately 70% of the victims in the United States are female and approximately 50% of the victims are under the age of 18 (McCabe, 2018). That means that many of the persons involved in sex trafficking are children. Research further suggests that one single trafficked child can net their trafficker up to $30,000 (Kangaspunta, 2006). However, across the globe, sex trafficking is not limited to prostitution, and TOC is involved in whatever ways the market dictates. Child victims of sex trafficking are forced into a variety of forms of sexual exploitation, including prostitution, pornography, bride trafficking, and sex tourism. The common element in all forms of sex trafficking is the total control of traffickers over their victims, or the term *forced*. Oftentimes, victims of sex trafficking are abused not only by their clients, but also by their traffickers; victims of sex trafficking face multiple situations of victimization—all for someone else's profit or pleasure.

Language and culture are other individual-level risk factors for many victims of sex trafficking, and especially those whose victimization is facilitated by TOC (Toney-Butler et al., 2020). For some victims of sex trafficking, their skills in the language spoken in the host country are nonexistent. For other victims, their culture has taught them to fear law enforcement, either as a result of experience with corrupt officials are as a result of their traffickers' narratives regarding the police; thus, they are unlikely to seek law enforcement's help to end their victimization (Clawson et al., 2009).

Debt bondage is another individual reason for sex trafficking (McCabe, 2008). Some victims of sex trafficking believe that they owe their trafficker a financial debt, and this perception is supported by the involvement of TOC. These debts, perhaps for movement into the area, for rent, or for food, place the victim in the position of debt bondage to their trafficker, and for many such victims the debt is repaid through sexual exploitation.

Another explanation of human trafficking is family involvement. Just as a family member often perpetrates the abuse of a child, a family member is often responsible for involving a woman or a child in sex trafficking. In exchange for money or even a television set, a family member will sell or trade their loved one into the world of sex trafficking (Farr, 2004). As the family member has allowed and even profited from the victimization of this person, the sex-trafficking victim cannot return to the family for fear of punishment by their trafficker or by that same family member. Hence, members of TOC may often play the role of "broker" in facilitating the deal for victims.

In addition, children, as well as lesbian, gay, bisexual, and transgender populations, face the additional dilemmas of parental acceptance or ignorance, their dependency on self-survival, and their desire to belong and be accepted. For these populations, the additional vulnerabilities of homelessness, depression, and lack of family support heighten their vulnerabilities for sex trafficking, and TOC is advantaged by these underlying factors (Toney-Butler et al., 2020). Just as there are a variety of individuals victimized through sex trafficking, there are a variety of individual reasons why the victimization continues.

In attempting to explain how sex trafficking can occur from a structural perspective, one of the earliest theoretical explanations for human trafficking is founded in Lee's (1966) **push-pull theory of migration**. Just as with migration in general, characteristics of both the host country and the destination country facilitate human trafficking. Specifically, characteristics of the host country push its natives out and conditions of the destination country pull the immigrants into the country. One common method of recruiting women for sex trafficking is by placing an advertisement in local newspapers asking for nannies or waitresses to work in another country (sometimes the United States). Once the women have been recruited, they are transported by TOC groups to the destination country, where their travel documents are confiscated and they are imprisoned by their traffickers and forced to repay their debts (i.e., the cost of their transportation, food, clothing, and shelter).

Another explanation for sex trafficking is military presence. Farr (2004) suggests that in areas with a strong military presence, there are often women engaging in prostitution. The prostitution serves both the military members and the prostitutes. When the military vacates the area, that demand for prostitution no longer exists; thus, prostitutes are in the area without work. It is these women who become targets of traffickers involved in TOC. Research also supports the idea that many sex-trafficked adults are simply aged prostitutes who have chosen to relocate for prostitution (Raymond & Hughes, 2001). Again, these women will endure the abuse of being a trafficking victim and will resist being arrested for fear of being sent back to a country where they cannot secure work. As always, TOC profits from this vulnerability of victims.

Finally, sex trafficking is related to the cultures of spousal prostitution and the **mail-order bride** industry. Cullen (2002) has reported that often the mail-order bride becomes trapped in the climate of slavery and prostitution. A young woman who wishes to escape the poverty and depression of her home country may choose to become a mail-order bride to a man in a "better" country. Of course, the mail-order bride industry, facilitated by TOC and technology, suggests to the victim that this decision will lead to a more secure environment in which her basic needs will be met and she may even find love. Unfortunately, this is rarely the case, as the mail-order bride business is essentially unregulated (McCabe, 2007). Instead, these women are perceived as material purchases—replaceable or even disposable. To give some perspective on the magnitude of this problem, there are over 200 mail-order bride businesses operating in the United States with over 5,000 women entering the United States each year as a potential bride (McCabe, 2018). The brokers of mail-order brides are not considered traffickers; however, they are often regarded as frauds for not disclosing all of the facts of the transaction. McCabe's (2007) term *spousal prostitution* is also an element of sex trafficking and the mail-order bride business in that in these cases the husbands give money or other goods in exchange for sex with their wives.

The structural conditions of poverty, inequality, and corruption are all related to sex trafficking and exist for both adult victims and child victims. The U.S. Department of State (2020), in an attempt to monitor human trafficking across the globe, produces an annual report that identifies countries and their efforts to address human trafficking. The Trafficking in Persons (TIP) Report provides general information on enforcement efforts at the country level, as well as identifying source, transit, and/or destination countries for human trafficking. In addition, countries are categorized in Tier Classifications (1–3) based upon their documented legal and enforcement efforts. These sources of information suggest that associations exist between poverty and sex trafficking (Deshpande & Nour, 2013), between gender inequality and sex trafficking (McCabe & Murphy, 2016), and between corruption and sex trafficking (Jonsson, 2018). Unfortunately, this report does not discuss aspects of TOC involvement in human trafficking.

Research suggests that human trafficking thrives on extreme poverty, and that this is especially true for victims of inequality (McCabe, 2018). In many countries, women and children are seen as property and as disposable, and it is these persons who will be recruited by members of TOC groups for human trafficking.

Traffickers and TOC

Explanations of the conditions that facilitate sex trafficking are often global, with far less attention paid to the local environments and those who traffick victims (Kragten-Heerdink et al., 2022). In the United States, research suggests that approximately one third of the cases of sex trafficking involve TOC (Tripp & McMahon-Howard, 2016). In Europe, specifically the Balkans, two thirds of human trafficking is facilitated by TOC (Djordjevic & Dobovsek, 2020). Hence, those interested in studying sex trafficking, a for-profit action, must also consider the opportunities of the local areas and the traffickers who pragmatically and rationally operate locally (Cockbain & Bowers, 2019). The United Nations has recognized the distinction between sex trafficking and prostitution and has advanced the notion of a participant-victim by their extension of the definition of *sex trafficking* to include payments or benefits to a person with control over another person for the purpose of exploitation—thus recognizing the role of TOC in human trafficking (McGinnis, 2004). Specifically, in the criminal activity of sex trafficking, the trafficker controls the type of sexual exploitation for his sex worker, his worker's "decision" to work or not work, and his worker's location; and TOC facilitates the distribution of product. Note that although in this narrative the trafficker is referred to using "his," especially in the cases of the sex trafficking of children the trafficker is a female, not a male (McCabe & Murphy, 2016).

Trafficker—A person who deals or trades in something illegal.

Research has suggested that with most crimes involving online networks, one of the best ways to identify the perpetrators is to identify the environment of the criminal action (McCabe, 2018). In cases of sex trafficking, environments that are prone to these crimes are usually areas that are prone to heavy-security establishments, including bars on the windows and strong locks on the doors. Thus, due to the secrecy of sex trafficking and the involvement of TOC, victims and traffickers are often hidden from public view. In an attempt to identify sex traffickers, one must consider the multiple aspects of the criminal activity and, in many cases, the relationship between the trafficker and the victim. Since many cases of sex trafficking involve multiple individuals involved in the victimization, many researchers

In October of 2021, a woman in San Jose, California, was convicted of recruiting victims for sex trafficking (U.S. Department of Justice, 2021a). The victims, both adults and minors, were forced to participate in sex rings advertised on social media.

also consider the client of the sex-trafficking victim as also being an offender in the process of trafficking. In addition, as demonstrated below the roles of women and technology must not be overlooked.

To identify the offenders (hereafter, traffickers) involved in sex trafficking, we must first consider the individual who has introduced the victim to the criminal organization and must also consider the interconnectivity of TOC. Research suggests that the individual who is often involved at the entry level of the victim's involvement is a family member, a close family acquaintance, or a boyfriend of the victim (McCabe, 2018). With child victims of sex trafficking, the individual most likely responsible for the child's entry into this type of victimization is a family member or a family acquaintance (also called a **recruiter**) (McCabe & Murphy, 2016). As discussed previously, some family members believe that their child will live a better life and will have more opportunities in other locations, and so they allow the movement of their child. Other family members, in need of money, may offer the child as trade (McCabe, 2008). Hence, it is difficult to provide demographic characteristics of family members involved in sex trafficking. Researchers suggest that most often these family members are male, as the family unit exists within a male-dominated culture. Others suggest it is the mother of the child who makes such arrangements, for the good of the remaining children (McCabe & Murphy, 2016).

Another person who is often involved in the entry of young women into the arena of sex trafficking is the "boyfriend" of the young victim. This boyfriend, much like a pimp in the arena of prostitution, begins to pursue the young woman with promises of love and security, when in actuality he is a recruiter for the sex-trafficking organization and will soon offer this young, unsuspecting female to the criminal world of sex trafficking (McCabe, 2018). In addition, and not to be overlooked, in many cases the recruiters of young women for sex trafficking are other young women who are themselves victims of sex trafficking (McCabe, 2008). These victims, to continue their relationship with their traffickers, will bring other young women into the world of sex trafficking; and so the process of recruiting victims for sex trafficking continues.

Also involved as traffickers of sex trafficking are the so-called middlemen, who are responsible for a variety of activities involved in the movement of victims. These individuals are likely to be members of TOC. Their activities include creating the documents for travel, arranging for the approval of travel, accompanying the victim from the source country (or area) to the destination country (or area), and in some cases facilitating the entry process (usually with a bribe) with the customs officials who allow "questionable" individuals to enter the destination country.

Much as in cases of counterfeiting and fraud, the individuals who arrange the travel documentation are experienced in this area, are often acquainted with local government employees, and are known throughout the criminal network (McCabe, 2018). In addition, the individuals who arrange for legitimate travel documents are often trained in law or in some other aspect of government-based regulations. Just as there is information on individuals involved in the smuggling of persons, there is information available on those individuals who travel with the victims of human trafficking; this information suggests that these individuals often are male and often pose as a family member of the victim (McCabe, 2018). However, as stated, with the trafficking of children, it is not unusual for the accompanying traveler to be a woman with the responsibility of childcare (McCabe & Murphy, 2016). In some extreme cases of child sex trafficking, these female members of TOC networks will travel with the very young children, care for the children until they are at an age to be profitable in the criminal activity, and then provide the children to the trafficker.

Nearly two decades ago, Bales (2004) suggested that a sex trafficker is usually a member of a network, involved in a "respectable" business in addition to owning a brothel (perhaps through an investment club), and that the profits from sex trafficking are hidden under the red tape of legitimate business bureaucracy. In these cases, the traffickers are most often male, they are most often involved in some sort of entertainment business, and in some cases they may have friends in high government positions (sometimes law enforcement). Finally, as Kangaspunta (2006) suggested, it is not unusual for many of the members of the sex trafficking criminal organization to share the nationality of the victim, whereas the client does not share the nationality of the victim. In every case of sex trafficking, the motivation for the trafficker is profit and the motivation for the client is pleasure (McCabe, 2018).

The Role of TOC in Facilitating Sex Trafficking

As with any type of criminal activity, there are multiple explanations for the success of sex trafficking. In particular, TOC recognizes sex trafficking as a multibillion-dollar industry with an endless supply of victims and traffickers. Unfortunately, there will always be poor countries with little opportunity for women and children and there will always be individuals willing to exploit others for personal gain. Until societies decide to address sex trafficking and TOC, human trafficking will continue for a variety of reasons.

First, investigative efforts by criminal justice systems are one aspect of the problem of sex trafficking that remains a challenge (McCabe, 2018). Globally, resources for law enforcement and prosecutors to reduce sex trafficking or human trafficking are limited. With little training on the recognition of cases of sex trafficking and little experience in identifying or investigating cases of sex trafficking, few officers and even fewer prosecutors are able to distinguish cases of sex trafficking from cases of prostitution. Therefore, victims remain unidentified and traffickers operate successfully. In addition, limited penalties for sex traffickers fuel the problem of sex trafficking. In particular, when cases of human trafficking are compared with cases of drug trafficking or firearms trafficking, the maximum penalty for sex trafficking is perhaps 10 years, whereas distributing a kilo of heroin or stolen weapons could mean a life sentence (McCabe and Manian, 2010). Again, without the recognition of victim and without legislative penalties, sex trafficking will continue at TOC will continue to be involved.

Second, reports by the victims of sex trafficking are still limited (McCabe, 2018). As suggested, many of the victims of sex trafficking are from countries outside of their destination country and therefore language is a barrier in reporting abuse. In addition, many of these victims have entered the destination country illegally or have had their travel documents taken from them by their traffickers. These victims are often from countries with negative perceptions of law enforcement, and in many cases they fear law enforcement and are unwilling to speak with officers even to report their own victimization. For those victims who do not fear the corruption of law enforcement, it is the fear of being returned to their home country that causes them to resist reporting their victimization to law enforcement.

> On her sixth birthday she was sold into the sex industry by her mother, who wanted to profit from child pornography. Until her escape, she was raped most nights while her mother told her to "smile and look pretty." This happened in her house on the East Coast of the United States (Eubanks, 2015).

In addition, those who are victims of sex trafficking within their own countries often are recruited into sex work as a result of a lack of social support in their homes or communities; because they became involved in sex trafficking to escape from those home conditions, they likely will not report their victimization as those conditions still exist. Without a victim to report an abuse, efforts by law enforcement to end that abuse are nonexistent.

Finally, the emerging entrepreneurs in the area of sexual exploitation are those who utilize the internet, the newest avenue for those interested in sex trafficking. TOC groups have used this technology very successfully to distribute pornography they've produced with victims of sex trafficking or to arrange sexual encounters. Just as with any online order, perpetrators interested in obtaining a victim for sexual exploitation may use email or a website to facilitate their desire. Unfortunately, this mode of communication is very difficult to monitor, and regulations frequently go unenforced. Therefore, the use of technology is often critical in fueling sex trafficking. Specifically, in this environment, the victim is a product, one that is worthy of much effort in its care and very profitable to its owner. In fact, a single victim may produce over $250,000 per year for their abuser (McCabe & Murphy, 2016). From the perspective that the victim is the product, the individual wishing for sexual exploitation is considered the consumer and the trafficker is simply the means of recruitment, production, and distribution for the product. Therefore, from a rational, objective, perspective, online sexual exploitation is a business. Two of the businesses that further facilitate sex trafficking are **sex rings** and sex tours.

Child sex rings, which usually occur within the category of extrafamilial (outside the family) abuse, involve multiple children and multiple abusers (McCabe, 2017). In this type of exploitation, there are organized venues for sexual activity among multiple child victims and multiple adult offenders. Traditionally, in sex rings there is communication (often online) among the offenders in terms of the desired demographic characteristic(s) of a child, such as the age and/or gender of the child, and the sex ring leader's ability to identify and locate a sought-after child. Historically, the communication took place in a phone call or an email; today, however, those communications are much more likely to occur in private chat rooms, via instant apps, and on websites operated as "discussion-only" forums from computer servers that are often based outside of the United States—and therefore outside U.S. regulations (McCabe, 2017). These forums, self-identified as discussion-only for individuals to share their thoughts on sexual activity, often lead to members moving to more private venues for sharing images and videos of child pornography as well as their plans for participation in a sex ring to abuse children. Thus, these crime rings are able to operate without police knowledge, without police jurisdiction, and without intervention. In addition, with multiple law enforcement jurisdictions, varying laws, and few children identified by name, the prosecution of those responsible is extremely difficult and, therefore, the investigation is always ongoing rather than completed (McCabe, 2017).

Regarding victims of sex tourism (or as the U.S. government defines it, "the extraterritorial sexual exploitation of children"), federal law prohibits any U.S. citizen from traveling to a foreign country with the intent to engage in any form of sexual conduct with a minor as well as to help organize or assist another person in traveling for this purpose. However, each year Americans are convicted of committing this crime. In 2005, the U.S. government's convictions of a pediatrician, a dentist, and a university professor helped put an end to the idea that those involved in these types of crime were poor, or uneducated, or feared criminals (Protect, 2016).

Historically, three of the most popular destinations for sex tourism are Thailand, Brazil, and Spain, and TOC facilitates these connections (Chawla, 2015). Also, these countries are often locations for educationally based study-abroad trips for American high school and college students. Advertising for these child victims is often done online via classified ads on Craig's List, Back Page, and various darknet sites (Calder, 2004).

For clarity, the term *darknet* refers to a network that requires special access and is characterized by its users and hosts being anonymous in order to conceal the production and distribution of illegal drugs, improper financial accounts, or illegal sexual activities (McCabe, 2017). To avoid detection and facilitate child abuse, most darknet users employ code words related to ordinary objects such as food to discuss the desired characteristics of children. For example, the food item *pasta* may represent a *young boy* and the food item *pizza* may represent a *young girl* (McCabe, 2017). Unfortunately, the relative ease and automation of international travel today has led to an increase in sex trafficking. Thus, one cannot underestimate the impact of technology and the internet on the trafficking of persons for sexual exploitation.

Other Forms of Human Trafficking

In January of 2012, six women in Mexico were arrested for their involvement in a child-trafficking ring providing adoptions to Irish families. In this case, 10 children were identified as victims (Pachino, 2012).

Although sex trafficking is the most common aspect of human trafficking by TOC, other aspects should be acknowledged. Specifically, TOC also facilitates labor trafficking, organ trafficking, adoption (as demonstrated here), and child soldiering.

Labor Trafficking

In the human-trafficking market, TOC traffickers act as intermediaries to provide employers with workers (Wheaton et al., 2009). Just as with most TOC efforts, success is measured by flexibility of product and by the ability to identify and provide that product in response to demand (McCabe & Murphy, 2016). As Bales (2005) suggested, anyone involved in business must take advantage of the disparity between product availability and product desire. Those involved in **labor trafficking** and TOC certainly understand this concept; labor traffickers recognize that unemployment and low wages in one part of the world will cause persons in the labor force to seek employment and opportunity in a different part of the world. As Becker (1995) suggested when he applied rational choice theory to employment, illegal access to work with little risk of detection is a rational decision. Employers who are in need of a labor force are unlikely to report these infractions to labor laws.

A young man from Mexico was recruited to work on a farm in California; however, once he borrowed 10,000 pesos from his trafficker, he was forced to share a single room with 34 other men while he worked off his debt. He was not allowed to leave the farm, not allowed visitors, not paid the salary he had been promised, and never allowed to work only 40 hours per week (Freedom United, 2020).

Human traffickers engaged with TOC offer differentiated products (i.e., people) based upon the needs of employers. Further, they limit the number and type of individuals they traffic to employers in order to ensure a consistency in demand (Wheaton et al., 2009). As demonstrated here, victims of labor trafficking are both male and female. This results in a constant demand for product supplied by TOC. Research suggests that in labor trafficking one person may yield TOC over $10,000 (Borjas, 2008). Vulnerable populations exist in every part of the world due to such factors as globalization, economic and political instability, disease, disintegration of families, and war—so the supply of victims for TOC is stable Many of these individuals initially agree to human smuggling but end up as victims of human trafficking, often unable to end the work if they desire as TOC groups hold them responsible for the costs associated with their recruitment, transportation, clothing, shelter, and false documentation. Since TOC groups incur the costs of establishing routes, recurring bribes, and forged travel documents, they are unlikely to "release" their victims (Wheaton et al., 2009).

> In Russia in 2020, the cost of a human life was approximately $250, as this was the cost for a victim of labor trafficking in 2015 (Waid, 2020). One male victim became a slave in a brick factory in Dagestan and is one of the over 700,000 living in conditions of modern slavery.

Organ Trafficking

While organ trafficking exists in all regions of the world (Interpol, 2021), its reach into communities through TOC has not fully been explored. The trafficking of organs, or transplant tourism, provides substantial profits for TOC. Unlike sex trafficking or labor trafficking, which can utilize the product (i.e., people) multiple times, **organ trafficking** is unique and specific and requires advanced specialization (such as a medical background) in addition to the skills generally acquired within TOC groups. Information suggests that a wide spectrum of actors is involved in organ trafficking in North Africa and West Africa, with connections to the medical sector in countries from Africa and beyond—notably, in Asia and the Middle East (Interpol, 2021). Transplants—which may be performed

> In 2001, the torso of a young boy was found floating in the River Thames in London. This young boy, later determined to be from Nigeria with clothing purchased in Germany, was found with his throat cut and with organs and limbs missing. This case remains unsolved (Crawford & Smith, 2021).

within Europe and North Africa with organs illegally sourced in the region, or done elsewhere illegally with organs sourced from vulnerable populations in areas such as Africa—often result in irreversible physical damage or death for victims.

TOC groups profit from the desperation of the unemployed, migrants, asylum seekers, and refugees by coercing them to sell an organ (Interpol, 2021).The techniques used for the recruitment and control of the victims are the same as those used for other types of human trafficking, such as promises of money or job opportunities abroad, as well as threats and the use of violence. In some cases, as demonstrated in the 2001 report on the previous page, the consequences are severe. In most cases, victims of organ trafficking receive a smaller amount of the money than had been agreed to with the recruiter or broker, and in some cases the victim may not get any of the promised payment (Interpol, 2021). Like many of the outcomes of current-day COVID-19, organ trafficking is expected to increase as vulnerable individuals sell their organs to improve their economic conditions.

Legislative Responses to Human Trafficking

In response to cases of human trafficking, legislative efforts have existed for over two decades. In addition, many nongovernmental organizations (NGOs) have been established to identify victims of sex trafficking and to provide assistance those victims. However, when asked about the problem of sex trafficking, most individuals still have no idea that the criminal activity exists, and especially that it exists in every country.

During the 20th century, there was no single department or agency responsible for collecting data on sex trafficking (McCabe, 2008). Surprisingly, it was not human rights groups or law enforcement that began to recognize this injustice; rather, it was the business industry, concerned about the competition for labor, that prompted the awareness of the problem of human trafficking for labor (Bales, 2004). Later, when then Secretary of State Colin Powell announced that monies acquired through human trafficking were used to support the activities of the 9/11 hijackers, legislative acts and law enforcement efforts began focusing on sex trafficking (McCabe, 2008).

THE VICTIMS OF TRAFFICKING AND VIOLENCE PROTECTION ACT OF 2000 DEFINES *HUMAN TRAFFICKING* AS

Sex trafficking in which a commercial sex act is induced by force, fraud, or coercion, or in which the person induced to perform such act has not attained 18 years of age

The recruitment, harboring, transportation, provision, or obtaining of a person for labor or services, through the use of force, fraud, or coercion for the purpose of subjection to involuntary servitude, peonage, debt bondage, or slavery. (22 U.S.C. § 7102[9]).

In 2000, with an estimate of nearly 700,000 individuals trafficked annually worldwide, the U.S. Congress passed the Victims of Trafficking and Violence Protection Act of 2000, P.L. 106-386, commonly referred to as the **Trafficking Victims Protection Act (TVPA)**. The TVPA mandated that the Secretary of State submit a report on severe forms of human trafficking to Congress on June 1st of that year. This report, which identifies countries as source, transit, and/or destination countries for human trafficking, has continued to be produced annually, citing a list of countries and their rankings in a Tier Classification system (McCabe, 2010). Specifically, those countries that fully abide by the TVPA's minimum standards for "elimination of trafficking" are placed on Tier 1. Countries that do not fully comply, but are making efforts to do so, are placed in either Tier 2 or Tier 2 Watch categories. Tier 3 countries are those countries that are not in compliance with the minimum standards for the elimination of trafficking and appear to not be making any significant efforts to become compliant.

The Victims of Trafficking and Violence Protection Act of 2000 is a federal statute passed by the U.S. Congress, signed by President Clinton, and then reauthorized by Presidents Bush, Obama, and Trump.

After the 2000 TVPA became law, other countries in various regions of the world began antitrafficking efforts on a larger scale in order to address human trafficking. Also, the United Nations Office on Drugs and Crime (often called UNODC) began focusing on strategies and developing policies to prevent human trafficking and assist victims (United Nations Office on Drugs and Crime, 2019). In 2003, then president George W. Bush signed the amended **Trafficking Victims Protection Reauthorization Act (TVPRA)**, which further supported government efforts to reduce human trafficking. In addition, and after the passing of the 2003 TVPRA, data on cases of sex trafficking within various countries began to be published in the annual Trafficking In Persons Report (on a limited basis) (McCabe, 2018). Legislative efforts in various countries have continued as more and more geographic locations attempt to identify and reduce cases of human trafficking. In the United States, the TVPRA has been reauthorized on multiple occasions, most recently in 2019, with its three-pronged approach of prevention, prosecution, and protection adopted globally. More specifically, during 2015–2019 a €11 million effort by the European Union and the UN has provided resources to government authorities and civil organizations in the "hot spot" countries of Belarus, Brazil, Colombia, Egypt, the Kyrgyz Republic, the Lao PDR, Mali, Morocco, Nepal, Niger, Pakistan, South Africa, and Ukraine (United Nations Office on Drugs and Crime, 2019).

Legislative responses to human trafficking have also gained momentum on the international level. Specifically, as recognized in 2005 by the Council of Europe Convention on Action against Trafficking in Human Beings, individuals engaged in trafficking were identified within the categories of exploitation of the prostitution of others, other forms of sexual exploitation, forced labor or services, slavery, practices similar to slavery, servitude, and removal of organs (Mattar, 2006).

In particular under international law, the Convention for the Suppression of the Traffic in Persons and the Exploitation of the Prostitution of Others criminalizes the procuring or enticing of a person for prostitution, and the UN's Protocol to Prevent, Suppress and Punish Trafficking in Persons, Especially Women and Children (United Nations Office of Human Rights, 2000) provides definitions of exploitation to be used within the global arena as related to sex trafficking and other forms of sexual exploitation. In addition, the Rome Statute of the International Criminal Court (discussed in Chapter 12) uses the phrase "crime against humanity" to enforce the prosecution of such cases.

In terms of specific international efforts to address child victimization through sex tourism, the international community recognizes the Preamble to the Optional Protocol to the Convention on the Rights of the Child on the Sale of Children, Child Prostitution, and Child Pornography, adopted in 2000 (United Nations Office of Human Rights, 2000a; Mattar, 2006). In this agreement, states (or countries) agree to strengthening cooperation among multilevel justice officials so that cases of child victimization can be detected, investigated, prosecuted, and eventually prevented. In this effort, states also (1) promote cooperation in assisting child victims in their recovery (physical and mental) and (2) attempt to address those underlying conditions that existed before the victimizations, such as poverty.

In addressing **forced labor**, since the Forced Labour Convention of 1930 the international community has acknowledged the victimization of vulnerable populations within the workforce (Mattar, 2006). Over the last two decades, through the Private Employment Agencies Conventions (1997), the Worst Forms of Child Labour Convention (1999) and the **UN's Protocol to Prevent, Suppress and Punish Trafficking in Persons, Especially Women and Children** (2000b), labor trafficking has been acknowledged as a significant threat to vulnerable populations and country stabilities as a whole. Hence, human trafficking, a problem within the global community, is receiving legislative attention at the global level.

Forced labor—When individuals are compelled to provide work or service through the use of force, fraud, or coercion.

UN PROTOCOL TO PREVENT, SUPPRESS AND PUNISH TRAFFICKING IN PERSONS ESPECIALLY WOMEN AND CHILDREN (PREAMBLE)—RATIFIED BY THE UN GENERAL ASSEMBLY IN NOVEMBER 2000

Preamble

The States Parties to this Protocol,

Declaring that effective action to prevent and combat trafficking in persons, especially women and children, requires a comprehensive international approach in the countries of origin, transit and destination that includes measures to prevent such trafficking, to punish the traffickers and to protect the victims of such trafficking, including by protecting their internationally recognized human rights.

Taking into account the fact that, despite the existence of a variety of international instruments containing rules and practical measures to combat the exploitation of persons, especially women and children, there is no universal instrument that addresses all aspects of trafficking in persons.

Concerned that, in the absence of such an instrument, persons who are vulnerable to trafficking will not be sufficiently protected, Recalling General Assembly resolution 53/111 of 9 December 1998, in which the Assembly decided to establish an open-ended intergovernmental ad hoc committee for the purpose of elaborating a comprehensive international convention against transnational organized crime and of discussing the elaboration of, inter alia, an international instrument addressing trafficking in women and children.

Summary

The United Nations has defined *human trafficking* as the recruitment, transfer, harboring, or receipt of persons by threat or use of force. The U.S. State Department's Trafficking Victims Protection Act (2000) identifies severe forms of human trafficking as (1) sex trafficking in which a commercial sex act is induced by force, fraud, or coercion, or in which the person induced to perform such an act has not attained 18 years of age; or (2) the recruitment, harboring, transportation, provision, or obtaining of a person for labor or services through the use of force, fraud, or coercion for the purpose of subjection to involuntary servitude, peonage, debt bondage, or slavery. In most cases, individuals are trafficked for one of two main reasons: labor or sex. This chapter focused on the trafficking of individuals for sex, also known as sex trafficking.

International estimates suggest that there are between 20 million and 40 million victims of human trafficking annually, and many of these individuals are victims of sex trafficking. Victims of sex trafficking usually become involved in sex trafficking through deception or coercion, with the destinations for many of the trafficking victims being urban areas or cities with large commercial trade centers. Unfortunately, in these densely populated areas, victims of sex trafficking and their traffickers can easily blend in and function unnoticed.

Explanations for sex trafficking include poverty, inequality, and family involvement. The United States is one of the most frequently reported destination countries for sex trafficking, as it is perceived by many of the poorer countries as the land of opportunity. Unfortunately, this appeal of the United States facilitates the criminal enterprise of sex trafficking.

Sex-trafficking offenders include the persons involved in the sex-trafficking of the victim and also the clients of the sex-trafficking victim, and these offenders are often tied to TOC groups. Due to the secrecy of this activity, little research exists on traffickers, and much of the information that does exist is based upon only a few cases (McCabe, 2018) and the role of TOC.

Poverty, inequality, corruption, and marketability all explain the consistency in cases of sex trafficking. In addition, victims' unwillingness to report sex trafficking and the use of the virtual community facilitate the criminal activity.

Finally, after the original 2000 TVPA (and the ratified TVPRA), countries in addition to the United States began more focused anti-trafficking efforts on a larger scale. After passage of the 2003 TVPRA, data on cases of sex trafficking within various countries began to be published annually in the Trafficking In Persons Report. In addition, various countries have continued their legislative efforts to identify and reduce cases of sex trafficking, such as through the UN's Protocol to Prevent, Suppress and Punish Trafficking in Persons, Especially Women and Children (2000b). However, the activity of sex trafficking and the role of TOC in it both remain undefined and misunderstood.

Questions for Further Thought

1. What are the conditions that support human trafficking, and how are children especially at risk under those conditions?
2. If human trafficking is one of the most widely recognized aspects of TOC, why is it so difficult to control?
3. What are some of the legislative efforts in place to deter human trafficking?

References

Bales, K. (2004). *New slavery: A references handbook* (2nd ed.). ABC-CLIO.

Bales, K. (2005). *Understanding global slavery.* University of California Press.

Becker, G. (1995). The economics of crime. *Cross Sections,* Fall, 8–15.

Borjas, G. (2008). *Labor economics.* McGraw-Hill Irwin.

Bouche, V. (2017). *An empirical analysis of the intersection of organized crime and human trafficking in the Unites States* [Office of Justice Programs #250955]. Retrieved June 30, 2021, from https://www.ojp.gov/pdffiles1/nij/grants/250955.pdf

Calder, M. (2004). *Child sexual abuse and the internet: Tackling the new frontier.* Russell House.

Chawla, A. (2015). The disturbing reality of human trafficking and children. *HuffPost,* December 18, 2015. Retrieved October 19, 2016, from http://www.huffingtonpost.com/

Clawson, H., Dutch, H., Salomon, A., & Grace, L. (2009, December). Study of HHS programs serving human trafficking victims. U.S. Department of Health and Human Services (HHSP233200600001T).

Cockbain, E., & Bowers, K. (2019). Human trafficking for sex, labour, and domestic servitude: How do key trafficking types compare and what are their predictors? *Crime, Law and Social Change, 72,* 9–34.

Crawford, A., & Smith, T. (2021, September 21). The torso in the Thames: A 20-year mystery. *BBC News*. Retrieved November 3, 2021, from https://www.bbc.com/news/uk-58415046

Cullen, S. (2002). The miserable lives of mail order brides. *Women in Action, 3*, 6–9.

Deshpande, N., & Nour, N. (2013). Sex trafficking of women and girls. *Review of Obstetric Gynecology, 6*(1), 22–27.

Djordjevic, S., & Dobovsek, B. (2020). Organised crime in Western Balkans Six at the onset of coronavirus. *International Journal of Sociology and Social Policy, 40*(9/10), 87–820. https://doi.org/10.1108/IJSSP-06-2020-0229

Eubanks, K. (2015, April 16). Sex trafficking victim shares story. *Clarion Ledger*. Retrieved May 15, 2022, from https://www.clarionledger.com/story/news/2015/04/16/sex-trafficking-victim-shares-story/25919625/

Farr, K. (2004). *Sex trafficking: The global market in women and children*. W. H. Freedman.

Federal Bureau of Investigation. (2020). *Transnational organized crime*. Retrieved November 3, 2020, from https://www.fbi.gov/investigate/organized-crime

Freedom United. (2020, May 26). *Help protect farmworkers like me from modern slavery*. Retrieved May 15, 2022, from https://www.castla.org/help-protect-farmworkers-like-me-from-modern-slavery/

Guinn, D., & Steglich, E., (Eds.). (2003). *In modern bondage: Sex trafficking in America*. Transnational.

Internet Watch Foundation. (2020 November 9). *Analyst's hunch leads to British schoolgirl's rescue from online child sexual abuse*. Retrieved December 30, 2020, from https://www.iwf.org.uk/news/analyst-s-%E2%80%98hunch%E2%80%99-leads-to-british-schoolgirl%E2%80%99s-rescue-from-online-child-sexual-abuse

Interpol. (2021, September 30). *North and West Africa: Interpol report highlights human trafficking for organ removal*. Retrieved November 3, 2021, from https://www.interpol.int/en/News-and-Events/News/2021/North-and-West-Africa-INTERPOL-report-highlights-human-trafficking-for-organ-removal

Jonsson, S. (2018). The complex relationship between police corruption and sex trafficking in origin countries. *Journal of Human Trafficking, 5*(2), 109–129.

Kangaspunta, K. (2006, April). *Trafficking in persons: Global patterns*. United Nations Office on Drugs and Crime. https://www.un.org/en/development/desa/population/events/pdf/other/turin/KANGASPUNTA.pdf

Kragten-Heerdink, S. L. J., van de Weijer, S. G. A., & Weerman, F. M. (2022, April). Crossing borders: Does it matter? Differences between (near-) domestic and cross-border sex traffickers, their victims and modus operandi. *European Journal of Criminology*. Accessed on August 19, 2022 at https://journals.sagepub.com/doi/full/10.1177/14773708221092314

Lee, E. (1966). A theory of migration. *Demography,* (*3*)1, 47–57. https://doi.org/10.2307/2060063

Mattar, M. (2006). *Comprehensive legal approaches to combatting trafficking in persons: An international and comparative perspective*. The Protection Project. Retrieved November 3, 2021, from https://www.icmec.org/wp-content/uploads/2015/10/The_Protection_Project_Comprehensive_Approaches_to_THB.pdf

McCabe, K. (2007). Spousal prostitution. In N. Jackson (Ed.), *Encyclopedia of domestic violence*, pp. 673–674. Routledge.

McCabe, K. (2008). *The trafficking of persons: National and international responses.* Peter Lang.

McCabe, K. (2017). *Protecting your children online.* Rowman & Littlefield.

McCabe, K. (2018). Common forms: Sex trafficking. In M. Burke (Ed.), *Human trafficking: Interdisciplinary perspectives* (2nd ed.), pp. 122–138. Routledge.

McCabe, K., & Manian, S. (2010). Part VII: North America. In K. McCabe & S. Manian (Eds.), *Sex trafficking: A global perspective* (pp. 147–158). Lexington Books.

McCabe, K., & Murphy, D. (2016). *Child abuseToday's issues.* Taylor & Francis.

McGinnis, E. (2004, December 12). *The horrifying reality of sex trafficking.* Concerned Women for America. Accessed on August 19, 2022 at https://lovesmessenger.net/the-horrifying-reality-of-sex-trafficking/

Niethammer, C. (2020, February 2). *Cracking the $150 billion business of human trafficking.* Forbes. Retrieved September 15, 2021, from https://www.forbes.com/sites/carmenniethammer/2020/02/02/cracking-the-150-billion-business-of-human-trafficking/?sh=65e037fa4142

Pachino, E. (2012, January 15). *Mexico adoption case points to child trafficking industry.* Insight Crime. Retrieved January 3, 2022, from https://insightcrime.org/news/analysis/mexico-adoption-case-points-to-child-trafficking-industry/

Pronczuk, M. (2022, January 19). Belgium convicts 18 people in people-smuggling case tied to UK truck death. *The New York Times.* Retrieved February 1, 2022, from https://www.nytimes.com/2022/01/19/world/europe/essex-lorry-deaths-verdict-belgium.html

Protect.org. (2016). *What is the magnitude of child exploitation?* Retrieved November 23, 2016, from http://www.protect.org/articles/what-is-the-magnitude-of-child-exploitation

Raymond, J., & Hughes, D. (2001). *Sex trafficking of women in the United States: International and Domestic Trends.* Coalition Against Trafficking in Women.

Tennis, T. (2020, June 9). Porn and human trafficking: The facts you need to know. *The Exodus Road.* Retrieved December 3, 2020, from https://blog.theexodusroad.com/porn-and-human-trafficking-the-facts-you-need-to-know

Toney-Butler, T., Ladd, M., & Mittel, O. (2020, November 16). *Human trafficking.* StatPearls Publishing. Retrieved December 5, 2020, from https://www.ncbi.nlm.nih.gov/books/NBK430910/

Tripp, Y. and McMahon-Howard, J. (2016). Perception vs. reality: The relationship between organized crime and human trafficking in metropolitan Atlanta. American Journal of Criminal Justice, 41 (2), 732–764.

United Nations Office of Human Rights. (2000a). *Optional protocol to the convention on the rights of the child on the sale of children, child prostitution, and child pornography.* Retrieved November 3, 2021, from https://www.ohchr.org/en/instruments-mechanisms/instruments/optional-protocol-convention-rights-child-sale-children-child

United Nations Office of Human Rights. (2000b). *Protocol to prevent, suppress and punish trafficking in persons, especially women and children.* Retrieved November 3, 2021, from https://www.ohchr.org/en/professionalinterest/pages/protocoltraffickinginpersons.aspx

United Nations Office on Drugs and Crime. (2009, February). *UNODC report on human trafficking exposes modern forms of slavery.* Retrieved May 11, 2022, from https://www.unodc.org/unodc/en/data-and-analysis/glotip_2009.html

United Nations Office on Drugs and Crime. (2012, July 19). *Human trafficking: Organized crime and multibillion dollar sale of people.* Retrieved September 3, 2012, from https://www.unodc.org/unodc/en/frontpage/2012/July/human-trafficking_-organized-crime-and-the-multibillion-dollar-sale-of-people.html

United Nations Office on Drugs and Crime. (2019). *EU-UNODC cooperation: Preventing and addressing human trafficking and migrant smuggling.* Retrieved December 30, 2020, from https://www.unodc.org/unodc/en/human-trafficking/glo-act2/Countries/eu-unodc-cooperation_-preventing-and-addressing-human-trafficking-and-migrant-smuggling.html

United Nations Office on Drugs and Crime. (2021). *Global report on trafficking in persons 2020.* Retrieved September 20, 2021, from https://www.unodc.org/documents/data-and-analysis/tip/2021/GLOTiP_2020_15jan_web.pdf

U.S. Department of Justice. (2020, August 5). *MS-13 members and associates arrested for sex trafficking a minor* [Press release]. Retrieved January 31, 2022, from https://www.justice.gov/usao-edva/pr/ms-13-members-and-associates-arrested-sex-trafficking-minor

U.S. Department of Justice. (2021a, October 6). *Federal jury convicts San Jose woman in sex trafficking conspiracy* [Press release]. Retrieved January 3, 2022, from https://www.justice.gov/usao-ndca/pr/federal-jury-convicts-san-jose-woman-sex-trafficking-conspiracy

U.S. Department of Justice. (2021b). *Human trafficking.* Retrieved November 15, 2021, from https://www.justice.gov/humantrafficking

U.S. Department of Justice. (2022, January 25). *Madison man sentenced to 4 years for conspiring to sex traffick a minor* [Press release]. Retrieved February 1, 2022, from https://www.justice.gov/usao-wdwi/pr/madison-man-sentenced-4-years-conspiring-sex-traffic-minor

U.S. Department of State. (2020). *Trafficking in persons report* (20th ed.). Retrieved October 5, 2021, from https://www.state.gov/wp-content/uploads/2020/06/2020-TIP-Report-Complete-062420-FINAL.pdf

Waid, L. (2020, November 25). *Human trafficking: The secret to Putin's economy.* Harvard International Review. Retrieved January 31, 2022, from https://hir.harvard.edu/putin-and-human-trafficking/

Wheaton, E., Schauer, E., and Galli, T. (2009). Economics of human trafficking. *International Migration,* 48(4), 114–141. Retrieved June 3, 2021, from https://www.amherst.edu/media/view/247221/original/Economics+of+Human+Trafficking.pdf

World Population Review. (2020). *Human trafficking statistics by state 2020.* Retrieved October 12, 2020, from https://worldpopulationreview.com/state-rankings/human-trafficking-statistics-by-state.

CHAPTER 8

Environmental Crimes and Wildlife Trafficking

Key Terms

Big cats
Blue economy
Convention on International Trade in Endangered Species of Wild Fauna and Flora (CITES)
Corruption
Eels
Elephants
Environmental crime
Environmental Investigation Agency (EIA)
Esmond Bradley Martin
Global Assessment Report on Biodiversity and Ecosystem Services
Green crime
International Tribunal for the Law of the Sea (ITLOS)
International Union for Conservation of Nature (IUCN)
Ivory trade
Jeddah Amendment
Joannah Stutchbury
Lacey Act
Maritime zones
Pangolins
Reptiles
Rhinoceroses
Rory Young
United Nations Environment Programme (UNEP)
Wildlife trafficking
World Wildlife Crime Report

CHAPTER OBJECTIVES

Chapter 8 will enable readers to understand the following:

- the various categories or environmental crimes as recognized by the international community
- the relationship between environmental crime and transnational organized crime (TOC)

(continued)

- the motivating factors that facilitate the involvement of TOC and environmental crimes
- legislative efforts to address environmental crimes
- the role of corruption in facilitating environmental crimes
- the relationship between environmental crimes and COVID-19
- the reasons why wildlife trafficking is viewed as the most significant environmental crime
- the relationship between environmental crime and other trafficking crimes, including the most severe consequences of environmental crime

FOR YEARS, THOSE attempting to address the consequences of the criminal activities for TOC have focused on security problems, drug- and human-trafficking profits, corruption, and coercion. Today, the relationship between TOC and the environment can no longer be ignored, as on a daily basis species are threatened, biodiversity is depleted, and public health is put at risk. In fact, illicit economies have emerged as one of the key factors in negative consequences to environments, nature, the climate, and societies (Brombacher et al., 2021).

> In December of 2019, a South Dakota man pleaded guilty to the change of conspiracy to commit wildlife trafficking. From 2014 through 2017 the defendant, along with his sons and other individuals within an organized crime network, had trafficked bald and golden eagles, hawks, and 15 other bird species, as well as parts of those birds (U.S. Department of Justice, 2019).

Environmental crimes, such as the December 2019 case described here, include any illegal activity that harms the environment, with profits to individuals and/or groups as the overarching motivating factor. Estimates suggest that, just within European Union (EU) countries, the cost of environmental crimes across the globe ranges from $7 billion to $23 billion annually with more than a 25% increase in just two years (United Nations Environment Programme, 2016). One of the most widely recognized aspects of environmental crimes is wildlife trafficking, which has been identified as a revenue source for not only TOC groups but also groups of violent extremists and those engaged in the actions of terrorism.

The United Nations Office on Drugs and Crime (2019) defines ***wildlife trafficking*** as the illegal trade, smuggling, poaching, capture, or collection of endangered species, protected wildlife, derivatives, or products. This illegal trade is driven by high profits for the sale of

Wildlife trafficking— The illegal trade, smuggling, poaching, capture, or collection of endangered species, protected wildlife, derivatives, or products.

rare species; estimates suggest a range from $90 billion to $250 billion annually, with profits to TOC continuing to increase (Interpol, 2015). In other words, illicit economies support the continued existence of environmental crimes.

Research suggests that the three dimensions of illicit economies by TOC and as applied to environmental crimes are extractive economies, nonextractive economies, and state's responses to illicit economies (Brombacher et al., 2021). Fueled by an insatiable demand for consumption, status, and traditional medicine, environmental crime is one of the world's most lucrative illegal businesses, often operated by sophisticated, international, and well-organized criminal networks seeking to exploit the high rewards and low risks of the trade (Global Environment Facility, 2020). Wildlife trafficking is only one aspect of environmental crime, as each of the dimensions is significant. Specifically, extractive illicit economies include the acts of poaching, the trafficking of wildlife, and illegal extractions such as mining, fishing, and timber trafficking (Brombacher et al., 2021). Nonextractive illicit economies include illegal cultivations, and the production and trafficking of illicit drugs, which results in deforestation, pollution of water, and the illegal dumping of chemicals. State's responses include aerial spraying of drug crops with potent herbicides that are fatal to other fauna, law enforcement's discretion to not arrest, and small or no fines for these crimes (Brombacher et al., 2021).

> Environmental crimes include any illegal activity that harms the environment with profits to individuals and groups as the motivation.

Environmental crime is an illegal act that directly harms the environment. Included within such criminal actions are the environmental crimes related to wildlife, biodiversity, and natural resources. In response, a variety of agencies (national and international) focus their efforts on reducing environmental crimes. In the United States, the largest of these is the Environmental Protection Agency (EPA), an independent federal agency established in the 1970s that focuses on matters of environmental protection. Within the global community, the **Environmental Investigation Agency** (EIA) is an international agency with offices in London and Washington, D.C. Since its inception in 1984, the EIA has been exposing environmental crime around the globe and has sought greater political support for stronger enforcement action against such international crimes (Banks et al., 2008).

CATEGORIES OF ENVIRONMENTAL CRIME

- illegal trade of wildlife
- illegal trade in ozone-depleting substances
- dumping of and illegal transport of various kinds of hazardous waste
- illegal, unregulated, and unreported fishing
- illegal logging and trade in timber (Banks et al., 2008)

International environmental crime can be defined across five broad areas of offenses: (1) illegal trade of wildlife; (2) illegal trade in ozone-depleting substances; (3) dumping of and illegal transport of various kinds of hazardous waste; (4) illegal, unregulated, and unreported fishing; and (5) illegal logging and trade in timber. Many African and Asian countries serve as source countries for the illegal wildlife trade. Underdeveloped or economically challenged countries such as Venezuela and Brazil have been identified as source countries for illegal mining. Ghana, Indonesia, and Zambia are among the destination countries for toxic waste (Biello, 2014). In terms of illegal fishing, China is the most vulnerable. Finally, with some of the largest rainforests in the world, Papua New Guinea (PNG), Brazil, and the Congo are identified as among the most vulnerable for illegal logging (Bohmer & Kalenga, 2019). Oftentimes, because of the profits produced, TOC is heavily involved in environmental crime.

For over a quarter century, the EIA has been recognized by government agencies, nonprofit organizations, and others for its extraordinary work addressing global environmental problems. The EIA, located in London since 1984 and in Washington, D.C., since 1989, has identified and implemented specific solutions to the world's most pressing environmental problems—including the international ban on **ivory trade** in 1989 and the passage of the 2008 **Lacey Act** Amendment in the United States to address a wide variety of prohibited animal and plant products (Environmental Investigation Agency, 2015).

Specifically, organized environmental crime, by its nature, requires the cross-border transportation that is embedded within TOC, and research suggests that environmental crime is one of the fastest growing types of TOC. This chapter examines environmental crimes, the categories of environmental crimes, and the roles of TOC in facilitating these crimes. Providing discussions on all five of the areas of international environmental crime, the chapter focuses on TOC and wildlife trafficking—including consequences of wildlife trafficking and the factors that facilitate wildlife trafficking, as well as the effects of COVID-19 on wildlife trafficking.

Lacey Act—First enacted in 1900 by the United States, it was the first conservation law for the country, which prohibits trade in wildlife. Specifically, today the Lacey Act makes it is unlawful to import, export, sell, acquire, or purchase fish, wildlife, or plants that are taken, possessed, transported, or sold (1) in violation of U.S. or Indian law, or (2) in interstate or foreign commerce involving any fish, wildlife, or plants taken, possessed, or sold in violation of state or foreign law (U.S. Fish and Wildlife Service, 2006).

In 2000, Europol concluded that environmental crime seldom attracted the attention of TOC (European Union Action to Fight Environmental Crime, 2015); a decade later, however, Europol recognized environmental crime as one of the emerging threats in the EU with exponential growth due to its profitability (European Union Action to Fight Environmental Crime, 2015). In particular, as Europol reported, the low risk and high profit of environmental crimes has resulted in attracting TOC groups, which had previously only been involved in money laundering, financial crime, thefts and drug trafficking (European Union Action to Fight Environmental Crime, 2015). In 2013, Europol further suggested that two of the most prominent environmental crimes featuring the involvement of TOC within the EU the trafficking in illicit waste and the trafficking of endangered species (European Union Action to Fight Environmental Crime, 2015).

Recent assessments from the United States are also focusing on environmental crimes. Specifically, the U.S. Financial Crimes Enforcement Network (FinCEN) released its 2021 financial threat analysis on wildlife-trafficking threat patterns and suggested that the illegal movement of wildlife accounted for a quarter of all the wildlife trade. Hence, wildlife trafficking is a major TOC activity that fuels **corruption** and exploits weaknesses in financial and nonfinancial sectors, which damages the economic integrity of a country (Financial Crimes Enforcement Network, 2021).

The Business of Environmental Crime

Wildlife crimes are most often considered in discussions on environmental crimes and on profits by TOC; however, the illicit trafficking and disposal of hazardous waste and trash is emerging as another lucrative business for TOC (Federation of American Scientists, 2000). *Environmental crime* includes the following:

> Corporate crime in the forestry sector, the illegal exploitation and sale of gold and minerals, illegal fisheries/fishing, and the trafficking of hazardous waste and chemicals (United Nations Environment Programme, 2016). Today, the value of the illegal wildlife trade is becoming dwarfed by profits to TOC through engagements in other environmental

> crimes. Specifically, forestry crimes account for an estimated $51–152 Billion, illegal fishing accounts for an estimated $11–24 Billion, illegal mining accounts for an estimated at $12–48 Billion, and the illegal disposal of waste accounts for an estimated $10–12 Billion annually (United Nations Environment Programme, 2016). In addition to environmental crimes, TOC groups often accompan[y] the crime of wildlife trafficking with the trafficking of guns and drugs as the connection and routes are established and only the product vary. (White, 2016)

In January of 2019, Uganda government authorities seized 750 pieces of ivory and thousands of pangolin scales hidden in melted wax that had been poured into hollowed logs for transportation out of the country (Nambi, 2019).

In many ways, as demonstrated in the January 2019 case here, wildlife trafficking is easier than the trafficking of other products, as regulatory checks are fewer and products are concealable. Thus, wildlife trafficking is yet another revenue stream for TOC and, depending on the product, a quite lucrative aspect of trafficking. Specifically, the U.S. State Department estimates that wildlife trafficking is the third largest type of illegal trade (after drugs and weapons), with profits of around $10 billion annually within the country (Hou, 2019). Research suggests that many of the TOC activities in illegal wildlife and/or wildlife products involve criminal groups with broad international reaches and profits; in addition, sometimes the indirect consequences of profits include use of finance civil conflict and violent extremist activities as well as money laundering (World Wildlife Fund, 2012). Most recently, epidemiologists have identified yet another negative consequence of wildlife trafficking: the transmission of disease. Specifically, illicit wildlife trafficking can provide an avenue of disease transmission that threatens the health of humans, other animals, and even ecosystems (World Wildlife Fund, 2012). This topic, as related to the recent COVID-19 pandemic, is discussed later in this chapter.

Green crime—Illegal activity that involves the environment, biodiversity, or natural resources.

Green crime refers to crimes that affect the environment. Wildlife trafficking, although not considered significant in the past, is quickly becoming a critical topic of discussion for green criminologists and those interested in protecting the environment. In fact, the international community has currently committed to addressing wildlife trafficking through the Convention on International Trade in

In September 2020, U.S. federal law enforcement arrested a wildlife-trafficking ring that had smuggled more than 10,000 pounds of shark fins into the country to be exported to Hong Kong (Sharpless, 2020).

Endangered Specifies of Wild Fauna and Flora (CITES). Yet TOC continues to form distribution networks across country boundaries by linking source countries and destination or consumer countries via indirect routes through transit states, often with violence and corruption as tools of practice.

History of Regulating Environmental Crime

As demonstrated in the 2020 case above, environmental crimes are not limited to land-based crimes; historically, crimes on the seas were the focus of environmental concerns. In the United States, the first environmentally specific law was the Rivers and Harbors Act of 1899, which attempted to address the polluting of waters (Uhlmann, 2009). The regulation of international wildlife trade began with a focus on African species and the signing in 1900 of the Convention Designed to Ensure the Conservation of various species of wild animals in Africa, which are useful to Man or inoffensive, which was identified as the first international treaty on nature conservation; however, it was never ratified. In 1933, the Convention Relative to the Preservation of Fauna and Flora in their Natural State was adopted (Rosen, 2020). This action, later known as the London Convention, focused mainly on the protection of African species by prohibiting hunting, killing, and capture through the regulation of international trade. The **International Union for Conservation of Nature (IUCN)**, established in 1948, institutionalized these efforts at the international level. During this same time period, several countries proposed that a permanent international body be established to address maritime safety and issues. This international organization, empowered in 1948 to address maritime pollution, became known as the International Maritime Organization, or IMO (International Maritime Organization, 2019). Today, the IMO is based upon four pillars: law of sovereign nations, law of freedom of the high seas, law of freedom of contract, and legal personality of a ship (Law Z Magazine, 2015). With the pillars as a foundation, the IMO provides a regulating framework for maritime security, environment concerns, and maritime safety.

International Union for Conservation of Nature (IUCN)—An organization for nature conservation and the sustainable use of natural resources; collects data, conducts projects, and provides educational awareness programs to assist countries in protecting their natural resources (McNeely, 2005).

At the seventh General Assembly of the International Union for Conservation of Nature (IUCN), in 1960, its delegates expressed concern over the threatened status of many species and urged governments to restrict imports of animals according to regulations of exporting countries. This brought to the forefront the realization that countries often did not know other countries' regulations regarding environmental crimes, especially those crimes affecting wildlife. To resolve this problem, in 1963 the IUCN General Assembly called for the creation of a new treaty to regulate international trade in wildlife (McNeely, 2005). In 1973, the **Convention on International Trade in Endangered Species of Wild Fauna and Flora (CITES)** was established.

The original CITES was an international agreement among 80 countries, including the United States, and was one of the first documented recognitions of the problems of environmental crime. Today, this agreement is a significant effort to address wildlife trafficking; in the 1960s and 1970s, however, discussions on endangered animals and transnational crimes were rare, as only a few countries considered crimes that occurred outside their borders to be worthy of criminal justice efforts. The most significant aspect of the CITES, as related to wildlife trade, is its identification of species with trade bans in place to prohibit the commercial movement or trafficking of specimens or their body parts that are caught in the wild (Frank & Wilcove, 2019).

Later, 1982, the **International Tribunal for the Law of the Sea (ITLOS)** was established as an independent judicial body through the UN Convention on the Law of the Sea with the purpose of settling disputes related to **maritime zones**, conservational of the resources of the sea, and the protection of the maritime environment (ITLOS, 2021). Of course, in hindsight, these legislative efforts helped to fuel the supply demand for products, which was met by TOC groups. Today, the CITES provides varying degrees of protection for more than 37,000 animals and plants and serves as international agreement among over 180 countries, including the United States and China, for the protection of environmental products (Convention on International Trade in Endangered Species of Wild Fauna and Flora, 2021).

In 2009, in response to the recognition of criminal gangs and their actions of piracy within the Western Indian Ocean region and the Gulf of Aden, the IMO facilitated the Djibouti Code of Conduct (hereafter, the Code) aimed to repress piracy and armed robbery on the seas (Chaudhury, 2020). In only a few years, the Code was used to address the emerging trends of criminal actions by TOC groups—specifically, human trafficking and illegal fishing as illicit maritime activities involving TOC (International Maritime Organization, 2019).

Jeddah Amendment—A revision to the Djibouti Code of Conduct, adopted in 2017, that recognizes the important role of the "blue economy," including shipping and fishing, and expresses concerns over crimes that occur at sea, such as piracy (International Maritime Organization, 2019).

Blue economy—The sustainable and integrated development of economic sectors for healthy seas (World Bank, 2017).

In June 2014, the **United Nations Environment Programme (UNEP)** dedicated much of its first UN Environment Assembly (UNEA) to addressing illegal wildlife trade. In 2017, the Code adopted a revised code of conduct known as the **Jeddah Amendment** to the Djibouti Code. This revised code recognized the importance of the **blue economy** and blue crimes, and the importance of repressing TOC in the maritime domain, maritime terrorism, illegal fishing, and other illegal activities that occur at sea (International Maritime Organization, 2019). For clarity, blue crimes include three categories: crimes against mobility, criminal flows, and environmental crimes. Specifically, crimes against mobility, such as piracy, target the movement of goods and international shipping across seas (Bueger & Edmunds, 2020). Criminal flows are sometimes called transit crimes or crimes of trafficking. Environmental crimes are activities that cause significant harm to the marine environment.

In 2019, the UN Security Council held its first discussion on the dangers on TOC and their crimes at sea. Within this meeting, the definition of *transnational* was discussed, as typically this involves the action of organized crime between two countries, which may not apply at sea. Specifically, the definition was expanded to include crimes that take place in or between spaces of specific, partial, or shared authority such as areas of port countries, territorial waters, contiguous zones (CZs), exclusive economic zones (EEZs), and the high seas or international straits (Bueger & Edmunds, 2020).

In 2020, UNEP launched the Wild for Life campaign in cooperation with the United Nations Development Programme, the United Nations Office on Drugs and Crime (UNODC), and CITES. This campaign extended international efforts for protecting species through the use of social media and media influences to promote the importance of protecting wildlife and combating wildlife trafficking (United Nations Environment Programme, 2020). However, as with all crimes committed by TOC groups, as profits continue to increase, unless laws

MARITIME ZONES AND BOUNDARIES

- Internal Waters: The waters on the landward side of the baselines from which the territorial sea is measured
- Territorial Sea: The area that extends seaward up to 12 nautical miles from its baselines
- Contiguous Zone: The area that extends up to 24 nautical miles adjacent to and beyond its territorial sea
- Exclusive Economic Zone: The area that extends up to 200 nautical miles adjacent to and beyond its baselines
- Continental Shelf: The seabed and subsoil of the submarine areas that extend beyond territorial seas
- High Seas: Areas not included in other zones to include all parts of the sea (National Oceanic and Atmospheric Administration, 2021)

and penalties are administered, the criminal actions of TOC in environmental crimes will increase.

The Problems of Wildlife Trafficking

Research suggests that, since 1970, the earth has lost approximately 60% of its vertebrate populations (Hou, 2019). The **Global Assessment Report on Biodiversity and Ecosystem Services** suggests that one third of marine animals, reef-forming corals, and sharks are on the brink of extinction and that approximately 40% of amphibians are in jeopardy (Lindwall, 2019). Currently, some species such as the Caribbean monk seal and the white rhino are extinct (Hou, 2019). In 2019, the International Union for Conservation of Nature (IUCN) listed 958 species as at risk for extinction by (Frank & Wilcove, 2019). Included within those species are elephants, black rhinoceroses, and pangolins. In addition, the illegal wildlife trade is judged to be one of the most significant factors in the extinction of species (Broad et al., 2003).

> The Intergovernmental Science-Policy Platform on Biodiversity and Ecosystem Services (IPBES), an independent intergovernmental body made up of over 130 member governments, was established in 2012 to provide policy makers with objective scientific assessments on the planet's biodiversity and ecosystems (Intergovernmental Science-Policy Platform on Biodiversity and Ecosystem Services, 2019).

These extinctions not only impact the species themselves but also pose risks to human populations. This is especially true for African countries, which are either suppliers or transit points for many products within the illegal wildlife trade (Gikonyo, 2019). Specifically, researchers suggest that climate change or other destruction of nature may lead to global warming and a reduction of healthy soils and crops that are required to support humankind in Africa, which experiences approximately 45% of the wildlife crimes (van Uhm and Nijman, 2020). In addition, climate change affects water quality, air quality, and weather patterns. Finally, an estimated four billion individuals who rely on natural medicines for their health may find that those ingredients no longer exist (Hou, 2019).

With the growth of international markets and limited governmental regulations on trade, corruption and violence often increase in conjunction with wildlife trafficking. Research suggests that wildlife trafficking and wildlife crime contribute to instabilities often experienced by underdeveloped countries. In fact, in Central African countries such as the Democratic Republic of the Congo, some armed groups fund their militant activities through money raised by poaching and selling animal parts (Hou, 2019). In addition, as highlighted later in this chapter, wildlife trafficking may result in the deaths of those attempting to prohibit these criminal activities and advocate for the preservation of nature and wildlife.

Finally, research suggests that wildlife trafficking spreads diseases and invasive alien species, which are harmful to animals, plants, and people. Given that *trafficking*, by definition, involves crossing borders without proper documentation or inspections, there is no question that wildlife trafficking has contributed to the 70% increase in invasive alien species transferring diseases to the human population since 1970 (Hou, 2019). Currently there are those who suggest that COVID-19 has been linked with the transportation of wildlife (Doody et al., 2021).

Specifically, the World Health Organization has determined that COVID-19—like SARS, Ebola, bird flu, and MERS—originated from an animal, and recently scientists have claimed that smuggling of pangolins in Southeast Asia could be one of the triggers of COVID-19, as these smuggled animals carried viruses closely related to coronavirus (Organisation for Economic Co-operation and Development, 2020). In fact, as pangolins are the most commonly illegally trafficked animal in Southeast Asia and are utilized both as food and in traditional medicine, the Organisation for Economic Co-operation and Development (OECD)'s Task Force on Countering Illicit Trade has been looking at the threat of wildlife trafficking as related to diseases and economic development, all of which impact humans.

Factors Facilitating Wildlife Trafficking

Globally, there is a high demand for wild plants and animals and products made from these products. However, empirical data identifying the specific factors that facilitate wildlife trafficking are sparse and incomplete. What is known regarding any form of trafficking is that the presence of demand combined with the lack of applied restrictions either by laws or by societies facilitates the illegal activities. Interventions that attempt to address wildlife trafficking often proceed on the assumption that the wildlife trade is based on commonsense thinking; thus, they generally fail to reduce the criminal activities because they fail to address the demanded supply of the product(s) that fuels the problem.

Research into the factors that facilitate wildlife trafficking suggests there are numerous conditions that facilitate the criminal activity, including socioeconomic factors, legal efforts, and societal awareness. Specifically, poverty has been suggested to be linked both directly and indirectly to poaching and trafficking of ivory and rhino horn from sub-Saharan Africa (Duffy & St. John, 2013).

In addition, West Africa has been affected by additional illicit TOC activities, including stolen oil and the dumping of toxic waste (United Nations Office on Drugs and Crime, 2019). In the case of stolen oil, before TOC groups can traffick the oil, they must obtain it. Classic oil bunkering involves attaching a secondary pipeline to a company main line; the theft of oil involves filling or overfilling containers, then paying less than the actual price. While more attention is given to bunkering, a lack of accounting and the corruption of oil officials must not be ignored (United Nations Office on Drugs and Crime, 2019). However, people involved in the trade are not necessarily poor, and poor individuals who are involved usually do not drive the trade. Specifically, improving the income or living standard of harvester communities will not necessarily reduce their participation in the wildlife trade.

Lastly, wildlife trafficking is profitable on its own; however, since it rarely receives the scrutiny given to other trafficked products, TOC groups have realized that wildlife trafficking provides opportunities for trafficking other commodities such as drugs or weapons (Wyatt et al., 2020). This realization has led to an emergence of multifaceted groups involved in wildlife trafficking as well trafficking of other products. Hence, when drug laws are strictly enforced and traffickers' drugs profits are minimized, then the same routes can be used to carry out wildlife trafficking instead. In other words, wildlife trafficking produces profits and creates diverging criminal careers for members of TOC groups.

Since 2016, legal controls have tightened in a number of wildlife markets, including those for ivory and pangolins (United Nations Office on Drugs and Crime, 2020b). Research suggests that laws and regulations often provide an effective mechanism for controlling illegal and unsustainable trade (Duffy & St. John, 2008). Law enforcement and broader governance conditions are also considered to be critical factors in determining their ultimate success and impact, as well as trade arrangements, traditional practices, and voluntary agreements. Unfortunately, these aspects of wildlife trafficking are often accompanied by corruption in the form of bribes, and corruption of legal authorities has been found to be a critical enabler of the illicit wildlife trade, taking place at sourcing, transit, and export stages and involving both public and private-sector abuse of power and trust (United Nations Office on Drugs and Crime, 2020b).

Lastly, research suggests that awareness of the problem of trafficking often reduces the incidents (McCabe, 2017). In particular, research on awareness campaigns has shown relatively high degrees of success in raising awareness about the illegality and negative conservation impacts of the wildlife trade among harvesters, traders, and consumers (Duffy & St. John, 2008). For example, the IUCN in Burma has resulted in a clear shift in the mindset of the people surveyed, with perceptions toward purchasing wildlife products shifting away from the demand for wildlife products (IUCN, 2017). However, there are still significant gaps in understanding about the links between awareness-raising and changes in the attitudes and behavior of participants in the wildlife trade.

Role of Corruption

Corruption is one of the most important elements of environmental crimes and the illicit wildlife trade (Zain, 2020). As wildlife trafficking and other similar crimes are perceived as high profit and low risk, TOC groups target these avenues of criminal activity, which are associated with a maximum monetary value (Zain, 2020). In the actions of TOC, corruption facilitates all aspects of wildlife trafficking. An example of the role of corruption in environmental crimes is the illicit trafficking and disposal of hazardous waste and trash as a lucrative activity for Italy's organized crime groups (Federation of American Scientists, 2000). According to reports, front companies and legitimate waste removal businesses, controlled by TOC groups, will earn billions of dollars by illicitly trafficking toxic waste from other countries and then dumping the waste in rural areas and in the country's waters. The same is true in Russia, where TOC members pay officials to allow the international exportation of stolen oil and precious metals and gems (Federation of American Scientists, 2000).

Wildlife trafficking is facilitated through a recognized five-step process that involves corruption at every stage:

1. *Obtaining the product*—In the trafficking of wildlife and/or wildlife parts, the first step, obtaining the product, is essential. Local individuals or individuals associated with the locals in the area facilitate the possession of poached animals by encouraging poachers to provide the products to them for financial remuneration. The more poachers, the wider the reach of the associate or buyer. The buyer, who in turn is either connected to the TOC group or is a member of the TOC group, now has the product to be trafficked for profit.
2. *Accumulating the product*—The second step in the illicit wildlife trade, the accumulation of product, is also critical to the criminal activity. Through the links, threats, and bribes of TOC, wildlife products are made ready to be moved across boundaries.
3. *Moving or transporting the product*—The third step of wildlife trafficking, moving or transporting the product, involves document(s) fraud as international trade is regulated and managed through various licenses, permits, and certifications. TOC groups, familiar with the documentation required in trade, provide the paperwork (forged, edited, or purchased illegally) required to move their product.

4. *Admitting the product into the consumer country*—In the fourth step, admitting the illicit product into the consumer country, TOC groups, familiar with the transportation hubs, facilitate these illegal trades through coercion, collusion, and bribes to private sectors, public regulators, and enforcement authorities at trade crossing such as seaports and airports. Since by definition TOC involves criminal activities that cross borders, the routes of trade are already established and are regularly used for wildlife trafficking.
5. *Gifting the illegal product, or corporate gifting*—The last step of the illicit wildlife trade involves delivery of the product. In many countries, gift-giving is an official practice that frequently involves luxury products. These gifts, often rare and exotic, demonstrate an abuse of entrusted power for private gain and are made possible through the actions of corruption by TOC (Zain, 2020).

COVID-19

Among the comparative rankings on perceptions of trafficking crimes, wildlife trafficking consistently ranks below the trafficking of drugs, humans, and weapons (Doody et al., 2021). Given the suggestion by the medical research community that COVID-19 is likely a zoonotic pathogen in wild bats that passed to humans possibly through the pangolin, an animal often trafficked for its meat and scales, wildlife trafficking is becoming a concern (United Nations Office on Drugs and Crime, 2020a). Specifically, the commercial trade in pangolins by TOC has been illegal in Malaysia since 2000 (Doody et al., 2021); however, given that both legal and illegal wildlife trade markets operate within the same location, obtaining unauthorized and unregulated wildlife species is not necessarily a difficult task.

Other consequences of COVID-19 as related to TOC activities and environmental crimes involve reactions to lockdowns by countries across the globe. As COVID-19 forced societies to quarantine and to rely of personal protective equipment (PPE) such as face masks and sanitizer, TOC was able to profit both from the shortage of products obtained through legitimate supply chains and from the price-gouging of products trafficked by their members (Djordjevic & Dobovsek, 2020). In these cases, while police were focused on monitoring community lockdowns and violations to public health policies, TOC was able to operate with even fewer cases of detection than in the pre-COVID era (Djordjevic & Dobovsek, 2020).

The result of introducing COVID-19 into the world was over 2.8 million human deaths (Worldometer, 2021). Through the consequences of COVID-19, the activities of TOC increased to include the increased exposure of humans to illegally trafficked wildlife and the increased abilities of TOC to fulfill supply demands through its operations. Given the cost of COVID-19 to society and the likelihood that wildlife trafficking was the host that introduced the pathogen into society and brought about the increase in TOC's abilities to engage in environmental crimes, these crimes may be among the most severe aspects of TOC.

Wildlife Trafficking

In the United States, the Lacey Act of 1900 made it unlawful to import, export, sell or purchase fish, wildlife, or plants that were in violation of U.S. or Indian law. Today, after multiple revisions and the introduction of additional legislation, the list of animals subjected to wildlife trafficking is even longer and now includes not only mammals, but also birds, reptiles, and ocean dwellers. Based upon the 2020 World Wildlife Report, the most common species are elephants and rhinoceroses, pangolins, reptiles, big cats, and eels (United Nations Office on Drugs and Crime, 2020b). These "more common" species are the focus of this section.

Elephants and Rhinoceroses

At one time, **elephants** that were poached for their ivory tusks and **rhinoceroses** (hereafter, rhinos) that were poached for their horns were discussed separately, as elephant tusks were used in art and jewelry while rhino horns were used in traditional medicines (United Nations Office on Drugs and Crime, 2020b). For the discussion here, however, they are discussed together as mammals with similar products of desire. In February of 2012, hundreds of elephants in Cameroon were slaughtered

> In June of 2020, poachers in Ethiopia were discovered to have killed six elephants in one day. The poachers immediately removed the elephants' tusks, which officials suspected are being slipped out of the country to China and Southeast Asia (Burke, 2020).

by poaching gangs believed to originate in Chad and Sudan and to have entered the country through adjacent borders (World Wildlife Fund, 2012). At the same time, evidence suggests that rhino horns are used as palliative medicine for cancer by affluent individuals in Vietnam (World Wildlife Fund, 2012). In fact, research suggests that rhino poaching increased 7700% from 2007 to 2013 (World Wildlife Fund, 2021).

As demonstrated in the June 2020 case of ivory poaching above, for both elephant tusks and rhino horns the source continent is Africa, with two of the largest ivory consumer markets located in China and the United States (United Nations Office on Drugs and Crime, 2020b); however, in 2016 both countries committed to closing their global markets by prohibiting import, export, and interstate trade of African elephant ivory. In addition, Thailand, another source country, has taken significant measures to criminalize the trade of African elephant ivory. These efforts resulted in a significant reduction in ivory for sale in the domestic market (United Nations Office on Drugs and Crime, 2020b), as it is suggested that these restrictions on the legal market also reduced the illegal market. However, the legal efforts to reduce the trade of these items did not eliminate the illegal market. In particular, because rhino horn is relatively portable and value-intensive, the vast majority is thought to be trafficked by air routes, concealed in luggage and personal carry-ons. Despite this prohibition, contingents of die-hard ivory buyers, primarily affluent individuals who travel abroad frequently and purchase the ivory and/or rhino horns while overseas, continue to participate in the trafficking of elephant ivory and rhino horns. Thus, TOC members who provide the products continue to profit from the trafficking of elephants and rhinos.

Pangolins

In 2019, an estimated 195,000 pangolins were trafficked for their scales, to be utilized in medical treatments (Rosen, 2020). **Pangolins** are reclusive nocturnal creatures and are the only mammal completely covered in scales. These animals are trafficked for their scales, which are used in traditional medicines, and their meat, which is thought of as a delicacy in many exotic food restaurants. Researchers, having limited knowledge of pangolin ecology, are now suggesting that the pangolin is the most heavily trafficked wild mammal in the world (United Nations Office on Drugs and Crime, 2020b).

There are eight identified species of pangolin found in the source regions of Asia and Africa (United Nations Office on Drugs and Crime, 2020b). Since 2014, it has been suggested that the trafficking of these animals has dramatically increased as there has been a significant increase in the number of whole pangolin equivalents seized globally. Currently, countries such as Nigeria, Uganda, and the Democratic Republic of the Congo serve as transit countries and logistical hubs for pangolin trafficking and other forms of wildlife trafficking (United Nations Office on Drugs and Crime, 2020b). Traffickers of pangolin, including government officials and foreign workers based in the country for development projects, tend to be members of TOC with enough wealth and political connections to ensure protection from the authorities. The two most common destination countries for pangolin scales and meat are Vietnam and Malaysia (also discussed previously in this chapter as related to pangolins and the possible transmission of COVID-19).

Reptiles

In the **2020 World Wildlife Crime Report**, several species of **reptiles** appeared among the most trafficked species in the world, including crocodilians, lizards, snakes, tortoises, and freshwater turtles (United Nations Office on Drugs and Crime, 2020b). Reptiles are trafficked for their meat, skins or shells, and venom, and for their use as pets. Since, 2016, as fashion brands and designers have limited their use of animal skins and have expanded their support to reptile conservation programs, it is suggested that the trafficking of reptiles has declined; however, as the movement of live reptiles often results in high mortality rates, the extent of reptile trafficking to result in a productive number for trade is vague. Live reptiles detected in illegal international trade are from several source parts of the world, including South Asia, Central Asia, Southeast Asia, East Africa, and West Africa. The reptiles most commonly seized have been identified as turtles and snakes.

In terms of shipment sizes, research suggests that the trafficking of wildlife involves a limited number of animals per shipment, as fewer than 15 reptiles per shipment accounted for 80% of seizures in the world (United Nations Office on Drugs and Crime, 2020b). Based on seizures, Asia is the main destination (or possibly a transit destination) for the illegal live reptile trade, followed by the United States and then the countries within Europe. In terms of source countries, Vietnam often provides meats to wildlife meat restaurants, including snakes, lizards, boas, and other animals (Ngoc & Wyatt, 2012). To avoid detection, the trafficking routes used by TOC are in constant flux, with traffickers seeking emerging transit opportunities and concentrating their activities in major air transit hubs for more direct flight options to reduce the likelihood of species deaths during transit (United Nations Office on Drugs and Crime, 2020b).

Big Cats

With the exception of the African lion, which is now officially classified as vulnerable, the international commercial trade of **big cats** (e.g., tigers, lions, jaguars) is illegal except under a few narrow conditions related to numbers and age. However, the sport hunting of lions has been a mainstay for South Africa's private game reserves for decades. In 2007, an examination of the adverse effects of trophy hunting on lion conservation and restrictions on trophy exports put pressure on game ranchers to find new outlets for their stock, which included the international sale of lion bones as a supplement to tiger bones in the trade (United Nations Office on Drugs and Crime, 2020b).

As tigers and tiger products such as their skin, claws, and teeth are still used ornamentally and are in demand, these items provide a good product for supply by TOC groups. The use of tiger bones, which continue to be used in tonics and medicines in East Asia, poses the most serious threat to the animal's survival (United Nations Office on Drugs and Crime, 2020b). In addition to medicinal purposes, tiger bones may also be soaked in wine to make tiger wine, boiled down to make glue or cake, and ground into powder for use in pills, plasters, and other manufactured medicinal products; hence, the utility of tiger bones results in its high demand.

Jaguars, mainly killed in retaliation for conflict with humans and their livestock, are also trafficked for parts across the states of Latin America (including Belize, Brazil, Costa Rica, Honduras, Panama, Peru, and Suriname) (United Nations Office on Drugs and Crime, 2020b). In addition, necklaces and keychains made of their teeth are found in local Asian markets. Traffickers link suppliers in source countries, both poachers and farms, with retailers in destination countries through the use of wildlife trade "hot spots." Source countries for big cats include China, India, Vietnam, and Indonesia, with China and Thailand identified as the largest of the destination countries (United Nations Office on Drugs and Crime, 2020b).

Eels

Eels are consumed by many cultures, and eel products are produced around the world. Research suggests that the use of eel is so great that not only are legal demands high but the demands of the illegal eel supply are high well (United Nations Office on Drugs and Crime, 2020b). The main source of eel that is illegally trafficked by TOC are the commercial fishing industries. In Europe, a type of eel, the glass eel, is caught for the legal market and knowingly or unknowingly is also supplied by illegal exporters and poachers, who fish clandestinely with the intent to support the illegal trade market. Established legal eel traders have been found to also be involved in illegal exports; therefore, any commercial fisherman selling glass eels to a trader could unwittingly be complicit in illegal exports (United Nations Office on Drugs and Crime, 2020b). Although it is not always acknowledged, few traders are ignorant of this fact.

Unlike contraband for drugs or weapons, there is no recognized black market for eel meat products. Instead, similar to some other wildlife products, legitimate eel products are tainted by illegitimate sources of supply. Specifically, in countries such as Japan and China, where eels are an important food source, providing these products is essential regardless of supply source and TOC is aware of this demand. In addition, many countries, including those in Europe as well as the United States, consume eel with little consideration to the effects that this large-scale consumption has on the ecosystem.

Wildlife trafficking is one of the most lucrative criminal actions for TOC groups involved in environmental crimes. These crimes, in addition to providing profits for TOC groups, also damage the ecosystems as well as threaten the longevity of the species being trafficked. However, another outcome of environmental crime that has only recently been identified is its role in facilitating other crimes. Specifically, as discussed in the next section of this chapter, wildlife trafficking and other environmental crime may provide the foundation for other crimes (McCabe, 2017) and security vulnerabilities within countries.

Implications for Security

International security organizations such as Interpol (2015) suggest that TOC groups involved in wildlife crimes often use the profits to fund rebel activities and purchase weapons. Research suggests that in Africa, ongoing armed conflicts and the profits from illicit wildlife trafficking are directly linked (Global Financial Integrity, 2012). Specifically, as the illegal ivory trade generates around $400 million annually and the illegal logging trade generates around $100 billion annually, investigations suggest that some of those profits by TOIC help to fund Islamist extremists and rebel movements, including Somalia's al-Qaeda (McNeish, 2014). In fact, the ivory trade was once the primary source of funding for the Lord's Resistance Army in Uganda (McNeish, 2014).

Another impact on security that results from the illicit trade of wildlife is the depletion of the social and economic resources of a country (World Wildlife Fund, 2012). Countries that are deprived of tax revenue from business transactions lack the financial resources to support their residents. Countries without educational programs, health care, and social services are often overwhelmed by populations with little promise of productive citizenship; hence, these individuals may resort to illegal activities to support their livelihoods.

Also, in countries that can offer little support to their populations, residents often experience corruption throughout all levels of government authority. Corruption reduces the effectiveness of governments, deters civil engagement, and erodes the rule of law (World Wildlife Fund, 2012). Corruption benefits TOC, increases a country's vulnerability, and limits the opportunities for legitimate business.

Finally, illicit wildlife trades often support unenforced laws and weakened criminal justice systems. These conditions enable criminal activities of all kinds, including violent extremism and terrorism. For those concerned about the implication on security for countries, wildlife trafficking provides many reasons to worry.

The Role of TOC in Environmental Crimes

TOC utilizes the illicit trade of wildlife, or wildlife trafficking, merely for profit. In fact, estimates suggest that wildlife trafficking is one of the most cost-effective aspects of TOC (Barber-Meyer,

2010). Assessments of wildlife species suggest that, in most cases, local residents harvest the wildlife specimens, then sell them to small retailers within their communities. These small retailers transfer the products to either provincial traders who transfer them to international traders or these community traders transfer the products directly to the international traders (General Department of Forestry, 2021). The profits for each of these actors are minimal, with the exception of the profits to the international traders or TOC members, who receive the most profit from the products (Nguyen, 2004). Until the context of wildlife crime as either the victimization of animals or the destruction of property and its correlation with penalties is clarified, TOC will continue to have a role in wildlife trafficking. In addition, with little importance placed on laws (Rawls, 1993), the low likelihood of law enforcement, minimal sentences being imposed, and fines being affordable, the role of TOC is likely to increase (Wyatt et al., 2020). Hence, profits for TOC will continue to grow.

In the actions of trafficking by TOC members, the mixing of illegal commodities may occur for reasons of convenience, expedience, or opportunity (Uhm et al., 2021). Specifically, when a TOC network is already established and operates without detection by police authorities, the mixing of products will occur. As displayed in the table below, this "mixing" of trafficking modes occurs through any and all of these: combined contraband, camouflage, multiple trade lines, shared smuggling routes, and the barter trade.

TOC facilitates the trafficking of wildlife through all steps in the process. The use of fraudulent shipping labels and unusual codes or product descriptions provides further access to the illegally distributed products (Sharma et al., 2019). In addition, the ease of obtaining the animal products or poaching further supports TOC groups' involvement (Pires et al., 2016). To suggest that wildlife trafficking is merely a part of criminal networks is an understatement, as it has the potential to provide significant revenues for TOC. Today's small-scale operations have the potential to engage with large-scale networks through TOC (White, 2016).

In addition, TOC continues to participate in blue crimes. In 2019, the prevalence of TOC in maritime crime was recognized when the UN Security Council held its first debate on TOC and

OVERVIEW OF TRAFFICKING MODES

Method: Combined contraband
Mode: The mixing of illegal commodities for convenience, expedience, or opportunity
Products: Illegal wildlife and illegal drugs

Method: Camouflage
Mode: A legal commodity is used as a vessel for smuggling/hiding the contraband
Products: Legal wildlife used to hide illegal drugs

Method: Multiple trade lines
Mode: Spread risks and increase controlled by dominating multiple trade lines and routes
Products: Illegal wildlife and illegal drug lines and routes controlled by the same network/group

Method: Shared smuggling routes and transport methods
Mode: Smuggling methods and/or paid corridors makes these routes profitable and multipurpose
Products: Illegal wildlife and illegal drugs

Method: Barter trade
Mode: Cashless transactions that are very hard to trace
Products: Illegal wildlife in exchange for illegal drugs (and vice versa)

(Uhm et al., 2021)

crimes at sea as being a threat to peace and security (Bueger & Edmunds, 2020). As the UN's current definition of *transnationality* is confined by its focus on the country, the fact that TOC at sea often occurs in or between spaces of specific authority—such as flag state jurisdictions (i.e., whose flag a ship flies), territorial waters, contiguous zones (areas beyond the edge of a country's jurisdiction), or exclusive economic zones (areas of the sea that a country has a special right to)—jurisdictional laws are unclear (Bueger & Edmunds, 2020). TOC is aware of this limitation and therefore continues its efforts on environmental crimes in these blue economies.

TOC has evolved with the wildlife market (Schaedla, 2017), with the infrastructure to provide opportunities for all interested parties to receive rare animals or animal parts. TOC is not a homogeneous group, and it adapts quickly to the niches in the market and the organizational preparations required to deliver the products (Wyatt et al., 2020). Thus, freelance poachers, family businesses, and corporations may all be involved with TOC and wildlife trafficking (Curtis, 1996) as the role of TOC continues to grow along with their profits.

Most Severe Consequences for Environmental Advocates

Unfortunately, in many criminal actions the most severe consequence is human death. This is also the case for environmental crimes. While these crimes may threaten public health, for some of the advocates against environmental crimes and wildlife trafficking the consequences are of the most severe nature.

In 2021, 227 activists working to protect the environment were killed.

Statistics indicate that in 2021, a record number of 227 activists working to protect the environment and land rights were murdered (Marshall, 2021). This was the highest number for the second year in a row, with nearly one third of these murders reportedly linked to the resource exploitation of logging, mining, large-scale agribusiness, hydroelectric dams, and other infrastructure (Marshall, 2021). In many cases, these victims include not only environmental activists but also community members and journalists. These victims were stabbed, beaten, or shot for reasons related to environmental crime and TOC groups. In addition, approximately 40% of those killed were indigenous community members who were simply protecting their homelands (Marshall, 2021). The following are three examples of these most severe consequences of environmental crimes committed by TOC groups.

In July of 2021, **Joannah Stutchbury**, a protester and advocate against the destruction of the Kambui Forest, was shot dead near her home in Kenya. Stutchbury had already received multiple death threats in response to her campaign against the development of wetlands in a national park (Burke, 2021).

In April of 2021, Ireland's **Rory Young**, founder of a wildlife NGO and recognized for his antipoaching efforts in West Africa, was ambushed in Burkina Faso by a gunman and killed along with two reporters (Beresford, 2021).

In February of 2018, **Esmond Bradley Martin**, a leading investigator of the illegal ivory trade, was killed in his Nairobi home by being stabbed in the neck. Known for his decades of undercover work investigating the black-market trade, Martin was concluding a report on the sale of elephant ivory and rhino horns (BBC News, 2018).

Summary

Environmental crimes and wildlife trafficking are still more profitable aspects of TOC. Each year, billions of dollars are provided to members of TOC groups as profit for their involvement in environmental crimes. Just a few of these are wildlife trafficking, the illegal trade of ozone-depleting substances, the dumping of waste, and illegal fishing. The environmental crime most commonly associated with TOC is wildlife trafficking, which until recently has been perceived as "less significant" than the trafficking of guns or people.

Environmental crimes, by definition, harm environments, with profits going to those involved in TOC. Environmental crimes—in particular, wildlife trafficking—are in many cases more appealing to TOC members, as regulations for trafficking drugs and guns are increasing, environmental crimes are less likely to be detected, and if environmental crimes are discovered, penalties are minimal. Environmental crimes, which receive the least attention from police, quite often utilize the same trafficking routes as other illicit products; they are an easy transition for TOC groups desiring to transport a different product for profit.

Unfortunately, the consequences of environmental crimes often go beyond damage to species and ecosystems. For many TOC groups, profits from environmental crimes help to support corruption by state officials and acts of violence by extremists and terrorists; for some who attempt to prohibit such events, the result may be death. Finally, the introduction of COVID-19 into society and the disease's link to the illicit animal trade, to wildlife trafficking, and to environmental crimes, although not yet considered concerning, may be the most detrimental of TOC's crimes against the world's population.

Questions for Further Thought

1. What are the conditions that support environmental crimes?
2. How has wildlife trafficking become the most widely recognized form of environmental crime?
3. What are some of the legislative efforts in place to deter environmental crimes?

References

Banks, D., Davies, C., Gosling, J., Newman, J., Rice, M., Wadley, J., & Walravens, F. (2008). *Environmental crime. A threat to our future.* Environmental Investigation Agency. Retrieved November 3, 2021, from https://www.unodc.org/documents/NGO/EIA_Ecocrime_report_0908_final_draft_low.pdf

Barber-Meyer, S. (2010). Dealing with the clandestine nature of wildlife-trade market surveys. *Conservation Biology, 24*(4), 918–923. http://www.jstor.org/stable/40864190

BBC News. (2018, February 5). *Esmond Bradley Martin: Ivory investigator killed in Kenya.* Retrieved October 19, 2021, from https://www.bbc.com/news/world-africa-42943503

Beresford, J. (2021, May 5). *Harrowing details behind the death of Irish conservationist Rory Young in Burkina Faso.* Irish Post. Retrieved January 10, 2022, from https://www.irishpost.com/news/harrowing-details-behind-the-death-of-irish-conservationist-rory-young-in-burkina-faso-emerge-211467

Biello, D. (2014, January 1). *E-waste dumping among top 10 most polluted sites.* Scientific American. Retrieved January 3, 2022, from https://www.scientificamerican.com/article/e-waste-dump-among-top-10-most-polluted-sites/

Bohmer, B., & Kalenga, M. (2019, March 21). *Corruption and illegal deforestation go hand in hand.* Transparency International. Retrieved January 10, 2022, from https://voices.transparency.org/corruption-and-illegal-deforestation-go-hand-in-hand-988854d931e5

Broad, S., Mulliken, T., & Roe, D. (2003). The nature and extent of legal and illegal trade in wildlife. In S. Oldfield (Ed.), *The trade in wildlife: Regulation for conservation* (pp. 3–22). Earthscan.

Brombacher, D., Garzon, J., & Velez, M. (2021). Introduction special issue: Environmental impacts of illicit economies. *Journal of Illicit Economies and Development, 3*(1), 1–9.

Bueger, C., & Edmunds, T. (2020). Blue crime: Conceptualizing transnational organized crime at sea. *Marine Policy, 119*, 1–6. https://doi.org/10.1016/j.marpol.2020.104067

Burke, J. (2020, June 2). *Six elephants killed in one day by poachers in Ethiopia.* The Guardian. Retrieved August 30, 2021, from www.theguardian.com/world/2020/jun/02/six-elephants-killed-in-one-day-by-poachers-in-ethiopia

Burke, J. (2021, July 16). *Environment activist shot dead outside Nairobi home after death threats.* The Guardian. Retrieved January 10, 2022, from https://www.theguardian.com/world/2021/jul/16/environment-activist-shot-dead-outside-nairobi-home-after-death-threats

Chaudhury, D. (2020, September 16). *India joins Djibouti code of conduct: Enhances Indian Ocean outreach.* The Economic Times. Retrieved January 3, 2022, from https://economictimes.indiatimes.com/news/politics-and-nation/india-joins-djibouti-code-of-conduct-enhances-indian-ocean-outreach/articleshow/78153310.cms?from=mdr

Convention on International Trade in Endangered Species of Wild Fauna and Flora (2021). *What is CITES?* Retrieved October 10, 2021, from https://cites.org/eng/disc/what.php

Curtis, R. (1996). *War on drugs in Brooklyn: Street-level drug markets and the tactical narcotics teams* [Doctoral dissertation]. Columbia University.

Djordjevic, S., & Dobovsek, B. (2020). Organized crime in Western Balkans six at the onset of coronavirus. *International Journal of Sociology and Social Policy, 40*(9/10), 807–820. https://doi.org/10.1108/IJSSP-06-2020-0229

Doody, J., Reid, J., Bilali, K. Diaz, J., & Mattheus, N. (2021). In the post-Covid-19 era, is the illegal wildlife trade the most severe form of trafficking? *Crime Scene, 19*(10), 1–12.

Duffy, R., & St. John, F. (2013, June). *Poverty, poaching and trafficking: What are the links?* Retrieved October 17, 2021, from https://eprints.soas.ac.uk/17836/1/EoD_HD059_Jun2013_Poverty_Poaching.pdf

Environmental Investigation Agency. (2015). *Environmental investigation agency: Protecting the environment with intelligence*. Retrieved January 10, 2021, from https://eia-global.org/

European Union Action to Fight Environmental Crime. (2015). *Organized crime and environmental crime: Analysis if EU legal instruments.* Retrieved June 30, 2021, from https://efface.eu/sites/default/files/EFFACE_Organised%20Crime%20and%20Environmental%20Crime_EU%20Level/index.pdf

Federation of American Scientists. (2000). *International crime threat assessment*. Retrieved January 10, 2022, from https://irp.fas.org/threat/pub45270chap3.html

Financial Crimes Enforcement Network. (2021, December 20). *FinCEN analysis reveals upward trend of SARs related wildlife trafficking.* U.S. Treasury. Retrieved January 2, 2022, from https://www.fincen.gov/news/news-releases/fincen-analysis-reveals-upward-trend-sars-related-wildlife-trafficking

Frank, E., & Wilcove, D. (2019, February). Long delays in banning trade in threatened species. *Science, 363*(6428), 686–688.

General Department of Forestry. (2021). "*Legal provisions on the management and license for wildlife trade, transport, export, and import"—Current situation and measures to improve the management of illegal wildlife trade.* National Conference on Prevention and Combating the Offenses against Wildlife, Biodiversity, and Natural Preservation, Hanoi, Vietnam. 25–30.

Gikonyo, C. (2019). The Jeddah Amendment and the fight against wildlife trafficking. *Criminal Law Forum, 30*(1), 181–200.

Global Environment Facility (2020). *Illegal wildlife trade.* Retrieved October 17, 2021, from www.thegef.org/topics/illegal-wildlife-trade

Global Financial Integrity. (2012). Testimony by GFI's Tom Cardamone before US Senate Foreign Relations Committee on Global Implications of Poaching. Accessed on August 19, 2022 at https://gfintegrity.org/press-release/testimony-gfis-tom-cardamone-u-s-senate-foreign-relations-committee-global-implications-poaching/

Hou, C. (2019). *Wildlife trade 101.* Natural Resources Defense Council. Retrieved October 11, 2021, from https://www.nrdc.org/stories/wildlife-trade-101

Intergovernmental Science-Policy Platform on Biodiversity and Ecosystem Services. (2019). The global assessment report on biodiversity and ecosystem services. Retrieved January 3, 2022, from https://ipbes.net/sites/default/files/inline/files/ipbes_global_assessment_report_summary_for_policymakers.pdf

International Maritime Organization. (2019). *Djibouti code of conduct.* Retrieved January 10, 2022, from https://www.imo.org/en/OurWork/Security/Pages/DCoC.aspx

International Tribunal for the Law of the Sea. (2021, December 29). *Latest news.* Retrieved January 13, 2022, from https://www.itlos.org/en/main/latest-news/

International Union for Conservation of Nature. (2017, March 3). *Hopeful signs in campaign against wildlife trafficking.* Retrieved October 17, 2021, from https://www.iucn.org/news/asia/201703/hopeful-signs-campaign-against-wildlife-trafficking

Interpol. (2015). *Environmental crime and its convergence with other serious crimes.* Environmental Security Sub-Directorate, INTERPOL. 2015/999/OEC/ENS/SLO

Law Z Magazine. (2015, October 20). *Four pillars of international maritime law.* Retrieved January 10, 2022, from https://lawzmag.com/2015/10/20/four-pillars-of-international-maritime-law/

Lindwall, C. (2019). *U.N. report: A million extinctions and ecological collapse are on the way.* National Resources Defense Council. Retrieved October 11, 2021, from https://www.nrdc.org/stories/report-million-extinctions-and-ecological-collapse-are-way

Marshall, C. (2021, September 13). *Record number of environmental activists murdered.* BBC News. Retrieved January 10, 2022, from https://www.bbc.com/news/science-environment-58508001

McCabe, K. (2017). *Protecting your children online.* Rowman & Littlefield.

McNeely, J. (2005). *Friends for life: New partners in support of protected areas.* International Union for Conservation of Nature. Retrieved January 10, 2022, from https://www.iucn.org/content/friends-life-new-partners-support-protected-areas

McNeish, H. (2014, June 27). *$213 BN illegal wildlife and charcoal trade funding global terror groups.* Our World. Retrieved January 3, 2022, from https://ourworld.unu.edu/en/contributors/hannah-mcneish

Nambi, C. (2019, January 31). *Uganda seizes ivory smuggled in timbers.* VOA News. Retrieved January 3, 2022, from https://www.voanews.com/a/uganda-seizes-ivory-smuggled-in-timbers-/4767476.html

National Oceanic and Atmospheric Administration. (2021, September 3). Maritime zones and boundaries. Retrieved January 10, 2022, from https://www.gc.noaa.gov/gcil_maritime.html

Ngoc, A., & Wyatt, T. (2012). A green criminological exploration pf illegal wildlife trade in Vietnam. *Asian Criminology, 8*(1), 129–142.

Nguyen, M. (2004). Status of the illegal trade in some mammals in Vietnam. *Journal of Agriculture and Rural Development, 8*(44), 1148–1149.

Organisation for Economic Co-operation and Development. (2020). Coronavirus (COVID-19) and Wildlife Trafficking. Retrieved October 11, 2021, from https://www.oecd.org/gov/illicit-trade/coronavirus-covid19-and-wildlife-trafficking-brief.pdf

Pires, S., Schneider, J., & Herrera, M. (2016). Organized crime or crime that is organized? The parrot trade in neotropics. *Trends in Organized Crime, 19,* 4–20. https://doi.org/10.1007/s12117-015-9259-7

Rawls, J. (1993). *Political liberalism* (*The John Dewey Essays in philosophy,* Vol. 4). Columbia University Press.

Rosen, T. (2020). *The evolving war on illegal wildlife trade.* International Institute for Sustainable Development. Retrieved October 17, 2021, from https://www.iisd.org/articles/evolving-war-illegal-wildlife-trade

Schaedla, W. (2017). Local socioculture, economic, and political facilitators of transnational wildlife crime. In L. Elliott & W. Schaedla (Eds.), *Handbook of transnational environmental crime* (pp. 45–67). Edward Elgar Publishing.

Sharma, C., Kumar, A., Sharma, V., Singh, B. Kumar, G., & Gupta, S. (2019). Online selling of wildlife part with spurious name: A serious challenge for wildlife crime enforcement. *International Journal of Legal Medicine, 133*(1), 65–69.

Sharpless, A. (2020, September 20). *Florida facilitates illicit shark fin trade without federal fin ban*. South Florida Sun Sentinel. Retrieved August 30, 2021, from www.sun-sentinel.com/opinion/commentary/fl-op-com-shark-fin-ban-20200921-ew33c4k2c5gl5bdxr4rrcybcsm-story.html

Uhlmann, D. (2009). Environmental crime comes of age: The evolution of criminal enforcement in the environmental regulating scheme. *Utah Law Review, 4*, 1223–1252.

United Nations Environment Programme. (2016). *The rise of environmental crime: A growing threat to natural resources peace, development, and security*. Retrieved June 30, 2021, from https://www.unep.org/resources/report/rise-environmental-crime-growing-threat-natural-resources-peace-development-and

United Nations Environment Programme. (2020). *New partnership aims to help put a stop to illegal wildlife trade*. Retrieved October 17, 2021, from www.unenvironment.org/news-and-stories/story/new-partnership-aims-help-put-stop-illegal-wildlife-trade

United Nations Office on Drugs and Crime. (2019). Module 3: Criminal justice responses to wildlife trafficking. Key issues: Criminalization of Wildlife Trafficking. *E4J University Module Series: Wildlife Crime*. Retrieved October 10, 2021, from https://www.unodc.org/e4j/en/wildlife-crime/module-3/key-issues/criminalization-of-wildlife-trafficking.html

United Nations Office on Drugs and Crime. (2020a). *Covid-19 UNODC ROMENA updates*. UNODC Regional Office for the Middle East and North Africa (ROMENA). Retrieved January 10, 2022, from https://www.unodc.org/romena/en/covid-19-response.html

United Nations Office on Drugs and Crime. (2020b). *World wildlife crime report: Trafficking in protected species*. Retrieved October 17, 2021, from https://www.unodc.org/documents/data-and-analysis/wildlife/2020/World_Wildlife_Report_2020_9July.pdf

U.S. Department of Justice. (2019, December 12). *Rapid City man pleads guilty to commit wildlife trafficking* [Press release]. U.S. Attorney's Office. District of South Dakota. Retrieved December 3, 2021, from https://www.justice.gov/usao-sd/pr/rapid-city-man-pleads-guilty-conspiracy-commit-wildlife-trafficking

U.S. Fish and Wildlife Service. (2006). Lacey Act. Crimes and Criminal Procedures. Retrieved January 10, 2022, from https://www.fws.gov/law/lacey-act-amendments-1981

Van Uhm, D. (2016). *The illegal wildlife trade: Inside the world of poachers, smugglers, and traders*. Springer.

Van Uhm, D., & Nijman, R. (2020). The convergence of environmental crimes with other serious crimes: Subtypes within the environmental crime continuum. *European Journal of Criminology*, 1–20.

Van Uhm, D., South, N., & Wyatt, T. (2021). Connections between trades and trafficking in wildlife and drugs. *Trends in organized Crime, 24*(4), 425–446.

Viollaz, J., Graham, J., & Lantsman, L. (2018). Using script analysis to understand the financial crimes involved in wildlife trafficking. *Crime, Law and Social Change, 69*(2), 595–614.

Von Essen, E., & Allen, M. (2017). Interspecies violence and crimes of dissent: Communication ethics and legitimacy in message crimes involving wildlife. *Critical Criminology, 25*(1), 261–274.

White, R. (2016). Building NESTS to combat environmental crime networks. *Trends in Organized Crime, 19*(1), 88–105.

World Bank. (2017, June 6). *What is the blue economy?* Retrieved January 10, 2022, from https://www.worldbank.org/en/news/infographic/2017/06/06/blue-economy

World Wildlife Fund. (2012). *Fighting illicit wildlife trafficking: A consultation with governments.* Retrieved October 19, 2021, from https://www.worldwildlife.org/publications/fighting-illicit-wildlife-trafficking-a-consultation-with-governments

World Wildlife Fund. (2021). *Illegal wildlife trade.* Retrieved October 19, 2021, from https://www.worldwildlife.org/threats/illegal-wildlife-trade

Worldometer. (2021). *COVID-19 coronavirus pandemic.* Retrieved from https://www.worldometers.info/coronavirus/

Wyatt, T. van Uhm, D., and Nurse, A. (2020). Differentiating criminal networks in the illegal wildlife trade: Organized, Corporate, and Disorganized Crime. *Trends in Organized Crime, 23*(2), 350–366. https://doi.org/10.1007/s12117-020-09385-9

Zain, S. (2020, July). *Corruption trade: An overview of corruption issues in illicit wildlife trade.* World Wildlife Fund. Retrieved October 19, 2021, from https://www.worldwildlife.org/pages/tnrc-introductory-overview-corrupting-trade-an-overview-of-corruption-issues-in-illicit-wildlife-trade

Illicit Trades of Art, Antiquities, and Other Goods

Key Terms

Alcohol
Alcohol poisoning
Antiquities theft
Art theft
Black markets
Blitz theft
Cigarettes
Contraband
Convention on the Means of Prohibiting and Preventing the Illicit Import, Export and Transfer of Ownership of Cultural Property
Copyrights
Counterfeit
Cultural antiquities
FBI Art Crime Team
Fence
Intellectual property (IP)
Interpol
Large-scale counterfeiting schemes
Patents
Piracy
Pirated goods
Pirated music
Product fraud
Provenance
Repatriation
Small-scale counterfeiting schemes
Trade secrets
Trademarks

CHAPTER OBJECTIVES

Chapter 9 will enable readers to understand the following:

- the role of transnational organized crime (TOC) in the illicit art trade
- the role of TOC in the illicit trade of cultural antiquities
- the role of TOC as related to intellectual property
- the role of demand in the supply of counterfeit products by TOC groups
- factors that facilitate art and antiquities crimes
- factors that facilitate the role of TOC groups in the illicit trade of art, antiquities, and counterfeit products
- factors that reduce criminal justice efforts to address the activities of TOC in the illicit trade of products

STOLEN ART, STOLEN cultural antiquities, smuggled cigarettes, pirated music, and counterfeit purses are all goods in demand by consumers around the globe. Unfortunately, these stolen goods are often not only illegal but in many cases illegally obtained. These illicit goods provide another line of profit for those wishing to engage in their production, distribution, and sale. In other words, these illicit goods are of significant interest to TOC groups. TOC groups make approximately $2 trillion annually through the trafficking of illicit goods and services, and the profits are expected to increase (Yancey-Bragg, 2017). For most individuals, these criminal actions by TOC groups are of little concern, since drug trafficking and human trafficking are the most recognized and most concerning of the illegal activities of TOC groups. However, these other less-recognized areas of illicit trades are also profitable for TOC groups, destabilizing for governments, and threatening to the rule of law.

The smuggling of illicit goods has resulted in severe consequences for many countries across the globe. As the smuggling of goods is often accompanied by the trafficking of other products, including drugs and humans, criminal activities within an area are increased. Also increased are competition and violence between TOC groups engaged in the activities—in many cases in conflicts over recognized territories, distribution lines, and products (Sofia, 2003). Hence, these criminal actions by violent TOC groups not only increase vulnerabilities for societies but also increase the risk for instability and conflicts within communities.

Research suggests that the goods most frequently subject to smuggling by TOC groups are those with high import tax rates, such as cigarettes, alcohol, motor vehicles, and motor vehicle parts (Sofia, 2003). However, it is also known that TOC groups also traffick in wildlife species, art, antiquities, strategic raw materials (e.g., aluminum, copper, lead), nuclear and radioactive materials, and hazardous and/or toxic substances. Depending on the nature of these "other goods," as well as the source and the end-buyer or destination, groups of individuals as well as community resources may also be directly victimized in the process, as human labor may be required in the production of the goods (Sofia, 2003).

Hence, these areas of other goods include the illicit trade of art, the illicit trade on antiquities, and the trafficking of counterfeited and other state-regulated contraband such as cigarettes and other pirated products, which continue to provide risk to communities and individuals.

Today, the involvement of TOC groups in the counterfeiting of goods and in other illicit trades is broadly acknowledged, as the management of these trades follows the models of TOC operations as found in other aspects of trafficking (United Nations Interregional Crime and Justice Research Institute, 2007). Specifically, a product of demand is identified, TOC groups facilitate its production or the accumulation of the product, and later the TOC group transports, distributes, and sells the products.

The trafficking of stolen art and antiquities has been estimated to produce approximately $6 billion in profits annually for TOC groups (Browning, 2007). In addition, trade in counterfeit and pirated goods is estimated to provide over $460 billion in profits on an annual basis (Organization for Economic Cooperation and Development, 2019). Lastly, an estimated $12 billion are lost from budgets, just in Europe, due to the trafficking of both genuine and counterfeit cigarettes (European Commission, 2010). Each of these products is accessible to TOC groups, trafficked by TOC groups, and expected to increase the profits of TOC groups.

Weapons and narcotics are goods that, because of their strong public demand, generate significant profits for TOC groups. Art, antiquities, and counterfeit and contraband products are similarly in demand, and thus they also significantly support the criminal activities of TOC groups (United Nations Interregional Crime and Justice Research Institute, 2007). This chapter provides information on some of the less recognized areas of profit for TOC groups. Specifically, this chapter discusses the trafficking of art, antiquities, contraband, and counterfeit goods, as well as crimes against intellectual property. Included in this chapter are discussions on the demand for these goods, as well as factors that facilitate their trafficking—including police efforts to address these crimes and the limitations on governments and regulatory authorities to address or reduce these criminal activities by TOC groups.

Art Trafficking

Art trafficking or **art theft** includes various types of art, such as paintings and sculptures. Hollywood's depiction of art theft often involves glamorous settings, fast cars, and beautiful people. In most of these cases, the media account of the crime is exaggerated and embellished to attract audiences and sell movie tickets. In reality, in most cases of art theft, the crimes are executed quickly and crudely and the art is distributed to customers who were identified prior to the criminal action. It is the flow of these goods within the global economy that has helped to facilitate the use of **black markets** for the sale of illicit goods (Basu, 2013).

Art theft—Criminal activity involving the theft of art or cultural property, including paintings, sculptures, and other objects identified as art.

According to reports, over 50,000 thefts of art occur each year across the globe, supporting a black-market profit of approximately $6 billion annually (Bishara, 2020). Art and cultural property crimes include theft, fraud, looting, and the trafficking of items across state and international lines (Interpol, 2021). Specifically, art crimes include theft, forgery, vandalism, and unauthorized import and export of works of art, with the most common forms of art crime identified as theft and the unauthorized transportation of the artistic media (Kuhar, 2020).

Research suggests that the true extent of art crime is unknown, as the crime is often unreported (O'Keefe, 2014). However, estimates over the last two decades suggest that members of TOC groups steal over $1 billion in art each year across the globe with less than 20% of these pieces ever recovered (Barrett, 1996). TOC groups are aware of the profits to be generated through art theft and the limited chance of detection and apprehension by law enforcement, and therefore they have embraced the crime as another mode for generating funds. Research suggests that art crimes have shifted from being rare and innocuous to playing a major role for TOC groups, with profits from art crimes noted as significant compared to the profits from drug trafficking and arms trafficking (Charney et al., 2012). When art forgery and fraud are added to the activities of TOC groups, art trafficking profits only increase in magnitude (Hill, 2008).

As displayed above, art theft is not a new problem. These crimes have occurred for many past centuries, and especially whenever there have been armed conflicts and the victorious troops have plundered churches, temples, homes, and other buildings of these conquered lands (Charney, 2018). Recently, Interpol suggested that criminal

TOP 10 MOST VALUED STOLEN ARTWORKS IN HISTORY

- Govaert Flinck, "Landscape with Obelisk" (1638) / Stolen from the Isabella Stewart Gardner Museum in 1990 / Value: priceless
- Rembrandt van Rijn, "Christ in the Storm on the Lake of Galilee" (1633) / Stolen from the Isabella Stewart Gardner Museum in 1990 / Value: priceless
- Jan van Eyck, "The Just Judges" (1430–1432) / Stolen from the Isabella Stewart Gardner Museum in 1990 / Value: priceless
- Édouard Manet, "Chez Tortoni" (c. 1875) / Stolen from the Isabella Stewart Gardner Museum in 1990 / Value: priceless
- Johannes Vermeer, "The Concert" (c. 1665) / Stolen from the Isabella Stewart Gardner Museum in 1990 / Value: $200 million
- Vincent van Gogh, "Poppy Flowers" (1887) / Stolen from the Mohamed Mahmoud Khalil Museum in Cairo, Egypt, in 2010 / Value: $55 million
- Claude Monet, "Charing Cross Bridge" (c. 1900) / Stolen from Kunsthal Museum in Rotterdam, Netherlands, in 2012 / Value: $35 million
- Claude Monet, "Waterloo Bridge, London" (1903) / Stolen from Kunsthal Museum in Rotterdam, Netherlands, in 2012 / Value: $35 million
- Lucian Freud, "Francis Bacon" (1952) / Stolen from Neue Nationalgalerie, in Berlin, Germany, in 1988 / Value: $35 million
- Michelangelo Merisi da Caravaggio, "Nativity with San Lorenzo and San Francesco" (1609) / Stolen from Oratorio di San Lorenzo, Palermo, Italy / Value: $20 million (Bishara, 2020)

groups involved in art theft adapted their criminal techniques during the COVID-19 lockdowns to allow their efforts to continue unabated, and the efforts have been exacerbated through the use of technology (Napier, 2021). In fact, Europol (2017) suggests that the surface web and darknets provide criminal vendors with the opportunity to purvey all manner of illicit commodities.

Blitz theft—A theft that occurs after the immobilization of a victim, where offenders steal items quickly and often recklessly.

German troops carried out massive thefts during World War II, and art recovered from that period is part of one of the biggest international crimes outside of the illicit drug trade (Charney, 2018). After the "**blitz thefts**" in the 1960s, research has suggested that TOC groups have come to dominate the world in these criminal actions (Charney et al., 2012). In the United States, the prime locations of art to be stolen include private homes and museums, while in Europe stolen art is often taken from churches (Barrett, 1996). Of course, much of this is related to the history of Europe and the significance of the church in medieval societies. In most cases, art stolen from private homes is the least likely to be reported, as in some cases such thefts are not immediately recognized or the owners themselves acquired the art through less than legitimate paths (Rea, 2020). TOC groups aware of this reduced likelihood of reporting continue to provide not only the incentives for thieves involved in these thefts but also the routes for distribution of the stolen art and the identification of potential consumers (Abadinsky, 2017).

Once stolen art is transported, sellers called ***fences*** are usually involved in its distribution. These individuals are often members of TOC groups (Abadinsky, 2017). Fences operate in two roles: they may help to identify consumers for stolen art, and they may provide ideas about what products are in demand. As demonstrated in the report here, much of the mechanics of art theft is not known to the public. However, when the chance for profit is high and the chance of recovery is low, TOC groups are often involved (Charney et al., 2012).

Fence—A person who buys or receives contraband, or stolen or counterfeit items, with the intention of reselling it later for profit.

In January of 2017, Spain's Interior Ministry announced the arrest of 75 people across Europe for trafficking in stolen art and artifacts. The investigation involved 18 countries and recovered some 500 pieces of art. Those charged are members of a TOC group that transported and sold illicitly acquired art and artifacts across Europe (Artsy Editors, 2017).

The smuggling of art and cultural antiquities is often an intense activity of logistics and transportation (Basu, 2013). TOC, with experience in both logistics and transportation, is a natural actor in the process. Unfortunately, law enforcement efforts to address art theft or the trafficking of art by TOC have had minimal impact. Just as in the case of most of the criminal activities by TOC, art theft profits are usually generated as cash or electronic transfers of funds through international financial services, and these transactions are most difficult to detect by regulating authorities. In addition, few countries have dedicated policing efforts to address art theft; therefore, policing organizations such as the FBI, Interpol, and Europol (discussed later in the chapter) are often utilized in cases of art theft. Countries with dedicated art crime policing units include the United States, the United Kingdom, the Netherlands, and Italy. However, most states do not have these dedicated units, and TOC groups are aware of these vulnerabilities and lack of police enforcement resources (Charney et al., 2012).

The overall absence of transparency or regulation within the art market also facilitates art theft by TOC groups (May, 2017). Specifically, the art market is often embedded in a veil of secrecy regarding the art that is owned, art that is available for sale, and art that is missing. In particular, most counterfeit products can be sold on the surface web either as presented as genuine products or combined with genuine products (Europol, 2017). If they're identifying a missing piece of art, the majority of private owners of these exclusive pieces may employ individuals outside of law enforcement, and sometimes outside of the legitimized security sector, to retrieve the work. In addition, fake **provenances** or paperwork is often utilized and produced by TOC group members and will receive little scrutiny (Barrett, 1996). As provenance is often established through original receipts, handwritten notes, or auction records, false provenances are not especially difficult to create if an individual is knowledgeable about the process.

Provenance—Documentation on the history of the ownership of a painting or other art form; can include its original source, a description of the piece, and an inventory of sales.

In terms of the actual value of art, individuals who wish to minimize the money they've invested or reduce the tax assessed on the work will publicly reduce the value of the art. Many countries provide minimum values for artwork to be shown in mandatory reports of sales, such as 15,000 euros per piece (Hill, 2008). Hence, the art theft market operates without the safeguards required in other high-value, high-risk markets and industries, such as real estate, insurance, casinos, and precious stones and metals (May, 2017). Unfortunately, as the vast majority of countries do not regulate the sale of art and there is often no transaction record of sale, with no reporting to authorities, in many cases no transfer or sale of the art is recorded. So, TOC groups continue to participate in the criminal activities associated with art theft and they continue to profit. This aspect of TOC, increasingly similar to the territorial structures that support the illicit drug trade, has been easily adapted to support the trafficking of goods such as art (United Nations Interregional Crime and Justice Research Institute, 2007). For many involved in cultural heritage projects, the theft of art and antiquities robs societies of their heritage, knowledge of past civilizations, and opportunities for learning.

Cultural Antiquities

Again, in many movies and depictions of the theft of cultural antiquities, the hero is victorious in their battle against the criminal organization for the stolen or smuggled sculpture. This is generally not the reality for cultural antiquities. Smuggling is a core competency for TOC groups and a very profitable aspect of their criminal activities. Unfortunately, the illicit trade of cultural property is another aspect of TOC that is often overlooked by police and by citizens as a whole (Basu, 2013). In many cases, the theft of cultural goods is a result of the impoverishment of the cultural heritage of the country of origin (Illicit Trade in Tobacco Products, 2018).

Theft of cultural antiquities—Illicit excavation, looting of archaeological sites, and the trafficking of cultural property.

For clarity, this section's discussion on theft of **cultural antiquities**, which may include art theft, includes the illicit excavation and looting of archaeological sites, the trafficking of cultural property during armed conflicts, and the use of faked or forged documentation to enable both illegal imports and illegal exports (May, 2017). As in the case of art theft, the demand for cultural antiquities usually comes from wealthy individuals or from developed countries, and the supply usually comes from developing or impoverished countries. **Antiquities theft** presents an even greater challenge in combatting art crime, as it is difficult to detect the theft of an artifact that may have been discovered only recently and so has never been identified. As displayed below, the roles of TOC members in the trafficking of cultural goods vary along with the process of the illicit trade.

ROLES OF TODAY'S TOC IN THE TRAFFICKING OF CULTURAL GOODS
Theft—Breaking and entering; corruption of security personnel within product venue; silencing security within product venue
Illicit Excavation—Payment of local residence; support of off-hours (nights and weekend) work; corruption of local law enforcement
Producing Fakes—Products with aging techniques utilized; combining legal and illegal works; through technology, focusing on current objects rather than classic works
Delivery and Sale—Providing product to consumer

(Illicit Trade in Tobacco Products, 2018)

Just as in the case of art theft, lack of oversight has allowed the illicit antiquities market to thrive. As demonstrated through the arrest described here, cultural antiquities continue to be available for trafficking by TOC groups. The global revenue

In November of 2021, police in northern Israel discovered a stolen Torah that was hundreds of years old and originally from Baghdad. Four suspects were arrested on suspicion of trafficking antiquities and possessing stolen property (TOI Staff, 2021).

generated from the illicit trade in cultural property is estimated conservatively to be approximately $12 billion annually (May, 2017).

The antiquities trade refers to the exchange of cultural property. These trades occur across the world and may occur legally or illegally. Legal trade in antiquities, regulated by national standards, enables historians, archeologists, and anthropologists to study cultural items and past civilizations scientifically and to educate the general population on the past. It has been suggested, however, that much of the antiquities trade is illegal. In fact, some suggest that for the majority of cultural antiquities, legal trades are questionable in either origin or trade authorities (Rea, 2020). As illustrated below, even internationally recognized organizations are often questioned regarding their property.

BRITISH MUSEUM SCULPTURES

In 1816, the British Museum purchased a set of ancient Greek marble sculptures from the Parthenon in Athens for £35,000 (about $4.8 million today). The 1801–1812 excavation of these objects—overseen by Lord Elgin, a Scottish diplomat—cost about two times that amount, but the works are now considered priceless. For that reason, they have been the subject of intense scrutiny, with many alleging that Elgin may not have purchased the works legally from the Ottoman Turks, who ruled Greece at the time (Greenberger, 2021).

The illegal or illicit trade of antiquities refers to the unregulated excavation or theft of cultural items. As demonstrated above in the British Museum account, in these cases artifacts are often unearthed or stolen by individuals, then transported internationally by TOC groups to collectors, museums, and other antiques dealers (Amineddoleh, 2013). Antiquities provide citizens a glimpse into past cultures and civilization that may otherwise be unknown. Individuals involved in the discovery and trade of such items deem them to be critical to the understanding of societies. However, for most individuals, and especially individuals living in poverty within source areas, the value on an ancient bowl does not outweigh the value of feeding one's family Therefore, the trafficking of cultural antiquities and the involvement of TOC groups in this trade is expected to continue—and, in most predictions, to increase (Rea, 2020), Unfortunately, the trade in counterfeit and pirated goods, which includes the theft of intellectual property, is also becoming one of the most profitable illicit activities for TOC today.

Intellectual Property

Intellectual property (IP) is a category of property that describes those items that are nontangible in nature; that is, they do not represent physical items, but rather ideas or concepts most often utilized in the business world. IP is protected by a variety of civil legal actions, depending on the country, with varying degrees of protection. TOC groups are aware of these inconsistencies across geographic regions as well as the limited penalties if a group is convicted of IP theft, and in most cases they use these conditions to their advantage. Although there are many categories of IP theft, the most common are violations of patents, copyrights, trademarks, and trade secrets (European Parliament, 2018).

Intellectual property (IP)—A category that describes those items of property that are nontangible in nature, such as patents, copyrights, trademarks, and trade secrets.

IP law was designed to encourage the creation of a wide variety of intellectual goods with economic incentives embedded in its creation (Lemley, 2005). Unfortunately, the intangible aspect of IP, unlike physical property, eliminates the use of structural barriers, such as fences or physical buildings, for the protection of the products.

In addition, as the majority of today's IP is stored electronically, the vulnerabilities of cyberspace provide another avenue for infractions such as theft or duplication, and TOC groups profiting from the theft of IP are well aware of these conditions. For clarity in this section, ***patents*** are rights granted by a country's government to an inventor to exclude others from making, using, selling, offering to sell, or importing their invention (Yu, 2007). A ***copyright*** gives the creator exclusive rights to the use of their artistic property, often writings or art. A ***trademark*** is a recognizable sign or symbol that distinguishes products from competitors' products if similar. Lastly, a ***trade secret*** is a design or formula that is not generally known but makes a product unique. An example of a trade secret would be a company's specific selection and curating process for tobacco.

Patent—right of ownership; *Copyright*—provides the creator exclusive rights to the utilization of their artistic property; *Trademark*—a recognizable sign or symbol that identifies a product; *Trade secret*—a design or formula for product production.

Violation of IP rights are referred to as infringements; however, these actions are often difficult to document in a court of law. In fact, research suggests that less than 5% of IP cases result in success for the inventor (Murphy, 2015). One of the most commonly noted ways

Piracy—Unauthorized duplication of protected products with the intent to profit.

in which TOC groups are involved in theft of IP is in the criminal action of piracy. Specifically, ***piracy***, or the unauthorized duplication of IP, especially film piracy, provides billions of dollars to TOC groups annually as these groups create multiple copies from an illegally obtained master copy of the original film and sell these copies through local and nationwide retail vendors (McIllwain, 2005). As displayed below, some artists are more likely to be pirated than others. Research suggests that one in three compact discs sold worldwide are counterfeit and that in many countries the **pirated music** market is more profitable that the market for legal music sales, with a revenue of $5 billion annually (Grahamton, 2022).

TEN MOST PIRATED MUSIC ARTISTS
1. Beatles
2. Fleetwood Mac
3. Bob Marley
4. Led Zeppelin
5. Cliff Richard
6. Stevie Wonder
7. Jimi Hendrix
8. Elvis Presley
9. ABBA
10. The Rolling Stones

(Polcaro, 2019)

In March of 2017, a Florida man pleaded guilty to software piracy in which profits of over $100 million were documented from illicit, unauthorized, and counterfeit Microsoft Office software products. These products, distributed across the United States and other countries, included approximately 10,000 items and a network of manufacturers and distributors (U.S. Department of Justice, 2017).

As illustrated in the 2017 case here, theft of IP often involves networks of individuals across multiple locations. In many cases, the role of technology is critical. In particular, most recently, advances in drone technology are expected to impact the transportation and delivery of illicit products by TOC groups (Europol, 2017).

For most consumers, IP theft seems insignificant. The copying of a logo or the duplication of a movie for personal use is a common everyday occurrence. Unfortunately, these actions rob the inventor of the profits they deserve. In addition, the mass duplication of IP by TOC groups provides profits to these criminal organizations; the profits may continue to fund not only these actions but also other criminal actions, such as the production of child pornography (McCabe, 2008), which may further victimize individuals and society as a whole.

Contraband, Counterfeit, and Pirated Goods

Most people equate the term *counterfeit* with the counterfeiting of currency. As demonstrated in the 2017 case here, however, although currency counterfeiting is a significant aspect of TOC criminal activities, it is not its only avenue of fake products. However, in the United States and countries that recognize the U.S. dollar, it is suggested that nearly $20 million is seized annually in fake money, with much of the currency produced in countries such as Peru and then distributed through TOC groups to the various countries (Cabitza, 2012). In reality, TOC groups are involved in the counterfeiting of not only currency but also cigarettes, alcohol, perfumes, clothing, electronics, and other goods (Abadinsky, 2017).

In August of 2017, airport authorities in Dublin, Ireland, seized over 29,000 smuggled cigarettes, 4 kilos of tobacco, and 155 liters of alcohol. The estimated total value of the seized product was over $20,000 (Revenue, 2018). In these cases, individuals involved were from the countries of Poland and Moldova and the city of Dubai.

GREY MARKETS VERSUS BLACK MARKETS

Grey market goods are legitimate goods that come from the correct manufacturer but are sold through unauthorized channels.

Black market goods are items that are illegal to manufacture or sell. In some cases, black-market goods are counterfeit. (Cal Micro Recycling, 2022)

Contraband, counterfeiting, and piracy affect global health, safety, and security as well as economic growth. Contraband reduces legitimate profits to manufacturers. Counterfeit and pirated products are tangible goods that violate a trademark, design rights, and/or patent (counterfeit), or a copyright (piracy) (May, 2017). For TOC groups, these goods operate within the same economies as the drug trade.

Just as legitimate enterprises do, if there is a demand for a product, then TOC groups will provide an avenue for delivery.

Annual estimates suggest that the global trade in counterfeit and **pirated goods** generates at least $900 billion for TOC groups (United Nations Office on Drugs and Crime, 2015). These profits continue to increase as individuals seek products for less cost. One of the most commonly traded counterfeit or contraband items is cigarettes (European Commission, 2010). Cigarettes, as discussed below, are not only high in demand across the globe, but significantly varied in price across the globe.

Two of the most common items of contraband: alcohol and cigarettes.

For clarity, a product is considered ***contraband*** if it is purchased in a low-tax country and then illegally resold in a market at higher prices, whereas a product is considered ***counterfeit*** if it is illegally produced and sold by a party other than the original trademark holder (European Commission, 2010). Across the globe, from 2012 to 2017 the illicit tobacco market was estimated to have grown over 200% (Illicit Trade in Tobacco Products, 2018). Two of the more common items of contraband are **cigarettes** and **alcohol**. In regard to cigarettes, it is estimated that around 10 billion euros (approximately $11 billion) are lost from European budgets each year due to the smuggling of both genuine and counterfeit cigarettes, with China being one of the largest source countries for counterfeit cigarettes. In addition, the United Kingdom appears to be a common destination for contraband cigarettes (Antonopoulos et al., 2020). Alcohol is another common product for contraband.

A variety of factors influence the smuggling of goods. In the European Union, counterfeit and pirated products account for up to 5% of imports (Europol, 2107). Specifically, differences in tax rates for products such as cigarettes and alcohol provide the motivation for the purchase of products in one state and the resale of those products without the tax base in another state (Illicit Trade in Tobacco Products, 2018). For large-scale smuggling operations, these profits are incentives for the illicit trade. Unfortunately, research suggests that ineffective cultures, corruption, weak government communities, and population perceptions also fuel the smuggling of contraband products (Illicit Trade in Tobacco Products, 2018). Notably, smuggled and counterfeit cigarettes and alcohol are sometimes dangerous for consumers as they are not subject to the same standards of quality control as in in legitimate manufacturing plants (Boesen, 2020). In fact, studies suggest that counterfeit cigarettes may contain as much as seven times the amount of lead as authentic brands (Boesen, 2020). This illicit trade of tobacco is a growing international problem that involves corruption, money laundering, and consumer health risk. TOC groups are aware of these conditions but continue the criminal activities for profit. TOC groups know of this demand for cigarettes and the prices differences in different countries (for example, $15 in the United Kingdom versus $2 in Serbia) and are willing to facilitate the transportation and distribution of cigarettes for significant profit.

In terms of alcohol, unrecorded alcohol is estimated to generate approximately $20 billion in sales in the United States alone (Illicit Trade in Tobacco Products, 2020). In these cases, as licit alcoholic beverages are legally produced and traded across borders, illicit alcohol involves the taxonomy of illegally home-produced products, smuggled contraband or counterfeit alcohol, and nonconforming products (Illicit Trade in Tobacco Products, 2020). The roles of TOC in these operations include production, falsification of trade documents, and tampering with product ingredients. As displayed in the table below, the consequences of unsafe alcohol or **alcohol poisoning** include risks to health—and even death for some consumers.

SYMPTOMS OF POISONING FROM FAKE ALCOHOL

Confusion
Loss of coordination
Vomiting
Irregular or slow breathing
Blue-tinged or pale skin
Low body temperature (hypothermia)
Stupor (being conscious but unresponsive)
Unconsciousness (passing out)
Death
(Interpol, 2021)

In many cases, *piracy* refers to the abuse of intellectual property; however, it may also apply to the production of specific products, as trade secrets are often utilized in the making of products. An estimate in 2019 suggests that the world trade in fake goods was already worth $509 billion, or 3% of world trade (Lewis, 2020). In fact, nearly 7% of all the products imported into Europe are now counterfeit, which equates to approximately $160 million per year (Lewis, 2020).

Research suggests that the rise in counterfeiting, contraband, and piracy is a result of the hyperglobalization of societies. Today, much of the counterfeiting of products involves a small group of entities collaborating for a single product (Abadinsky, 2017). For many of these products, technology also plays a role: specifically, the development and spread of digital technologies, the evolution of new and developed container freight systems, postal and courier services, reduced travel costs, and more globalized banking systems (Lewis, 2020). In particular, the operation of online platforms in the legal economy has had a profound impact on business models. This development has been experienced in the online trade of illicit goods and services (Europol, 2017). Of course, TOC groups are aware of the demand for these products and utilize the vulnerabilities of today's society to further their illegal profits.

Just as human trafficking often operates on the demand for cheap labor, counterfeiting thrives on the global demand for cheap goods (May, 2017). TOC groups are involved in both the **small-scale counterfeiting schemes** and the large-scale ones. The small-scale schemes usually involve individuals living in the source country for short or temporary periods of time, whereas large-scale schemes involve members of TOC groups involved in a significant volume of counterfeiting products (Savona & Riccardi, 2015).

For many of these operations, members are recruited either through current TOC group members or through ties within the areas to family who are aware of the illicit activities but feel that the actions are acceptable as a source of income. Because many of the counterfeit items are small-scale, one-time, or limited-availability items, the structure of the TOC organization that supports the counterfeiting exists until the product(s) area is acquired and/or the product is delivered, and then these organizational ties are disengaged. These small-scale members may participate in future TOC criminal activities or may be once-and-done participants. This temporary structure of TOC provides not only a short window for detection by law enforcement but also minimal contact among TOC members, and thus a reduced opportunity for TOC members to be identified and criminal activities to be detected.

Large-scale counterfeiting schemes by members of TOC groups typically are more permanent, with large qualities of products produced (Savano & Riccardi, 2015). These TOC organizations are often embedded in the legal production and trade of the legitimate goods (Antonopoulos et al., 2020). In these cases, oftentimes countrywide production is employed and illicit products are transported along with legitimate products. In the United States, the most commonly identified country for counterfeit goods is China (Briggs, 2018). Also, in these cases TOC organizations provide the entire supply chain, including manufacture, transportation, storage, and distribution (Antonopoulos et al., 2020). For the most part, wealthy individuals already living in wealthy countries provide the demand for such products. The entry of TOC groups into the counterfeiting market also has other consequences. Specifically, as counterfeiting requires a workforce, many individuals (including children) producing the items are subjected to long hours, unsafe working conditions, and other aspects of exploitation (McCabe, 2008).

Research suggests that the United States and Europe are the most popular destinations for such counterfeit goods (Briggs, 2018). Low production costs for counterfeit goods result in higher profits for TOC groups. Unfortunately, counterfeiting and piracy have often been seen as victimless crimes, yet there are many potential hazards to threaten the health and safety of the public while serving as a solid source of financing for TOC groups.

Tax policy can never be overlooked as a factor fueling the criminal enterprise. Research suggests that the high and inconsistent rates of cigarette taxes have added to the increase in cigarette smuggling across the globe (Boesen, 2020). As counterfeit goods are the basis for a global, multibillion-dollar crime, TOC groups have not hesitated to profit from their trade (United Nations Office on Drugs and Crime, 2015). In addition, in many parts of the world, international, regional, and national law enforcement authorities have uncovered intricate links between this crime and other serious offenses, including illicit drugs, money laundering, and corruption. TOC groups' involvement in the production and distribution of counterfeit goods has been documented by both national and international authorities. In particular, many TOC groups have diversified into the illicit trafficking of counterfeit goods, while at the same time being involved in crimes varying from drug trafficking to human trafficking (United Nations Office on Drugs and Crime, 2015).

Specifically, TOC groups in Italy and Greece are often involved in fashion, while TOC groups in Lithuania may focus on alcohol (Antonopoulos et al., 2020). Unfortunately, the levels of profit from counterfeiting and the illicit trade of other products are similar to those in the drug trade but with reduced levels of risk (United Nations Interregional Crime and Justice Research Institute, 2007). In addition, the low levels of deterrence by systems of law and the generally benevolent attitudes of citizens fuel the actions (United Nations Interregional Crime and Justice Research Institute, 2007). With exchanges of illicit products conducted with little chance of detection, large profits, and an unconcerned public, the criminal actions continue.

The illicit trafficking of counterfeit goods offers criminals a complementary source of income, and monies received from the sale of counterfeit products can be utilized in the continued production of fake goods or in other illicit activities. In the United States, it is suggested that 15% of the pharmaceuticals that enter the country each year are counterfeit (National Crime Prevention Council, 2017). In addition, subpar products such as automobile parts cost the U.S. auto industry billions of dollars and place consumers at risk (Council of Europe, 2008). Criminals also feed fake goods into the legitimate supply chain, which provides them with "clean" money (Council of Europe, 2008).

The illicit trafficking of counterfeit goods is often linked to other serious crimes, and Europol has suggested that counterfeiting is an increasingly attractive avenue for organized crime to widen their areas of criminal actions (United Nations Interregional Crime and Justice Research Institute, 2013). In fact, evidence suggests that TOC networks use the same routes and modi operandi to move counterfeit goods as they do to smuggle drugs, firearms, and people (United Nations Interregional Crime and Justice Research Institute, 2013). In addition, just as the licit market for online sales of goods is increasing, so too is the opportunity for the online sale of counterfeit goods by organized crime groups, with the extent of the role of TOC in distributing these products online undetermined. In addition to their links to other crimes, TOC group members often compel clients to participate in the counterfeit process in exchange for payment on their debts. Specifically, a TOC group member may engage a client involved in drug trafficking to peddle counterfeit products on the street, in bars, and at community markets as a way to fulfill their financial obligations to the TOC group (Abadinsky, 2017). Hence, with counterfeiting embedded in the legal production and trade of products as well as its connection to other criminal activities by TOC groups, counterfeiting is expected to continue with little chance of detection.

> Manufacturers creating fake goods often use pollution-creating and dangerous machinery and materials (Borrell, 2020). In addition, after large quantities of counterfeits are seized by law enforcement, often the products are destroyed by incineration, which leads to massive amounts of air pollution (Borell, 2020).

The environmental costs of counterfeiting are also often overlooked. As these actions operate without strict regulations, the production of such goods often presents particular challenges to the environment (United Nations Office on Drugs and Crime, 2015). In particular, toxic dyes and chemicals disposed of unlawfully contribute to environmental harm. Because these actions occur without a clear line of responsibility, legal recourse or consumer rights are virtually nonexistent; not only do present-day individuals suffer from such illegal activities; future individuals and communities suffer as well.

In addition, as the use of technology increases, counterfeiting increases (Antonopoulos et al., 2020). The use of technology provides the TOC group with an additional level of secrecy. For many TOC groups, the counterfeiting group was infiltrated as an investment for TOC profits and, as suggested by many, is a common target for reinvestments by TOC groups (Antonopoulos et al., 2020). Through diversification of actions, TOC groups engage in counterfeiting and contraband smuggling as additional revenue streams.

Lastly, given the high levels of profit, counterfeiting and illegal trade of goods serves a dual function as a source of funding for TOC groups and as a tool to launder money (United Nations Interregional Crime and Justice Research Institute, 2007). For terrorist groups, as well as TOC groups, profits from these activities can be equal to or greater than profits from drug trafficking, but with much less risk of detection. Today, terrorist organizations have taken a more active role in counterfeiting by organizing the production and distribution of goods. An example of this aspect of profits is the financing for the attack on the Charlie Hebdo offices in Paris in January 2015, which was achieved in part through counterfeiting as the terrorist Kouachi brothers received funding from their sale of counterfeit products—particularly, footwear and clothing—which they purchased from China (May, 2017). In states without strong legislation and legal remedies to prevent these crimes, TOC groups face little deterrence.

The Role of Technology in Illicit Product Trades

Counterfeiting is no longer confined to street corners and flea markets, with research suggesting that the illegal trade in art, culture, and counterfeited items has increased over 150% in the United States alone (U.S. Department of Homeland Security, 2020). As is the case for many TOC criminal activities, technology and e-commerce have expanded the reach of TOC groups. Historically, many counterfeits were distributed at swap meets and by individual sellers on street corners; today, however, the ability to reduce transportation costs and search costs for consumers has given e-commerce platforms an advantage over brick-and-mortar retailers (U.S. Department of Homeland Security, 2020). Today, the level of commercial access offered by the cybercommunity has increased as these venues serve as points for supply and demand while at the same time promoting the counterfeit goods (United Nations Interregional Crime and Justice Research Institute, 2007). Selling counterfeit and pirated goods through e-commerce (as illustrated in the table below) is rarely detected and is highly profitable for TOC groups.

SEIZURES BY U.S. CUSTOMS AND BORDER PATROL, 2019

Goods Being Sold Illegally	Amount Seized
Apparel	18%
Footwear	14%
Handbags/wallets	11%
Electronics	10%
Pharmaceuticals	7%

(U.S. Department of Homeland Security, 2020)

As demonstrated in the account here, counterfeit drugs may have serious consequences. Once limited to pharmaceuticals, counterfeiting has spread into over-the-counter medicines like cough syrup and to weight loss drugs, with many consumers unaware of the potential dangers of purchasing counterfeit drugs from internet pharmacies. In particular, counterfeit pharmaceutical products provide over $20 billion annually to TOC (Illicit Trade in Tobacco Products, 2018). Specifically, unlike legitimate drug manufacturers, which are subject to inspections by regulating authorities, labs that manufacture counterfeits have no such oversight. As shown below, the most common pharmaceutical products seen in the illicit trade are antibiotics.

In 2019, doctors around the globe called for an urgent international effort to combat a pandemic of bad drugs that are thought to kill hundreds of thousands of people annually (Sample, 2019). In particular, this surge in counterfeit and poor-quality medicines results in the deaths of approximately 250,000 children every year (Sample, 2019). Most vulnerable are those individuals living in impoverished countries where poor or counterfeit vaccines and antibiotics are administered for infections and diseases such as hepatitis, yellow fever, and meningitis.

TYPES OF PHARMACEUTICALS SMUGGLED
Antibiotics (35%)
Sexual Impotence Treatment (15%)
Painkillers (10%)
Anti-Malarial (9%)
Diabetes Treatment (5%)

(Illicit Trade in Tobacco Products, 2018)

For consumers, use of counterfeit medicines may cause serious health issues and even death. Research suggests that both the sale of counterfeit goods and the distribution of counterfeit goods typically require central coordination—and thus a role for TOC groups. In addition, with child labor available to manufacture and sell counterfeit goods and the proceeds from counterfeit sales sometimes supporting terrorism, this market is even more of a concern for international security organizations (U.S. Department of Homeland Security, 2020). Counterfeit products rob governments of tax revenue, fuel government corruption, and often subsidize other forms of illicit trade, such as drug trafficking and human trafficking (Illicit Trade in Tobacco Products, 2018).

Factors facilitating the trafficking of these goods are related to profits, as production costs are low, millions of consumers are online, transactions are convenient, and listing goods on well-known platforms provides an air of legitimacy. In addition, TOC groups are often in countries outside of the sale country, so they are exposed to relatively little risk of criminal prosecution. Unfortunately, consuming countries are left with the consequences of more damage to residents' health (Illicit Trade in Tobacco Products, 2018). It comes as no surprise that the role of TOC in these criminal activities are expected to continue and increase.

Legal Efforts to Address Theft and Counterfeiting

The illegal trade of arts and antiquities, also known as the trafficking of arts and cultural property, is a criminal activity well known for being associated with TOC groups (Congressional Research Service, 2021). As a result, many countries have enacted laws to address TOC; however, most are targeted toward the crimes of drug trafficking or human trafficking (McCabe, 2008). Among the collaborating agencies are the FBI, Interpol, Europol, and the National Crime Agency. In 2021, **Interpol** developed a new app aimed at identifying reported stolen works of art. This new app allows collectors, dealers, and citizens to access the international organization's database of over 50,000 stolen artworks (McGreevy, 2021). Estimates over the years suggest annual profits in the billions of dollars—with challenges in provenance documentation, in legal efforts, and in police detection only making these criminal actions move forward. In reaction, many countries have attempted to address these illegal activities. Since 2001, interest by the U.S. Congress has increased amid evidence of links to money laundering, sanctions evasion, and terrorist financing (Congressional Research Service, 2021). Prior to the 9/11 terrorist attacks, the United States and the United Nations participated in the UN's Educational, Scientific, and Cultural Organization (UNESCO) 1970 **Convention on the Means**

> In March of 2021, the FBI offered a $10,000 reward for information regarding national treasures stolen from the Truman Presidential Library in Missouri (Federal Bureau of Investigation Kansas City, 2021).

Interpol—An international law enforcement organization that facilitates worldwide police cooperation and crime control.

of Prohibiting and Preventing the Illicit Import, Export and Transfer of Ownership of Cultural Property. Through initiatives such as these, states have supported provisions related to safeguarding cultural property, and intergovernmental entities that address arts and antiquities trafficking are also attempting to address the problem.

In April of 2022, the **FBI Art Crime Team** returned 16 stolen cultural items to Peru's government (Federal Bureau of Investigation Los Angeles, 2022). This **repatriation** of another country's cultural goods demonstrates goodwill between countries and underlines the importance of restoring items of importance to a country's history and culture.

Unfortunately, some arts and antiquities professionals argue that foreign governments seek restrictions on too broad a range of items and that such restrictions could jeopardize the treatment of cultural items, as purchasers in destination countries may be able to provide higher-quality care for valuable objects than is provided in the objects' home country (Congressional Research Service, 2021). Other states suggest that countries that have persecuted minority groups should not receive priority over diaspora communities in debates over ownership of such groups' cultural objects and that, in some cases, the process for import restrictions is too burdensome and without the proper infrastructure to enforce regulations. Without question, while it is acknowledged that common preservation goals can strengthen bilateral relations and improve public sentiment toward art and cultural antiques, to address these criminal activities by TOC groups will require more concentrated efforts and support throughout the entire global community.

Repatriation—The return of someone or something to their home country.

Counterfeiting, contraband, and aspects of IP theft by TOC groups are often considered victimless crimes, and they continue to provide difficulties for police and government officials. Research suggests that the United States and other industrialized countries are not only the greatest producers of IP but also the largest victims (National Crime Prevention Council, 2017). In fact, because the role of IP in these economies is significant, estimates suggest that approximately one third of software products, music, and videos are counterfeit (National Crime Prevention Council, 2017).

Product fraud and counterfeiting are sources of financing for terrorism (Spink, 2016).

Unfortunately, research also suggests that **product fraud** and counterfeiting are sources of financing for terrorist groups (Spink,

2016). Given that the financing of most terrorist organizations is decentralized and very lucrative, it is often difficult to distinguish between TOC groups that sometimes support terrorist actions and terrorists who commit crimes to finance their goals (Heinonen et al., 2014). Studies have suggested that products that are in high demand with consumers and with established TOC networks are attractive to terrorists' funding opportunities. Hence, a product-counterfeiting scheme would provide the necessary funding for violent activities. The same can be applied to the criminal enterprises of movie and music piracy and the involvement of terrorist groups. Thus, while the primary objective of TOC groups is profit, a secondary objective may be the financing of terrorist activities (Abadinsky, 2017).

These perceived "victimless" crimes are, for the most part, not victimless. In fact, faulty products harm individuals every day, while inappropriate medicines and illegal drugs (discussed in Chapter 1) provide billions of dollars to TOC groups every year. Combined with the profits from products such as counterfeit air-bags and counterfeit electronics, these actions by TOC groups not only rob countries of potential revenue from legitimate supply chain processes but also threaten real public health risks for people throughout the world.

Summary

The illicit trades of art, antiquities, and other goods are yet another aspect of the criminal actions of TOC groups. Profits from the illicit trade in art and cultural antiquities produce billions of dollars annually for TOC groups. Combined with profits from intellectual property theft, contraband, and counterfeit products, this adds up to trillions of dollars in profits for TOC groups every year.

Throughout history, the theft of art and antiquities has been a lucrative criminal activity. For the most part, the consumers of such illicit products are from wealthier countries, while the supplies come from less developed countries. Members of TOC groups facilitate not only the distribution of such products but also the identification and source of potential product. Like counterfeiting and the trafficking of contraband, IP theft has also emerged as a profitable avenue for TOC groups.

Unfortunately, these aspects of illicit trade are often facilitated by the legitimate trade of such products, such as through regulating authority's actions, requiring minimal reporting, and making use of technology. TOC groups, well aware of this limitation in the trade of such items, are eager to exploit such vulnerability to the extent that counterfeiting and intellectual property theft, often facilitated by globalization and technology advancements, continue to increase. Internationally connected police organizations such as Interpol have had some success in addressing these criminal actions by TOC groups. Unfortunately, across the globe, increases in these criminal actions provide risk to economies, democracies, and public health and safety, while at the same time providing trillions of dollars to members of TOC groups.

Questions for Further Thought

1. If regulating authorities in the legal trade of art and cultural antiquities choose to limit their actions, are they really concerned about the illicit trade of such items?
2. If discrepancies in the tax revenues of items such as cigarettes facilitate the counterfeiting and smuggling of contraband, would consistent tax rates be worth examining as a way to reduce these illegal activities?
3. How might counterfeiting products help to diversify the criminal actions of TOC groups?

References

Abadinsky, H. (2017). *Organized crime* (11th ed.). Cengage Group.

Amineddoleh, L. (2013). The role of museums in the trade of black market cultural heritage property. *Art, Antiquity, and Law, 18*(2), 1–28.

Antonopoulos, G., Hall, A., Large, J., & Shen, A. (2020). Counterfeit goods fraud: An account of its financial management. *European Journal on Criminal Policy and Research, 26*(2), 357–378.

Artsy Editors. (2017, January 23). 75 members of art trafficking ring arrested in major bust. Retrieved March 1, 2022, from https://www.artsy.net/article/artsy-editorial-75-members-art-trafficking-ring-arrested-major-bust

Barrett, J. (1996). Crimes involving art. *Journal of Criminal Law and Criminology, 87*(1), 334–358.

Basu, G. (2013). The role of transnational smuggling operation in illicit supply chains. *Journal of Transparency Security, 6*, 315–328.

Bishara, H. (2020, March 18). *The most valuable stolen artworks across time.* Hyperallergic. Retrieved April 12, 2022, from https://hyperallergic.com/545938/the-most-valuable-stolen-artworks-across-time/

Boesen, U. (2020, November). *Cigarette taxes and cigarette smuggling by state, 2018.* Tax Foundation. Retrieved March 30, 2022, from https://taxfoundation.org/cigarette-taxes-cigarette-smuggling-2020/

Borrell, D. (2020, February 5). *The knockoff effect: The hidden environmental and social impact of counterfeit goods.* Total Retail. Retrieved March 3, 2022, from https://www.mytotalretail.com/article/the-knockoff-effect-the-hidden-environmental-and-social-impact-of-counterfeit-goods/

Browning, F. (2007, May 31). *Stolen fine art: Organized crime's fine commodity.* NPR. Retrieved March 21, 2022, from https://www.npr.org/templates/story/story.php?storyId=10588693&t=1647940641460

Briggs, F. (2018, November 20). *Fake fashion items top EU border seizures, Kroll analysis shows.* Retail Times. Retrieved April 3, 2022, from https://www.retailtimes.co.uk/fake-fashion-items-top-eu-border-seizures-kroll-analysis-shows/

Cabitza, M. (2012, August 16). *Why fake dollars are big business in Peru.* BBC News. Retrieved April 3, 2022, from https://www.bbc.com/news/world-latin-america-19240999

Cal Micro Recycling. (2022). *The difference between grey, black market, and counterfeit goods.* Retrieved March 30, 2022, from https://www.calmicrousa.com/the-difference-between-grey-black-market-and-counterfeit-goods/

Charney, N. (2018, July 9). *What's the motive behind most art thefts? These Mafia heists provide clues.* Observer. Retrieved March 3, 2022, from https://observer.com/2018/07/mafia-heists-provide-clues-to-motive-behind-famous-art-thefts/

Charney, N., Denton, P., & Kleberg, J. (2012, March). Protecting cultural heritage from art theft. *FBI Law Enforcement Bulletin*, 1–8.

Congressional Research Service. (2021, March 1). *Transnational crime issues: Arts and antiquities trafficking.* Retrieved March 3, 2022, from https://www.everycrsreport.com/files/2021-03-01_IF11776_f742f1db4fadd9a260af7384790481713cea72a4.pdf

Council of Europe. (2008). *MONEYVAL: Committee of experts on the evaluation of anti-money laundering measures and the financing of terrorism.* Retrieved March 3, 2022, from http://www.coe.int/t/dghl/monitoring/moneyval/typologies/MONEYVAL%282008%2922RRepTyp_counterfeiting.pdf.

European Commission. (2010). *Contraband and counterfeit cigarettes.* Retrieved March 20, 2022, from https://ec.europa.eu/commission/presscorner/detail/fr/MEMO_10_334

European Parliament. (2018). *Intellectual, industrial, and commercial property.* Retrieved March 30, 2022, from https://www.europarl.europa.eu/factsheets/en/sheet/36/intellectual-industrial-and-commercial-property

Europol. (2017, December 10). *Crime in the age of technology. Europol unclassified—Basic protection level.* Retrieved May 7, 2022, from https://www.europol.europa.eu/media-press/newsroom/news/crime-in-age-of-technology-%E2%80%93-europol%E2%80%99s-serious-and-organised-crime-threat-assessment-2017

Federal Bureau of Investigation Kansas City. (2021, March 24). *FBI offers reward of up to $10,000 for information regarding stolen national treasures* [Press release]. Federal Bureau of Investigation. Retrieved May 8, 2022, from https://www.fbi.gov/contact-us/field-offices/kansascity/news/press-releases/fbi-offers-reward-of-up-to-10000-for-information-regarding-stolen-national-treasures

Federal Bureau of Investigation Los Angeles. (2022, April 22). *The FBI's art crime team returns 16 cultural items to Peruvian officials at a ceremony held today at the FBI's Los Angeles field office* [Press release]. Federal Bureau of Investigation. Retrieved May 8, 2022, from https://www.fbi.gov/contact-us/field-offices/losangeles/news/press-releases/the-fbis-art-crime-team-returns-sixteen-cultural-items-to-peruvian-officials-at-a-ceremony-held-today-at-the-fbis-los-angeles-field-office

Francesco, C., Favarin, S., Ingrascì, O., & Smit, A. (2013). *Illicit Trade in Tobacco Products, 2018 The factbook on the illicit trade in tobacco products.* Accessed on August 19, 2022 at http://www.transcrime.it/wp-content/uploads/2013/10/Factbook_on_the_ITTP_1-UK1.pdf

Grahamton, N. (2022, April 24). IFPI: *Music piracy funding organized crime.* A6Soft. Retrieved May 7, 2022, from https://a6soft.com/ifpi-music-piracy-funding-organized-crime/

Greenberger, A. (2021, February 26). *Looting, plundering, and more: 20 cultural treasures that have faced claims of theft.* ARTnews. Retrieved March 3, 2022, from https://www.artnews.com/list/art-news/artists/most-important-looted-plundered-works-1234584727/

Heinonen, J., Spink, J., & Wilson, J. (2014). When crime events defy classification. The case of product counterfeiting as white-collar crimes. *Security Journal, 18*(3), 1057–1065.

Hill, C. (2008). Art crime and the wealth of nations. *Journal of Financial Crime, 15*(4), 444–448.

Illicit Trade in Tobacco Products. (2018). The factbook on the illicit trade in tobacco products 3 - Ireland. *Trends in Organized Crime, 21*(1), 189–214. https://doi.org/10.1007/s12117-018-9339-6

Interpol. (2021). *Stolen works of art database.* Retrieved March 3, 2022, from https://www.interpol.int/en/Crimes/Cultural-heritage-crime/Stolen-Works-of-Art-Database

Kuhar, S. (2020). Art crime and preventive measures for museums, churches and sacred objects. *Journal of Criminal Justice and Security, 2*, 202–217.

Lemley, M. (2005). Property, intellectual property, and free riding. *Texas Law Review, 83*(1031), 1003.

Lewis, P. (2020, April 23). *Counterfeiting and organized crime.* World Trademark Review. Retrieved March 3, 2022, from https://www.worldtrademarkreview.com/global-guide/anti-counterfeiting-and-online-brand-enforcement/2020/article/counterfeiting-and-organised-crime

May, C. (2017, March). *Transnational crime and the developing world.* Global Financial Integrity. Retrieved March 3, 2022, from https://secureservercdn.net/50.62.198.97/34n.8bd.myftpupload.com/wp-content/uploads/2017/03/Transnational_Crime-final.pdf?time=1646839567

McCabe, K. (2008). *The trafficking of persons: National and international responses.* Peter Lang.

McGreevy, N. (2021, May 12). Interpol's new app combats art crime and protects cultural heritage. *Smithsonian Magazine*. Retrieved May 7, 2022, from https://www.smithsonianmag.com/smart-news/interpol-launches-app-help-people-report-stolen-art-180977700/

McIllwain, J. (2005). Intellectual property and organized crime: The case of film piracy. *Trends in Organized Crime, 8*(4), 15–39.

Murphy, I. (2015, August 26). *The rise of copyright infringement lawsuits—and what retailers can do about it.* Retail Dive. Retrieved March 23, 2022, from https://www.retaildive.com/news/the-rise-of-copyright-infringement-lawsuitsand-what-retailers-can-do-about/404336/

Napier. (2021, October 29). *Art theft of the rise as financial criminals get more creative.* Retrieved May 8, 2022, from https://www.napier.ai/post/interpol-art-theft-covid

National Crime Prevention Council. (2017). *Intellectual property theft: Facts and figures illustrate the extent of intellectual property theft.* Retrieved March 5, 2022, from http://archive.ncpc.org/topics/intellectual-property-theft/facts-and-figures-1.html

O'Keefe, P. (2014). Difficulties in investigating crime and recovering its proceeds: An international perspective. In D. Chappell & S. Hufnagel (Eds.), *Contemporary perspectives on the detection, investigation and prosecution of art crime: Australasian, European and North American perspectives* (pp. 151–167). Routledge.

Organization for Economic Cooperation and Development. (2019). *Trade in fake goods is now 3.3% of world trade and rising.* Retrieved March 22, 2022, from https://www.oecd.org/newsroom/trade-in-fake-goods-is-now-33-of-world-trade-and-rising.htm#:~:text=18%20March%202019%20%2D%20Trade%20in,the%20EU's%20Intellectual%20Property%20Office.

Polcaro, R. (2019, September 4). *The Beatles and the most pirated artists in the world.* Rock and Roll Garage. Retrieved May 7, 2022, from http://rockandrollgarage.com/the-beatles-are-the-most-pirated-artists-in-the-world-see-the-complete-list/

Rea, N. (2020, April 6). *Almost 98 percent of eastern Mediterranean antiquities sold in Germany are of questionable origin, a new report has found.* Artnet News. Retrieved April 3, 2022, from https://news.artnet.com/art-world/germany-illicit-antiquities-1826016

Revenue. (2017, August 29). *Revenue seizes contraband alcohol and tobacco products at Dublin airport and port* [Press release]. Irish Tax and Customs. Retrieved April 3, 2022, from https://revenue.ie/en/corporate/press-office/press-releases/2017/pr-290817-alcohol-tobacco.aspx

Sample, I. (2019, March 11). *Fake drugs kill more than 250,000 children a year, doctors warn.* The Guardian. Retrieved March 3, 2022, from https://www.theguardian.com/science/2019/mar/11/fake-drugs-kill-more-than-250000-children-a-year-doctors-warn

Savona, E., & Riccardi, M. (2015). *From illegal markets to legitimate businesses. The portfolio of organized crime in Europe.* Transcrime.

Sofia. (2003). *Corruption, contraband, and organized crime in Southeast Europe.* Center for the Study of Democracy. Retrieved April 12, 2022, from https://www.files.ethz.ch/isn/29778/2003_Corruption.pdf

Spink, J. (2016). Product fraud and product counterfeiting as a source of terrorist financing. *Security Journal, 30*(2), 640–645.

TOI Staff. (2021, November 17). *Cops find stolen Torah originally from Baghdad that alleged thief planned to sell.* Times of Israel. Retrieved April 12, 2022, from https://www.timesofisrael.com/cops-find-stolen-torah-originally-from-baghdad-that-alleged-thief-planned-to-sell/

United Nations Interregional Crime and Justice Research Institute. (2007). Counterfeiting: A global spread, a global threat. *Trends in Organized Crime, 12*(1), 59–77.

United Nations Interregional Crime and Justice Research Institute. (2012). Ministero dello Sviluppo Economico (Italia), "La contraffazione come attività gestita dalla criminalità organizzata Transnazionale: Il caso Italiano", p. 12, 2012. Retrieved March 3, 2022, from http://www.unicri.it/in_focus/files/contraf_unicr2.pdf.

United Nations Office on Drugs and Crime. (2015). *The illicit trafficking of counterfeit goods and transnational organized crime.* Retrieved March 3, 2022, from https://www.unodc.org/documents/ropan/Campaign/Counterfeit_Goods/The_Illicit_Trafficking_of_Counterfeit_Goods_and_Transnational_Organized_Crime.pdf

U.S. Department of Homeland Security. (2020, January 24). *Combating trafficking in counterfeit and pirated goods.* Retrieved March 3, 2022, from https://www.dhs.gov/sites/default/files/publications/20_0124_plcy_counterfeit-pirated-goods-report_01.pdf

U.S. Department of Justice. (2017, March 2). *Florida man pleaded guilty to software piracy scheme* [Press release]. U.S. Attorney's Office. Western District of Missouri. Retrieved April 2, 2022, from https://www.justice.gov/usao-wdmo/pr/florida-man-pleads-guilty-software-piracy-scheme

Yancey-Bragg, N. (2017, March 28). *NGO: Transnational organized groups make $2.2 trillion a year.* Organized Crime and Corruption Reporting Project. Retrieved March 20, 2022, from https://www.occrp.org/en/daily/6240-ngo-transnational-organized-crime-groups-make-us-2-2-trillion-a-year

Yu, P. (2007). *Intellectual property and information wealth: Copyright and related rights.* Greenwood.

Violent Extremism, Terrorism, and Transnational Organized Crime

Key Terms

Al-Qaeda
Al-Shabaab
Boko Haram
Counterterrorism
COVID-19
Edmund Burke
Global Terrorism Index (GTI)
Hate crimes
Irish Republic Army (IRA)
Islamic State (ISIS)
Islamic State in Iraq and the Levant (ISIL)
Mass media
Radicalization
Rational choice theory
Rule of law
September 11, 2001
Social disorganization theory
Subculture theory
Terrorism
Trafficking
Violent extremism
Wolverine Watchmen
United Nations Universal Declaration of Human Rights

CHAPTER OBJECTIVES

Chapter 10 will enable readers to understand the following:

- the problem of defining *violent extremism* and *terrorism*
- the relationships among violent extremism, terrorism, and transnational organized crime (TOC)
- the more common methods of funding by terrorist organizations
- the common TOC crimes adopted by terrorist groups
- the similarities and differences between terrorist groups and TOC groups
- the impact of the COVID-19 pandemic on terrorism and TOC
- the connection between TOC and acts of terrorism
- international efforts to address terrorism

PRIOR TO THE September 11th attacks in the United States, terrorism was of little concern to Americans. For most U.S. citizens, their safety was assured and their vulnerability to violence from those outside of the country was not an issue. This feeling of security changed on **September 11, 2001**. For Americans and many others across the globe, the demonstrated vulnerability of the United States to a terrorist attack created a fear of future attacks and focused governmental actions on addressing terrorism or the use of violence to intimidate the public (Banks & Baker, 2016).

Of course, terrorist acts are not unique to the United States. In April of 2020, seven people were killed by two suicide bombers in Cameroon (Human Rights Watch, 2020). In April of 2017, a group of terrorists kidnapped 200 villagers and killed dozens in an attack within the country of Nigeria (Shelley, 2017). In March of 2016, three separate bombings in Brussels resulted in the deaths of 35 people and over 300 injured (Shoichet, 2016). In April of 2013, two brothers planted bombs at the finish line of the Boston Marathon; the explosion killed three people and injured hundreds (CNN Staff, 2013). In July of 2003, 18 people were killed when two Chechen female bombers blew themselves up at an open-air rock festival in Moscow (U.S. Department of State, 2005). Each of these events was considered a terrorist attack and each was related, in some manner, to groups involved with TOC.

Across the globe, there is a history of crimes against governments and crimes against a government's citizens. For some of these activities extremists are involved, and with some of these activities terrorists are involved. For clarity, *extremism* generally refers to both violent and nonviolent acts of political expression while *terrorism* is violent acts. In addition, extremism includes encouraging acts of violence while terrorism focuses on the commission of such acts of violence. These attacks are not limited to underdeveloped countries or countries with internal conflicts; the September 11, 2001, attack in the United States, the 2005 London Underground bombing, and the 2015 terrorist attack in Paris are examples of attacks within countries that have relatively high levels of economic growth and security. In these cases, in the United States nearly 3,000 American lives were lost when 19 hijackers crashed three planes into the World Trade Center, the Pentagon, and the Pennsylvania countryside (*The Atlantic*, 2016). In the United Kingdom, over 50 people lost their lives (BBC News, 2015b), and the three explosions outside a football stadium in Paris resulted in over 125 people dead (BBC News, 2015a). The topics of extremist activities and terrorism are critical in any text dedicated to discussions on the significantly negative consequences of TOC, and in this chapter, acts of **violent extremism** and **terrorism** are discussed as related to actions of violence against groups of individuals within a country.

Violent extremism—Encouraging, condoning, justifying, or supporting the commission of a violent act to achieve political, ideological, religious, social, or economic goals (Futures Without Violence, 2017).

Terrorism—The unlawful use of force and violence against persons or property to intimidate or coerce a government, the civilian population, or any segment thereof, in furtherance of political or social objectives (Federal Bureau of Investigation, 2015).

In addressing the topics of TOC and terrorism, this chapter provides an overview of the roles of TOC in extremist activities perpetrated against a government or its citizens, as well as an overview of terrorism as one of today's most common concerns within societies. Included in this chapter is a historical examination of terrorist acts as well as discussion on the identified categories of **radicalization**, and the links among radicalization, violent extremism, and terrorism. In addition, this chapter addresses the role of technology in facilitating these acts of destruction as well as the influence of **COVID-19** on today's TOC and terrorism. Therefore, this chapter provides information on the nexus between TOC and terrorism, demonstrated in many forms, with the goal of threatening international peace and security across the globe (Global Counterterrorism Forum, 2018).

Defining Radicalization, Violent Extremism, and Terrorism

Terrorism generally refers to actions that produce fear and violence. As with the term *terrorism*, there is also no universally agreed definition of the phrase *violent extremism* and therefore the two terms are often applied interchangeably to label an action of destruction (United Nations Office on Drugs and Crime, 2020b). In the 1930s, the League of Nations defined *terrorism* as criminal acts directed against a state or country that are intended or calculated to create terror in the minds of particular persons, or a group of persons, or the general public (United Nations Office on Drugs and Crime, 2018). Thus, in general, the term *terrorism* refers to an action that most often produces a significant amount of fear and panic among potential victims.

The U.S. Code of Federal Regulations defines *terrorism* as the unlawful use of force and violent actions against persons or property to intimidate or coerce a government, the civilian population, or any segment thereof, in furtherance of political or social objectives

(28 C.F.R. Section 0.85). *Violent extremism*, a phrase more contemporary in use than the term *terrorism*, is often applied to explanations of a less significant (i.e., few deaths and injuries) violent event. In terms of a more global definition, USAID defines *violent extremist activities* as the "advocating, engaging in, preparing, or otherwise supporting ideologically motivated or justified violence to further social, economic or political objectives" (United Nations Office on Drugs and Crime, 2020b).

Defining *terrorism* is difficult because most definitions of criminal behaviors refer to the actions (e.g., robbery indicates that someone was robbed); however, the term *terrorism* refers to elements present in the action(s) rather than one simple definition. Thus, *terrorism* includes a reference to violence or force that is intended to generate fear among individuals, a reference to harm or death to civilians, the use of words for intimidation or coercion, and a reference to a political or religious objective (Banks & Baker, 2016). In research, those studying terrorism often focus upon the process of terrorism rather than the end results, as terrorism is essentially the systematic use of intimidation and coercion to create a climate of fear among members of a target group (Wilkinson, 2001).

Whereas definitions of both *violent extremism* and *terrorism* vary across governments and within intergovernmental agencies, for the purpose of this chapter *terrorism* means the use of force or violence against a government or its citizens with goals of death, destruction, and fear. *Violent extremist activities* are defined in terms of participating in or supporting ideologically motivated violence against a specific government or population. For the purpose of this chapter, and in discussions on their associations with TOC, *terrorism* and *violent extremism* may be used interchangeably with the assumption that common to both of them is the outcome of death to an innocent victim.

Historically, TOC and terrorism have been researched as different entities, with unique dynamics associated with each. TOC is related to profit and terrorism is related to fear. Since 9/11 there has been a growing operational, organizational, and conceptual convergence of research suggesting that terrorist groups and members of TOC groups are known to have cooperated with, coexisted with, and even learned from each other (Global Counterterrorism Forum, 2018). Specifically, in some countries terrorists benefit from the criminal experiences of members of TOC groups. Two Middle Eastern terrorist groups, Hezbollah and Hamas, have historically been linked to the drug trade (Levitt, 2013). In particular, many terrorists have expertise in counterfeiting of documents, access to weapons, and access to financial resources from their illicit activities of trafficking, smuggling, kidnapping, and extortion (Global Counterterrorism Forum, 2018). In other regions, TOC groups have utilized the violence of terrorist groups to maintain control over populations and to secure territories for operations. Terrorist groups are benefiting from TOC, and TOC groups are benefitting from the use of radicalization and terrorist groups. The result of this cooperation is the undermining of security, stability, and governance within countries.

> Radicalization is a process that occurs over time.

The United Nations has attempted to address radicalization for many years. Most recently, the radicalization of youth (McCabe, 2017) and the promotion of violent extremism have been at the front of the issue as the world combats the global COVID-19 pandemic and people spend more time online. In these cases, the UN suggests that extremist groups are taking advantage of the lockdown situations across the globe and intensifying efforts to spread hatred and radicalize youth through social media (United Nations, 2021). In addition, as travel restrictions continue, TOC groups are capitalizing on the new vulnerabilities by shifting products, based upon demand, and altering transit patterns to best supply products and incorporate new members into the organization.

For clarity, *radicalization* is a process that occurs over time (i.e., weeks or months) with a change in philosophy varying by individual characteristics and circumstances based upon the social and political conditions that exist within an area (Langat & Kushner, 2015). For the most part, radicalization is classified into four categories based upon context and time period (Center for Prevention of Radicalization, 2020): right-wing, politico-religious, left-wing, and single-issue. Specifically, right-wing radicalization is a form of radicalization associated with fascism and racism. This form of radicalization is characterized by the violent defenses of a racial, ethnic, or pseudo-national identity, and is often associated with radical hostility toward state authorities, minorities, immigrants, and/or left-wing political groups.

Politico-religious extremism is associated with a political interpretation of religion by violent means, of a religious identity perceived to be under attack. In this form of radicalization, any religion may spawn these types of violent actions. Left-wing extremism focuses on anticapitalist demands and calls for the transformation of political systems considered responsible for producing social inequalities. This category most often includes anarchist and Marxist groups that use violence to advocate for their cause. Single-issue radicalization is generally motivated by one issue. This category includes animal rights groups, antiabortion extremists, certain antigay/antifeminist movements, and other independent extremist movements. Unfortunately, it is this last category of radicalization that most often involves individuals who participate in the mass murders of populations.

In November of 2021, **counterterrorism** police in London detained three men, between the ages of 21 and 29, in connection to an explosion at a hospital in the city of Liverpool. The explosion killed one person and injured another (Center for Prevention of Radicalization, 2020).

Some suggest that this process of radicalization is fueled by many factors, including negative experiences with police and an exposure to the state's criminal justice system, negative perceptions of the area's **rule of law**, and a desire for group acceptance (Hamm, 2009). For example, the threat posed by **al-Shabaab** and other extremists in the Horn of Africa continues to evolve in West Africa, where the terrorist organization Boko Haram already exists and is funded through the criminal activities of TOC (Adisa, 2021).

Specifically, the trafficking of drugs, people, and wildlife provides financing for terrorist groups. In particular, research suggests that **Boko Haram** as well as ISIS have managed their campaigns based on financing from the complex transnational criminal networks (Adisa, 2021).

In fact, despite significant blows to its organizational leadership, Boko Haram continues to orchestrate attacks in Nigeria. In 2016, Boko Haram attacked a mosque and a suicide bomber killed over 20 individuals. In August of 2017 a suicide attack by Boko Haram resulted in the deaths of over 30 individuals; later that same year over 50 individuals were killed in another attack (Wilson, 2018).

As suggested by the UN, violent extremists pose a direct threat to human rights and the right to liberty and security (United Nations,

Al-Shabaab—Somalia-based terrorist jihadist fundamentalist group active in East Africa and Yemen.

Boko Haram—An Islamic sect that believes politics in northern Nigeria has been seized by a group of corrupt Muslims. The phrase translates to "Western education is forbidden."

Counterterrorism—Efforts by police or the military that are designed to prevent or thwart terrorism.

2015). Factors that facilitate an individual's propensity to engage in extremist activities vary based upon the conditions of their community. Specifically, the UN suggests that conditions facilitating violent extremism include (1) a lack of socioeconomic opportunities in countries that fail to generate high and sustainable levels of growth or create jobs for their young people; (2) marginalization of diverse populations such as when a country experiences insecurities in relation to scarce resources, and one group acts monopolistically in the political and economic sectors at the expense of other groups; (3) poor governance, with violations of human rights and the rule of law; (4) prolonged and unresolved conflicts; and (5) radicalization in prisons (United Nations, 2015). When these risk factors for terrorism are examined, the common elements of risk for TOC can be seen as well.

Lastly, as suggested by the U.S. Department of Justice, the process of radicalization includes not only the factors of the community but also the types and context of belief systems (U.S. Department of Justice, 2021). In particular, potential risk factors for radicalizing individuals to commit acts of violent extremism include experiencing identity conflicts, feeling there is a lack of meaning in life, having a desire to belong, experiencing mental health issues, feeling emotionally unstable, and having little or no knowledge of religion and ideologies (National Institute of Justice, 2021). Those involved in recruiting members for terrorist activities are well aware of the vulnerabilities of individuals, especially the vulnerabilities of young people.

Theoretical Explanations of Terrorism and TOC

Historically, TOC was regional in scope with only the rarest of links to terrorism; however, today, TOC networks are ever-changing and they adjust based upon the market for their products and their engagement in a wide range of illicit activities, including support for terrorism (Abadinsky, 2017). Contemporary research suggests that to understand the link between TOC and terrorism, one must first understand the needs of a community (Funk et al., 2013). Historically, the presence of ideological motivations has encouraged criminologists to endorse the belief that violent extremism and terrorism together form an exclusive phenomenon that is outside the explanatory scope of traditional theories (Mullins, 2019). However, recent studies, suggest that this trend is changing as more criminological theories such as subcultural theory (Pisoiu, 2015), rational choice (Perry & Hasisi, 2015), and social disorganization (Fahey & LaFree, 2015) are applied in general to explanations for membership within criminal organizations and for actions of destruction.

On October 8, 2020, in the United States, six men were arrested and charged with conspiring to kidnap Michigan's governor. These men, charged under the Anti-Terrorism Act, are thought to be connected to a little-known extremist militia group called the **Wolverine Watchmen** (Macklin, 2021).

Wolverine Watchmen—A recently established Michigan militia group.

Subculture

Subculture theory, as applied to terrorism and TOC, suggests that groups or subcultures in society have values and attitudes that are conducive to crime and violence (Blackmon, 2014). In these organization, the skills of toughness, fearlessness of the police, and engagement in criminal behaviors are valued. Hence, it would not seem unreasonable that individuals who assimilate into the subculture of TOC may also participate in actions of terrorism. In particular, the development of a subculture of terrorism and its ideology of apocalyptic violence is essential for understanding and countering this worldwide phenomenon (Hamm, 2004).

Research suggests that individuals within these subcultures utilize subcultural products of money and material possessions to promote their ideology and inspire a new generation of homegrown terrorists. The stimuli of the subculture support the attitudes and behaviors of its members, which are designed to bring praise, acceptance, and a sense of self-worth within that cultural context (Hamm, 2004). Thus, the subculture supports membership not only in groups dedicated to TOC but also in groups dedicated to mass destruction.

Rational Choice

Rational choice theory states that individuals make decisions after weighing the costs and benefits of an action (McCabe & Martin, 2005). In the criminal actions of terrorism and TOC, the perpetrator(s) decide that their actions are worth the risk with a limited possibility of negative consequences. Specifically, for engagement with TOC the product must be in great demand with a high value, and for the members of a TOC group to decide to commit a criminal act, the penalty for engaging in the act must be unlikely or minimal.

Choosing to be a suicide bomber, which is a common act of terrorism, requires a specific kind of rationality. Its particular balance between costs and benefits suggests that martyrdom videos and biographical information on suicide attackers, as well as interviews with would-be suicide bombers, make it plausible to suggest that suicide missions are acceptable (Tosini, 2010). Militants frequently refer to a series of absolute values to support their ideologies, so their response that a suicide mission is reasonable is based on their adhesive principles that require the ultimate sacrifice as well as indifference to others (Tosini, 2010). Therefore, the actions of TOC as well as terrorism are considered rational decisions.

Social Disorganization

Social disorganization theory suggests that a society characterized by the breakdown of effective social controls will also experience at least a lack of positive interactions between groups or even a state of conflict between parties. As applied to terrorism and the criminal actions of TOC groups, social disorganization suggests that as the demographic characteristics of poverty, residential mobility, and ethnic diversity increase, the risk for extreme actions of destruction also increase (Akyuz & Armstrong, 2011). In other words, societies without structure and the rule of law will produce individuals who are involved in criminal activities and in crimes against governing authorities (i.e., terrorism).

Early social disorganization theory predicts that areas with high levels of poverty and heterogeneity will have more crime; thus, in these societies there will be more members within TOC groups. In social disorganization theory, the relationship between the sociostructural characteristics of poverty, heterogeneity, and residential instability as related to crime is believed to be mediated by a number of characteristics, including the tendency of citizens to exercise informal social control and the existence of subcultures that support delinquent behavior (Akyuz & Armstrong, 2011). An examination of terrorism or TOC finds that social disorganization theory continues to support the notion that poverty, heterogeneity, and residential instability are indeed strong predictors of instability. The instability of a society is a strong predictor of victimization and criminal activity. The bottom line is that instability supports TOC and terrorist incidents.

Similarities and Differences Between Terrorist Groups and TOC Groups

Terrorist groups and transnational organized crime (TOC) have many similarities that must be acknowledged in discussion of either or both. At the structural core of their similarities, both entities exploit porous national borders, corrupt law enforcement, and corrupt government officials (Baldwin & DiPerna, 2007). In particular, both are generally rational-thinking actors who plan for either their criminal activity or their terrorist attack (Sanderson, 2004). **Trafficking** networks do not instantaneously emerge, they are established; and bombs or explosives do not simply ignite, they are built and detonated for a terrorist attack. In addition, both terrorist groups and TOC are comfortable using violence and threats to gain or maintain power within a region. In both of these groups, members seek a sense of belonging that they may feel does not exist outside of the organization, and both groups are dedicated to a specific goal. Specifically, terrorist groups and TOC memberships are based around the concept of multiple members within the organization. Although there are "lone wolf" terrorists, all are embedded in an organization and have a common mission of either profit and power or power and destruction. Hence, both terrorist groups and TOC seek power within a region, and to maintain that power both structures consist of backup leaders and foot soldiers (Sanderson, 2004). In addition, both terrorist groups and TOC generally share the same geography as well as the same victim pools, and it is not unusual to discover cells of terrorist groups operating within areas that have a heavy presence of TOC (Baldwin & DiPerna, 2007). Also, as the two groups are in literal proximity to each other, they often share some of the same members—with both groups highly adaptable, innovative, and resilient—all while operating secretly, with members rarely leaving their groups (Sanderson, 2004). Lastly, both terrorist groups and TOC members have incorporated the use of technology and the cyber world in their efforts. TOC utilizes technology to identify, transport, and deliver products (McCabe & Murphy, 2016), while terrorist groups utilize technology to disseminate information on the groups and to recruit members. However, there are also differences between terrorist groups and TOC members.

The goal for TOC is always profit. The members of TOC may seek power and influence within a region based upon threats or violence; however, the rational for TOC is to operate as a business with large margins of financial return. The goal for terrorist groups is political. Members of terrorist groups may seek power and control within a region, also through threats or violence, but in general the members of terrorist groups are disenchanted with their current governments and, by definition of the acts of terrorism, seek a change in government as their overarching mission. Terror groups welcome attention to their actions, while TOC groups prefer that their criminal actions remain undetected. In addition, members of both groups defy the rule of law; however, TOC often acts to form levels of authority parallel to the current governments, or they simply coexist within the realms of the current governments that allow their criminal actions to continue and flourish. Terrorist groups, by definition, defy the state and have the desire to overthrow or control the existing governments. In addition, terrorist groups are less discriminating in their choice of victims (Sanderson, 2004). Lastly, although terrorist groups and TOC may share members within a particular location, TOC—through its structure of secrecy and maximizing profits—will restrict its members to only those individuals who currently serve a specific need, such as a forger for customs documentation. Terrorist groups actively recruit members as they wish to have an abundance of followers for participation in current or future acts of destruction.

History of Terrorism

Over the last decade, over 20,000 people worldwide have been killed in terrorist attacks (Richie et al., 2019). Although the majority of these deaths in recent years are geographically focused within the Middle East, Africa, and South Asia, terrorism is a concern for all countries. Unfortunately, terrorism has existed in all civilizations and is not a new phenomenon. For example, the Sicarii, a first-century Jewish group, was known to have murdered their enemies and collaborators with small daggers hidden in their cloaks, stabbing people as they walked through the crowd—in their effort to drive the Roman rulers from Judea (Zalman, 2020). Prior to these attacks, leaders such as Julius Caesar were casualties of assassinations, or what today we would label terrorism.

Research suggests that the first use of the term *terrorism* occurred in the writings of **Edmund Burke** in the late 1700s (Law, 2016). It was also during this time period that we saw the shift from premodern terrorism, which dismissed terrorists as evil or insane, to today's modern terrorism, involving planned and calculated acts for the murder of many.

The English Parliamentarian Edmund Burke used the phrase "reign of terror" in the 1700s during the French Revolution to describe the government's slaughter of nobles, their families, and sympathizers (Heywood, 2003).

Prior to the 18th century, terrorism shifted from a very specific target—a king, a pope, or an emperor—to groups of individuals or populations. Given that terrorist acts were intended to cause change to the governing system or to maintain control by a governing system, this change in scope and size of targets is reasonable. During this period, changes to governments came with a change in leadership. If a terrorist act such as the assassination of a leader is successful, a new power begins; and this new power or leader is usually accompanied by a new government. Therefore, in these cases, terrorist acts targeted specific individuals to facilitate change.

After the 18th century, society was experiencing what some philosophers have termed an Age of Enlightenment—a time of considering punishments that fit the crimes. Based upon social contracts and empirical assessments of social conditions, societies evolved into communities governed more by groups and policies than by individual personalities. During this era, terrorist acts began targeting not simply the leader of the government but also the groups in control of the government, as well as populations benefiting from the current governmental policies (Law, 2016).

In the United States, the attacks on September 11, 2001, were a series of four attacks coordinated by a militant Islamic terrorist group called **al-Qaeda**. During the day, four airplanes were hijacked with the goal of crashing them into significant American buildings. Two of the planes struck the Twin Towers of the World Trade Center in New York. The third plane struck the Pentagon, and the fourth was crashed into a field in Pennsylvania after the passengers took control of the plane from the hijackers. The result of this attack were the deaths of nearly 3,000 Americans, and "9/11" has been identified as the worst terrorist attack on U.S. soil (Morgan, 2009).

The roots of modern terrorism can be found in 19th-century revolutionary radicalism, and in particular the emergence of "anarchist," "collectivist anarchist," and "anarchy-communist" teachings being read by millions across the globe (United Nations Office on Drugs and Crime, 2020a). In particular, groups led by some of the more popular individuals of the mid-19th century (e.g., Karl Marx) promoted antiestablishment efforts. For example, the German revolutionary and author Karl Heinzen was one of the first to articulate the use of violence, even mass murder, by individuals to effect political change (United Nations Office on Drugs and Crime, 2020a). In addition, although the majority of antiestablishment efforts were nonviolent, Vladimir Lenin, a Russian revolutionary, politician, and political theorist who headed the governments of Soviet Russia from 1917 to 1924 and the Soviet Union from 1922 to 1924, supported power by force and systematically advised and instructed his comrades to resort to executions on a large scale (Global Security, 2020). His successor Joseph Stalin continued these actions of mass destruction.

At the turn of the 20th century, most reports of terrorism involved attacks within Europe, the Middle East, and Africa. Research suggests that three factors contributed to these attacks: (1) a collapse of the International Workingmen's Association, an organization of socialists and anarchists (i.e., groups that are skeptical about authority and reject government hierarchies); (2) the failure of antigovernment efforts; and, (3) the introduction of government-based social reforms to improve the lives of laborers (Law, 2016).

Irish Republican Army (IRA)—A paramilitary group in Ireland (still recognized today), established at the beginning of the 20th century with the philosophy that Ireland should be separate from the United Kingdom.

One of the most publicized of these groups was a paramilitary group called the Irish Republican Army (History Channel, 2019), or IRA. The IRA, established in 1919, was formed to halt British rule in Northern Ireland using armed forces. In 1969, demanding British withdrawal from Northern Ireland but differing on tactics, the IRA split into two factions: officials and provisional. In these two groups, officials sought independence through peace while provisional utilized violence—resulting in an estimated 1,800 deaths, including more than 600 civilians (Angelos, 2019). Even today, the scars of the IRA's battles over British rule are still raw, as those concerned with the 21st-century United Kingdom's Brexit withdrawal plans worry that conflicts will resume with Northern Ireland and that the IRA will be rejuvenated.

Another publicized account involving terrorism was the Six-Day War in the Middle East. Specifically, the Six-Day War was a bloody conflict in June of 1967 between Israel and the Arab states of Egypt, Syria, and Jordan. Following years of diplomatic friction and small battles between Israel and its neighbors, including increasing attacks by Palestinian guerrilla groups, Israeli forces launched preemptive air strikes against Egypt and its allies. Israel also staged a successful ground offensive and seized the Sinai Peninsula and the Gaza Strip from Egypt, the West Bank and East Jerusalem from Jordan, and the Golan Heights from Syria (History Channel, 2018). On June 10, 1967, a UN–brokered ceasefire took effect and the Six-Day War came to an abrupt end. It was later estimated that approximately 20,000 Arabs and 800 Israelis had died in just 132 hours of fighting. In addition, the Six-Day War had momentous geopolitical consequences in the Middle East as victory in the war led to an increase in national pride in Israel, which had tripled in size. Unfortunately, this pride also fanned the flames of the Arab-Israeli conflict. Since 1967, the lands that Israel seized in the Six-Day War have been at the center of efforts to end the Arab-Israeli conflict (History Chanel, 2018).

In addition, 20th-century discussions of terrorism were dominated by conversations about ISIS or ISIL. For clarity, the **Islamic State in Iraq and the Levant (ISIL)** and **Islamic State (ISIS)** began as an offshoot of al Qaeda, those who have made a pledge of loyalty to Osama bin Laden. The goal of ISIS continues to be the creation of an Islamic state, called a caliphate, across Iraq and Syria. The group implements Sharia law, rooted in eighth-century Islam, to establish a society that mirrors the region's ancient past and is known for public executions, crucifixions, and other acts of violence towards groups (CNN World, 2019). In addition, ISIS utilizes modern tools like social media (to also be discussed later in this chapter) to promote reactionary politics and religious fundamentalism and to recruit young followers (McCabe, 2017).

Lastly, terrorism in Africa during the 20th century resulted in victims across the lands and seas. Specifically, terrorism through violent actions and terrorism through piratical acts continue to be major security challenges in Africa. On Africa's west and east coasts, the Boko Haram have spearheaded attacks in the Lake Chad Basin and piracy in Djibouti and Kenya (Oriola & Knight, 2019). For clarity, Boko Haram is a militant Islamic group, working out of Nigeria; established in the late 20th century, Boko Haram is home-stationed in the African state of Borno and its purpose is to institute Sharia, or Islamic law. Boko Haram militants mainly inhabit areas in the northern states of Nigeria, specifically Yobe, Kano, Bauchi, Borno, and Kaduna (CNN World, 2019). The group does not engage in Nigeria's political system, out of an adherence to a fundamentalist form of Islam, which forbids participation unless the system is based on Islamic law; however, their actions of destruction are not unrecognized.

The 21st century has seen terrorism expanding from the less-developed countries to the more economically successful ones, including the United States, the United Kingdom, and France. Although the United States had experienced domestic terrorism—such as the Oklahoma City Bombing in 1995, which resulted in the deaths of over 160 people—the terrorist attacks on September 11, 2001, in New York and the U.S. capital brought terrorism to the forefront of the global stage, and instantaneously other countries, previously perceived as safe and secure by their citizens, began noting the vulnerabilities of their states.

Throughout this century, communities across the globe have experienced anthrax attacks (USA), terrorist seizures (Moscow), bombings on public transportation (Madrid and London), the kidnapping of groups of citizens (Nigeria), and targeted attacks (Istanbul, Paris, and Brussels) (Law, 2016). However, reports from the Global Terrorism Index indicate a decrease in the number of deaths attributed to terrorism (Institute for Economics and Peace, 2019). The **Global Terrorism Index (GTI)**, a report published annually by the Institute for Economics and Peace, provides a summary of global trends in terrorism since 2000.

2020 GLOBAL TERROR INDEX SUMMARY

- Deaths from terrorism are now 59% lower than their peak in 2014. The fall in the number of deaths has been largest in Iraq, Syria, and Nigeria.
- The overall fall in the number of deaths from terrorism has also led to a reduction in the number of *countries* experiencing deaths from terrorism. Still, in 2019 63 countries recorded at least one death from terrorism.
- The impact of terrorism lessened in seven of the nine regions of the world in 2019.
- South Asia recorded the largest deterioration, followed by Central America and the Caribbean.
- However, Central America and the Caribbean remain the region with the lowest impact of terrorism, a position the area has held for the past 17 years.
- More recently, terrorist activity has been concentrated in South Asia and sub-Saharan Africa.

(Institute for Economics and Peace, 2019)

Specifically, based on the GTI, deaths from terrorism fell for the fourth year in a row, with this decline corresponding to military successes against ISIL and Boko Haram. For the first time since 2003, Iraq is no longer the country most impacted by terrorism. The fall in the total number of deaths from terrorism accompanies a reduction in the impact of terrorism around the world, with 98 countries recording an improvement on their GTI score (Institute for Economics and Peace, 2019).

Unfortunately, as the GTI reports, the intensity of terrorism has diminished its breadth, as over 100 countries recorded at least one terrorist incident in 2018 and over 70 of those countries suffered at least one fatality (Institute for Economics and Peace, 2019). Lastly, conflict remains the primary driver of terrorism, with over 95% of deaths from terrorism occurring in countries that are already in conflict, and many of the countries existing with a high prevalence of TOC groups in operation. Terrorism and violent extremism, although not new to most countries, continue to be global issues for all.

Facilitating Terrorism Through TOC

In order for the rule of law to serve a legitimate function within a society, it must be supported by the citizens of that society. International agreements establish procedures and rules intended to facilitate peace and security among states, and those agreements must also be supported if the rule of law is to continue. Unfortunately, the legitimacy of a country's conduct depends upon other countries executing their international relations through foreign policy in accordance with these laws (Baldwin & DiPerna, 2007). If countries act unilaterally and without the constructs of the international community, the legitimacy of the entire international system is vulnerable, and members of TOC as well as terrorist organizations are aware of these vulnerabilities. One example of this vulnerability is found in the Paraguayan city of Ciudad del Este. The city has experienced activities by the Islamic fundamentalist groups of Hamas and Hezbollah, which fund their terrorist activities by engaging in contraband smuggling, trafficking of narcotics, and money laundering (Baldwin & DiPerna, 2007).

> A study by the Norwegian Defence Research Establishment (FFI) examined the financing of 40 jihadi cells that plotted attacks against European targets between 1994 and 2013 and concluded that in over 25% of the attacks, the funding was through illicit trades, which included drugs, cars, forged documents, and weapons (CT MORSE, 2017).

Thus, the relationship between TOC and terrorist groups to provide military skills and weapons strengthens both the terrorist and TOC powers within a region. Another example of TOC profits being used to finance terrorism is narcotics trafficking to support groups such as the Kosovo Liberation Army (KLA), Basque Homeland, and the Islamic Movement of Uzbekistan (IMU) (Dishman, 2005).

The global war on terrorism has constricted the flow of financial support to terror groups (Sanderson, 2004). In particular, narcotics trafficking remains one of the most common and lucrative forms of criminal activity on which terrorist groups rely in order to finance their activities (Clarke, 2016). To address these efforts, terrorist organizations are moving deeper into criminal activity beyond narcotics trafficking. Specifically, after 9/11, when the U.S. government reduced its funding to various "humanitarian" groups worldwide, the illicit funding that some terrorist groups were receiving was also reduced. Specifically, when the United States exerted pressure on various countries to prevent charities from funding terrorists, some terrorist organizations created "in-house" criminal capabilities in order to generate loss revenue (Sanderson, 2004). Thus, the connection between terrorist groups and TOC became solidified. Specifically, many of the criminal activities associated with TOC were now a part of the terrorist group.

Historically, research has rarely identified a link between TOC and terrorism, although after the fall of the Berlin Wall in 1989, Warsaw Pact nations found themselves flush with weapons. Many of these weapons found their way to the illegal arms market, with conflicts in the former Yugoslavian countries and West Africa servings as consumers of the products (Sanderson, 2004). In these cases, vulnerable international borders and corrupt or untrained police in a multitude of countries have facilitated TOC and, in turn, facilitated terrorism. Most recently, the terrorist organization Hezbollah has been involved with methamphetamine labs and cigarette smuggling in the United States and Canada, which has funded their activities. Another example, the Real Irish Republican

> In 2012, the Global Counterterrorism Forum (GCTF) addressed the issue of kidnapping for ransom (KFR)—a tool used by terrorists to finance their activities—by developing the Algiers Memorandum on Good Practices on Preventing and Denying the Benefits of KFR. In 2015, the GCTF adopted an *Addendum to the Algiers Memorandum*, providing further recommendations relating to KFR prevention and deterrence measures (CT MORSE, 2017).

Army (RIRA) was identified as a terrorist organization in 2001; however, according to the Irish government, the RIRA consists of approximately 100 active members, who get their financial support from sympathizers in the United States and from TOC organizations that engage in weapons trafficking (U.S. Department of State, 2018).

Terrorist groups and TOC networks seeking to profit from the African continent's poor governance systems have continued to unleash terror on innocent citizens and security forces. The Boko Haram terrorist group is reported to have survived on multiple sources of income and through various criminal dealings, including selling gold and other precious metals, selling farm products, arms trafficking, cattle rustling, squeezing money from local residents, and robbing banks (Adisa, 2021). Thus, the link between TOC and terrorist groups is strong, and getting stronger every day.

The Role of the Online Community

Many governments are recognizing the online community's role on hate, violent extremism, and terrorist acts, and the governments are designing efforts to reduce these impacts (U.S. Department of Justice, 2013). For the most part, bias crimes or **hate crimes** are nonviolent offenses and involve the destruction of property (Bouman, 2003). In addition, a violent hate crime is most often an assault or a threat(s) against one person. This is not the case for violent extremism or terrorism. Approximately 20% of hate crimes in the United States occur within the school setting or on a college campus (Bouman, 2003). Approximately 50% of all hate crimes are outcomes of bias based upon either race or ethnicity, approximately 25% are outcomes of bias based upon religion, and approximately 25% are based upon a bias toward sexual orientation (Bouman, 2003). Hence, crimes of violent extremism and terrorism often are founded within the same ideologies of hate crimes.

> Young people are a vital source of support for many terrorist groups, with roles ranging from cooks to armed fighters. However, the ways that young people are recruited vary widely across contexts—including fraud, trafficking, and kidnapping (Darden, 2019).

The majority of these perpetrators of hate crimes are under the age of 25, with nearly 30% of those individuals considered minors. Common within this group of individuals is the everyday use of technology, and unfortunately, through a variety of posts, discussions on various topics of hate occur every day within the online community (McCabe, 2017). It is not uncommon for groups that facilitate discussions on committing acts of violence to attempt to recruit new and young individuals into their subculture of hate and sometimes violence toward other groups or individuals (DeVoe and Murphy, 2011). In these cases, the cybercommunity not only affects those being targeted for extremist activities but also may be damaging to specific groups within a society—such as the young, who are often online. Therefore, when considering violent extremism and terrorism, one must acknowledge the utility of technology.

> The vulnerability of youth to terrorist recruitment can be affected by a multitude of factors, including their geographic proximity to a terrorist group, economic vulnerability, perceptions of social or political marginalization, and exposure to permissive social networks (Darden, 2019).

COVID-19, TOC, and Terrorism

During the COVID-19 pandemic, authorities across all levels of government throughout the world have noted that TOC and violent extremist groups have taken advantage of the situation, capitalizing on and exploiting supply pressures, shortages of medical equipment, and the lack of stability in government since 2020. Specifically, the vulnerabilities of people, businesses, and governments are exploited by TOC for profit, as well as by terrorist groups that prey on the vulnerable aspects of impoverished societies and political systems.

In particular, as suggested by the United Nations (2020), the world has yet to fully understand the impact of the pandemic and consequences it has forced upon global peace and security. Even more, the world has yet to understand the relationships among COVID-19, TOC, and terrorism. TOC groups are utilizing the poverty and strain of obtaining medical equipment and personal protection equipment for profit. Terrorists are exploiting the significant disruption and economic hardships caused by COVID-19 to spread fear, hate, and division and to radicalize and recruit new followers. In addition, the work-from-home regulations have increased internet usage among most populations; thus, the pandemic further compounds the problem of misinformation (United Nations, 2020). One example of such vulnerability is in the Sahel region of Africa, where terrorist groups are imposing informal taxation on goods that cross their territories. They are also using TOC networks to finance the activities through kidnapping for ransom; the trafficking of drugs, people, and wildlife; and illegal migration (United Nations, 2020). Another example, in the country of Tunisia, is the actions of terrorist groups exploiting local grievances and thriving on political instability, armed conflict, corruption, poor economic conditions, and social unrest to recruit members to their organization (United Nations, 2020). Clearly, in terms of the social and economic conditions that are resulting from COVID-19, the platforms for recruitment into TOC and terrorist groups are thriving.

Terrorist groups have also maliciously used social media to disseminate conspiracy theories about the origin of COVID-19. These efforts usually attribute the origin of the virus to governments, religious or ethnic groups, secret networks, companies, or business people who, according to these interpretations, are trying to push through secret agendas such as globalist depopulation (United Nations Interregional Crime and Justice Research Institute, 2020). With messages customized for the specific audience of interest (for example, those against immigration), the commonality of thoughts brings the terrorist groups and sympathizers together. Particular groups that have adopted a similar narrative are Blanche Europe and the online based Eco-Fascist Central, both of which combine the traditional anti-Semitic and Islamophobic narratives with fallacious theories related to the COVID-19 pandemic to recruit members (United Nations Interregional Crime and Justice Research Institute, 2020). Thus, COVID-19 has indirectly fueled the expansion of terrorist networks.

Criminal organizations have also taken advantage of COVID-19 to portray a *positive* image of themselves and to reinforce their presence and control in the territory. A number of organized criminal groups have succeeded in maintaining a monopoly on illegal activities at the local level by imposing protection on all types of economic businesses and corrupting local political institutions (United Nations Interregional Crime and Justice Research Institute, 2020). To enforce this form of territorial control, these criminal groups often build images of a "state within the state" and are able to provide aid and support (such as COVID-19 vaccination cards) to the local community while at the same time, through intimidation and violence, discouraging any form of criticism and dissent. From this perspective, the COVID-19 crisis has provided an excellent opportunity to reinforce this rhetoric and to promote the idea that, in an emergency, criminal groups can replace the government and perform its role. The main goal of TOC, however, is not to assist the community but rather to produce a profit for TOC members.

It is important to acknowledge that the current economic crisis created by COVID-19 facilitates the possibility that criminal groups will acquire, either directly or indirectly, control over or ownership of legitimate companies. With the current financial crisis, and the potential bankruptcy of several enterprises (including shops and other economic activities), TOC has the opportunity to infiltrate the legal economy. Once TOC is operating in "legitimate" businesses, money is laundered and detection is even less likely. In this way, COVID-19 has provided a significant boost for those involved in TOC.

Media Attention

Lastly, one must consider the role of the media in relation to violent extremism and acts of terrorism. For decades, young people (McCabe et al., 2020) have examined the role of the media in relation to crimes of violence, serial killers, and crimes such as school shootings. So-called copycat cases are often associated with high levels of media coverage. Most recently, it has been suggested that media coverage may also be related to acts of terrorism. In fact, the investigative role of the media in communication terrorism has become a new field of research in criminology (Fahmy, 2017).

By decree, a journalist's job is to provide stories about the news and of interest to the public. As a result, terrorist acts are often sensationalized in media accounts (Organization for Security and Cooperation in Europe, 2018). Hence, one must look at the influence of media attention on terrorism from two perspectives. First, terrorism is by definition related to actions designed to produce fear in citizens. Research suggests that as media coverage of terrorist acts increases, fear within consuming populations also increases (Fahmy, 2017). Also, terrorist groups welcome the media coverage, as it facilitates their ultimate goal of provoking fear. Second, research suggests that media accounts influence human behavior and that these influences are often related to the degree and quantity of coverage (Slone, 2000). Therefore, continued coverage of a terrorist act may help to build solidarity and sympathy among those who may be related to the terrorist groups (Fahmy, 2017). That is, the **mass media** may serve as a propaganda tool for terrorist groups (Slone, 2000). Thus, one cannot ignore the role of the media in discussions on factors that may facilitate terrorism.

Prevention of Terrorism

It is suggested that most of today's efforts to counter violent extremism and terrorism are often ambiguous in scope and that they lack the metrics needed for terrorism's impact to be evaluated—further compounding concerns about ambiguity, subjectivity, and overreach (Ingram, 2018). To best address violent extremism and terrorism in the United States, specific definitions, policies, and efforts should be implemented. Specifically, in recommendations for preventing violent extremism and terrorism in the United States, the approach most recognized involves the four elements of the rule of law, the person, proportionality, and public outreach, with each of these elements to be included in a process of education and training.

In general, participation in a federal intervention program would need to be voluntary, as the First Amendment (i.e., freedom of religion and freedom of expression) provides constitutional and civil rights protections to all individuals within the United States, although authorities would also have the option of directing individuals toward intervention programs based on risk and threat assessments. In addition, efforts to address violent extremist activities and terrorism must empower communities and individuals to sideline those who are championing terrorism or related offenses via a community safety campaign; further, it must empower them to protect democratic freedoms and responsibilities, to confront the belief that violence is a necessary and legitimate means of exerting political influence, to apply the rule of law, and to utilize strategic communications and public awareness to decrease the incentives associated with supporting extremist or terrorist violence (Ingram, 2018).

In response, the following policy recommendations are among the elements that are most essential for reducing extremist violence and terrorism in the United States: (1) legislative change, (2) intervention strategies, and (3) public awareness campaigns (Ingram, 2018). In addition, parents and young adults must be aware of the recruiting methods that members of extremist groups use to find individuals who identify or sympathize with feelings of victimization or the philosophies of the extremists (McCabe, 2017). In particular, through a variety of posts and discussions, topics related to violent extremism and terrorism occur every day within the online community; hence, governments attempting to reduce violent extremism and terrorism must be aware and counteract these attempts to facilitate destruction. It is in these key ways that terrorism prevention seeks to reduce the recruitment of new members and confront terrorist influencers, as well as to address the psychosocial and strategic factors that contribute to the terrorist threat more broadly.

United Nations Recommendations

In 2016, the United Nations provided their global partners with a framework for designing efforts to prevent violent extremism and terrorism (United Nations, 2016). This plan, an outcome of the UN's commitment and obligation under the principles and values enshrined in the Charter of the United Nations, the **Universal Declaration of Human Rights**, and other international human rights instruments, is detailed to address the drivers of these actions, through seven specific priority areas. In effect, as suggested by the UN, each state should develop a national plan of action that identifies strategies for fighting counterterrorism and violent extremist and makes it a national priority to do so. Specifically, based on the principle of national ownership and in accordance with international law, member states may wish to consider the following elements in establishing such plans: National plans should be developed in a multidisciplinary manner to address dialogue and conflict prevention, strengthening good governance, human rights and the rule of law, engaging communities, empowering youth, gender equality and empowering women, education, skill development and employment facilitation, and strategic communications and internet and social media (United Nations, 2016).

Specifically, in the key area of dialogue and conflict prevention, suggestions include ensuring that—if military action becomes necessary—these responses are in full compliance with international law in order to counter the expansion of violent extremist groups. In addition, efforts should be made to engage opposing parties and regional actors earlier on and to seek consensus so that solutions may be discovered. Also, individuals should be encouraged to leave violent extremist groups; states can help facilitate that by developing programs that provide those individuals with an education and economic opportunities. States should explore opportunities to introduce alternative dispute resolution mechanisms, such as mediation, arbitration, and restorative justice, so that conflicts can be resolved and sustainable peace can be achieved. Lastly, religious leaders should be provided the venue for intra- and interfaith discussions to promote tolerance and understanding (United Nations, 2016).

In 2015, UN Resolution 2199 underlined the obligations of member states to take steps to prevent terrorist groups in Iraq and Syria from benefiting from trade in oil, antiquities, and hostages, and from receiving donations (CT MORSE, 2017).

In support of strengthening good governance, states should review all national legislation, policies, strategies, and practices aimed at preventing and countering violent extremism and terrorism, and ensure that they are grounded in the foundation of respect for human rights and the rule of law. States should also provide access to fair justice for all and should engage community members to protect them from recruitment by extremist groups. Community-oriented policing models should be implemented to solve local issues. Local and family-based mentorship programs should be established that focus on those who are vulnerable to extremist group recruitment. Lastly, medical, psychosocial, and legal service support should be provided throughout communities (United Nations, 2016).

In empowering youth, states must acknowledge the strengths of the world's 1.8 billion young women and men, who constitute invaluable partnerships in attempting to prevent violent extremism (United Nations, 2016). In particular, states should support these individuals by prioritizing meaningful engagement mechanisms at the national, regional, and global levels by integrating young people into the decision-making processes at all levels. Fostering trust between decision makers and youth will make antiextremist efforts more successful.

Also, gender equality and empowering women are critical forces for sustainable peace. As cases have been identified with women serving in critical positions for violent extremist actions, these efforts are also more likely to occur within societies with large measures of gender inequality. Thus, countries should ensure that the protection and empowerment of women is a central consideration in strategies designed to counter terrorism and violent extremism. Further, countries should invest in gender-sensitive research on women's roles in violent extremism. All of this is part of including women and other underrepresented groups in national law enforcement and other security agencies, and building on the capacity of women to counter the actions of violent extremism.

In addition, education, skill development, and employment are all significant in countering violent extremism. States should invest in education at all levels by including preschool education, implementing educational programs to promote citizenship, collaborating with local governments to create social and economic opportunities for the country's citizens, and providing young people with multiple options for careers through entrepreneurship (United Nations, 2016).

States should support strategic communications, the internet, and social media in their efforts to prohibit violent extremism and terrorism. Just as violent extremists have demonstrated the usefulness of media tools in the recruitment of members (McCabe, 2017), so should states work closely with social media companies and the private sector to develop and implement national communications strategies that are tailored to local contexts, are gender-sensitive, and are based on international human rights standards. These will challenge the narratives associated with violent extremism as well as providing more research on the relationship between violent extremists' misuse of the internet and social media and the factors that drive individuals towards violent extremism (United Nations, 2016). Through the use of the media, efforts to promote tolerance, pluralism, and understanding may be implemented to empower and enable victims and other community members to transform their losses into positive forces for preventing violent extremism and terrorism.

Lastly, the United Nations has provided four strategies or pillars in its attempt to address terrorism: (1) measures to address the conditions conducive to terrorism, (2) measures to prevent and combat terrorism, (3) measures to build capacity and prevent terrorism, and (4) measures to ensure respect for human rights and the rule of law (Aolain, 2020). Included within these strategies is the acknowledgment that terrorism may only be addressed through the strengthening of human rights and the rule of law. In addition, as suggested, human rights language must be strengthened to make clear and concrete the obligations of the state to protect and promote the rights of individuals. Particularly urgent in these recommendations is stronger language disavowing the abuse of counterterrorism law and practices.

Summary

Violent extremism, terrorism, and TOC are concerns for all countries across the globe. For countries experiencing war as well as those living in peace, TOC and terrorist groups continue to operate on a daily basis. Estimates suggest that annually hundreds if not thousands of individuals are killed or injured through the actions of violent extremists and terrorists. TOC plays a significant role in the support of the operations of many of these terrorist groups. In fact, recent research has suggested that over time, groups involved in terrorism also become involved in TOC. Similar in structure and often having members in common, terrorist organizations benefit from the criminal activities of TOC and TOC benefits from the instability caused by terrorist organizations. In particular, it is not unusual for the criminal activities of TOC groups to provide the financial resources to support acts of radicalization, violent extremism, and terrorism. These consequences of TOC are often demonstrated through the violent attacks on individuals in the Middle East, Europe, Africa, and the United States. Whereas the trafficking of drugs continues to be the most lucrative form of criminal activity for terrorist groups, other criminal activities have emerged, including weapons trafficking, human trafficking, and the illicit trade of medical supplies (such as those required for public health during the COVID-19 pandemic).

Countries attempting to address the actions of violent extremist, terrorists, and those individuals involved in TOC have offered theoretical explanations and crisis planning as well as proactive efforts in their attempts to address these actions. Cross-culturally, terrorism, violent extremism, and TOC appear in all socioeconomic strata, with efforts to combat these actions appearing at the local, state, and regional levels. Individuals and countries throughout the world must acknowledge and address the relationships among violent extremism, terrorism, and TOC groups in order to provide all persons the safety and security of community.

Questions for Further Thought

1. How are violent extremism, terrorism, and TOC related?
2. How do terrorist groups and TOC groups benefit each other?
3. How have technology and COVID-19 facilitated the "partnerships" between TOC and terrorism?

References

Abadinsky, H. (2017). *Organized crime* (11th ed.). Cengage Group.

Adisa, W. (2021). Transnational organized crime, terrorist financing, and Boko Haram insurgency in Nigeria. *Journal of Terrorism Studies, 3*(1), 1–26.

Akyuz, K., & Armstrong, T. (2011). Understanding the sociostructural correlates of terrorism in Turkey. *International Criminal Justice Review, 21*(2), 134–155.

Angelos, J. (2020, January 6). Will Brexit bring the troubles back to Northern Ireland? *New York Times*. Retrieved May 4, 2020, from https://www.nytimes.com/2019/12/30/magazine/brexit-northern-ireland.html?auth=linked-facebook

Aolain, F. (2020, March 30). Negotiating a global counter-terrorism strategy in a time of COVID-19. Just Security. Retrieved November 20, 2021, from https://www.justsecurity.org/69408/negotiating-a-global-counter-terrorism-strategy-in-a-time-of-COVID-19/

The Atlantic. (2016, September 11). How much really changed about terrorism on 9/11? Retrieved May 4, 2020, from https://www.theatlantic.com/international/archive/2016/09/jenkins-hoffman-crenshaw-september-11-al-qaeda/499334/

Baldwin, F., & DiPerna, T. (2007). The rule of law. An essential component of the financial was against organized crime and terrorism in the Americas. *Journal of Financial Crime, 14*(4), 405–437.

Banks, C., & Baker, J. (2016). *Comparative, international, and global justice*. Sage.

BBC News. (2015a, December 9). *Paris attacks: What happened on the night?* Retrieved May 4, 2020, from https://www.bbc.com/news/world-europe-34818994

BBC News. (2015b, July 6). *7/7 London bombings: What happened on 7 July 2005?* Retrieved May 4, 2020, from https://www.bbc.co.uk/newsround/33401669

Blackmon, S. (2014). Subculture theory: A historical and contemporary assessment of the concept for understanding deviance. *Deviant Behavior, 35*(6), 496–512.

Bouman, W. (2003). Best practices of hate/bias crime investigations. *Law Enforcement Bulletin, 72*(3), 21–25.

Burgess, A., Regehr, C., & Roberts, A. (2013). *Victimology: Theories and applications* (2nd ed). Jones & Bartlett Learning.

Center for Prevention of Radicalization. (2020, May 4). *Categories of radicalization 2020*. Retrieved May 4, 2020, from https://info-radical.org/en/types-of-radicalization/

Clarke, C. (2016). Drugs and thugs: Funding terrorism through narcotics trafficking. *Journal of Strategic Security, 3*(9), 1–15.

CNN Staff. (2013, April 18). *What we know about the Boston bombing and its aftermath*. Retrieved November 3, 2021, from https://www.cnn.com/2013/04/18/us/boston-marathon-things-we-know/index.html

CNN World. (2019, September 8). *Boko Haram fast facts*. Retrieved February 16, 2020, from https://www.cnn.com/2014/06/09/world/boko-haram-fast-facts/index.html

CT MORSE. (2017). *Examining the nexus between organized crime and terrorism and its implications for EU programming*. Retrieved December 3, 2021, from https://icct.nl/app/uploads/2017/04/OC-Terror-Nexus-Final.pdf

Darden, J. (2019, May). *Tackling terrorists' exploitation of youth*. American Enterprise Institute. Retrieved November 3, 2021, from https://www.un.org/sexualviolenceinconflict/wp-content/uploads/2019/05/report/tackling-terrorists-exploitation-of-youth/Tackling-Terrorists-Exploitation-of-Youth.pdf

DeVoe, J. and Murphy, C. (2011). Student Reports of Bullying and Cyber-Bullying: Results from the 2009 School Crime Supplement to the National Crime Victimization Survey (NCES 2011-336). U.S. Department of Education, National Center for Education Statistics. Washington, DC: U.S. Government Printing Office. Retrieved August 20, 2022 at: http://nces.ed.gov/pubs2011/2011336.pdf

Dishman, C. (2005). The leaderless nexus: When crime and terror converge. *Studies in Conflict and Terrorism, 28*(3), 246–258.

Fahey, S., & LaFree, G. (2015). Does country-level social disorganization increase terrorist attacks? *Terrorism and Political Violence, 27*(1), 81–111.

Fahmy, S. (2017). Media, terrorism, and society: Perspectives and trends in the digital age. *Mass Communications and Society, 20*(6), 735–739.

Federal Bureau of Investigation. (2015). *Terrorism*. Retrieved November 3, 2021, from https://www.fbi.gov/stats-services/publications/terrorism-2002-2005

Funk, N., Romuk, P., & Barakal, R. (2013). *Evaluating country violent extremism programming: practice and progress*. Center on Global Counterterrorism Cooperation.

Futures Without Violence. (2017). *What is violent extremism?* Retrieved November 3, 2021, from https://www.futureswithoutviolence.org/wp-content/uploads/FWV_blueprint_3-What-is-VE.pdf

Global Counterterrorism Forum. (2018). *The Hague good practices on the nexus between transnational organized crime and terrorism*. Retrieved November 3, 2021, from https://www.thegctf.org/Portals/1/Documents/Framework%20Documents/2018/GCTF-Good-Practices-on-the-Nexus_ENG.pdf?ver=2018-09-21-122246-363

Global Security. (2020). Lenin and terror. Retrieved February 12, 2020, from https://www.globalsecurity.org/intell/world/russia/lenin-and-terror.htm

Hamm, M. (2009). Prison Islam in the Age of Sacred Terror, *The British Journal of Criminology*, 49(5), 667–685.

Heywood, A. (2003). *Political ideologies: An introduction* (3rd ed.), p. 74. Palgrave Macmillan.

History Channel. (2018, August 21). Six Day War. Retrieved February 16, 2020, from https://www.history.com/topics/middle-east/six-day-war

History Channel. (2019, May 15). Irish Republican Army. Retrieved February 16, 2020, from https://www.history.com/topics/21st-century/irish-republican-army

Human Rights Watch. (2020). Cameroon: Boko Haram Suicide bombers strike displacement site. Retrieved October 30, 2021, from https://www.hrw.org/news/2020/08/25/cameroon-boko-haram-suicide-bombers-strike-displacement-site

Ingram, H. (2018, November). *Terrorism prevention in the United States.* Program on Extremism. The George Washington University. Retrieved February 12, 2020, from https://www.un.org/sites/www.un.org.counterterrorism/files/plan_action.pdf

Institute for Economics and Peace. (2019, November). *Global Terrorism Index, 2019.* Retrieved January 29, 2020, from https://www.visionofhumanity.org/maps/global-terrorism-index/#/

Langat, A., & Kushner, J. (2015, July 29). *Kenya's anti-terror police are inflicting terror of their own.* OPRI News. Retrieved January 20, 2020, from https://www.pri.org/stories/2015-07-29/kenyas-anti-terror-police-are-inflicting-terror-their-own

Law, R. (2016). *Terrorism: A History* (2nd ed.) (pp. 63–67). Policy Press.

Levitt, M. (2013). *Hezbollah: The global footprint of Lebanon's parity of God* (p. 320). Georgetown University Press.

Macklin, G. (2021). The conspiracy to kidnap governor Gretchen Whitmer. *CTC Sentinel, 14*(6). Retrieved November 3, 2021, from https://ctc.usma.edu/the-conspiracy-to-kidnap-governor-gretchen-whitmer/

McCabe, K. (2017). *Protecting your children online.* Rowman & Littlefield.

McCabe, K., & Martin, G. (2005). *School violence, the media, and criminal justice responses* (pp. 78–92). Peter Lang.

McCabe, K., & Murphy, D. (2016). *Child abuse—Today's issues.* Rowman & Littlefield.

McCabe, K., Egan, B., & Eagle, T. (2020). *Acts of Violence in the school setting: National and international responses.* Rowman & Littlefield.

Morgan, M. (2009, August 4). *The impact of 9/11 on politics and war: the day that changed everything.* Palgrave Macmillan.

Mullins, S. (2019). Parallels between crime and terrorism: A social psychological perspective. *Studies in Conflict and Terrorism, 32*(9), 811–830.

National Crime Prevention Council. (2016, October 23). *Tolerance for teens.* Retrieved October 23, 2020, from http://www.ncpc.org/topics/hate-crime/tolerance

National Institute of Justice. (2021). *Radicalization and violent extremism: Lessons learned from Canada, the U.K. and the U.S.* U.S. Department of Justice. Retrieved October 3, 2021, from https://www.ojp.gov/pdffiles1/nij/249947.pdf

Organization for Security and Cooperation in Europe. (2018). *Reporting on violent extremism and terrorism: Guidelines for journalists.* OSCE Mission to BiH. https://www.osce.org/files/f/documents/9/2/442381.pdf

Oriola, T., & Knight, A. (2019). Combating violent extremism in Africa: Terrorism and piracy. *African Security, 12*(3/4), 269–271.

Perry, S., & Hasisi, B. (2015). Rational choice rewards and the jihadist suicide bomber. *Terrorism and Political Violence, 27*(1), 53–80. http://dx.doi.org/10.1080/09546553.2014.962991

Pisoiu, D. (2015). Subculture theory applied to jihadi and right-wing radicalization in Germany. *Terrorism and Political Violence, 27*(1). http://dx.doi.org/1080/09546553.2014.959406

Richie, H., Hasell, J., Mathieu, E., Appel, C., & Roser, M. (2019, November). *Terrorism.* Our World in Data. Retrieved February 12, 2020, from https://ourworldindata.org/terrorism

Sanderson, T. (2004). Transnational terror and organized crime: Blurring the lines. *SAIS Review of International Affairs, 24*(1), 49–61.

Shelley, L. (2017, April 14). *ISIS, Boko Haram, and the growing role of human trafficking in 21st century terrorism.* Daily Beast. Retrieved November 3, 2021, from https://www.thedailybeast.com/isis-boko-haram-and-the-growing-role-of-human-trafficking-in-21st-century-terrorism

Shoichet, C. (2016, March 28). *Brussels attacks: Charges filed, a man freed and suspects on the run.* CNN World. Retrieved November 3, 2021, from https://www.cnn.com/2016/03/28/europe/brussels-investigation/index.html

Slone, M. (2000). Responses to media coverage of terrorism. *Journal of Conflict Resolution, 44*(4), 508–522.

Tosini, D. (2010). Calculated, passionate, pious extremism: Beyond a rational choice theory of suicide terrorism. *Asian Journal of Social Science, 38*(3), 394–415.

United Nations. (2015, December 24). *Plan of action to prevent violent extremism.* UN General Assembly. Retrieved October 3, 2021, from https://undocs.org/pdf?symbol=en/A/70/674

United Nations. (2016, January 15). *Plan of action to prevent violent extremism, presented to General Assembly on January 15, 2016.* Retrieved February 12, 2020, from https://www.un.org/counterterrorism/plan-of-action-to-prevent-violent-extremism

United Nations. (2020, August 6). *Briefing security council on linkages between terrorism, organized crime, executive director notes greater efforts needed in cross-border cooperation* [Press release]. Retrieved December 3, 2021, from https://www.un.org/press/en/2020/sc14273.doc.htm

United Nations. (2021). *75 minutes of conversation: Rethinking radicalization.* Retrieved November 29, 2021, from https://www.un.org/en/academic-impact/75-un75-conversation-rethinking-radicalization

United Nations Interregional Crime and Justice Research Institute. (2020, November). *Stop the virus of disinformation: The risk of malicious use of social media during COVID-19 and the technology options to fight it.* Retrieved November 30, 2021, from http://www.unicri.it/sites/default/files/2020-11/SM%20misuse.pdf

United Nations Office on Drugs and Crime. (2018). *The League of Nations and terrorism.* Retrieved November 3, 2021, from https://www.unodc.org/e4j/en/terrorism/module-1/key-issues/league-of-nations-and-terrorism.html

United Nations Office on Drugs and Crime. (2020a). Module 1: Introduction to international terrorism. *E4J University Module Series: Counter-terrorism.*

Retrieved February 12, 2020, from https://www.unodc.org/documents/e4j/18-04932_CT_Mod_01_ebook_FINALpdf.pdf

United Nations Office on Drugs and Crime. (2020b). *Radicalization and violent extremism*. Retrieved January 20, 2020, from https://www.unodc.org/e4j/en/terrorism/module-2/key-issues/radicalization-violent-extremism.html

U.S. Department of Justice. (2013, February 5). *Working to counter online radicalization to violence in the United States*. Retrieved January 22, 2020, from https://www.justice.gov/archives/opa/blog/working-counter-online-radicalization-violence-united-states

U.S. Department of State. (2005). Chechen female suicide bombers: The new face of terrorism in Moscow. Retrieved November 3, 2021, from https://www.hsdl.org/?view&did=14112

U.S. Department of State. (2018, September 19). Country reports on terrorism 2017—Foreign Terrorist Organizations: Real IRA. Retrieved November 3, 2021, from https://www.refworld.org/docid/5bcf1f2d13.html https://www.visionofhumanity.org/maps/global-terrorism-index/#/

Wilkinson, P. (2001). *Terrorism vs. democracy: The liberal state response*. Routledge.

Wilson, M. (2018, January 25). *Nigeria's Boko Haram attacks in numbers—As lethal as ever*. BBC News. Retrieved January 20, 2020, from https://www.bbc.com/news/world-africa-42735414

Zalman, A. (2020, January 7). *History of terrorism* [Search term]. ThoughtCo. Retrieved February 12, 2020, from https://www.thoughtco.com/search?q=history+of+terrorism

PART III

Global Responses

CHAPTER 11

Law Enforcement and Transnational Organized Crime

Key Terms

Centralized policing
Constable
Corruption Perceptions Index
Decentralized policing
Democratic policing
Deputy
Diversity
Illicit financial flows
Integrated policing
Law enforcement
Law enforcement office
Night watch
Night watchmen
Police
Police corruption
RICO Act (Racketeer Influenced and Corrupt Organizations Act)
Sheriff
Transnational crimes
Underground economy

CHAPTER OBJECTIVES

Chapter 11 will enable readers to understand the following:

- the problems posed by transnational organized crime (TOC) for police across the globe
- the models of policing as applied to police efforts
- the vulnerabilities to policing as created by underground economies
- the roles of diversity and corruption as applied to policing efforts and TOC
- the role of police in addressing terrorism
- the challenges to police in a hyperglobalized world
- the better practices or efforts by police to address TOC

CRIMINAL JUSTICE SYSTEMS across the globe are all characterized by three components (i.e., police, courts, and corrections) of the system, and all of these components are designed to work together to ensure the goal of justice for all (Schmalleger, 2004). In modern criminal justice systems, the process begins with the reporting of a crime, which is under the purview of **law enforcement**. That is, law enforcement provides the entry into the criminal justice system for victims, perpetrators, and witnesses. For most researchers in criminal justice, the term ***police*** refers to the sworn first responders employed by a municipal police agency and the term ***deputy*** refers to county-level law enforcement officers. For this chapter, the terms *police*, *deputy*, and ***law enforcement officer*** are utilized interchangeably to describe first responders and criminal investigators sworn to uphold the laws of their jurisdictions. This critical position of a law enforcement officer is most associated with the law and with the safety of citizens, as the police officer is known as the keeper of the peace. The office is the role model for keeping children safe and is the rescuer in a time of crisis. In fact, the law enforcement officer's position is the position most often coveted by those employed within the criminal justice system. It is also the position most open to criticism and public judgment, as it is the position most visible to those in the community and those in TOC groups. In attempting to address TOC, law enforcement uses police relationships both domestically and abroad to combat the influences of organized crime activities. Today, TOC is no longer a matter of concern for specialists in crime-fighting organizations; instead, TOC is an essential strategic activity for corrupt politicians and groups wishing to commit crimes against the state (International Peace Institute, 2009). Although most individuals understand and appreciate the gravity of TOC in terms of economics, law enforcement recognizes TOC for its flexible structure and for the sophisticated criminal actions TOC takes that occur undetected and without punishment (Allum & Sands, 2004). In other words, law enforcement has realized the strategic threats posed by TOC.

Law enforcement—The agencies and employees responsible for ensuring public safety, managing social order, and enforcing laws (Bureau of Justice Statistics, 2021).

In every country around the world, law enforcement officials are on the front line in efforts to combat TOC. Law enforcement officers, often underpaid and overworked, with little time for their families, must identify and attempt to combat the criminal actions of TOC groups. This chapter focuses on policing around the world as related to the reality of TOC. It includes a discussion on the greatest concerns for law enforcement today around aspects of TOC and provides a history of policing efforts in various countries. Also in this chapter is a brief discussion on the three structural models of policing (centralized, decentralized, integrated); the vulnerabilities to policing as created by underground economies, diversity, and corruption; and the effects of hyperglobalization and the digital age as police attempt to control the criminal actions of TOC.

The Reach of TOC

In the past, police efforts to control the activities of TOC often focused on the criminal actions of trafficking, in an effort to include products such as drugs, people, and wildlife. Unfortunately, today the domain of local law enforcement is not limited simply to low-level criminal actions and petty crimes (Clarke, 2016). For the most part, law enforcement officers have been trained to identify human victims and areas of high drug trafficking, and to engage in search and seizure operations for discovering concealed illicit products. In recent years, TOC activities have expanded to include criminal actions that threaten not only certain vulnerable populations but also banking systems, securities markets, border security, and cybercommunities, putting even more pressure on police attempts to control TOC. The U.S. Department of Justice and its international partners have identified eight strategic areas of vulnerability threatened by today's TOC groups, and law enforcement officers are considered to be responsible for guarding those areas (U.S. Department of Justice, 2008).

TOC has penetrated the energy sector and other strategic sectors of the economy, and they now control significant positions in the global energy and strategic materials markets. Therefore, TOC is an important element in the vulnerabilities that are vital to national security interests. Specifically, the surveillance and arrests of TOC members with ties to extremists and terrorist groups require a significant amount of police strength and resources, and as a result, most police forces are understaffed and underfunded. As TOC provides logistical and other support to terrorists, to foreign intelligence services, and to many governments, they are helping to facilitate an already significant aspect of violence. Research suggests that involvement

STRATEGIC THREATS BY TOC

- International organized criminals have penetrated the energy and other strategic sectors of the economy.
- International organized criminals provide logistical and other support to terrorists, foreign intelligence services, and governments.
- International organized criminals smuggle/traffic people and contraband goods into the United States.
- International organized criminals exploit U.S. and international financial systems to move illicit funds.
- International organized criminals use cyberspace to target U.S. victims and infrastructure.
- International organized criminals are manipulating securities exchanges and perpetrating sophisticated frauds.
- International organized criminals corrupt and seek to corrupt public officials in the United States and abroad.
- International organized criminals use violence and the threat of violence as a basis for power.

(U.S. Department of Justice, 2008)

in the narcotics trade also brings together insurgent groups and drug cartels (Dishman, 2005). Law enforcement must not only target the violent actions of those groups but also target the process that produces the violent outcomes. For example, in Europe, preventing attacks such as the November 2015 attack in Paris or the March 2015 attack in Brussels would have required the cooperative efforts of local police as well as national and European Union officials (Clarke, 2016).

In November of 2015, Europe experienced its worst terrorist attack in 11 years when over 130 people were killed in Paris. Those killed included an architect, an American college student, and an Algerian violinist (*New York Times*, 2015).

In March of 2016, two separate bombing by a terrorist group at a Brussels airport and a metro station killed 32 people and injured many more (BBC News, 2016).

At the same time, TOC groups smuggle and/or traffick people and contraband goods into countries such as the United States, compromising border security. To combat instances such as these, police across the globe must remain vigilant in their enforcement of regulations that address the illegal transport of persons or items across borders. TOC also exploits financial systems to move illicit funds, and police must be aware of these actions. International organized crime groups transfer billions of dollars of illicit funds annually through financial systems, resulting in the corruption of financial and nonfinancial intermediaries globally. TOC utilizes cyberspace to target victims and infrastructure, which results not only in crimes against individuals but also in the loss of millions of dollars for consumers (U.S. Department of Justice, 2008). To combat these threats, law enforcement must understand how technology, cybercommunities, and the darknet can be used for illegal purchases. TOC groups manipulate securities exchanges and perpetrate sophisticated fraud, with highly organized groups of overseas criminals victimizing consumers across the globe. This is yet another reason why police must cooperate and exchange information with similarly positioned individuals around the world. In addition, TOC groups seek to corrupt public officials both nationally and internationally, using these individuals to facilitate illegal TOC operations and to increase TOC's sphere of influence (U.S. Department of Justice, 2008). Law enforcement personnel, often significantly underpaid for their responsibilities and the hours they work, are themselves especially vulnerable to corruption by TOC groups. Finally, TOC groups use violence and the threat of violence as a basis for power, which results in the injury or death of hundreds of people whom police, by some duty, are responsible for protecting.

Not only do groups involved in TOC put more pressure on police to successfully combat crime, but their planned, organized criminal activities require law enforcement officers to put forth similarly planned and organized efforts. The reach of TOC is beyond local jurisdictions and across international borders and levels of security and governments, and this reach places police at local and isolated areas of jurisdiction at a particular disadvantage.

COVID-19 has also provided more challenges for police, not only in expanding their responsibilities to now include the monitoring of public health measures but also in expediting the process of digitalization within regions; reports indicate an increase of 70% in social media use by TOC groups (United Nations Office on Crime and Justice Research Institute, 2021). Finally, the reach of TOC within cybercommunities and banking systems is especially frustrating to law enforcement, who often are not trained to investigate crimes involving technology or financial systems.

History of Policing

In many ways the history of policing is related to the history of organized crime, as policing and organized crime evolved from individual efforts to access the organizational structures that facilitate and/or address criminal behaviors. In addition, as discussed in previous chapters, the organization and structure of policing today is, in many ways, similar to the organization and structure of TOC groups. The word *police* comes from the ancient Greek word *polis*, meaning "city" (Badge & Wallet, 2021). This term was adopted because these individuals were essentially the caretakers of the city. When the first policing organizations began, around 3000 BCE in Egypt, pharaohs appointed officials to oversee and enforce justice and security in the pharoahs' jurisdictions. In ancient Greece, the role of police was unknown until the fifth century BCE, when police authorities began to form; at that time, publicly owned slaves were used as personnel to formalize police forces (Tsolakidou, 2013). After the fifth century BCE, as Greece developed economically, police authorities were established with the missions of surveillance and accident prevention, similar to the missions of police today.

In particular, one of the first official duties identified for a police officer was to monitor foreigners, as criminal actions were attributed primarily to immigrants and were not often subjected to review by governments or human rights advocates (Tsolakidou, 2013). That same duty rests with law enforcement and security agents today in terms of documentation required for entry into different countries.

In history, while Greeks utilized slaves for their police officers, ancient Romans continued the practice of recruiting lower-class citizens (sometimes with criminal pasts) to be part of the police force. In many cases, early police officers may have shared common traits with early criminals. In fact, the United States, during its infancy, utilized its "undesirable" individuals as police officers. Specifically, many Irish immigrants, unable to obtain other jobs (i.e., NINA, or No Irish Need Apply), were employed in policing, and so the majority of police officers in the early eastern towns of America were Irish. Also, in the early days of the American West it was also not unusual for lawmen to have a history of gunfighting, theft, and/or robbery before being offered a position as a law enforcement officer; for example, Wyatt Earp was a horse thief before becoming a U.S. marshal.

After the collapse of the Roman Empire in the fifth century, the Byzantine Empire returned to the original model of law enforcement, where most crimes were left to be dealt with by individual victims, who could pay police officers if they wanted their assistance (Badge & Wallet, 2021). In England, however, a new structure of policing was being formed, and this structure laid the framework for the United States and other British territories. In this English model, groups of men were responsible for enforcing good conduct among themselves while also protecting the community. These groups were headed by a "shire-reeve," with the role of the shire-reeve eventually developing into what we know in the United States today as a **sheriff**, a position seen often in county police agencies across America. In the United States today, the position of sheriff remains one of the positions of law enforcement in government. By the late 13th century in England, the role of **constable** was created, with constables being responsible for overseeing the **night watch** and for providing security.

Night watchmen—A group of men, established by England's Ordinance of 1233, with the responsibility of patrol and crime prevention at night on the dark streets of London.

This foundation of the **night watchmen** carried over from England to the colonies of America as law and order quickly became a concern in the rapidly developing towns. In 1631, Boston became the first U.S. city to establish a night watch; New York City followed in 1647 (Badge & Wallet, 2021) and other policing systems in the United States emerged soon after. In the late 18th and 19th centuries, regulators or vigilantes became commonplace in many U.S. cities, with their perceived role of enforcing order in areas where there was none—a practice that, although illegal, sometimes continues today in the United States, as is referenced in the 2018 case here.

In January of 2018, in Louisiana (USA), two individuals were convicted of the murder of a convicted sex offender whom they killed when he was released early from his prison sentence. One of those convicted in the 2018 crime reported to be a victim of childhood sexual abuse by the convicted sex offender (WBRZ Staff, 2018).

Later, in the early 1930s, the Metropolitan Police Department was established in London and this organization established the framework for modern policing across the globe. Around the same time, the Greek Gendarmerie, the first organized police force in Greece, was formed (Douvlis & South, 2016). Today in France, the French Gendarmerie is a military agency within the Ministry of Defense with a position of authority over the police force (Hunter, 1990). As an example of its current efforts, in 2018 the French Gendarmerie arrested over 30 TOC members believed to be involved in organized burglaries across Europe. Also in the 1930s, although China's police force was documented to exist in 2000 BCE during the first dynasty of China, the government of China began to have police forces similar to those used in China today (Ma, 2000). In addition, in the early 19th century, police forces were forming in other parts of the world, including Brazil's Royal Police Guard and Italy's Carabinieri.

During the middle of the 19th century in the United States, laws were passed in order to regulate social behavior. Also at that time, penitentiaries, asylums, and official police forces were established, with New York City establishing the first official police department in 1844. Soon after, police departments were established in many of the major cities in the United States, and all were modeled after the London Metropolitan Police Department. Today, for a comparison between police and TOC, just as the term *intergenerational* applies to TOC, so it also applies to policing: children of TOC members often become TOC members and children of police officers often become police officers.

Law enforcement agencies across the globe continue to make progress in advancements in technology, science, research, equipment, and training (Badget & Wallet, 2021). With computer-based technology, departments are becoming more centralized and information is more easily shared between them. As expected (and displayed below), countries that have large police forces for the safety and security of their large populations also identify large numbers of members of TOC groups. This helps to ensure better data collections, more arrests of suspects, more crime prevention capabilities, and safer communities. In other words, today's law enforcement now recognizes that a purely targeted approach to controlling crime may no longer be the answer to addressing TOC and that they must also address the process of recruitment into TOC groups and the planning and process of organized criminal activities.

The Structure of Law Enforcement

Good governance, policing efforts, and crime are all related. Research suggests that countries with poor governance and corrupt police forces will experience high crime rates as well as reductions in economic

POLICE FORCES SIZES AND TOC MEMBERS BY COUNTRY

Country	Number of Police Officers	TOC Members (Group)
India	1.58 million	5,000 (D Company)
USA	794,300	2,500 (Hell's Angels)
Russia	782,001	300,000 (Bratva)
Mexico	544,000	60,000 (Sinaloa Cartel)

Sources: Police forces sizes: Deakin (2014); TOC group sizes: Levin (2019)

growth (Habibullah et al., 2016). In association with the concept of good governance is the concept of effective policing. The structure of a law enforcement organization within a country, an aspect of governmental authority, is related to the safety of its citizens and the security of a country (Blackburn & Forgues-Puccio, 2009). Reports by international groups suggest that a country is afflicted with TOC because its immunity is low and because the pathogens themselves are mostly foreign in origin (United Nations Office on Drugs and Crime, 2009).

Police must understand that the mechanism that sustains criminal networks, member recruiting, and resource acquisition will also affect public plans to address TOC (Djordjevic & Dobovsek, 2020). The structure of police organizations within a country is associated with the country's system of law. One way for police to address TOC is to address the problems fueling these criminal acts within source countries (United Nations Office on Drugs and Crime, 2009). For countries with common law systems, police organizations are usually decentralized, with policing authorities and services recognized at the local level. For countries with civil systems of law, police organizations are generally centralized, with national police forces existing under the control of central governments. As societies develop, economies grow, and global exchanges become more common, a third integrated organizational structure has emerged. Thus, policing structures across the globe are classified through one of three policing models: (1) centralized, (2) decentralized, and (3) integrated. This section provides a general discussion on each model as well as some information on the advantages and disadvantages of each model as related to TOC.

Centralized

A police force is identified as ***centralized*** if there is a national police force under the control of the national government (Banks & Baker, 2016). In cases of international security today, to address the effects of TOC police must become more effective in building capacity within countries (Clarke, 2016). Historically, centralized police forces are the most common model of policing (Bayley, 1985). In these organizations, the national government is accountable for the success or failure of the actions of law enforcement officers. The centralized police structure is common in Europe and Russia, with some variation among the centralized police organizations of Western European countries. In particular, most of the police forces are highly centralized, with a small number of national police forces or some regional centralization. Other commonalities among these centralized structures of police include strong emphasis on domestic security and unarmed police forces for the enforcement of local laws.

Centralized policing—A model of policing in which the authority of the police rests generally within one centralized command.

Although some suggest that centralized police systems operate counter to democratic ideals, with fears of "police states" in practice, the majority of the countries utilizing a centralized police structure do not express concerns for civil liberties, which are often discussed in common law systems (Hunter, 1990). Nations that employ the centralized model of policing include countries such as Denmark, France, Israel, Italy, Morocco, South Korea, Sweden, and Thailand (Levin, 2019). Of these, Italy is known for its large presence of TOC (Levin, 2019).

Decentralized

A police force is classified as ***decentralized*** if the responsibilities of police service are embedded in the mission of local governments. In the decentralized model, policing responsibilities are divided by numerous criteria to include land boundaries, types of crimes (e.g., theft or animal control), and level of crime sophistication (i.e., physical or cyber). In the United States, police forces include local entities, state-level policing, and federal policing organizations such as the FBI, DEA, Marshals Service, and ATF.

U.S. Federal Law Enforcement Agencies: Federal Bureau of Investigation (FBI), Drug Enforcement Agency (DEA), Marshals Service, and Bureau of Alcohol, Tobacco, Firearms and Explosives (ATF).

Decentralized policing—A model of policing in which the authority of the police rests within multiple command levels.

In decentralized police forces, a variety of political, cultural, and economic factors influence the organizational structures and the management of these structures (Hunter, 1990). Small police agencies may focus on towns, while larger police agencies may focus on supporting the efforts of those smaller departments as well as larger towns and communities that do not have dedicated police forces. Police agencies with specialized skills such as search and rescue or technical knowledge may also provide support for those same areas. Hence, all three police forces may serve the same area within a decentralized police structure as viewed appropriate by the communities they serve and the criminal action in question. Countries identified as operating with a decentralized police structure include Belgium, Canada, Egypt, Kenya, Netherlands, Switzerland, and the United States.

In examining the decentralized system within the United States, researchers acknowledge that many of the complexities of policing in the United States are confusing to those in countries that do not have the land boundaries of the United States (i.e., 50 states, various state laws, and many levels of policing). In the United States, there are approximately 18,000 federal, state, and local law enforcement agencies. As demonstrated, each of these agencies operates based upon the laws of their particular venue or the laws afforded them by Congress—for example, federal law enforcement officers work to enforce the **RICO Act**.

RICO Act (Racketeer Influenced and Corrupt Organizations Act)—A 1970 U.S. federal law that provides for extended criminal penalties and a civil cause of action for acts performed as part of an ongoing criminal organization. Crimes committed under the RICO Act include gambling, murder, kidnapping, extortion, and bribery, which are all crimes commonly committed by TOC members.

The advantage for the decentralized policing forces of the United States is demonstrated in focused local areas police efforts. The disadvantages for the decentralized police organizations in the United States include a lack of communication, a lack of uniform standards, and fragmented services (Hunter, 1990), as well as the potential for territorial disputes. One example of this lack of communication among police and emergency response agencies occurred in 1999 with the Columbine school shooting: Multiple agencies responded to the incident, but their communications systems were not compatible with each other so in some cases actions were delayed until assurances of tactical efforts and officer safety could be offered (McCabe & Martin, 2005). Unfortunately, in many decentralized policing systems, the sharing of information related to TOC and other criminal activities is limited. TOC groups are aware of this limitation and may purposely organize themselves to target their efforts within varying police jurisdictions in order to avoid detection.

Integrated

An ***integrated*** model of policing exists in countries when the administration of policing is shared by local and national agencies (Banks & Baker, 2016). In developing nations, oftentimes integrated policing systems will emerge when countries evolve from their colonial period of policing structure (often a common law system from British influences) to a more formalized rules-based (often civil law) system. For clarity, *integrated systems of policing* are also referred to as moderately decentralized systems, combined systems, or comprised systems (Hunter, 1990). Typically, integrated police organizations have fewer police forces than decentralized structures, and more police forces that centralized structures. Countries with integrated policing systems include Australia, Japan, and the United Kingdom.

Integrated policing—A model of policing in which the authority of the police is often divided between one centralized command and multiple lower levels of command.

As indicated, countries implement policing systems based upon the needs of their population and their system of law. Specifically, these systems of law provide the foundation for the operations of police. In addition to the structure and mission of law enforcement agencies, other factors must be considered in understanding the threat posed by TOC and the police responses to those threats. One of those factors is the presence of TOC criminals who do not need to reside in the United States (U.S. Department of Justice, 2008). Also, the most powerful international organized crime groups benefit from the symbiotic relationship that their leaders have developed with corrupt public officials and business tycoons within other countries. In addition, TOC group members in the highest ranks are far removed from the streets and often have billions of dollars at their disposal, with members often highly educated and occupying some of the most powerful occupational positions, such as lawyer, banker, and lobbyist (U.S. Department of Justice, 2008). Notably, TOC groups often portray themselves as legitimate businesspeople or benefactors for local charities. Finally, there are still very large gaps in police intelligence on TOC, which fuels the threats by TOC as they exist and emerge. Hence, if law enforcement is expected to address TOC, then cooperation, training, and professionalization are essential, as well as a level of democratic policing.

For clarity, ***democratic policing*** is a phrase that has its origins in the developing countries of the world (Muntingh et al., 2021). Democratic policing is regarded as a consolidation of principles that should be apparent within all systems of policing. Its fundamental principles of policing are often cited within the international community in conversations on police reform and best practices (Muntingh et al., 2021). Some researchers suggest that democratic policing helps to eliminate police torture, minimizes damage to civility, and provides for better quality of life, including reductions in crime. The opposite of democratic policing is *regime policing*, which is found in many military-based countries and in many countries with a large presence of TOC (e.g., Russia).

Democratic policing has three minimum requirements: democratic accountability of and for the police; adherence to rule of law by the police; and police behaviors that are fair and in service to the public. These principles are at risk when TOC members succeed in corrupting police forces. The ultimate result of democratic policing is a legitimate police service, which results in public confidence in police; however, public confidence in police is usually low in countries with high levels of TOC. As displayed below, in democratic policing there are nine dimensions or elements that are essential for the highest-quality policing. However, TOC compromises those elements.

Unfortunately, TOC directly affects each of the dimensions through fueling police turnover or through corruption. Specifically, in countries with a large presence of TOC, police often feel powerless to provide security and justice for the citizens, and so they often become disengaged from the profession and practice a hands-off approach to TOC activities. As a result of turnover, both the knowledge of police and their capacity to develop effectiveness and efficiency are compromised because the focus is on training new officers. In addition, in areas with a large presence of TOC, police often fail to observe the rights of non-TOC citizens as well to failing to show empathy toward citizens. Lastly, with the corruption of police by TOC, public trust in police is lost along with their abilities to protect and serve. Hence, through democratic policing, police forces may be better able to address (1) global or transnational crimes, (2) police and/or government corruption and accountability, and (3) terrorism that is funded by TOC groups.

NINE DIMENSIONS FOR DEMOCRATIC POLICING

1. Knowledge: Police officers are highly skilled in their work and can apply skills to their post level. In addition, policing is based on knowledge of what works.
2. Capacity development to fulfill a particular job function is thus central to this dimension. Thus, managers use data to evaluate policing, identify success and challenges, and learn lessons.
3. Effectiveness and efficiency: Effective policing in a democratic society refers to the successful maintenance of an environment of order, security, and trust—one in which the public's ability to go about their daily routines without fear can be attributed to the quality of police services they receive. Police effectiveness is ultimately about what and how much the police have accomplished in the eyes of the public, and efficiency refers to the cost-effective utilization of resources.
4. Ethics and accountability: Police conduct is ethical and lawful, and transgressors are held accountable. Internal accountability mechanisms (e.g., disciplinary processes) are effective and are complemented by strong external checks and balances. Further, police hold each other accountable for disciplinary misconduct and criminal activity (including corruption), with the ultimate aim being to modify unlawful behavior and institutional practices that fuel such behavior. Lastly, ethical and accountable policing generates trust from the policed, with different spheres of government collaborating in the spirit of cooperative governance.
5. Rights-based: Policing is based on adherence to and the protection of human rights, and on the values of transparency, fairness, equality, and justice. Thus, the rights of all people, including suspects, are enshrined in the Constitution and all people are treated fairly.
6. Police as citizens: The rights of police officers are protected by the Constitution, in their interactions with colleagues and in their interactions with the public. In addition, police are treated fairly and objectivity. Thus, it is the task of police (with other stakeholders) to protect democratic political life.
7. Responsivity: Police are responsive to the needs of the public and victims of crime, and to this end they exhibit community-centered policing practices.
8. Empathy: Police demonstrate empathy with people and with victims of crime.
9. Trust: The public trusts the police and particular attention is paid to how accessible and approachable the police is perceived to be with particular reference to the diversity in a population.

(*Muntingh et al., 2021*)

Globalization Issues for Today's Law Enforcement

Law enforcement has changed significantly over the years, and in today's world of hyperglobalization and the increasing criminal activities of TOC, it is expected that the roles and responsibilities of policing will change even more. In particular, in addition to understanding the increasing threat of a global society, police officers are often challenged in addressing extensive and complex investigations within cyber-communities or in cases involving data-heavy environments that fall outside of their traditional areas of expertise (United Nations Interregional Crime and Justice Research Institute, 2021). The global perspective of TOC cannot be denied, as profits from crime are enormous, rule of law is often in jeopardy, and individuals are victimized. For law enforcement, TOC has become a persistent challenge. Included within those challenges are illicit financial flows, underground economies, transnational crimes, diversity, and corruption.

Illicit Financial Flows

Illicit financial flows—Money that is earned, transferred, or used illegally, often by TOC groups.

The phrase ***illicit financial flows*** is a relatively new concept as related to the criminal activities of TOC (World Bank, 2015). However, it has emerged as one more of the criminal activities for law enforcement concern to be concerned about, as it relates to members of TOC being able to move funds and assets across national borders within the scope of national or international laws (Goredema, 2011). Although specific activities are not always recognized by legal systems, the common notion over the last decade has been that *illicit financial flows* can be defined as money that is illegally earned, transferred, or used (United Nations Economic Commission for Africa, 2015). Although research studies show a lack of consensus on what constitutes illicit financial flows, most researchers agree that the term should cover money earned from criminal (illegal) activity or money that was legally earned but became illegal because of its use in financing actions such as terrorism (Goredema, 2011). There are several sources of money earned from illicit flows, including corruption, crime (including TOC), and illegal commercial practices such as manipulation of custom duties, mispricing, and tax evasion (Global Financial Integrity, 2014).

Ultimately, due to the differences in national legal frameworks, a concept of what constitutes illicit financial flows will always depend on the legislation of the particular state (Tropina, 2017). Specifically, any international policing efforts implemented to tackle illicit financial flows may be limited by differences in national legislation and by the fact that in some countries there may be laws on the books but there is no capacity or willingness to enforce them. Members of TOC are aware of these limitations, and they often exploit these legal loopholes.

Unfortunately for law enforcement officials, who often are not trained to use technology to fight criminal activities, information and communications technologies have created new ways of earning and laundering money illegally; TOC groups simply add these new ways to their traditional money-laundering activities. In addition, any illegal activity can be facilitated with the possibility of transferring funds anonymously or generating large amounts of money via aggregation of small sums (Tropina, 2017). Hence, despite officers' lack of training for these types of investigations, the link between digital technologies and illicit financial flows has been widely recognized as an issue for today's law enforcement and for policing tomorrow.

Underground Economies

An **underground economy** involves the exchange of goods and services that are hidden from official view (i.e., in the United States the Internal Revenue Service provides just one official avenue for monitoring open economies). In the United States, it is estimated that the underground economy produces approximately 12% of U.S. gross domestic product (GDP), or about $2.5 trillion, annually (Kenton, 2020).

> In the United States, approximately $2.5 trillion in profits flows through underground economies each year (Kenton, 2020).

The rise of an underground economy supported by TOC groups is another concern for law enforcement across the globe. In the early days of cybercrime, individuals or groups of loosely connected hackers who committed these attacks out of boredom or to demonstrate their technical skills (SecureWorks, 2014) dominated the crime scene. This is not the case today, nor is it expected to be the case tomorrow. Recently, the nations with the three largest shadow economies were Zimbabwe (60%), Bolivia (62%), and Georgia (65%) (Kenton, 2020).

The development and growth of the digital economy has dramatically changed both the criminal landscape and the motivations for offenders (Tropina, 2017). Now TOC members, skilled in the use of technology for criminal activities, may utilize these technologies to extort money from victims within cybercommunities. The primary targets of the cybercriminals are the wealthier developed countries, which depend heavily on information technologies (Europol, 2015).

As demonstrated in the 2021 account provided below, specific criminal activities have been developed and are being constantly improved in order to obtain data information or to facilitate access to otherwise secure servers. For example, police data on the undercover operations of the U.S. Drug Enforcement Administration, or DEA, may be of real interest to those members of TOC attempting to identify and eliminate police agents hidden within their organization. Access to credit card information may be of interest to TOC groups attempting to obtain funds and material goods through fraud. Access to computer servers controlling the electricity of a city may be of interest to TOC members wishing to ransom funds from governmental authorities that are trying to maintain services to their communities.

> In April of 2021, the breach of Colonial Pipeline demonstrated the vulnerabilities of large corporations to the organized criminal actions of TOC groups. A TOC group disrupted gas supplies all along the East Coast of the United States. The result was the identification of the potential TOC group (The DarkSide), which Colonial Pipeline paid $4.4 million dollars in Bitcoin to avoid further disruption (Touro College Illinois, 2021).

In addition to being a platform for the new type of criminal activity analyzed above, cyberspace and digital technologies serve as a new medium for facilitating the criminal business of traditional Mafia-style organized crime groups (Williams, 2002).The underground economy is structuring its operations similarly to business models from legitimate economy sectors (Tropina, 2017). As technological developments have affected business structures, making them more decentralized and collaborative with regard to external partners, their vulnerability has been exposed to those wishing to do harm for profit. This means that in the same way digital technologies are facilitating illicit financial flows, they are also creating illicit economies—with law enforcement often unable to prohibit these criminal actions.

Transnational Crimes

Many aspects of living today have become part of a global village, and crime is no exception. In particular, the same political and economic changes and technological advances that support easy international travel, communication, and business transactions also facilitate a criminal's ability to commit crimes that transcend borders (Finckenauer, 2000) or facilitate what is termed ***transnational crimes***.

Crimes by TOC are gaining much attention within the global arena, not only for their criminal actions and human rights violations, but also for the assumed inability of law enforcement and other criminal justice officials to control these types of criminal actions. As demonstrated in the 2021 account here, many transnational crimes involve organized crime or TOC groups. On the list of crimes more commonly associated with TOC are drug trafficking, weapons trafficking, human trafficking, and wildlife trafficking, as well as cybercrimes, the counterfeiting of goods, and money laundering. For policing agencies, transnational crimes add even more work to their already exhausting days. For those wishing to profit from transnational crimes, estimates suggest that TOC is earning up to $2.2 trillion dollars per year (Clough, 2017).

In July of 2021, 286 people were arrested in a global human-trafficking operation. Interpol and law enforcement officials from 47 countries were involved. In this operation, the result was the rescue of over 430 human-trafficking victims from 74 different countries (Interpol, 2021b).

In a market-based society, the trafficking of drugs and other products within illicit markets generally is categorized as open in the case of street-corner purse snatching or as closed when sellers sell only to individuals who are known to them. In these cases, the more open the market, the higher the risk to the perpetrators. Through technology such as the mobile applications in use today, sellers are now able to be more open regarding their products but closed regarding their distribution (Berry, 2018), and police are limited in their ability to detect such crimes. In these cases, sellers are now able to arrange more closed sales of their products and avoid detection by police (Wainwright, 2016).

Human trafficking also exists within a market-based economy; however, where drugs are products to be used once and replaced, humans may be exploited repeatedly. TOC understands that this investment in a human will provide revenue beyond the first sale. In the cases of exploitation by TOC, direct and indirect victimization occurs for profit (McCabe, 2017), and police are once again limited in their skills to detect and later investigate the crimes. Individuals and members of TOC utilize the internet and technology for the production and distribution of pornography as well as to arrange for the sale of humans as victims of sex trafficking, with the police unable to react (McCabe & Johnson, 2014).

Lastly, technology is used to facilitate the illicit flow of financial gains—and most often without police detection. Through online and mobile banking, electronic payments made by unregulated intermediaries, digital currencies, online gambling, and e-commerce or online manipulation of the supply of goods, profits for criminal actions are increased and the risk for apprehension by law enforcement is rare (Tropina, 2017).

The challenges to law enforcement are numerous when applied to transnational crimes. Specifically, some crimes arise out of particular cultural or societal conditions and experiences that differ from one country to another (Finckenauer, 2000). For example, behaviors like as child marriage that are acceptable in one country may be illegal in another. For policing, the challenges from TOC stem from the orientations of laws and law enforcement, as every country has its own laws and law enforcement system to deal with crime; however, when crimes cross borders the laws of one country may not apply. Since transnational crimes are committed within the secrecy of a criminal organization, they are often undetected, or if they are detected they are ignored by the police after financial compensation by the TOC group; in this way, the structure of the international system is also associated with TOC. Specifically, if one country views a behavior as legal but another government has criminalized it, then crime organizations take advantage of the discrepancies between competing legal jurisdictions (Block & Chambliss, 1981). In summary, research suggests that the structural factors assumed to create opportunities for transnational crime are (1) the differences in countries' ability to implement border controls, (2) the disparity in the distribution of resources, (3) the discrepancies in countries' ability to prevent other types of crimes, and (4) the disintegration of legal systems within an area (United Nations Office on Drugs and Crime, 2019).

Structural factors, which create opportunities for transnational crime, include differences in countries as related to border controls, disparities in police resources, discrepancies in countries to prevent other types of crimes, and the disintegration of legal systems or rule of law within countries (United Nations Office on Drugs and Crime, 2019).

Diversity

The world's 7.8 billion people are incredibly diverse and with this **diversity** comes an array of languages, customs, religions, races and ethnicities, values, traditions, and more (World Population Review, 2021). Racism in policing is often thought of as an American problem;

however, some researchers suggest that many countries have problems with heterogeneity, as suggested by actions such as the European Commission's co-opting of the framing of xenophobic parties across Europe, which reported that Europe needs to be protected from migrants in order to protect the European way of life (Nwabuzo & Siklossy, 2020). Hence, differences among populations, which in itself leads to a varying of customs, foods, and activities, also provides for conflicts in ideas, and perhaps conflicts in what might be considered criminal actions. For law enforcement across the globe, diversity provides its own set of challenges.

Diversity creates unique opportunities for those individuals in first-responder fields, and in particular, it is commonly discussed in relation to police actions. Research suggests that diversity presents challenges, including individuals feeling as though they are not being heard, individuals feeling as though they are not valued, misunderstandings in communication, misunderstandings in professional etiquette, and conflicts in working styles (Reynolds, 2018). Individuals from different backgrounds communicate differently. For example, in a one-on-one discussion with a police officer, an individual from an Asian community may be less likely to express disagreement, especially if the person is new to the area; on the other hand, individuals from Western cultures (such as the United States or the United Kingdom) may view it as appropriate to challenge ideas and police authority if they feel the police officer is not acting within the law. In addition, while language barriers may be a challenge, nonverbal miscommunications are also significant to police challenges. Law enforcement officers are trained to be aware of not only the words from a person of interest but also the person's nonverbal modes of communicating. In some cases, nonverbal communications are a delicate and nuanced part of cultural interaction that can lead to misunderstandings or even offenses between individuals (Reynolds, 2018). Both for law enforcement and for members of TOC groups, who may be from different backgrounds than the police officers, diversity is another challenging element that requires attention.

Police Corruption

One of the most commonly discussed structural factors related to criminal behaviors and policing is corruption. For clarity, *corruption*

In July of 2020, the operations of an entire police organization in northern Italy were ended and the station was closed after multiple police officers were charged with drug dealing, torture, and extortion (Euronews Staff, 2020).

is the act of unfairly or illegally influencing a decision-making process by giving or receiving a benefit for a third party connected to the decision maker (Transparency International, 2021). Corruption is the illegal activities, which are deliberately hidden and come to light only through scandals, investigations, or prosecutions. One of the most recent measures of corruption within a country is the **Corruption Perceptions Index**, a composite index calculated annually by Transparency International.

Transparency International is a global movement, registered as a German voluntary association, founded in the 1990s by former employees of the World Bank. The focus of Transparency International is advocacy and research to expose systems and networks that facilitate corruption (Transparency International, 2021).

Police corruption, sometimes referred to as public corruption, poses a fundamental threat to rule of law, human rights, and global security (Federal Bureau of Investigation, 2021). Police corruption can affect everything from how well borders are secured and neighborhoods protected, to how verdicts are handed down in courts, to how public infrastructure such as roads and schools are built. In the United States alone, it is estimated that public corruption costs the government and the public billions of dollars each year (Federal Bureau of Investigation, 2021).

Police corruption is either external or internal and, as demonstrated below, involves a variety of actions. External corruption involves police contacts with the public, and internal corruption involves contacts among fellow police officers. External corruption, what most people consider in discussions on police corruption, consists of one or more of the following: (1) payoffs to police by essentially noncriminal elements who consequently fail to comply with stringent statutes or city ordinances; (2) payoffs to police by individuals who continually violate the law as a method of making money (for example, prostitutes, narcotics addicts and pushers, and professional burglars); and (3) "clean graft," where money is paid to police for services, or where courtesy discounts are given to the police as a matter of course (Beigel, 1974). Members of TOC groups are often the funding source behind external corruption.

COMMON ACTIONS TO DEMONSTRATE FORMS OF POLICE CORRUPTION

Form of Corruption	Common Actions
Corruption of Authority	free coffee, free meals, gifts
Kickback	cash, gratuities, gifts
Protection of Illegal Activity	cash from an underground gambling ring
Direct Criminal Activity	theft, family violence
Internal Payoff	shift changes, abuse of overtime

(Chene, 2010)

Internal corruption is less likely to be detected, as all parties involved are police officials. Internal corruption exists as a result of a desire by individual officers to improve their working conditions or to achieve higher status in the police department. It may include (1) payment of money to join the police force, (2) payment of money to higher-ranking officers for better shifts or assignments, (3) payment for choice vacation time, (4) strict adherence to a code of silence concerning external police corruption, (5) payment for a promotion, and (6) payment for an assignment, which will yield lucrative kickbacks (Beigel, 1974).

The overarching goal of preventing police corruption is to change the underlying structures that encourage corruption. Research suggests that by reforming the management systems, training, and organizational culture of the police agency and promoting integrity at all levels of the police institution, police corruption will be reduced (Dammer & Albanese, 2014). Addressing police corruption, which often supports TOC activities, is essential to maintain public order and the rule of law, to support the legitimacy of the state, and to maintain or restore public trust in democratic processes and institutions.

Police Efforts to Control TOC

For law enforcement who are trying to address the criminal activities of TOC, changes are being identified and implemented. These are in addition to attempts to raise awareness through outreach to public and private organizations, which typically begin with efforts to reduce specific crimes such as human-trafficking through public awareness campaigns. In the United States, federal agencies that often address the criminal activities of TOC include Customs and Border

Protection (CBP), Immigration and Customs Enforcement (ICE), the Coast Guard, and the Department of Defense (DOD). In particular, as suggested in reports by the U.S. Department of Justice (2008), law enforcement must employ strategic initiatives in order to achieve any sort of measurable results in combating the threats posed by TOC.

The first initiative for police to address TOC includes a plan to prioritize and target TOC leaders. The intent is to ensure a concerted and high-impact action in order to most effectively utilize resources and identify the TOC groups that pose the greatest and most immediate threats to national and international interests (U.S. Department of Justice, 2008). Law enforcement must pursue high-impact laws against TOC as well as collecting and organizing critical information on TOC crime targets. In addition, as law enforcement agencies often pursue parallel operations with each other in their attempts to address TOC, they must recognize and implement team approaches with their foreign counterparts for joint operations against TOC. Examples of such recognition are demonstrated in the accounts just below.

In December of 2021, the Korean National Police Agency of the Republic of Korea and the European Union Agency for Law Enforcement Cooperation (Europol) signed a Working Arrangement to assist in preventing and combating serious crime and terrorism across over 40 countries (Europol, 2021). In addition to the exchange of information, the agreement includes the exchange of specialist knowledge, general situation reports, and results of strategic analyses of TOC criminal activities. Also within the Working Arrangement are plans to train police on performing criminal investigations.

In July of 2021, Interpol hosted a five-day exercise referred to as Operation STOP (Smuggling Training and Operations Programme), which included training frontline officers in Ghana to optimize the use of policing capabilities within the country and internationally (Interpol, 2021a). Included in the training is the introduction of Interpol's criminal, stolen, and lost travel documents databases, designed to better track the movement of criminals and identify potential victims. After the training session, officers from various enforcement services, including Aviation Security, Customs, Immigration, Narcotics, and Ghana's Interpol National Central Bureau, were deployed to Accra Airport, where they carried out almost 33,000 checks against the various databases managed by Interpol. At the heart of Operation STOP are (1) the provision and extension of access for enforcement officers at strategic border points to secure a global police communications network and (2) the use of mobile technology to allow frontline officers the information required to combat TOC.

To better address the menace of TOCs in West Africa, including drug trafficking, a number of international organizations—among them the United Nations Office on Drugs and Crime (UNODC) and Interpol—launched the West African Coast Initiative (WACI) to support the implementation of the ECOWAS Action Plan to

(continued)

Address the Growing Problem of Illicit Drug Trafficking, Organized Crime and Drug Abuse in West Africa (United Nations Office on Drugs and Crime, 2020). The goal of WACI is to create Transnational Crime Units (TCUs), meant to enhance national and international coordination as well as to enable intelligence-based investigations. These elite interagency units will train and equip police to fight TOC and to coordinate their activities in an international framework (United Nations Office on Drugs and Crime, 2020). As of 2016, TCUs were operational in Liberia, Sierra Leone, and Guinea Bissau. TCUs, which form close ties with prosecutorial services or include prosecutors, are used to enhance the effectiveness of TOC investigations by applying tools from Interpol and other policing organizations to support intelligence-gathering and sharing as well as analysis for investigations and eventual prosecution of TOC group members involved in crimes across borders.

As discussed in the operations of illicit fund financial flows and underground economies, law enforcement should facilitate the engagement of non–law enforcement actors to include those within the banking systems, securities and commodities markets, and the commercial assets market with global influence. Law enforcement and criminal justice organizations must train and retain skilled analysts, investigators, and prosecutors to combat the criminal activities of TOC groups. Finally, to address crimes of an international nature and the challenges of TOC, police must also reach across borders and cooperate with other law enforcement agencies. In summary, to address the criminal activities of TOC groups, law enforcement must be aware if their limitations, must understand the state of TOC activities today, and must have insight into the criminal activities of TOC—since TOC will likely continue and increase in the future.

Summary

Policing within the international community provides even more difficulties than patrolling traditional home jurisdictions. In international cases, law enforcement must not only be knowledgeable about their levels of procedures and practice; they must also be cooperative, share information, and share successes and failures with other police across those communities. The chapter discusses policing across the globe, including the specific issues related to TOC and policing. It provides a brief history of policing in various countries as well as information on the three structures of policing that exist in our societies today: the notion of democratic policing, the relationship between police structures and the systems of law, and the reality of hyperglobalization and cybercommunities.

In addition, this chapter discusses some of the critical issues facing law enforcement in our global society, such as policing of transnational crimes; the notion of racism in the police, and the corruption of police as well as of government officials. Further, this chapter covers the topic of police violence as a function of police action and police victimization. Terrorism, another topic of concern within the international arena of security, is discussed in terms of policing efforts and global efforts to address TOC. Lastly, this chapter provides readers the opportunity to explore the efforts police have made to address TOC on an international level.

Questions for Further Discussion

1. What are today's issues of concern related to policing and TOC?
2. How are the structure and organization of TOC similar to the structure and organization of police forces?
3. How are cooperative international policing efforts helping to address TOC?

References

Allum, F., & Sands, J. (2004). Explaining organized crime in Europe: Are economists always right? *Crime, Law and Social Change, 41*(1), 133–160.

Badge & Wallet. (2021). A brief history of law enforcement. Retrieved April 3, 2021, from https://www.badgeandwallet.com/news/brief-history-law-enforcement

Banks, C., & Baker, J. (2016). *Comparative, international, and global justice*. Sage.

Bayley, D. (1985). *Patterns of policing: A comparative international analysis*. Rutgers University Press.

BBC News. (2016, April 9). *Brussels explosion: What we know about the airport and metro attacks*. Retrieved February 20, 2022, from https://www.bbc.com/news/world-europe-35869985

Berry, M. (2018, October 29). Technology and organized crime in the smart city: An ethnographic study of the illicit drug trade. *City, Territory, and Architecture, 16*, 1–8.

Beigel, H. (1974). The investigation and prosecution of police corruption. *Journal of Criminal Law and Criminology, 65*(2), 135–148.

Blackburn, K., & Forgues-Puccio, G. (2009). Why is corruption less harmful in some countries than in others? *Journal of Economic Behavior & Organization, 72*(3), 797–810.

Block, A., & Chambliss, W. (1981). *Organizing crime*. Elsevier Science.

Bureau of Justice Statistics. (2021, February 18). *Law enforcement*. Retrieved June 30, 2021, from https://bjs.ojp.gov/topics/law-enforcement

Chene, M. (2010, May 31). Anti-corruption and police reform. Anti-Corruption Resource Centre. Retrieved October 30, 2021, from https://knowledgehub.transparency.org/assets/uploads/helpdesk/247_Anti_corruption_police_reform.pdf

Clarke, C. (2016). Drugs and thugs: Funding terrorism through narcotics trafficking. *Journal of Strategic Security, 9*(3), 1–15.

Clough, C. (2017, March 27). *Transnational crime is a $1.6 trillion to $2.2 trillion annual business, finds new GFI report* [Press release]. Retrieved June 30, 2020, from https://gfintegrity.org/press-release/transnational-crime-is-a-1-6-trillion-to-2-2-trillion-annual-business-finds-new-gfi-report/

Dammer, H., & Albanese, J. (2014). *Comparative criminal justice systems* (5th ed). Wadsworth.

Deakin, D. (2014, February 27). *Freeze! The world's biggest police forces*. Therichest.com. Retrieved January 13, 2022, from https://www.therichest.com/the-biggest/freeze-the-10-biggest-police-forces-in-the-world/

Dishman, C. (2005). The leaderless nexus: When crime and terror converge. *Studies in Conflict and Terrorism, 28*(3), 246–258.

Djordjevic, S., & Dobovsek, B. (2020). Organized crime in Western Balkans Six at the onset of coronavirus. *International Journal of Sociology and Social Policy, 40*(9/10), 807–820.

Douvlis, K., & South, N. (2016). Police reform and social change in Greece: The development and merger of the gendarmerie and urban police forces. *Revija kriminalistiko in kriminologijo, 67*(4), 288–299.

Euronews Staff. (2020, July 22). *Entire police station shut in northern Italy amid "drug dealing," "torture," and extortion charges*. Euronews. Retrieved April 3, 2021, from https://www.euronews.com/2020/07/22/entire-police-station-shut-in-northern-italy-amid-drug-dealing-torture-and-extortion-charg

Europol. (2015). The Internet Organised Crime Threat Assessment (IOCTA) 2015. Retrieved on August 20, 2022 at https://www.statewatch.org/media/documents/news/2015/oct/eu-europol-iocta-2015.pdf

Europol. (2021, December 22). *Republic of Korea and Europol sign arrangement to combat cross-border serious organized crime*. Retrieved February 20, 2022, from https://www.europol.europa.eu/media-press/newsroom/news/republic-of-korea-and-europol-sign-arrangement-to-combat-cross-border-serious-organised-crime

Federal Bureau of Investigation. (2021). *What we investigate: Public corruption*. Retrieved November 3, 2021, from https://www.fbi.gov/investigate/public-corruption

Finckenauer, J. (2000, July). Meeting the challenge of transnational crime. *National Institute of Justice Journal* (NCJ 183454), 1–6. https://www.ojp.gov/pdffiles1/jr000244b.pdf

Global Financial Integrity. (2014). *Illicit financial flows*. Retrieved January 30, 2022, from http://www.gfintegrity.org/wpcontent/uploads/2014/09/GFI-Analytics.pdf https://gfintegrity.org/issue/illicit-financial-flows/

Goredema, C. (2011, October). *Combating illicit financial flows and related corruption in Africa: Towards a more integrated and effective approach* (U4 Issue 2011:12).

Anti-Corruption Resource Centre. Retrieved January 3, 2022, from www.cmi.no/publications/file/4214-combating-illicitfinancial-flows-and-related.pdf

Habibullah, M., Din, B., & Hamid, B. (2016). Good governance and crime rates in Malaysia. *International Journal of Social Economics, 43*(3), 308–320.

Hunter, R. (1990). Three models of policing. *Police Studies, 13*(3), 118–124.

International Peace Institute. (2009). *Transnational organized crime: Task forces on strengthening multilateral security capacity* (IPI Blue Paper No. 2). Retrieved January 31, 2022, from https://www.ipinst.org/wp-content/uploads/2015/06/toc_final.pdf

Interpol. (2021a, August 3). *Operation STOP: Securing borders from transnational crime.* Retrieved February 20, 2022, from https://www.interpol.int/en/News-and-Events/News/2021/Operation-STOP-securing-borders-from-transnational-crime

Interpol. (2021b, July 26). *286 arrested in global human trafficking and migrant smuggling operation.* Retrieved October 3, 2021, from https://www.interpol.int/en/News-and-Events/News/2021/286-arrested-in-global-human-trafficking-and-migrant-smuggling-operation

Kenton, W. (2020, April 30). *Underground economy.* Investopedia. Retrieved February 5, 2022, from https://www.investopedia.com/terms/u/underground-economy.asp#:~:text=The%20nations%20with%20the%20three,%2C%20and%20Switzerland%20(7.2%25).

Levin, N. (2019, August 2). *10 Largest Criminal Organization to ever exist.* Largest.org. Retrieved January 13, 2022, from https://largest.org/people/criminal-organizations/

Ma, Y. (2000). A research note on the history of Chinese police. *International Journal of Comparative and Applied Criminal Justice, 24*(1), 115–123.

McCabe, K. and Marin, G. (2005). School violence, the media, and criminal justice responses. NY: Peter Lang.

McCabe, K. (2017). *Protecting your children online.* Rowman & Littlefield.

McCabe & Johnson. (2014). Perceptions on the legality of sexting. *Social Science Computer Review,* 32(6), 1–4.

Muntingh, L., Faull, A., Redpath, J., & Petersen, K. (2021). Democratic policing: A conceptual framework. *Law, Democracy and Development, 25,* 121–147. http://www.scielo.org.za/scielo.php?script=sci_arttext&pid=S2077-49072021000100005

New York Times. (2015, November 19). *Paris attack suspect killed in a shootout had plotted terror for 11 months.* Retrieved February 3, 2022, from https://www.nytimes.com/news-event/attacks-in-paris

Nwabuzo, O., & Siklossy, G. (2020, October 8). *Why Europe has a racism problem.* Social Europe. Retrieved October 30, 2020, from https://socialeurope.eu/why-europe-has-a-racism-problem

Reynolds, K. (2018). 13 benefits and challenges of cultural diversity in the workplace. *Hult.edu.* Retrieved November 3, 2021, from https://www.hult.edu/blog/benefits-challenges-cultural-diversity-workplace/

Schmalleger, F. (2004). *Criminal justice: A brief introduction* (5th ed). Pearson/Prentice Hall.

SecureWorks. (2014, December). *Underground hacker markets*. Retrieved January 3, 2022, from http://www.secureworks.com/assets/pdf-store/white-papers/wp-underground-hackingreport.pdf

Touro College Illinois. (2021, November 12). *The 10 biggest ransomware attacks of 2021*. Retrieved February 4, 2022, from https://illinois.touro.edu/news/the-10-biggest-ransomware-attacks-of-2021.php

Transparency International. (2021). *Corruption perceptions index, 2021*. Retrieved October 3, 2021, from https://www.transparency.org/en/cpi/2020/index/nzl

Tropina, T. (2017). *Do digital technologies facilitate illicit financial flows?* World Development Report 2016 Background Paper: Digital Dividends. Retrieved January 20, 2022, from https://thedocs.worldbank.org/en/doc/396751453906608518-0050022016/original/WDR16BPDoDigitalTechnologiesFacilitateIllicitFinancialFlowsTropina.pdf

Tsolakidou, S. (2013, May 30). *The police in ancient Greece*. Greek Reporter. Retrieved April 3, 2021, from https://greekreporter.com/2013/05/30/the-police-in-ancient-greece/

United Nations Economic Commission for Africa. (2015). *Illicit financial flows: Report of the high level panel on illicit financial flows from Africa*. Retrieved January 3, 2022, from https://repository.uneca.org/handle/10855/22695

United Nations Office on Crime and Justice Research Institute. (2021). *Countering terrorism online with artificial intelligence*. Retrieved February 20, 2022, from http://www.unicri.it/News/-Countering-Terrorism-Online-with-Artificial-Intelligence

United Nations Office on Drugs and Crime. (2009). Transnational trafficking and the rule of law in West Africa: A threat assessment. *Trends in Organized Crime, 12*(1), 307–324.

United Nations Office on Drugs and Crime. (2019). *Human trafficking*. Retrieved January 16, 2020, from https://www.unodc.org/nigeria/en/human-trafficking.html

United Nations Office on Drugs and Crime. (2020). *Transnational crime units*. Retrieved February 3, 2022, from https://www.unodc.org/westandcentral-africa/en/west-africa-coast-initiative.html

U.S. Department of Justice. (2008, April). *Overview of the law enforcement strategy to combat international organized crime*. Retrieved January 10, 2022, from https://www.justice.gov/sites/default/files/criminal-icitap/legacy/2015/04/23/04-23-08combat-intl-crime-overview.pdf

Wainwright, T. (2016). *Narconomics: How to run a drug cartel*. PublicAffairs.

WBRZ Staff. (2018, January 19). *Couple sentenced in 2015 vigilante justice murder case*. WBRZ.com. Retrieved April 5, 2021, from https://www.wbrz.com/news/couple-sentenced-in-2015-vigilante-justice-murder-case/

Williams. J. (2002). *Organized crime and cyber-crime: Implications for business*. CERT Coordination Center. Retrieved January 3, 2022, from http://www.cert.org/archive/pdf/cybercrime-business.pdf

World Bank. 2015. *Illicit financial flows (IFFs)*. Retrieved January 3, 2022, from http://www.worldbank.org/en/topic/financialmarketintegrity/brief/illicit-financial-flows-iffs

World Population Review. (2021). *Most diverse countries*. Retrieved November 3, 2021, from https://worldpopulationreview.com/country-rankings/most-diverse-countries

CHAPTER 12

International Courts and Justice

Key Terms

Amnesty International
Community Court of Justice (CCJ)
Court of last resort
Crimes against humanity
Crimes of aggression
Double jeopardy
European Court of Human Rights (ECHR)
European Union (EU)
General jurisdiction
Genocide
Human trafficking
In absentia
Inter-American Court of Human Rights (IACHR)
International Court of Justice (ICJ)
International courts
International Criminal Court (ICC)
International justice
International law
International Military Tribunal for the Far East
International Tribunal for Law of the Sea (ITLOS)
League of Nations
Permanent Court of Arbitration (PCA)
President Woodrow Wilson
Protocol Against the Illicit Manufacturing of and Trafficking in Firearms, Their Parts and Components and Ammunition
Protocol Against the Smuggling of Migrants by Land, Sea and Air
Protocol to Prevent, Suppress and Punish Trafficking in Persons, Especially Women and Children
Rome Statute
The Hague
Tribunal
United Nations
War crimes
Wilson's Fourteen Points
World Court

CHAPTER OBJECTIVES

Chapter 12 will enable readers to understand the following:

- the definition of *international law*
- the foundation for establishing international courts
- the roles (past and present) of the United States in establishing international courts
- the role of the League of Nations in international courts
- the variety of international courts
- the difference between the International Court of Justice (ICJ) and the International Criminal Court (ICC)
- the link between transnational organized crime (TOC) and the case criteria of the ICC
- the potential for prosecution of TOC through international courts

In June of 1985, the International Court of Justice (ICJ) ruled that the United States, by using force against another country, was in breach of its obligations under international law. Specifically, in the Case Concerning Military and Paramilitary Activities in and Against Nicaragua—in short, *Nicaragua v. United States of America*—it was alleged that the United States, in recruiting, training, and funding military and paramilitary actions against the country of Nicaragua, had violated customary international law in the killing, wounding, and kidnapping of Nicaraguans (Pax, 1985).

The creation of **international courts** helped to solidify the cooperative efforts among countries to address crimes of the most severe nature. These courts facilitated the operations of a global criminal justice system in which perpetrators could not escape prosecution and extradition by seeking refuge in the legal obstacles of country jurisdiction (Schloenhardt, 2005). Unfortunately, the crimes by TOC were rarely addressed, as the majority of their efforts (e.g., drug trafficking, money laundering)

By definition, TOC involves crimes that occur across jurisdictional boundaries. So once the crimes are detected and arrests are made, the countries (source, transit, and destination) involved in the criminal actions generally determine the venue for prosecution. In most cases, this venue for prosecution rests with the state of arrest; in some cases, however, other courts may be involved. In particular, in the United States, with both federal and state systems, crimes by TOC are often addressed at the federal level if the crime has been documented to have occurred within

(continued)

multiple states. However, as the United States is governed by two legal systems, the prosecution of such crimes may depend upon the product of illicit trade or upon the criminal activity (U.S. Courts, 2022). Specifically, crimes such as embezzlement, mail or wire fraud, and drug trafficking are prosecuted by the federal courts (Luftman et al., 2019). Crimes of a violent nature such as the sexual exploitation of children are most often prosecuted at the state level.

With the exception of the United States and the United Kingdom, with the latter made up of multiple countries and three separate criminal justice systems (England and Wales, Scotland, and Northern Ireland), most countries are governed by one legal system. Whereas this phenomenon of multiple systems of laws seems convoluted, for those wishing to address TOC, once the crime has resulted in an arrest, the prosecution generally falls within the jurisdiction of the arresting authority.

In the United States, crimes that are committed by TOC groups and occur in multiple states are prosecuted by the federal system, with state systems occasionally choosing to prosecute the crimes within their system. Furthermore, in the United Kingdom, if a crime is committed only in Scotland, then the Scottish court will arrest and prosecute.

were not within the jurisdictional charges of the international courts, particularly not within the bounds of the international criminal court. However, today's criminal activities of human trafficking by TOC groups have forced international courts to consider their applications to TOC as being under the focus of crimes against humanity.

As illustrated in the 1985 case named above, one government (the United States) was determined to be involved in funding efforts against another government (Nicaragua) as a result, international courts have attempted to address, in general, organized crime.

Establishment of the Wickersham Commission—appointed in 1931 by then president Herbert Hoover to study law enforcement and recommend improvements to the judicial system—while also pointing out the difficulties in local law enforcement, was the first written acknowledgement by the U.S. government that a greater centralization of authority is needed to control many forms of cross-border crimes (CQ Researcher, 2021). Of course, for the United States, this centralization was applied in the founding of federal agencies with authority in cross state boundaries in order to address organized crime within jurisdictions. These concepts of centrality and cooperation across borders are applied in the efforts of international laws and courts to address crimes such as those committed by groups involved in TOC. **International justice** applies transparency and accountability for some of the most serious crimes, including genocide, torture, and crimes against humanity (Amnesty International, 2021).

International justice— Ensuring accountability for some of the most serious crimes, including genocide, crimes against humanity, war crimes, torture, and enforced disappearances.

Amnesty International— A London-based international nongovernmental organization focused on human rights.

As the phrase implies, *international justice* is associated with addressing international crimes. For clarity, *international crimes* involve the most serious crimes of concern to the global community and include genocide, war crimes, and crimes against humanity (these are also often referred to as *atrocity crimes* (Open Society, 2016). Characterizing atrocities as crimes against humanity recognizes that large-scale violence is different from ordinary domestic crime, as this characterization requires examining systems and patterns of crime, which is a lengthy process. In response, there are no statute of limitations for international crimes for the international court system (Open Society, 2016).

One crucial element for achieving international justice at the global level is the concept of an international court. Specifically, in today's world of globalization, justice is not served only within the exclusive realm of sovereign nations. In fact, global justice depends on cooperation across the world and in courts with recognized international jurisdictions. Specific to the topic of transnational organized crime, as TOC is involved in criminal activities coordinated across national borders and involves individuals in multiple countries conducting illegal businesses, a globally coordinated effort of justice is mandatory to ensure human safety, quality of life, and global security. In response, in the last century, two major international courts have been established—the International Court of Justice in 1945 and the International Criminal Court in 1998—to address **international law** and crimes of a mass and/or sometimes transnational nature.

International law—A body of rules, established by custom or treaty, that are recognized by nations as binding in their relations with one another.

This chapter focuses on international courts of justice and the concept of international crime, and provides examples of such courts around the globe. In addition, the chapter examines the various legal jurisdictions of these courts and reviews specific cases. The primary focus of the chapter will be on the **International Court of Justice** (**World Court**) and the **International Criminal Court**. In addition, this chapter discusses the concept of TOC as related to prosecution, accountability, and potential expansion of prosecution within the international courts.

In the 18th century, offenses such as the use and sale of illegal drugs and psychotropic substances were recognized as violations of international law and were documented to be of concern to nations within the Shanghai International Opium Conference of 1909 (Schloenhardt, 2005). Specifically, these violations of international law required an international response. These multinational justice courts, not new in concept, evolved in response to the events of the early 20th century, which brought the need for global justice forums to the forefront of international politics, diplomacy, and the rule of law. Within the last two decades, researchers documenting the increasing activities of TOC are calling for better applications from militaries, security forces, intelligence agencies, and the international courts, as hyperglobalization has impacted crimes, criminal activities, and justice systems (Edwards & Gill, 2002).

WOODROW WILSON'S FOURTEEN POINTS

1. Open diplomacy without secret treaties
2. Economic free trade on the seas during war and peace
3. Equal trade conditions
4. Decrease armaments among all nations
5. Adjust colonial claims
6. Evacuation of all Central Powers from Russia and allow it to define its own independence
7. Belgium to be evacuated and restored
8. Return of Alsace-Lorraine region and all French territories
9. Readjust Italian borders
10. Austria-Hungary to be provided an opportunity for self-determination
11. Redraw the borders of the Balkan region creating Romania, Serbia, and Montenegro
12. Creation of a Turkish state with guaranteed free trade in the Dardanelles
13. Creation of an independent Polish state
14. Creation of the League of Nations

(*National WWI Museum and Memorial, 2022*)

In 1918, the last year of World War I, U.S. **President Woodrow Wilson** realized that national security was not possible without international stability. In particular, Wilson recognized the connection between an individual's safety, a country's security, and the need for global stability. In the waning days of World War I, Wilson put forth his ***Fourteen Points*** as a framework to ensure national security and world peace (National WWI Museum and Memorial, 2022). This framework outlined the ideas of "a general association of nations ... affording mutual guarantees of political independence and territorial integrity to great and small States alike," which framed future international organizations to enhance global stability and promote international justice (Britannica, The Editors of Encyclopaedia, 2018). These 14 points and Wilson's proposal led to the formation of the

League of Nations, which gave the world an international forum in which to address issues of crime and security between and among nations in an attempt to diffuse military conflicts and wars before they begin.

League of Nations (1920–1946)—The first worldwide intergovernmental organization with the principal mission to maintain world peace.

On January 10, 1920, the League of Nations was created, and the Palace of Nations, in Geneva, Switzerland, was chosen as its headquarters (International Court of Justice, 2018b). Although President Wilson was a founding force and urged the United States to join the League of Nations (hereafter, the League) in a demonstration of U.S. support for international cooperation, the United States never became a member. President Wilson predicted that without the support of the United States, the League would fail and that the world would see a second world war. True to his prophecy, on September 1, 1939, 19 years after the formation of the League, German forces under Adolf Hitler invaded Poland; in reaction, Great Britain and France, as allies of Poland, declared war on Germany. The countries that aligned themselves with Germany were known as the Axis powers and the countries that sided with Great Britain and France were known as the Allies. As the different countries aligned themselves with either the Axis or the Allies, the world found itself in a second global conflict and unable to focus on crimes of an international level. Once World War II started, the role of the League was essentially nullified, even though the official end of the League did not occur until 1946, when the triumphant Allies sought a legal process to address the atrocities committed by the losing Axis countries (United Nations, 2018). This desire for international criminal justice was pursued through War Crimes Tribunals in Nuremberg, Germany, and Tokyo, Japan. These international tribunals brought war criminals of both the Nazi and Japanese regimes to face charges for the crimes they committed during the war. The Nuremberg Trials, which occurred from 1945 to 1946, resulted in the conviction of 22 out of 24 defendants, with 11 defendants sentenced to death (History.com Editors, 2018).

Later, the **International Military Tribunal for the Far East** was convened and lasted from 1946 to 1948. Of the 28 Tokyo defendants, 25 were convicted and 7 received the death penalty (History.com Editors, 2018). Both the Nuremberg Trial and the Tokyo Tribunal contributed to the Geneva Convention of 1949, which established

Tribunal—A court of justice often formed to address specific criminal matters.

many of the legal foundations for modern international criminal cases. The Geneva Convention codified customary law and adapted some of the legal procedures and practices of both tribunals (History.com Editors, 2018). Although even today it is difficult to draft measures and responsibilities to address crimes occurring across countries, these international tribunals helped to establish the foundation for future international courts.

World War II proved to be the catalyst for attempt at forming a new League of Nations through the concept of the **United Nations** (UN), which was formed on October 24, 1945 (United Nations, 2018). In a demonstration of unity, the United States joined the organization and became a primary decision maker in the UN as a permanent member of the UN Security Council. New York City was selected as the location for the original UN headquarters. Today, as originally designed, the UN provides an international forum for discussing disputes between member nations, with additional offices in Geneva, Switzerland, Vienna, Austria, and Nairobi, Africa.

United Nations office locations: New York, New York; Geneva, Switzerland; Vienna, Austria; Nairobi, Kenya.

The International Court of Justice (ICJ)—also known as the World Court—was established in 1945 under the UN's original charter as a part of the organization. Housed at the Peace Palace in **The Hague**, the Netherlands, the World Court began operation in 1946 (International Court of Justice, 2018c). In an attempt to address crimes within unclear jurisdictions, specifically those crimes that occur at sea, the International Tribunal for the Law of the Sea (ITLOS) was established in 1982. This effort, discussed earlier in this book as it relates to environmental crimes, helped to facilitate cooperation among countries in addressing TOC activities.

The Hague—A city on the North Sea coast of the western Netherlands where the 16th-century Noordeinde Palace is located. The city is also the home to the UN's International Court of Justice (ICJ) and the International Criminal Court (ICC).

Subsequent to the formation of the World Court, the International Criminal Court (ICC) was established through the ratification of the **Rome Statute** in 1998 at the United Nations Diplomatic Conference in Rome, Italy. Like the World Court, the ICC is located in The Hague, the Netherlands; however, the ICC, which began operations in 2002, is independent of the United Nations (International Court of Justice, 2018c). Also, the World Court is a civil court for disputes between countries, while the ICC is a criminal court focused on the prosecution of individuals. Relevant to TOC, the ICC may be utilized in the prosecution of those members of TOC groups accused of crimes against humanity, while the World Court may be used to determine venue.

Our global society also needs other international courts, to address regional, continental, or other transnational legal issues. One example is the **Inter-American Court of Human Rights (IACHR)**, located in San José, Costa Rica, an international court focused on the Americas (Inter-American Court of Human Rights, 2019). The **International Tribunal for the Law of the Sea (ITLOS)**, located in Hamburg, Germany, is an example of an international court with a specific legal focus: the ITLOS is concerned with maritime law, a specific area of international law (International Tribunal for the Law of the Sea, 2019). Over the last 100 years, various nations have come together to form different institutions to deal with a range of international issues, including crimes against humanity.

The existence of these international courts offers countries a way to have wrongs redressed without resorting to adverse political, economic, or military action. These courts also provide smaller, less powerful countries a venue for lodging complaints and having them heard on an equal footing with bigger states. The smallest of nations, marginalized groups, and even individuals may have a voice in these international courts, thereby furthering the ideal of justice for all on a global level within the World Court.

Inter-American Court of Human Rights— An international court (formed in 1979) based in San José, Costa Rica. Together with the Inter-American Commission on Human Rights, it was formed by the American Convention on Human Rights and serves as a human rights treaty that has been ratified by members of the Organization of American States.

International Tribunal for the Law of the Sea (ITLOS)—An intergovernmental organization created by the mandate of the Third United Nations Conference on the Law of the Sea, and established in 1982 by the United Nations Convention on the Law of the Sea.

International Court of Justice

The primary global court is the International Court of Justice (ICJ) or World Court (located at The Hague, the Netherlands). This court provides two major functions for member states of the United Nations: (1) to settle disputes between UN nations, referred to as contentious cases; and (2) to give advisory opinions on legal questions brought forth by international organizations, known as advisory proceedings (ICJ, 2018b). Cases are designated contentious when a member state of the UN brings a case before the World Court against another member state. Individuals, nonprofits, nongovernmental organizations, or private entities, even if they exist within a UN member state, cannot

> In January of 2022, a German court sentenced a Syrian colonel to life in prison for crimes against humanity (58 murders and the torture of at least 4,000 people), which occurred between 2011 and 2012 (Hill, 2022). This was the first state-led criminal case as the colonel was arrested in Germany where he had sought asylum in 2019.

INTERNATIONAL COURT OF JUSTICE (ICJ), OR WORLD COURT

- Founded at the San Francisco Conference (California, USA) on June 26, 1945. Authorized by UN Charter, Statute of the International Court of Justice.
- Operational in April 1946; the first case was heard in May 1947.
- Located in The Hague, the Netherlands (same city as the ICC, but at a different location).
- Has two primary functions: (1) to settle disputes between member nations of the UN and (2) to provide legal opinions on questions brought forth by international organizations.

WORLD COURT ORGANIZATION

1. The Court: 15 Judges elected to 9-year terms.
   A. Court has three chambers:
      1. Chamber of Summary Procedure (five judges).
      2. Chamber with three judges.
      3. Ad Hoc Chamber with unelected judges.
2. The Registry (administrative and support functions).

Jurisdiction: ICJ may hear any case that is not within the exclusive jurisdiction of another court. This is also known as ***general jurisdiction***.

Territorial jurisdiction: Any issue between member states of the UN (over 190 nations). Unlike the ICC, the World Court is not a criminal court.

Working Languages: English and French.

One of six principal organs of the UN (ICJ is the only organ not located at the UN in New York City).

(International Court of Justice, 2018b)

present a case to the World Court, as the court has no jurisdiction to deal with complaints from such parties; however, if an individual or an entity within a UN member state alleges wrongdoing by another member state, the country of the individual or entity may take up the case on the complainant's behalf in the country's name against another UN member nation. The World Court is one of six major organs or departments of the UN, and English and French are the two main working languages of the ICJ (International Court of Justice, 2018b).

The World Court has general jurisdiction, which means that the it may hear any case that is not already exclusively within the jurisdiction of another court (International Court of Justice, 2018b). In addition, the World Court does not stand alone in providing a venue for international justice, as several other international courts or tribunals deal with a variety of matters of international concern. However, these courts tend to focus more narrowly or to specialize in a specific area as compared to the World Court. In particular, despite the strict limitations of the World Court's jurisdiction, the creation of the court strengthens the idea of cooperation between states and strengthens international authorities to address transnational crimes (Schloenhardt, 2005).

As referenced earlier, one example of an international tribunal dealing with specific legal issues is the ITLOS, located in Hamburg, Germany. The ITLOS is an independent judicial body ready to settle disputes involving the interpretation and application of the UN Convention on the Law of the Sea (International Tribunal for the Law of the Sea, 2019). If a member state disagrees with another member country regarding the UN laws of the seas, the case would be heard at the International Tribunal for the Law of the Sea in Germany since the ITLOS has the specific jurisdiction for such matters while the ICJ only has general jurisdiction.

WHALING IN THE ANTARCTIC (*AUSTRALIA V. JAPAN*)

The World Court opened proceedings in May 2010 over a dispute between two member nations, Australia and Japan. Australia had lodged a complaint about Japan's practices of whaling in the Antarctic.

A year later in May 2011, Australia filed written arguments outlining the allegation that Japan was actually conducting commercial whaling against specific species of protected whales in the Antarctic region, which had been designated a sanctuary from hunting for such whales. Japan, according to Australia, continued killing the whales under the justification of whale research. Australia alleged that the actions of Japan violated the International Convention for the Regulation of Whaling.

Japan responded in March 2011 by presenting written arguments that their whaling activities were in support of their whaling research and that the studies were self-funded through the sale of whale products such as whale meat from the killer whales. Such sales, per Japan, provided the funding necessary for continuing the research and therefore did not violate any restriction or convention on whaling.

In November 2012, the country of New Zealand, which is also a member nation of the UN and a party to the International Convention for the Regulation of Whaling, filed additional written arguments against the activities of Japan. New Zealand alleged that they were also affected by the Japanese whaling.

(continued)

Throughout 2013, all three countries filed additional written arguments and provided testimony from various experts before the World Court. Finally, Australia, Japan, and New Zealand individually presented oral arguments to support their positions before the World Court.

The case ended on March 31, 2014, when the World Court ruled that Japan was violating the moratorium on whaling under the pretext of scientific research and ordered Japan to stop the practice. (International Court of Justice, 2015)

The legal disputes between member countries are also referred to as contentious cases. These cases begin with a disagreement concerning a question of law or a fact, a conflict, or a clash of legal views or interests; however, per international law the ICJ may accept a case only if it is brought forth by one or more of the member states. Any member state of the UN may present a case before the World Court. Unlike the International Criminal Court, however, the World Court itself cannot launch inquiries or investigations into an issue. There are two nonmember states of the UN that are allowed to participate as observers of the sessions and of the work of the General Assembly, but they cannot present a case in the World Court. These nonmember states are the Holy See (the Vatican in Rome, Italy) and the Palestinian Territory, which lies within the member state of Israel.

Once a state presents a case to the ICJ, that state and the other states named in the disagreement are referred to as the parties (International Court of Justice, 2018d). All parties listed in the dispute before they may be heard in the World Court must accept these cases. However, without the agreement of all the member states involved, the World Court would not have jurisdiction unless there was a previous binding agreement in place that would allow a case to be brought by a member state without the approval of all the parties (International Court of Justice, 2018d).

World Court proceedings are generally open to the public, as the judgments from the World Court are final with no opportunity for appeal. In addition, if one or more parties fail to comply with the court's decision, the case may be referred to the UN Security Council for action, as occurred in the 1985 *Nicaragua v. United States* case discussed previously.

The World Court renders judgments utilizing various sources of law, including international treaties, international custom, principles

THE WORLD COURT JURISDICTION IS TYPICALLY ACHIEVED VIA THESE CONDITIONS

Special Agreement: Every member state involved in the dispute agrees to have the issue heard before the World Court.

Matters provided for in Treaties and Conventions: There is already a binding legal agreement in force with other member states that would permit just one member state to submit the case to the World Court.

Compulsory Jurisdiction: Member states that have previously granted the World Court jurisdiction by filing a declaration with the office of the UN Secretary-General must accept the case going before the World Court when the specific criteria outlined in their declaration are met.

The Hearing Procedures for the World Court are outlined in the ICJ statute and comprise four phases:

- Written Phase: Written arguments outlining the contested issue are filed with the ICJ judges by all parties in addition to being shared with the other parties.
- Oral Phase: Oral arguments by all parties are presented before the ICJ judges in court.
- Deliberations Phase: The judges consider the presented arguments *in camera* (away from the open courtroom) and then make a decision under the applicable laws.
- Judgment Phase: The decision of the judges is announced in open court.

(International Court of Justice, 2018d)

of law, and legal conventions in force. The court may also consider judicial decisions and legal opinions of legal experts of various fields and may provide legal advice through advisory proceedings. These proceedings are typically limited to the other departments of the UN; however, the court may provide advisory proceedings for the specialized agencies of the UN or affiliated organizations.

The World Court's advisory proceedings are similar to the procedures for contentious cases in that the court first assembles the facts through written and oral hearings, then conducts deliberations in camera, and finally concludes with the announcement of the advisory opinion at a public session. These proceedings are not binding on the requesting organ or agency unless the court's judgment was designated in advance to be binding on the party or parties. Since 2018, the World Court has issued approximately 25 advisory opinions since becoming operational in 1946, including legal opinions regarding the consequences of the West Bank Security Wall separating Israel and Palestine, as well as various issues surrounding nuclear weapons

(International Court of Justice, 2018a). Finally, agencies are international organizations that are legally independent of the UN, but that coordinate their work with the UN through negotiated agreements such as the World Bank, which focuses on poverty reduction and better quality of life through interest-free credit and grants or the World Health Organization, an organization involved in promoting and protecting the health of the world's population. The specific number of UN specialized agencies changes from time to time, with 15 such agencies (located in Geneva, Vienna, and New York City) in existence at the end of 2021 (United Nations Dag Hammarskjold Library, 2018).

International Criminal Court

The International Court of Justice and the various other courts with international or transnational jurisdiction are not always the correct forum to handle international justice; specifically, these courts do not always address criminal actions. Unfortunately, despite early attempts to address organized crime, most TOC occurred outside the jurisdiction of the International Criminal Court, or ICC; today, however, based upon the demographics of victims (such as women or children), the ICC, may be used to address TOC.

Historically, when major issues of unaddressed criminality occurred, they were often surrounding a governmental conflict and the UN would periodically convene ad hoc international tribunals to deal with such matters. Two such post-conflict ad hoc tribunals were assembled to deal with issues arising out of the conflicts in Rwanda (genocide) and Yugoslavia (war crimes). Additionally, the UN has worked with other local countries to form tribunals (internationalized courts) to deal with such issues arising from conflicts in East Timor, Kosovo, Cambodia, and Sierra Leone (Georgetown Law Library, 2018).

All of these tribunals were typically a temporary judicial body formed to deal with types of criminality occurring over a specified period and during a specific conflict. The periodic need for such temporary tribunals had been a subject of UN discussion since its inception after World War II. In addition, as the ICC's focus on crimes against humanity requires proof of a specific act before a conviction, the list of acts that apply to "other inhumane acts" includes offenses such as

INTERNATIONAL CRIMINAL COURT

Established by the Rome Statute, July 17, 1998 in Rome, Italy. Became operational July 1, 2002 (the ICC cannot charge any crime that was committed before July 1, 2002).

The ICC is not a UN court (the ICJ or World Court is a UN court).

Located in The Hague, the Netherlands (same city as the ICJ but at a different location).

The court is organized into four organs:

1. The Presidency
2. Judicial Divisions (three "chambers")
   A. Pretrial Chamber
   B. Trial Chamber
   C. Appeals Chamber
3. Office of the Prosecutor
4. The Registry (support functions)

Crimes authorized for the ICC:

1. Genocide
2. Crimes against humanity
3. War crimes
4. Crimes of aggression (only since July 17, 2018)

Territorial jurisdiction: Any state that is a party to the Rome Statute (over 120 nations). The ICC can intervene only when a state is unable or unwilling to investigate and prosecute offenders. Therefore, the ICC is a *court of last resort*.

Languages: Primary: English and French. Translators provided for all defendants regardless of their language.

(International Criminal Court, 2018)

trafficking in persons, enslavement, and enforced prostitution (Schloenhardt, 2005), which are often associated with TOC.

Formation of the Court

In 1998, the Rome Statute was adopted at the UN Diplomatic Conference in Rome, Italy, by 120 signatory nations from around the world, which authorized the formation of the International Criminal Court (ICC). Originally, only seven countries voted against the ICC: the United States, China, Libya, Iraq, Israel, Qatar, and Yemen; however, another 21 countries abstained from voting (Scharf, 1998). The establishment of the ICC concluded decades of discussion and debate, beginning in 1948 when a resolution by the UN General Assembly suggested a study to examine the possibility of an international judicial organ for the trial of persons charged with genocide. The court officially began operation in 2002 and is housed in The Hague, the Netherlands, the same city as the UN International Court of Justice. While both courts are located in The Hague, the ICC and the ICJ are housed in different facilities distanced a few miles apart; however, unlike the ICJ, the ICC is not part of the UN—although it has links to the UN. As of December 2020, there are over 120 country members of the ICC. However, the world's most powerful countries—the United States, Russia, and China—are not members.

Jurisdiction and Crimes

Court of last resort—Court having the highest and final appellate authority.

The ICC does not have jurisdiction over all crimes, and the court does not have the venue of primary jurisdiction for the crimes it prosecutes; therefore, the ICC is known as a **court of last resort**. The ICC is utilized when countries that have ratified the Rome Statute are unwilling or unable to intervene via their national systems of justice (primary courts). This jurisdiction is also called the complementarity principle in that the ICC complements the signatory nation's criminal justice system only when such involvement is required. One of the more publicized situations involving the ICC are the allegations that both the Taliban and the U.S.-led coalition forces may have committed war crimes in the long-running conflict in Afghanistan (International Criminal Court, 2017).

While most of the coalition force members in Afghanistan are from countries that are member nations of the ICC, and therefore fall within the jurisdiction of the court, the United States is not a signatory nation of the ICC. However, Article 12(2) of the Rome Statute states that the ICC has jurisdiction over any crimes committed in the territory of Afghanistan since May 1, 2003, regardless of nationality, since Afghanistan is a signatory to the Rome Statute (Hakimi, 2018). Given that the United States is not part of the ICC, but U.S. actions occurred inside the geographic confines of Afghanistan, the ICC would still have the authority to prosecute the crimes of **genocide, crimes against humanity**, and **war crimes** that were committed on or after July 1, 2002 (just as in the case concerning Nicaragua, at the beginning of this chapter). For clarity, in cases of crimes against humanity, the people who carry out the crime may not have planned or instigated the violence—since the actual act may be carried out by soldiers or by members of a drug gang, but ordered by a senior commander, a cartel leader, or a politician (Open Society, 2016). Therefore, in charging individuals with crimes against humanity, superiors are responsible for crimes committed by their subordinates and for failing to prevent or punish those crimes, and these crimes can be applied to any organized body, including armed forces of police, militias, or TOC.

ELEMENTS OF CRIMES AGAINST HUMANITY

Widespread or systematic attacks; against civilian populations; by a perpetrator; pursuant to governmental policy or tolerated by the country; and with knowledge of the attack. (Schloenhardt, 2005)

Of interest to this text are the crimes of international terrorism and transnational drug trafficking that were considered but later rejected for ICC authority; however, the parties to the Rome Statute could not agree on a definition of *terrorism* so that crime was excluded. Drug crimes were seen as placing too many demands on the court's investigative resources, so that crime was not added to ICC jurisdiction. Human trafficking, a crime often committed by TOC groups, is under the umbrella of transnational criminal law, as a result domestic courts may be limited (Esser & Dettmeijer-Vermeulen, 2016). But this realization of the aspects of human trafficking leaves room for an international interpretation of its components. In 2017, the signatory nations of the ICC added a fourth crime to the crimes that the court has the authority to address: **crimes of aggression** that are committed by one nation against another nation. Currently, the ICC may prosecute crimes of aggression committed on or after July 17, 2018.

The components of the Rome Statute included outlining the criminal procedural law to be followed by the ICC judges and lawyers during legal action against a defendant. These rules of procedure were drawn from a variety of UN sources, including covenants, treaties, and agreements protecting individual and state rights. In addition, legal precedents established by Yugoslavia, Rwanda, and other international

THE FOUR CRIMES UNDER ICC JURISDICTION

The *Crime of Genocide* is defined as the specific intent to destroy a part or the whole of a national, ethnic, racial, or religious group by killing or inflicting serious bodily harm or mental harm to group members. Genocide also includes imposing life conditions on the targeted group that are intended to cause the physical destruction of a portion or the entire group, preventing births within the group, and transferring the assignment of children from the targeted group to another group.

Crimes against Humanity are serious violations committed as part of widespread or systematic attacks knowingly focused on a civilian population. There are many forms of crimes against humanity listed in the Rome Statute, including offenses such as murder, extermination, enslavement, the forcible transfer of a population, various forms of sexual violence, apartheid, the enforced disappearance of people, torture, and other grave inhumane acts.

War Crimes are grave breaches of the Geneva Conventions, which are a series of treaties on the treatment of civilians, prisoners of war (POWs), and soldiers who are no longer able to fight, such as those severely wounded during warfare. Included in this form of crime are the use of child soldiers (under the age of 15), the killing or torture of noncombatants (civilians or POWs), and deliberately attacks on hospitals, historical monuments, or structures utilized for religious, educational, art, science, or charitable activities.

A *Crime of Aggression* is the action of an armed force committed by one state against another state. Actions such as invasion, military occupation, blockading of ports, or the forceful annexation of borders constitute acts of aggression. These acts are judged by their gravity and scale, and when the crime of aggression has been committed, the defendant to be charged is the person or persons in the positions that control or direct the political or military action of the state. One significant difference between crimes of aggression and the three other ICC crime charges is that with crimes of aggression the ICC will also have jurisdiction over nonsignatory nations and their citizens who commit crimes of aggression if the situation is referred to the ICC by the UN Security Council. Therefore, nation states not accepting the authority of the ICC may now fall under the court's jurisdiction for this crime.

In addition to the date on which the crime was committed and the offense type, at least one of the following conditions must be present for the ICC to prosecute the case (International Criminal Court, 2019):

- The crimes were committed by a citizen of a signatory nation.
- The crimes occurred within the geographical boundaries of a signatory nation.
- The signatory nation or other nation has deferred to or accepted the jurisdiction of the ICC.
- The UN Security Council has referred the crimes to the ICC prosecutor in accordance with the UN charter. Note: A referral from the UN Security Council may allow the ICC to investigate crimes occurring outside of the court's typical geographical jurisdiction of only signatory nations.
- The ICC prosecutor may initiate an investigation after receiving authorization from the ICC Pre-Trial Division. The prosecutor may launch such an inquiry on their own or upon request from a signatory nation. (International Criminal Court, 2019)

tribunals were incorporated into ICC legal procedure. Therefore, ICC legal procedures reflect concepts drawn from both common (adversarial) and civil (inquisitorial) criminal law systems, making the ICC a hybrid court whose functions do not precisely mirror any one nation's system of justice (Haddad, 2018). Other aspects of the Rome Statute include protecting individuals against **double jeopardy** in that the ICC may not try a person for the same crime that the person has already been tried for in another court. Also, anyone under the age of 18 may be charged as a juvenile, and anyone responsible for a crime committed before their 18th birthday is exempt from prosecution for that crime by the ICC. In addition, defendants are considered innocent until proven guilty, and the burden of proof falls upon the prosecutor. The court does not try individuals **in absentia**, meaning that suspects must be arrested and brought to the court in The Hague in order for the trial process to be completed. Lastly, there is no statute of limitations for the prosecution of crimes under the court's authority, the only qualifier being that the crime occurred after the initial jurisdiction date of the specific ICC crime.

In absentia—A Latin phrase meaning "not present at the event"; usually applied to defendants not being present in a criminal trial.

A preliminary examination is the initial look by the Office of the Prosecutor (OTP) into a situation or potential issue to be dealt with by the ICC. The OTP verifies that the situation is serious enough for ICC involvement, that the court has jurisdiction, and that the country's national legal system is not properly addressing the problem. In many cases, the mere act of the ICC prosecutor initiating a preliminary examination may be sufficient to cause some nations to take responsible legal action themselves. For example, in October of 2021 after an ICC inquiry, Colombian officials agreed to launch their own investigation into the deaths of over 100 civilians by military officials (Bates & Zvobgo, 2021). Individuals, groups, or countries may send information to the OTP alleging that crimes have been committed that deserve the attention of the court, without a period specified by the Rome Statute for opening or closing a preliminary examination; therefore, the OTP may open and conduct these inquiries when and for as long as they deem appropriate. As of 2018, more than 10,000 reports of potential issues had been submitted to the OTP (International Criminal Court, 2018); the following example demonstrates ICC efforts in the Democratic Republic of the Congo.

THE ICC PROSECUTOR V. THOMAS LUBANGA DYILO

In February 2006, Thomas Lubanga Dyilo (Lubanga), President of the Union of Congolese Patriots (UPC) militia group in the Democratic Republic of the Congo (DRC), was charged by ICC with war crimes of using children under the age of 15 years as soldiers in hostile actions. The ICC investigation began two years earlier in June 2004, and centered on the use of children fighters in the ethnic violence occurring in the DRC's Ituri region. Allegations included recruiting children as young as 11 years old as combatants, the use of drugs and physical abuse to control the youth, and finally that some of the young girls had been used as sex slaves. The ethnic fighting in the DRC had been violent, and Human Rights Watch estimates that more than 60,000 people were killed in the conflict.

When the ICC warrant was issued, Lubanga was already incarcerated in the DRC on other charges, and he was transferred to ICC custody in March of 2006.

The original trial date was set for June 2008, more than two years after Lubanga had been arrested by the ICC. However, just days before the trial was to begin, legal issues arose questioning whether Lubanga could receive a fair trial due to actions by the prosecutor. The OTP had failed to disclose exculpatory evidence to Lubanga's defense team and the prosecutor had failed to comply with a court order to identify an intermediary utilized to provide witnesses for the prosecution. These issues halted the trial, and it was not for more than another two years that the trial began in October 2010, an incredible four and one-half years after Lubanga had been transferred to ICC custody.

Once the trial began, it lasted about one and a half years, and the ICC found Lubanga guilty in March 2012 of war crimes for the use of child soldiers. Lubanga was sentenced in July 2012 to 14 years in prison, and he subsequently appealed the sentence. The ICC Appellate Division upheld the sentence in December 2014, and finally, in December 2015, Lubanga was transferred back to the DRC to serve out the remainder of his sentence. By the time Lubanga was sent back to the DRC, he had been in the custody of the ICC for eight years and about nine months.

Lubanga was the first person convicted by the ICC since it began operations. (International Justice Monitor, 2018)

The existence of the ICC is not without debate, and some of the nations at the 1998 diplomatic conference in Rome raised objections to the court. Specifically, seven nations—Iraq, Israel, Libya, China, Qatar, Yemen, and the United States—voted against the Rome Statute on various grounds (Scharf, 1998). To date, a number of countries are still not signatory nations of the ICC, and other countries signed the statute but have not ratified it, such as China, Egypt, Iran, Israel, Russia, and initially the United States (BBC News, 2015). In addition, of the nine countries in the world that possess nuclear weapons (China, France, India, Israel, North Korea, Pakistan, Russia, the United Kingdom, and the United States), only France and the United Kingdom are member nations of the ICC (Chuck, 2016).

Other International Courts and Efforts

Along with the International Court of Justice (ICJ, or World Court) and the International Criminal Court (ICC), the international community is also served by the **Permanent Court of Arbitration (PCA)**. Both the World Court and the PCA are housed at the Peace Palace in The Hague, the Netherlands. The PCA predates the World Court in that the PCA was first authorized in 1899 as part of the First Hague Peace Conference, and the Peace Palace was constructed in 1913 to serve as the permanent home of the PCA. The PCA also predates the UN, and therefore is open to organizations outside of the UN, including nonprofit entities, private organizations, and individual persons. If these various entities seek arbitration through the PCA, the court's decision is binding on all parties. However, the PCA may also provide nonbinding resolution services (much like the advisory proceedings of the World Court), such as the mediation of particular issues, as well as fact-finding commissions of inquiry.

The **European Union (EU)**, a collection of sovereign states spread over the continent of Europe, has two international courts dealing with issues arising from the countries that make up the EU. The first is the **European Court of Human Rights (ECHR)**, located in Strasbourg, France, which accepts cases brought by individuals, groups, or nongovernmental organizations against European nations if their claims have been denied or dismissed in the original European state system of justice. The ECHR acts both as a pseudo-appellate system to the original jurisdiction of individual EU countries and as a check and balance against EU states failing to take action in certain matters (European Court of Human Rights, 2018).

European Court of Human Rights—An international court (also known as the Strasbourg Court) of the Council of Europe that interprets the European Convention on Human Rights.

Another international court of the EU is the Court of Justice of the European Union (CJEU), which is located in Luxembourg, a small country in Western Europe bordering Belgium, Germany, and France. The CJEU, which is the supreme or highest court of the EU, renders judgments on issues involving EU laws, and the court may also arbitrate conflicts between EU institutions. Judges for the CJEU are selected from every member country of the EU, and they serve renewable six-year terms. Unlike the International Court of Justice or the World Court, the CJEU will potentially address complaints from individuals (Court of Justice of the European Union, 2018).

The **Community Court of Justice** (**CCJ**) of the Economic Community of West African States (ECOWAS) is an example of another international court focused on a regional area. The court sits in Abuja, Nigeria, and hears cases originating in more than 12 West African countries. The CCJ examines contentious cases that were initiated in member states but were not properly dealt with per the law, and the court also provides advisory and arbitration services to ECOWAS members (Community Court of Justice, 2018). In addition, in the Western Hemisphere the Inter-American Court of Human Rights (IACHR), located in San José, Costa Rica, hears cases alleging human rights violations occurring in member nations in North America, Central America, and South America. The IACHR does not have jurisdiction over human rights disputes in the United States or Canada since neither country is a ratifying member of the court.

Regarding TOC on the seas, the European Court of Human Rights (ECHR) addressed the crime of drug smuggling in 2010 through its reference in the *Medvedyev v. France* cases that concluded interdiction and enforcement jurisdiction applied to drug-smuggling vessels on the high seas (Papastavridis, 2010). In addition to the abovementioned courts, the UN's Office on Drugs and Crime (UNODC) also has established legal tools to address crimes across borders. Specifically, the United Nations Convention against Transnational Organized Crime not only directs attention to the problems of TOC but also provides a foundation for specific protocols for addressing various aspects of TOC.

UN EFFORTS TO ADDRESS TOC

The United Nations Convention against Transnational Organized Crime, adopted by General Assembly resolution in 2000, is the main international instrument in the fight against TOC. It opened for signature by member states at a High-level Political Forum convened for that purpose in Palermo, Italy, on December 12–15, 2000, and entered into force on September 29, 2003.

The Convention is further supplemented by three protocols, which target specific areas and manifestations of organized crime.

- The **Protocol to Prevent, Suppress and Punish Trafficking in Persons, Especially Women and Children**, was adopted by General Assembly resolution in 2003 and is the first global legally binding instrument with an agreed definition of *trafficking in persons*.

(*continued*)

- The **Protocol Against the Smuggling of Migrants by Land, Sea, and Air** was adopted in 2004 and addresses the growing problem of organized criminal groups that smuggle migrants, often at high risk to the migrants and at great profit for the offenders.
- The **Protocol Against the Illicit Manufacturing of and Trafficking in Firearms, Their Parts and Components, and Ammunition** was adopted in 2001 and implemented in 2005, and is the first legally binding instrument on small arms that has been adopted at the global level, is to promote, facilitate, and strengthen cooperation among countries. (United Nations Office on Drugs and Crime, 2018)

International Courts and TOC

In regard to the prosecution of TOC at the international level, the Rome Statute of the International Criminal Court (ICC) establishes the criteria for a prosecution in the ICC. However, since the end of World War II it is difficult to recall any crimes against humanity that did not involve groups involved in TOC. Human trafficking, the drug trade, kidnapping, and the illicit trade of environmental resources are all crimes committed by TOC, and all are crimes that contribute to the actions of terrorists, extremists, insurgents, and paramilitary organizations, which often result in dramatic extractions of populations—hence, crimes against humanity.

According to the U.S. Department of Homeland Security, in the United States TOC causes over 70,000 drug overdose deaths annually, fosters corruption, and decreases citizens' confidence in governments (Klein, 2020).

Specifically, consider the Lord's Resistance Army (LRA) in Central Africa, which has committed numerous crimes against humanity since the 1980s and continues to kidnap children to be trained as soldiers in support of their illegal ivory trade (Kersten, 2021). Also, in 2014, 276 girls were abducted from their school in the northeast Nigerian town of Chibok by the militant Islamist group Boko Haram, and 100 of those girls are still missing (BBC News, 2017).

In Syria and Iraq, the Islamic State of Iraq and the Levant (ISIL) has been accused of a variety of international crimes committed by TOC groups, including the attempted genocide of the Yazidi population; however, such transnational crimes have permitted ISIL to survive (Kersten, 2021). In addition, the Kosovo Specialist Chambers and Specialist Prosecutor's Office has shed new light on the actions by the Kosovo Liberation Army engagement in human organ trafficking by

> In December of 2020, the ICC issued a preliminary report stating that crimes against humanity had been committed in the Philippines under the reign of President Rodrigo Duterte, whose drug war has left thousands of people dead since 2016. Specifically, the ICC's report suggested that there was "a reasonable basis to believe that the crimes against humanity of murder, torture, and the infliction of serious physical injury and mental harm" had taken place under the orders of the president. According to the Philippine National Police, roughly 8,000 people accused of being involved in the illegal drug trade had been killed as human rights groups reported higher numbers, with the violence continuing even as the country was under a coronavirus lockdown (Gutierrez, 2020).

TOC members following its war and their alleged counter-ethnic cleansing campaign against Serbia in the late 1990s and early 2000s (Kersten, 2021). Finally, the UN Office on Drugs and Crime estimated that of the approximately 464,000 people murdered in 2007, approximately were killed as a result of TOC (Todd, 2019). Therefore, many of the crimes committed by TOC are theoretically within the criteria of the ICC, and at some point this may be applicable to the ICC or (as demonstrated below) influenced by the ICC.

Under the current international courts system, the International Criminal Court is the only judicial body capable of adjudicating crimes beyond the responsibility of domestic jurisdictions (Morello & Schweighoferova, 2021). While the crime of **human trafficking** is not criminalized under treaty of the ICC, the inclusion of TOC crimes such as human trafficking could be warranted given the scale, gravity, and brutality of the crime. As of February of 2020, all but seven ICC state parties had ratified or signed the Protocol to Prevent, Suppress and Punish Trafficking in Persons, Especially Women and Children (the Trafficking Protocol), which requires states to adopt national legislation in line with the treaty so they can then prosecute human trafficking domestically; thus, the lines of distinction that may have existed decades ago may not be relevant in today's global societies. International legal responses to TOC and political crime have varied based upon country.

The ICC and other international courts have attempted to address TOC. However, with only a limited number of core crimes (genocide, war crimes, crimes against humanity, aggression), many have perceived their efforts to be less than significant (Van der Wilt, 2010). The perpetrators of TOC may face direct criminal responsibility under international law, but for the most part their crimes have been pursued at the country level. Unfortunately, in attempts to address TOC, the horizontal, interstate character of jurisdiction is not always applicable (Van der Wilt, 2010). Hence, international efforts, international courts, and cooperation across countries are essential in addressing global crimes committed by members of TOC.

Summary

The events of the last century highlighted the increasing need for institutions of international justice. To that end, the world has seen the initiation of several courts and organizations with an international focus. Since the Permanent Court of Arbitration (PCA) was first authorized in 1899, many of the world's nations have come together on several occasions to establish venues to address justice on an international level. World War I became the catalyst for the formation of the League of Nations, which, while it failed to stop World War II, did provide the basis for the United Nations, which serves as a forum for international dialogue to this day. The UN created the International Court of Justice (ICJ), also known as the World Court, to give member nations a place to settle disputes (contentious cases) between UN nations, and to offer opinions on legal questions brought forth by international organizations. The World Court has general jurisdiction, meaning that the court may hear only those cases that are not already exclusively within the jurisdiction of another court. Finally, the ICJ gives a voice to all member nations, permitting small nations a forum in which to stand up against larger, more powerful countries as equal adversaries in a courtroom.

Over the years, additional courts have been established to deal with specific areas of international law, or sometimes to focus on a particular region of the world and on TOC. One type of court dealing with a specific area of international law is the International Tribunal for the Law of the Sea (ITLOS), which deals with maritime issues. An example of a regional international court is the Inter-American Court of Human Rights (IACHR), which hears cases involving complaints of human rights abuses from member nations in the Americas. Several of these regional courts exist today, covering various areas of the world and dealing with a variety of issues.

Out of the atrocities committed during World War II and during the conflicts in Yugoslavia and Rwanda came the formation of the International Criminal Court (ICC). The ICC is the first full-time criminal court ready to address grave issues of criminality as they occur, instead of forming tribunals or other temporary courts to deal with the problem. Jurisdiction of the ICC applies when a state that has ratified the Rome Statute is unwilling or unable to intervene with their national system of justice. TOC is an international problem in need of a solution, and many suggest that the ICC is a solution in need of problems. Therefore, the existence of these international courts suggests an end to blanket impunity for grave violations of law committed by rogue nations, tyrants, and dictators. However, the idea of a global rule of law and its application to TOC have not been fully recognized. Every year, TOC groups generate billions of dollars of revenue through their criminal activities. In many cases, these crimes by TOC may also be considered crimes against humanity—and thus crimes of concern for international courts.

Questions for Further Thought

1. How might the ICC expand its jurisdiction over citizens of nonsignatory nations by investigating those citizens for crimes committed within the boundaries of a signatory nation?
2. Using the four types of crimes under the jurisdiction of the ICC, what type of scenario would justify the prosecution of each specific crime?
3. How might international courts be used to specifically address TOCs?

References

Amnesty International. (2021). *International justice*. Retrieved November 10, 2021, from https://www.amnesty.org/en/what-we-do/international-justice/

Bates, G., & Zvobgo, K. (2021, October 8). The ICC doesn't look so interventionist after all. *Foreign Policy*. Retrieved January 5, 2022, from https://foreignpolicy.com/2021/12/08/icc-colombia-farc-special-jurisdiction-peace-complementarity-interventionism/

BBC News. (2015, June 25). *What does the International Criminal Court do?* Retrieved December 30, 2018, from https://www.bbc.com/news/world-11809908

BBC News. (2017, May 8). *Nigeria Chibok abductions: What we know*. Retrieved November 3, 2021, from https://www.bbc.com/news/world-africa-32299943

Britannica, The Editors of Encyclopaedia. (2018, February 21). League of Nations. *Encyclopedia Britannica*. Retrieved December 8, 2018, from https://www.britannica.com/topic/League-of-Nations

Chuck, E. (2016, March 31). *Fact sheet: Who has nuclear weapons, and how many do they have*. NBC News. Retrieved January 17, 2019, from https://www.nbcnews.com/news/world/fact-sheet-who-has-nuclear-weapons-how-many-do-they-n548481

Community Court of Justice. (2018). *About us*. Economic Community of West African States (ECOWAS). Retrieved December 29, 2018, from http://www.courtecowas.org/mandate-and-jurisdiction-2/

Court of Justice of the European Union. (2018). Overview. *European Union*. Retrieved December 29, 2018, from https://europa.eu/european-union/about-eu/institutions-bodies/court-justice_en

CQ Researcher. (2021). *The federal government and organized crime*. Retrieved November 3, 2021, from http://library.cqpress.com/cqresearcher/cqresrre1934081000

Edwards, A., & Gill, P. (2002). Crime as enterprise? The case of transnational organized crime. *Crime, Law and Social Change, 37*(1), 203–223.

Esser, L., & Dettmeijer-Vermeulen, C. (2016). The prominent role of national judges in interpreting the international definition of human trafficking. *Antitrafficking Review, 6*, 91–105.

European Court of Human Rights. (2018, December 31). *Pending applications allocated to a judicial formation* [Graphic]. Retrieved January 19, 2019, from https://www.echr.coe.int/Documents/Stats_pending_month_2018_BIL.pdf

Georgetown Law Library. (2018, October 22). War crimes research guide: Courts and tribunals. Retrieved December 9, 2018, from https://guides.ll.georgetown.edu/c.php?g=365751&p=2471272

Gutierrez, J. (2020, December 15). Court finds evidence of crimes against humanity in the Philippines. *The New York Times*. Retrieved June 30, 2021, from https://www.nytimes.com/2020/12/15/world/asia/philippines-duterte-drugs-icc.html

Haddad, H. (2018, July 17). The International Criminal Court was established 20 years ago. Here's how. *Washington Post*. Retrieved December 28, 2018, from https://www.washingtonpost.com/news/monkey-cage/wp/2018/07/17/the-international-criminal-court-turns-20-heres-a-look-at-how-it-got-here/?noredirect=on&utm_term=.6ec5b1a9113e

Hakimi, M. (2018, August 31). Forum: The ICC and Afghanistan—Time to end impunity? *Yale Journal of International Law*. https://www.yjil.yale.edu/forum-the-icc-and-afghanistan-time-to-end-impunity/

Hill, J. (2022, January 13). German court finds Syrian colonel guilty of crimes against humanity. *Deutsche Welle*. Retrieved January 13, 2022, from https://www.dw.com/en/german-court-finds-syrian-ex-colonel-guilty-of-crimes-against-humanity/a-60407021#:~:text=News-,German%20court%20finds%20Syrian%20ex%2Dcolonel%20guilty%20of%20crimes%20against,during%20the%20Syrian%20civil%20war

History.com Editors. (2018). *Nuremberg trials*. History.com. Retrieved December 9, 2018, from http://www.history.com/topics/world-war-ii/nuremberg-trials

Inter-American Court of Human Rights. (2019). *History*. Retrieved January 3, 2019, from https://www.corteidh.or.cr/historia.cfm?lang=en

International Court of Justice. (2015). *Whaling in the Antarctic (Australia v. Japan: New Zealand intervening)*. Retrieved December 9, 2018, from https://www.icj-cij.org/en/case/148

International Court of Justice. (2018a). *Advisory proceedings: 1996 Nuclear Weapons; 2004 Palestine*. Retrieved December 21, 2018, from https://www.icj-https://www.icj-cij.org/en/advisory-proceedings

International Court of Justice. (2018b). *The court*. Retrieved December 19, 2018, from https://www.icj-cij.org/en/court

International Court of Justice. (2018c). *History: Rome Statute*. Retrieved December 20, 2018, from https://www.icj-cij.org/en/court

International Court of Justice. (2018d). *How the court works: Contentious cases*. Retrieved December 21, 2018, from https://www.icj-cij.org/en/how-the-court-works

International Court of Justice. (2018e). *The permanent Court of International Justice*. Retrieved December 19, 2018, from https://www.icj-cij.org/en/history

International Criminal Court. (2017). *The preliminary examination of the situation in the Islamic Republic of Afghanistan*. Retrieved August 9, 2022, from https://www.icc-cpi.int/afghanistan

International Criminal Court. (2018). *About the court*. Retrieved January 4, 2019, from https://www.icc-cpi.int/about

International Criminal Court. (2019). *Understanding the International Criminal Court: Crimes within the jurisdiction of the ICC*. Retrieved January 4, 2019, from https://www.icc-cpi.int/iccdocs/pids/publications/uicceng.pdf

International Justice Monitor. (2018, October 17). *Thomas Lubanga / Background*. Retrieved January 18, 2018, from https://www.ijmonitor.org/category/thomas-lubanga/

International Tribunal for the Law of the Sea. (2019). The tribunal. Retrieved August 9, 2022, from https://www.itlos.org/en/main/the-tribunal/the-tribunal/

Judiciary Staff. (2022). *The justice system and the constitution*. Courts and Tribunals Judiciary. Retrieved May 11, 2022, from https://www.judiciary.uk/about-the-judiciary/the-judiciary-the-government-and-the-constitution/jud-acc-ind/justice-sys-and-constitution/

Kersten, M. (2021, July 17). To stop mass atrocities, follow the money. *Aljazeera*. Retrieved December 3, 2021, from https://www.aljazeera.com/opinions/2021/7/17/to-stop-mass-atrocities-follow-the-money

Klein, D. (2020, October 12). *DHS: Transnational organized crime, a "devastating threat" to the US*. Organized Crime and Corruption Reporting Project. U.S. Department of Homeland Security. Retrieved November 3, 2021, from https://www.occrp.org/en/daily/13229-dhs-transnational-organized-crime-a-devastating-threat-to-the-us#:~:text=Transnational%20organized%20crime%20is%20%E2%80%9Can,Department%20of%20Homeland%20Security%20said

Luftman, Heck, & Associates. (2019, August 30). *What's the difference between state and federal courts in Ohio?* Retrieved May 12, 2022, from https://www.columbuscriminalattorney.com/whats-the-difference-between-state-and-federal-courts/

Morello, R., & Schweighoferova, F. (2021). Taking down one of the world's largest and more profitable criminal industries: Trafficking in persons (Part I). *Harvard International Law Journal*. Retrieved on August 20, 2022 at https://harvardilj.org/2021/05/taking-down-one-of-the-worlds-largest-and-more-profitable-criminal-industries-trafficking-in-persons-part-i/

National WWI Museum and Memorial. (2022). *The fourteen points*. Retrieved January 3, 2022, from https://www.theworldwar.org/learn/peace/fourteen-points

Open Society. (2016). *Fact sheet: International crimes*. Retrieved November 10, 2021, from https://mail.google.com/mail/u/0/?tab=rm&ogbl#inbox?projector=1

Papastavridis, E. (2010). European Court of Human Rights Medvedyev et al France (Grand Chamber, Application No 3394/03) Judgement of 29 March 2010. *International and Comparative Law Quarterly, 59*(3), 867–882.

Pax, T. (1985). Nicaragua v. United States in the International Court of Justice: Compulsory jurisdiction or just compulsion? *Boston College International and Comparative Law Review, 8*(2), 471. Retrieved November 3, 2021, from https://lawdigitalcommons.bc.edu/iclr/vol8/iss2/7

Scharf, M. (1998). Results of the Rome conference for an international criminal court. *American Society of International Law, 3*(10).

Schloenhardt, A. (2005). Transnational organized crime and the International Criminal Court developments and debate. *University of Queensland Law Journal, 24*(1), 93–122.

Todd, A. (2019, July 9). *UN: Organized crime accounts for a fifth of murders worldwide*. Organized Crime and Corruption Reporting Project. Retrieved November 3, 2021, from https://www.occrp.org/en/daily/10158-un-organized-crime-accounts-for-a-fifth-of-murders-worldwide

United Nations. (2018). *Historical overview of the League of Nations*. Retrieved August 20, 2022 from https://www.ungeneva.org/en/league-of-nations

United Nations Dag Hammarskjold Library. (2018). *What is an Advisory Opinion of the International Court of Justice (ICJ)?* Retrieved December 21, 2018, from http://ask.un.org/faq/208207

United Nations Office on Drugs and Crime. (2018). *United Nations convention against transnational organized crime and the protocols thereto*. Retrieved December 3, 2021, from https://www.unodc.org/unodc/en/organized-crime/intro/UNTOC.html

U.S. Courts. (2022). *Comparing federal and state courts*. Administrative Office of the U.S. Courts. Retrieved May 10, 2022, from https://www.uscourts.gov/about-federal-courts/court-role-and-structure/comparing-federal-state-courts

Van der Wilt, H. G. (2010). Expanding criminal responsibility in transnational and international organized crime. *Groningen Journal of International Law, 4*(1), 1–9.

Conclusion

Transnational organized crime (TOC) is a response to the demand for illicit products and/or services as well as an indication of a state's ability to enforce laws as related to criminal activity within the state's own domestic populations. Essentially, there are four categories of TOC: (1) organized criminal gang activities for crimes such as murder and kidnapping; (2) racketeering; (3) syndicate crimes such as drug trafficking; and (4) smuggling, such as people smuggling. TOC is a growing concern for all aspects of criminal justice, as it poses a significant and growing threat to national and international security. In addition, the outcomes of the criminal activities by TOC groups often provide the most negative of consequences for public safety, public health, democratic institutions, and economic stability across the globe.

TOC groups' annual global profits are estimated to be in the billions of dollars, with suggestions that these profits are equivalent to approximately 10% of GDP. Today, TOC is an enterprise with significant profits for its members. Unfortunately, these criminal networks are expanding and diversifying their criminal activities. The result is the increasing victimization of vulnerable populations and the convergence of threats that were once distinct but now have far-reaching implications—not only for criminal justice issues but also for issues of social justice within the international arena.

Across the globe, TOC networks are recognized for their profits and their consequences. Specifically, within the Western Hemisphere, TOC networks have expanded and matured and are threatening the safety of citizens and the stability of governments throughout the region, with direct security implications for those within the United States. TOC groups within Central America remain involved in the illicit trafficking of drugs, weapons, and people. In Afghanistan and other Asian countries, the convergence of TOC and violent extremism is apparent as the Taliban and other drug-funded terrorist groups threaten the efforts of many international partners to build a peaceful and democratic future for that nation. In Russia and Eurasia, TOC networks represent a significant threat to economic growth and democratic institutions, with Russian organized crime syndicates attempting to collude with government officials to undermine competition in strategic markets such as gas, oil, aluminum, and precious metals. The Balkans have become an ideal environment for the cultivation and expansion of TOC, with weak institutions in Albania, Kosovo, and Bosnia and Herzegovina enabling criminal groups to seize control of significant drug-trafficking and human-trafficking routes as well as economic markets. TOC groups in West Africa have become a major transit point for illegal drug shipments such as heroin to Europe and the United States, in addition to being a source, transit, and destination region for illicit goods of all types. Finally, in Asia, due to the region's global economic ties, the criminal activities of TOC continue to heighten the threats posed to intellectual property rights, human trafficking, and smuggling.

TOC crosses the boundaries of legal jurisdictions as well as the boundaries of virtual communities such as the darknet. The actions of TOC groups often continue undetected and without limits to products, profits, or victims.

TOC groups are self-perpetuating associations of individuals who operate, wholly or in part, by illegal means and across state or country boundaries. These groups seek profit, power, and influence, with globalization or hyperglobalization fueling the problem. Unfortunately, there is no single structure for TOC groups; they vary from hierarchies to clans and networks, and they often evolve into other structures in reaction to criminal justice enforcement efforts and products. TOC groups are typically insular and protect their activities through corruption, violence, international commerce, complex communication mechanisms, and an organizational structure exploiting national boundaries. For those reasons, the study of TOC is often limited.

This text attempts to address those limitations. Therefore, the book is divided into three sections: (1) Foundations of TOC, (2) Issues and Consequences of TOC, and (3) Global Responses to TOC. Knowledge about this global crime problem is often based upon an awareness of TOC groups within a particular area and their criminal actions there. It is the goal of this text not only to provide accurate and objective information on TOC and the criminal activities of TOC groups but also to inspire readers to study the actions of TOC as part of an effort to better protect victims, economies, and democracies.

Index

D

E

Printed in the USA
CPSIA information can be obtained
at www.ICGtesting.com
LVHW080203231024
794596LV00005B/147